6.95

JOHN KEATS

Selected Poems and Letters

RIVERSIDE EDITIONS

RIVERSIDE EDITIONS

UNDER THE GENERAL EDITORSHIP OF

Gordon N. Ray

JOHN KEATS

Selected Poems and Letters

EDITED WITH AN INTRODUCTION AND NOTES BY

Douglas Bush

HARVARD UNIVERSITY

HOUGHTON MIFFLIN COMPANY

BOSTON

Acknowledgment is made to the Harvard University Press for permission to reprint the texts of some letters from *The Letters of John Keats,* Hyder E. Rollins, Editor; Cambridge, Mass., Harvard University Press; copyright, 1958, by The President and Fellows of Harvard College. Also to the Oxford University Press for some texts from *The Letters of John Keats,* Maurice B. Forman, Editor, fourth edition, Oxford, 1952.

PREFACE

THIS BOOK, being designed mainly for college students, includes not only all of Keats's best poems but a number of his early and poorer ones, since without these one cannot fully appreciate the development of his mind and craftsmanship. The texts of most of the poems are of course taken from Keats's three published volumes; most of the others are based more or less on the versions in the *Life, Letters, and Literary Remains, of John Keats* (1848) by Richard Monckton Milnes, later Lord Houghton. Because of manuscript copies made by Keats or his friends, it is not always clear which variants represent his final choice. Obvious misprints have been corrected, but punctuation and spelling are not ordinarily altered unless there is danger of misreading; some obsolete, peculiar, and inconsistent forms are therefore retained.

The notes — unusually full for this series of editions — are addressed to different kinds of readers and perhaps require different kinds of apology (people who abhor all annotation have an obvious remedy). I have tried, with imperfect success, to keep interpretative notes to the minimum, since these can be especially unwelcome. A good deal of space is needed for run-of-the-mill notes on mythological allusions and the like (these, by the way, follow Keats in his frequent use of Roman names for Greek divinities). It is hoped that sophisticated readers may not resent the space given to literary parallels, chiefly from poetry. Keats, while not learned, was a highly literary poet, in the sense that he continually echoed other writers, and some students wish to follow his reading and taste, to be aware of both relatively insignificant importations and of significant transmutations. Such illustrative material, first assembled on a large scale in De Selincourt's edition, has been augmented by other scholars, and citations here, though abundant, are necessarily far from exhaustive; some of them are new. Many items may not be actual sources but are of interest anyhow. All of them have to be recorded in bony bareness, without comment.

Of Keats's letters, the invaluable complement to the poems, only a sampling can be given here. They are reprinted, with the kind permission of the Oxford University Press and the Harvard University Press, from the fourth edition (1952) of Maurice B. Forman and the new and magisterial edition (1958) of Professor Hyder E. Rollins. (Letters of which the Houghton Library has the originals have also, rather superfluously, been checked with them.) For the sake of authentic flavor it has seemed best to reproduce Keats's hasty misspellings, alterations, and erratic punctuation rather than to provide smoothly corrected versions. Lack of space forbids annotation of the letters, beyond the identifying of Keats's more open quotations from Shakespeare *et al.*

The editorial apparatus has had the benefit of being looked over by three expert students of Keats, Miss Mabel A. E. Steele, curator of the Keats collection in the Houghton Library, and Professors Rollins and W. J. Bate. (This was perhaps the last piece of work Professor Rollins did — and did with his accustomed generosity and vigilance — before his fatal illness.) Any errors or shortcomings that remain are of course my own. For much miscellaneous information, including the correction of hitherto mistaken or uncertain dates, I am indebted to the omniscience and infallibility of Professor Rollins' two editions, *The Keats Circle* (1948) as well as *The Letters of John Keats.*

D.B.

CONTENTS

Poems

viii · *Contents*

Letters *

* An asterisk indicates that a letter is not given in full.

x · *Contents*

INTRODUCTION

by Douglas Bush

THE MEAGRE "events" of Keats's life are recorded in the Chronological Table. He died four months after his twenty-fifth birthday, and tuberculosis had ended his poetic life over a year before his death. As critics have observed, no other major English poet would rank as a major poet if he had been cut off at that early age; and the miracle of Keats's growth and achievement is none the less remarkable in that he was not precocious and had, besides, some deficiencies of education and taste to overcome. At school he was known chiefly for his "terrier courage" in fighting (the phrase is a reminder that even in manhood he was only an inch over five feet), though his last year or more was marked by a new passion for reading. He left school at fifteen, and for the next five years his time was largely absorbed by his medical studies. But, with Charles Cowden Clarke's friendly guidance, he carried on reading; and he began to write. Most of his earliest verse was an escape from medicine and the dingy Borough into leafy luxuries and romance — not that he lacked professional conscientiousness and competence, but his heart was increasingly elsewhere. Soon after receiving his certificate, Keats gave himself wholly to poetry, living on the small income from his inheritance. By his twenty-first birthday, October 31, 1816, he had written a fair amount of poor verse (some of which is touching in its eagerness and ardor), some respectable bits, and one great sonnet, a poem not merely of promise but of signal mastery.

At this time the letters begin, and henceforth they are an indispensable accompaniment to poetry of slowly growing power. To postpone for the moment their poetic concerns, the letters give a picture of Keats the man in his relations with his two younger brothers and sister, who were at the center of his affections, and his friends. The four young people, orphaned in childhood, were bound together by especially strong ties, and these were not weakened by George's marriage and emigration to the United States; six months later came Tom's death. Before that time, by the end of 1817, Keats had become acquainted with such eminent or rising writers as Wordsworth, Hazlitt, Lamb, and Shelley; but two lesser spirits, Leigh Hunt and Haydon the painter, were his special mentors and friends. (All of these men were more or less outside the pale of the orthodox ruling circles of literature represented by the powerful magazines, the *Edinburgh*, the *Quarterly*, and *Blackwood's*.) Both Hunt and Haydon gave enthusiastic encouragement to the poetic novice, but they had qualities which in time somewhat alienated Keats, and he remained closer to a number of young men whose names live now chiefly or only because they were his friends; one was John Hamilton Reynolds, a very minor poet and journalist, to whom Keats wrote so many of his most thoughtful letters. The kind and degree of affection and loyalty that Keats both gave and inspired may be seen in his own letters and in those of his friends about him. With these last may be put the letters of Fanny Brawne to Fanny Keats, written after the poet's death; but this testimony is a very partial alleviation of the pain we still feel, notwithstanding the long passage of time, in reading Keats's letters to her, letters that carry the ravages of disease, passion, frustration, and despair.

These few pages must concern themselves with Keats's poetry, not his biography, and, since the notes include introductions to the major poems, we may here look briefly at some general questions. In spite of his limited reading and limited acquaintance with his elders, even the youthful Keats was an instinctive participant and standard-bearer in the romantic movement. As a schoolboy, quite unaware that European romanticism was revitalizing myth, Keats devoured the mythological lore in the unexciting volumes of Tooke and Lempriere and Joseph Spence. Later he went through Spenser, said Clarke, "as a young horse would through a spring meadow — ramping." His own early verse, thin as most of it is, shows his intense feeling for nature and myth and the interfusion of the two. He inveighed against what he saw as the barren rationalism and formalism of the eighteenth century, and affirmed his profound faith in the senses and imagination and "the holiness of the Heart's affections." When Keats exclaims "O for a Life of Sensations rather than of Thoughts," he means "O for the direct, concrete apprehensions of the artist rather than the logical abstractions of the thinker." But, though Keats's name is identified with sensuous richness, he was never the aesthete or voluptuary of sensation that, to the later nineteenth century, he often seemed to be. For one thing, he was — except in genius — too normal and sensible: if we can imagine ourselves contemporaries, and in urgent need of wise advice, we would never think of consulting Shelley or Byron or Blake or Coleridge or even Wordsworth, but we would turn with confidence to Keats, the youngest of the lot. It is part of his fundamental wisdom that he was never carried away by ideological mirages or into misjudgments of other people or himself; along with a manly self-respect and high ambition, he had a healthy and humble capacity for self-criticism, an incapacity for self-deception. Speaking in a wider sense of the poet and critic, W. J. Bate observes: "He is a part of our literary conscience." Although he was so utterly devoted to poetry, he remains very human and approachable, an inhabitant, at least in part, of our world.

The articles of Keats's romantic faith owed something to Hunt, and far more to Wordsworth and Hazlitt. But whatever ideas he encountered were not assimilated until they had been tried on his own pulses, and they were more or less modified in becoming part of his being and outlook. In such letters as those on the "Mansion" of life or "the vale of Soul-making," we are not concerned with the novelty or lack of novelty in Keats's ethical-poetical creed, but only with the value it has acquired for him through his own reflection. Keats did not start with a full-fledged set of principles, aesthetic or philosophical, but worked them out as he went along. And some central problems were never worked out, but some of the attempts at resolution were his finest poems.

One main impulse of European romanticism was a striving toward the ideal and the infinite, and the young author of *I Stood Tip-toe* and *Endymion* had his full share of it. Experience that begins in the senses may in the end "burst our mortal bars," may attain a vision of "truth" or reality that is denied to mere reason. But even the young Keats, and much more the older Keats, had also a realistic awareness of human limitations and of the pains and sorrows of life. The tension between the ideal and the actual takes a variety of related forms. Indeed the ambiguities latent in both words cover most of them: the ideal suggests the perfection of art or imaginative vision, but also the imperfection of the remote and inhuman; the actual embraces both warm, substantial human experience and the ills that flesh and spirit are heir to.

In *Sleep and Poetry,* Keats is dwelling happily in the world of Flora and old Pan, the world of sensuous luxury, but he feels that he must in time leave this for "the agonies, the strife Of human hearts." The extraordinary intensity of his sensuous faculties confirms his faith in them; the senses yield an indubitable kind of beauty, beauty which is surely an element of whatever reality gives meaning to the world. Yet the senses are inferior to imaginative intuition, and beauty of form and color is inferior to the beauty born of man's tragic experience.

Thus, in his desire to achieve poetry of the Wordsworthian, and ultimately the Shakespearian, kind, the poetry of the human heart, Keats is at once seeking to fulfill and running counter to his strongest instincts. The attempted reconciliation of the ideal and the actual in *Endymion*, though wholly sincere, was premature and partly unreal; but deepening experience gives deepening reality to the conflict when it comes up again in *Hyperion*, the odes, and *The Fall of Hyperion*,

Within that general conflict are related tensions. Keats vacillates — and knows that he vacillates — between passive responsiveness to "sensations" and the desire for intellectual knowledge; passiveness may be the prelude to poetic fertility, yet even bookish knowledge enlightens the spirit and fortifies it against the buffets of circumstance. (As a rule, "knowledge" for Keats means an effort to grasp "the burthen of the mystery," but at times it has its ordinary sense.) Then there are moments when he doubts even the value of poetry; in his more normal moods, fine writing is pronounced, next to fine doing, the top thing in the world. But the qualification is important, and the problem of humanitarian action versus contemplation, of involvement versus detachment, receives its most urgent and earnest expression in Keats's last philosophic utterance, *The Fall of Hyperion*.

One other form of Keats's central polarity must be mentioned. Quite early he evolved the artistic ideal of "negative capability," that is, a refusal to seek for clear-cut answers, a willingness to maintain a state of suspension, to let the mind and imagination be a thoroughfare for all kinds of ideas — in short, to emulate the disinterested, morally neutral creativeness of Shakespeare, who had as much delight in conceiving an Iago as an Imogen. (We need not ask here if this was an altogether right notion of Shakespeare.) Thus Shakespeare, the ideal artist, has no personal identity, whereas Keats's two other great but lesser ideals, Milton and Wordsworth, are in their different ways exemplars of the "egotistical sublime" (to use the phrase Keats applied only to Wordsworth); each has a strong personal identity which leaves its positive, doctrinaire impress on his poetry. (Without disputing this, we may note that Keats's view, at least his early view, of Milton's ideas has the inevitable romantic inadequacy.) Shakespeare being a supreme and inimitable ideal, Keats fluctuated between the two more imitable poets; with reservations, we may say that in his mind Wordsworth and Milton stand respectively for the heart and the art of poetry. In the end, he feels that what is life for Milton would be death for him. How long negative capability remains an active ideal for Keats it would be hard to say. But, as he undergoes more and more painful experience, his letters show a stronger ethical concern, an increasing effort to achieve understanding, fortitude, and stability (the lesson of *The Excursion*), and the ideal of chameleon non-identity seems to give place to its opposite. In the sober letter on "the vale of Soul-making" the attainment of a positive ethical identity is the goal. And the "knowledge" that floods in upon Apollo and makes him a god, or the illumination seen in the face of Moneta, is surely a world away from Keats's earlier ideal.

Keats the artist matured slowly (as time is measured in Keatsian chronology). In some of the very early poems, and much more in *Endymion* and *Isabella*, there are incidental beauties that bear his hallmark, yet the most devout modern admirer, if he had been a sympathetic reviewer of the *Poems* of 1817, might — though the book contained the sonnet on Chapman's *Homer* — have failed to discern great promise. The earlier poetry, up through *Isabella*, manifests almost all the faults that can be comprised under slackness of structure, versification, style, and taste. The reasons are obvious: Keats's youth and inadequate culture and inadequate critical sense, and his assimilation of the weak elegance of much conventional and especially "Spenserian" verse of his own and preceding generations. Leigh Hunt is often made the scapegoat, since Keats was for a while a worshipful protégé. But a resemblance to Hunt's mixture of colloquial looseness, jauntiness, and lushness was as much a symptom of affinity as an effect of imitation. For the same reason of affinity, in reading such discursive Spenserians as the early William Browne or the late James Beattie and Mrs. Tighe, Keats was likely to pick up more vices than virtues. To such small poets he responded for a time with an instinctiveness that was not corrected by his early reading in Spenser, Shakespeare, Milton, and Wordsworth. His first poem of sustained and relatively flawless power was *Hyperion*, which remained a magnificent fragment and was, as Keats knew, off the line of his natural evolution; yet to move from *Isabella* to *Hyperion* is to realize the enormous advance he made in firmness of control, strength and concentration of phrase, weighted and expressive rhythm, indeed almost every element of poetic art. Whatever his later revulsion, it was chiefly discipleship to Milton that transformed a versifying pet-lamb into a great poet.

Some of Keats's early weaknesses can appear as late as the *Ode to Psyche* or *Lamia*, yet these become as nothing when set against the fully disciplined art and the ripe complexity of thought and feeling displayed during the marvelous year from the autumn of 1818 to the autumn of 1819. The nature of that power, as of any other fine artist's, can only be approached, even by the analytical subtlety of modern criticism, and these general or marginal comments attempt no subtleties. Keats has, for one thing, a genius for entering into and becoming and recreating in words an object or sensation. That capacity may not be the greatest of poetic gifts, but it is a rare one; various modern terms, empathy, kinaesthesia, and the like are perhaps no more precise than the phrase Arnold used about Keats, "natural magic." Even when he is hovering in or near a dream-world, his natural magic is never misty but is marked by clarity of line and more or less tactile solidity, whether he is imagining a little Greek town for ever desolate, or makes us simultaneously see, touch, smell, and almost hear "hush'd, cool-rooted flowers, fragrant-eyed." Even if we regard *The Eve of St. Agnes* as no more than a romantic tapestry of unique richness of color, we may react to individual images, bits of the "material sublime," as Keats reacted to northern scenes:

> they can never fade away — they make one forget the divisions of life; age, youth, poverty and riches; and refine one's sensual vision into a sort of north star which can never cease to be open lidded and stedfast over the wonders of the great Power . . . I cannot think with Hazlitt that these scenes make man appear little. I never forgot my stature so completely — I live in the eye; and my imagination, surpassed, is at rest. —

Of countless images and epithets in Keats we may say what Abt Vogler says of the musician, that out of three sounds he frames, not a fourth sound, but a star.

Such images and epithets, if often first thoughts, were often too the result of inspired revision, at the moment or sometimes much later. On the side of aesthetic and technical understanding, nothing takes us farther inside Keats's sensibility and the processes of his art than study of his revisions, notably in *Hyperion* and *The Eve of St. Agnes* but also in the odes and some lesser poems. Two extended examples are the opening picture of stillness in *Hyperion* and the casement window in the *Eve* (stanza 24). The largest example, of course, is *The Fall of Hyperion*, which involved a basic change in conception and technique. Revisions, as conscious changes, are a clue to what doubtless became more and more a matter of unconscious instinct. As Professor Bate has fully shown, Keats exploited every means of achieving greater intensity and restraint, a more effective blend of concentration and suggestion, for instance, the substitution of verbs or past participles for less forceful and less concrete words, the placing of vowels in patterns of simple or complicated assonance, and so on. While most of these multitudinous and minute changes tend toward greater concreteness, some of the most effective can be abstract: thus in *Hyperion* i.19 the description of Saturn's eyes is altered from the merely pictorial "white-browed" to the abstract but commonplace "ancient" to the abstract and tragically suggestive "realmless."

Both in themes and manner, even some poems of Keats's great year may have suffered somewhat from the ideas of "beauty" and "the poetical" that were in the atmosphere of his age; and recent poets, intent at times on pure perception, tend to shy away from the sumptuous in phrase and rhythm — although they may none the less give the impression of strain, whereas Keats's rich, warm density of texture, whatever hard work went into it, seems quite spontaneous and effortless. And modern critics have asked if the wisdom that Keats the man and the letter-writer won from life and thought got, or got very far, into the poems his brief maturity allowed him to write. Some have held that at his finest he was still a poet of luxury and sensation; others have seen him moving some way toward Shakespearian humanity, toward "the agonies, the strife Of human hearts," most clearly in the greater odes and *The Fall of Hyperion*. Certainly, if Keats's senses remained one avenue to "truth," his conception of beauty widened and deepened from the merely sensuous to the beauty that comprehends passion and sorrow. The verbal and rhythmical richness of the odes does not — like Keats's northern lakes and mountains — make one forget youth and age, life and death, permanence and transience, joy and suffering, which are at the center of the poems; the sensuous images, individually so potent — Ruth "amid the alien corn" — are elements in a view of life. The dealings of such a poet as Wallace Stevens with the senses and imagination and the nature of reality are doubtless far more subtle and complex than Keats's, yet they may be thought far more remotely and even inhumanly intellectual. Most of Keats's major poems have to do with the nature and experience of the poet, and might therefore seem foreordained to be precious; but Keats is in a way the natural man raised to the nth degree, and his meditations are so central that he speaks, with "the true voice of feeling," for no small part of humanity.

CHRONOLOGICAL TABLE

1795   October 31. Keats born, at a livery stable, the Swan and Hoop, at 24 Moorfields Pavement Row in London, just north of the City. His father Thomas, head ostler, had in 1794 married Frances, daughter of John Jennings, the owner, and later became the owner himself.

       George Keats born in 1797; Thomas in 1799; Frances (Fanny) in 1803.

1803   John and George sent to the Clarke school at Enfield, ten miles north of London.

1804   April 16. Father killed by a fall from his horse.

       June 27. Mrs. Keats marries William Rawlings. Her mother takes the children to live with her and her husband at Ponders End, near Enfield. Mrs. Rawlings soon leaves her husband and joins them.

1805   March. Death of John Jennings. Mrs. Jennings moves to Edmonton, eight miles north of London.

1809   At 14 Keats develops a passion for reading. Literary friendship with Charles Cowden Clarke, the young son of the headmaster and an assistant teacher.

1810   March. Death of Keats's mother, from tuberculosis, after a long illness.

       July. Mrs. Jennings arranges a trust fund of £8000 for her grandchildren and names as their guardians Richard Abbey, a tea-merchant, and J. R. Sandell (Abbey eventually became sole guardian).

1811   Keats wins the last of his several school prizes, John Bonnycastle's *Introduction to Astronomy*.

1811   Keats leaves school. Apprenticed by his guardian to an apothecary-surgeon, Thomas Hammond, in Edmonton. Carries on friendship with C. C. Clarke, borrowing books and reading with him. Finishes a prose translation of the *Aeneid* begun at school.

1814   Early attempts at verse: *Imitation of Spenser, To Lord Byron*, etc.

       December. Mrs. Jennings' death breaks up the family home.

1815   Poems multiply, more or less weak and imitative. Keats leaves Hammond and begins (October 1) the next stage in his medical training, at Guy's Hospital in the Borough, London (south side of the river).

1816 First publication: the sonnet *To Solitude* (written in November, 1815) printed in Hunt's *Examiner,* May 5. Becomes acquainted with Joseph Severn.

July 25. Receives Apothecaries' Certificate.

August–September. With Tom at Margate, on the southeast coast.

October. Keats's first great poem, on Chapman's *Homer.*

December 1. The Chapman sonnet printed, with praise, in the *Examiner,* in Hunt's article, "Young Poets" (Reynolds, Shelley, Keats).

Autumn and early winter. *I Stood Tip-toe* (begun in the summer?); *Sleep and Poetry.* Keats becomes acquainted with Hunt, Haydon, Reynolds, Shelley, and perhaps Hazlitt and Lamb.

Between autumn and spring, 1816–17, Keats gives up any notion of medical practice.

1817 March 1 or 2. Views the Elgin Marbles, under Haydon's guidance.

March 3. First volume, *Poems,* published. (At intervals six reviews, three by friends, including Hunt; mostly favorable.)

Late March. Living with his brothers in Well Walk, Hampstead.

Spring and summer. Becomes a friend of Benjamin Bailey, James Rice, Charles Dilke, Charles Brown, and perhaps Richard Woodhouse.

April. Begins *Endymion,* in the Isle of Wight

May–June. At Margate, Canterbury, etc.

June–August. In Hampstead.

September. With Bailey at Oxford. Writes *Endymion* iii.

November 28. *Endymion* finished, at Burford Bridge, Surrey.

December 21. As substitute for Reynolds, dramatic critic of the *Champion,* writes "Mr. Kean," the first of three theatrical reviews.

December 28. Haydon's "immortal dinner" (Keats, Wordsworth, Lamb, *et al.*).

1818 January–February. Meetings with Wordsworth. Hears Hazlitt's lectures on the English poets.

February–April. *Isabella.*

March 6–7—May 4–5. At Teignmouth, Devon, with the consumptive Tom.

March 25. *Epistle to John Hamilton Reynolds.*

Late April. *Endymion* published.

May 28 (?). George Keats marries Georgiana Wylie.

June–August. Keats sees the pair off for the United States and proceeds from Liverpool, with Charles Brown, on a walking tour in northern England, Scotland, and Ireland. His first experience of rugged mountain scenery.

August 18. Keats returns to London, having been compelled by a severe cold to abandon the tour. Tom much worse.

August–September. Meets Fanny Brawne (b. August 9, 1800).

c. September 1. Keats's *Poems* and *Endymion* coarsely abused in *Blackwood's Magazine* (August issue), in a review by J. G. Lockhart.

c. September 27. A harsh review of *Endymion* by John Wilson Croker, *Quarterly Review,* XIX (April), 204–8.

September–November. Keats begins *Hyperion,* while nursing Tom through the last stages of tuberculosis.

December 1. Death of Tom.

December. Keats goes to live with Charles Brown in his half of a double house, Wentworth Place, in Hampstead; the other half was occupied by the Dilkes. (This is now the Keats Museum.)

December 25. An avowal of love between Keats and Fanny Brawne.

1819 January 18–19—February 1–2. Keats with Brown at Chichester and Bedhampton. Writes *The Eve of St. Agnes* (revised in September).

February 13–17. *The Eve of Saint Mark.*

April (?). The Brawnes move into the Dilkes' half of Wentworth Place. Keats and Brown in the other half.

April 11. Walk and talk with Coleridge.

April. Unable to finish *Hyperion*, Keats gives the MS. to Woodhouse. *La Belle Dame sans Merci* (the second version done before May 10, 1820). *Ode to Psyche.*

May. Odes: *Nightingale, Grecian Urn, Melancholy, Indolence.*

June. Brown, as usual, rents his house for the summer; Keats and Fanny Brawne separated. Perhaps a provisional engagement, Keats hoping to make enough money to marry.

July–August 12. Keats in the Isle of Wight with James Rice, and later Brown. Working on *Lamia, The Fall of Hyperion,* and, with Brown, on *Otho the Great.*

August 12– *c.* October 8. With Brown in Winchester. *King Stephen* (August or November?). *Lamia* and the *Fall* continued.

September 19. *To Autumn.*

September 21. Writes to Reynolds that he has given up the *Fall* (or/and *Hyperion?*). Some revision done in November–December.

September–October. Short-lived plans to make money in journalism.

October. Formally engaged to Fanny? With Brown in Hampstead (late October). *The Cap and Bells:* October or November to December or January.

November (or August?): *King Stephen.*

A mainly unhappy summer and autumn because of growing illness, separation from and inability to marry Fanny Brawne, acute need of money for George and himself, and a sense of failure.

1820   January. George Keats in England to raise money.

February 3. Keats seriously ill (a haemorrhage). Slow and incomplete recovery.

May–August. Brown away. Keats living in Kentish Town, near, and then with, the Hunts, until August 12.

Early July. Third volume published: *Lamia, Isabella, The Eve of St. Agnes, and Other Poems. La Belle Dame, The Eve of Saint Mark. The Fall of Hyperion,* etc., not included.

July 27. Shelley sends invitation to Keats to live with him and his family in Pisa. Keats declines (August 16).

August–September. In Hampstead, under the care of Mrs. Brawne and Fanny.

August. Francis Jeffrey's largely favorable but belated review of *Endymion* and of the 1820 volume, *Edinburgh Review*, XXXIV, 203–13.

September 18. Keats sails for Italy, with Joseph Severn looking after him.

October 31. They land at Naples, after quarantine.

November 15. Arrival at Rome. They lodge at 26 Piazza di Spagna (now the Keats-Shelley Memorial House).

December 10. Serious haemorrhages.

1821   February 23. Keats's death.

February 26. Buried in the Protestant Cemetery, Rome.

POEMS

IMITATION OF SPENSER

Now Morning from her orient chamber came,
And her first footsteps touch'd a verdant hill;
Crowning its lawny crest with amber flame,
Silv'ring the untainted gushes of its rill;
Which, pure from mossy beds, did down distill,
And after parting beds of simple flowers.
By many streams a little lake did fill,
Which round its marge reflected woven bowers,
And, in its middle space, a sky that never lowers.

There the king-fisher saw his plumage bright   10
Vieing with fish of brilliant dye below;
Whose silken fins, and golden scales' light
Cast upward, through the waves, a ruby glow:
There saw the swan his neck of arched snow,
And oar'd himself along with majesty;
Sparkled his jetty eyes; his feet did show
Beneath the waves like Afric's ebony,
And on his back a fay reclined voluptuously.

Ah! could I tell the wonders of an isle
That in that fairest lake had placed been,   20
I could e'en Dido of her grief beguile;
Or rob from aged Lear his bitter teen:
For sure so fair a place was never seen,
Of all that ever charm'd romantic eye:
It seem'd an emerald in the silver sheen
Of the bright waters; or as when on high,
Through clouds of fleecy white, laughs the cœrulean sky.

And all around it dipp'd luxuriously
Slopings of verdure through the glossy tide,
Which, as it were in gentle amity,   30
Rippled delighted up the flowery side;
As if to glean the ruddy tears, it tried,
Which fell profusely from the rose-tree stem!
Haply it was the workings of its pride,
In strife to throw upon the shore a gem
Outvieing all the buds in Flora's diadem.

3

TO LORD BYRON

BYRON! how sweetly sad thy melody!
   Attuning still the soul to tenderness,
   As if soft Pity, with unusual stress,
Had touched her plaintive lute, and thou, being by,
Hadst caught the tones, nor suffered them to die.
   O'ershading sorrow doth not make thee less
   Delightful: thou thy griefs dost dress
With a bright halo, shining beamily,
As when a cloud the golden moon doth veil,
   Its sides are tinged with a resplendent glow,   10
Through the dark robe oft amber rays prevail,
   And like fair veins in sable marble flow;
Still warble, dying swan! still tell the tale,
   The enchanting tale, the tale of pleasing woe.

TO CHATTERTON

O CHATTERTON! how very sad thy fate!
   Dear child of sorrow — son of misery!
   How soon the film of death obscured that eye,
Whence Genius mildly flashed, and high debate.
How soon that voice, majestic and elate,
   Melted in dying numbers! Oh! how nigh
   Was night to thy fair morning. Thou didst die
A half-blown flow'ret which cold blasts amate.
But this is past: thou art among the stars
   Of highest Heaven: to the rolling spheres   10
Thou sweetly singest: nought thy hymning mars,
   Above the ingrate world and human fears.
On earth the good man base detraction bars
   From thy fair name, and waters it with tears.

WRITTEN ON THE DAY THAT MR. LEIGH HUNT LEFT PRISON

WHAT though, for showing truth to flatter'd state,
   Kind Hunt was shut in prison, yet has he,
   In his immortal spirit, been as free
As the sky-searching lark, and as elate.
Minion of grandeur! think you he did wait?

Think you he nought but prison walls did see,
  Till, so unwilling, thou unturn'dst the key?
Ah, no! far happier, nobler was his fate!
In Spenser's halls he strayed, and bowers fair,
  Culling enchanted flowers; and he flew   10
With daring Milton through the fields of air:
  To regions of his own his genius true
Took happy flights. Who shall his fame impair
  When thou art dead, and all thy wretched crew?

ODE TO APOLLO

In thy western halls of gold
  When thou sittest in thy state,
Bards, that erst sublimely told
  Heroic deeds, and sang of fate,
With fervour seize their adamantine lyres,
Whose chords are solid rays, and twinkle radiant fires.

Here Homer with his nervous arms
  Strikes the twanging harp of war,
And even the western splendour warms,
  While the trumpets sound afar: 10
But, what creates the most intense surprise,
His soul looks out through renovated eyes.

Then, through thy Temple wide, melodious swells
  The sweet majestic tone of Maro's lyre:
The soul delighted on each accent dwells, —
  Enraptured dwells, — not daring to respire,
The while he tells of grief around a funeral pyre.

'Tis awful silence then again;
  Expectant stand the spheres;
  Breathless the laurell'd peers,   20
Nor move, till ends the lofty strain,
Nor move till Milton's tuneful thunders cease,
And leave once more the ravish'd heavens in peace.

Thou biddest Shakspeare wave his hand,
  And quickly forward spring
The Passions — a terrific band —
  And each vibrates the string
That with its tyrant temper best accords,
While from their Master's lips pour forth the inspiring words.

A silver trumpet Spenser blows,   30
    And, as its martial notes to silence flee,
From a virgin chorus flows
    A hymn in praise of spotless Chastity.
'Tis still! Wild warblings from the Æolian lyre
Enchantment softly breathe, and tremblingly expire.

Next thy Tasso's ardent numbers
    Float along the pleased air,
Calling youth from idle slumbers,
    Rousing them from Pleasure's lair: —
Then o'er the strings his fingers gently move,   40
And melt the soul to pity and to love.

But when *Thou* joinest with the Nine,
And all the powers of song combine,
    We listen here on earth:
The dying tones that fill the air,
And charm the ear of evening fair,
From thee, great God of Bards, receive their heavenly birth.

TO SOLITUDE

O SOLITUDE! if I must with thee dwell,
    Let it not be among the jumbled heap
    Of murky buildings; climb with me the steep, —
Nature's observatory — whence the dell,
Its flowery slopes, its river's crystal swell,
    May seem a span; let me thy vigils keep
    'Mongst boughs pavillion'd, where the deer's swift leap
Startles the wild bee from the fox-glove bell.
But though I'll gladly trace these scenes with thee,
    Yet the sweet converse of an innocent mind,   10
Whose words are images of thoughts refin'd,
    Is my soul's pleasure; and it sure must be
Almost the highest bliss of human-kind,
    When to thy haunts two kindred spirits flee.

Among the rest a shepheard (though but young
Yet hartned to his pipe) with all the skill
His few yeeres could, began to fit his quill.
Britannia's Pastorals. — BROWNE.*

TO GEORGE FELTON MATHEW

SWEET are the pleasures that to verse belong,
And doubly sweet a brotherhood in song;
Nor can remembrance, Mathew! bring to view
A fate more pleasing, a delight more true
Than that in which the brother Poets joy'd,
Who with combined powers, their wit employ'd
To raise a trophy to the drama's muses.
The thought of this great partnership diffuses
Over the genius-loving heart, a feeling
Of all that's high, and great, and good, and healing.   10

Too partial friend! fain would I follow thee
Past each horizon of fine poesy;
Fain would I echo back each pleasant note
As o'er Sicilian seas, clear anthems float
'Mong the light skimming gondolas far parted,
Just when the sun his farewell beam has darted:
But 'tis impossible; far different cares
Beckon me sternly from soft "Lydian airs,"
And hold my faculties so long in thrall,
That I am oft in doubt whether at all   20
I shall again see Phœbus in the morning:
Or flush'd Aurora in the roseate dawning!
Or a white Naiad in a rippling stream;
Or a rapt seraph in a moonlight beam;
Or again witness what with thee I've seen,
The dew by fairy feet swept from the green,
After a night of some quaint jubilee
Which every elf and fay had come to see:
When bright processions took their airy march
Beneath the curved moon's triumphal arch.   30

But might I now each passing moment give
To the coy muse, with me she would not live
In this dark city, nor would condescend

* Prefixed to the group of Epistles.

'Mid contradictions her delights to lend.
Should e'er the fine-eyed maid to me be kind,
Ah! surely it must be whene'er I find
Some flowery spot, sequester'd, wild, romantic,
That often must have seen a poet frantic;
Where oaks, that erst the Druid knew, are growing,
And flowers, the glory of one day, are blowing;   40
Where the dark-leav'd laburnum's drooping clusters
Reflect athwart the stream their yellow lustres,
And intertwined the cassia's arms unite,
With its own drooping buds, but very white.
Where on one side are covert branches hung,
'Mong which the nightingales have always sung
In leafy quiet: where to pry, aloof,
Atween the pillars of the sylvan roof,
Would be to find where violet beds were nestling,
And where the bee with cowslip bells was wrestling.   50
There must be too a ruin dark, and gloomy,
To say "joy not too much in all that's bloomy."

Yet this is vain — O Mathew lend thy aid
To find a place where I may greet the maid —
Where we may soft humanity put on,
And sit, and rhyme and think on Chatterton;
And that warm-hearted Shakspeare sent to meet him
Four laurell'd spirits, heaven-ward to intreat him.
With reverence would we speak of all the sages
Who have left streaks of light athwart their ages: 60
And thou shouldst moralize on Milton's blindness,
And mourn the fearful dearth of human kindness
To those who strove with the bright golden wing
Of genius, to flap away each sting
Thrown by the pitiless world. We next could tell
Of those who in the cause of freedom fell;
Of our own Alfred, of Helvetian Tell;
Of him whose name to ev'ry heart's a solace,
High-minded and unbending William Wallace.
While to the rugged north our musing turns   70
We well might drop a tear for him, and Burns.

Felton! without incitements such as these,
How vain for me the niggard Muse to tease:
For thee, she will thy every dwelling grace,
And make "a sun-shine in a shady place:"
For thou wast once a flowret blooming wild,
Close to the source, bright, pure, and undefil'd,

Whence gush the streams of song: in happy hour
Came chaste Diana from her shady bower,
Just as the sun was from the east uprising;   80
And, as for him some gift she was devising,
Beheld thee, pluck'd thee, cast thee in the stream
To meet her glorious brother's greeting beam.
I marvel much that thou hast never told
How, from a flower, into a fish of gold
Apollo chang'd thee; how thou next didst seem
A black-eyed swan upon the widening stream;
And when thou first didst in that mirror trace
The placid features of a human face:
That thou hast never told thy travels strange,   90
And all the wonders of the mazy range
O'er pebbly crystal, and o'er golden sands;
Kissing thy daily food from Naiad's pearly hands.

HOW MANY BARDS

How many bards gild the lapses of time!
   A few of them have ever been the food
   Of my delighted fancy, — I could brood
Over their beauties, earthly, or sublime:
And often, when I sit me down to rhyme,
   These will in throngs before my mind intrude:
   But no confusion, no disturbance rude
Do they occasion; 'tis a pleasing chime.
So the unnumber'd sounds that evening store:
   The songs of birds — the whisp'ring of the leaves —   10
The voice of waters — the great bell that heaves
   With solemn sound, — and thousand others more,
That distance of recognizance bereaves,
   Make pleasing music, and not wild uproar.

TO ONE WHO HAS BEEN LONG IN CITY PENT

To ONE who has been long in city pent,
   'Tis very sweet to look into the fair
   And open face of heaven, — to breathe a prayer
Full in the smile of the blue firmament.
Who is more happy, when, with heart's content,
   Fatigued he sinks into some pleasant lair
   Of wavy grass, and reads a debonair
And gentle tale of love and languishment?

Returning home at evening, with an ear
  Catching the notes of Philomel, — an eye   10
Watching the sailing cloudlet's bright career,
  He mourns that day so soon has glided by:
E'en like the passage of an angel's tear
  That falls through the clear ether silently.

TO MY BROTHER GEORGE

MANY the wonders I this day have seen:
  The sun, when first he kist away the tears
  That fill'd the eyes of morn; — the laurel'd peers
Who from the feathery gold of evening lean; —
The ocean with its vastness, its blue green,
  Its ships, its rocks, its caves, its hopes, its fears, —
  Its voice mysterious, which whoso hears
Must think on what will be, and what has been.
E'en now, dear George, while this for you I write,
  Cynthia is from her silken curtains peeping   10
So scantly, that it seems her bridal night,
  And she her half-discover'd revels keeping.
But what, without the social thought of thee,
Would be the wonders of the sky and sea?

TO MY BROTHER GEORGE

FULL many a dreary hour have I past,
My brain bewilder'd, and my mind o'ercast
With heaviness; in seasons when I've thought
No spherey strains by me could e'er be caught
From the blue dome, though I to dimness gaze
On the far depth where sheeted lightning plays;
Or, on the wavy grass outstretch'd supinely,
Pry 'mong the stars, to strive to think divinely:
That I should never hear Apollo's song,
Though feathery clouds were floating all along   10
The purple west, and, two bright streaks between,
The golden lyre itself were dimly seen:
That the still murmur of the honey bee
Would never teach a rural song to me:
That the bright glance from beauty's eyelids slanting
Would never make a lay of mine enchanting,
Or warm my breast with ardour to unfold
Some tale of love and arms in time of old.

But there are times, when those that love the bay,
Fly from all sorrowing far, far away;   20
A sudden glow comes on them, nought they see
In water, earth, or air, but poesy.
It has been said, dear George, and true I hold it,
(For knightly Spenser to Libertas told it,)
That when a Poet is in such a trance,
In air he sees white coursers paw, and prance,
Bestridden of gay knights, in gay apparel,
Who at each other tilt in playful quarrel,
And what we, ignorantly, sheet-lightning call,
Is the swift opening of their wide portal,   30
When the bright warder blows his trumpet clear,
Whose tones reach nought on earth but Poet's ear.
When these enchanted portals open wide,
And through the light the horsemen swiftly glide,
The Poet's eye can reach those golden halls,
And view the glory of their festivals:
Their ladies fair, that in the distance seem
Fit for the silv'ring of a seraph's dream;
Their rich brimm'd goblets, that incessant run
Like the bright spots that move about the sun;   40
And, when upheld, the wine from each bright jar

Pours with the lustre of a falling star.
Yet further off, are dimly seen their bowers,
Of which, no mortal eye can reach the flowers;
And 'tis right just, for well Apollo knows
'Twould make the Poet quarrel with the rose.
All that's reveal'd from that far seat of blisses,
Is, the clear fountains' interchanging kisses,
As gracefully descending, light and thin,
Like silver streaks across a dolphin's fin,   50
When he upswimmeth from the coral caves,
And sports with half his tail above the waves.

These wonders strange he sees, and many more,
Whose head is pregnant with poetic lore.
Should he upon an evening ramble fare
With forehead to the soothing breezes bare,
Would he naught see but the dark, silent blue
With all its diamonds trembling through and through?
Or the coy moon, when in the waviness
Of whitest clouds she does her beauty dress,   60
And staidly paces higher up, and higher.
Like a sweet nun in holy-day attire?
Ah, yes! much more would start into his sight —
The revelries, and mysteries of night:
And should I ever see them, I will tell you
Such tales as needs must with amazement spell you.

These are the living pleasures of the bard:
But richer far posterity's award.
What does he murmur with his latest breath,
While his proud eye looks through the film of death?   70
"What though I leave this dull, and earthly mould,
Yet shall my spirit lofty converse hold
With after times. — The patriot shall feel
My stern alarum, and unsheath his steel;
Or, in the senate thunder out my numbers
To startle princes from their easy slumbers.
The sage will mingle with each moral theme
My happy thoughts sententious; he will teem
With lofty periods when my verses fire him,
And then I'll stoop from heaven to inspire him.   80
Lays have I left of such a dear delight
That maids will sing them on their bridal night.
Gay villagers, upon a morn of May,
When they have tired their gentle limbs with play,
And form'd a snowy circle on the grass,

And plac'd in midst of all that lovely lass
Who chosen is their queen, — with her fine head
Crowned with flowers purple, white, and red:
For there the lily, and the musk-rose, sighing,
Are emblems true of hapless lovers dying: 90
Between her breasts, that never yet felt trouble,
A bunch of violets full blown, and double,
Serenely sleep: — she from a casket takes
A little book, — and then a joy awakes
About each youthful heart, — with stifled cries,
And rubbing of white hands, and sparkling eyes:
For she's to read a tale of hopes, and fears;
One that I foster'd in my youthful years:
The pearls, that on each glist'ning circlet sleep,
Gush ever and anon with silent creep,   100
Lured by the innocent dimples. To sweet rest
Shall the dear babe, upon its mother's breast,
Be lull'd with songs of mine. Fair world, adieu!
Thy dales, and hills, are fading from my view:
Swiftly I mount, upon wide spreading pinions,
Far from the narrow bounds of thy dominions.
Full joy I feel, while thus I cleave the air,
That my soft verse will charm thy daughters fair,
And warm thy sons!" Ah, my dear friend and brother,
Could I, at once, my mad ambition smother,   110
For tasting joys like these, sure I should be
Happier, and dearer to society.
At times, 'tis true, I've felt relief from pain
When some bright thought has darted through my brain:
Through all that day I've felt a greater pleasure
Than if I'd brought to light a hidden treasure.
As to my sonnets, though none else should heed them,
I feel delighted, still, that you should read them.
Of late, too, I have had much calm enjoyment,
Stretch'd on the grass at my best lov'd employment   120
Of scribbling lines for you. These things I thought
While, in my face, the freshest breeze I caught.
E'en now I'm pillow'd on a bed of flowers
That crowns a lofty clift, which proudly towers
Above the ocean-waves. The stalks, and blades,
Chequer my tablet with their quivering shades.
On one side is a field of drooping oats,
Through which the poppies show their scarlet coats;
So pert and useless, that they bring to mind
The scarlet coats that pester human-kind.   130
And on the other side, outspread, is seen

Ocean's blue mantle streak'd with purple, and green.
Now 'tis I see a canvass'd ship, and now
Mark the bright silver curling round her prow.
I see the lark down-dropping to his nest,
And the broad winged sea-gull never at rest;
For when no more he spreads his feathers free,
His breast is dancing on the restless sea.
Now I direct my eyes into the west,
Which at this moment is in sunbeams drest:
Why westward turn? 'Twas but to say adieu!
'Twas but to kiss my hand, dear George, to you!

140

TO CHARLES COWDEN CLARKE

OFT have you seen a swan superbly frowning,
And with proud breast his own white shadow crowning;
He slants his neck beneath the waters bright
So silently, it seems a beam of light
Come from the galaxy: anon he sports, —
With outspread wings the Naiad Zephyr courts,
Or ruffles all the surface of the lake
In striving from its crystal face to take
Some diamond water drops, and them to treasure
In milky nest, and sip them off at leisure.   10
But not a moment can he there insure them,
Nor to such downy rest can he allure them;
For down they rush as though they would be free,
And drop like hours into eternity.
Just like that bird am I in loss of time,
Whene'er I venture on the stream of rhyme;
With shatter'd boat, oar snapt, and canvass rent,
I slowly sail, scarce knowing my intent;
Still scooping up the water with my fingers,
In which a trembling diamond never lingers.   20

By this, friend Charles, you may full plainly see
Why I have never penn'd a line to thee:
Because my thoughts were never free, and clear,
And little fit to please a classic ear;
Because my wine was of too poor a savour
For one whose palate gladdens in the flavour
Of sparkling Helicon: — small good it were
To take him to a desert rude, and bare,
Who had on Baiæ's shore reclin'd at ease,
While Tasso's page was floating in a breeze   30
That gave soft music from Armida's bowers,
Mingled with fragrance from her rarest flowers:
Small good to one who had by Mulla's stream
Fondled the maidens with the breasts of cream;
Who had beheld Belphœbe in a brook,
And lovely Una in a leafy nook,
And Archimago leaning o'er his book:
Who had of all that's sweet tasted, and seen,
From silv'ry ripple, up to beauty's queen;
From the sequester'd haunts of gay Titania,   40
To the blue dwelling of divine Urania:

One, who, of late, had ta'en sweet forest walks
With him who elegantly chats, and talks —
The wrong'd Libertas — who has told you stories
Of laurel chaplets, and Apollo's glories;
Of troops chivalrous prancing through a city,
And tearful ladies made for love, and pity:
With many else which I have never known.
Thus have I thought; and days on days have flown
Slowly, or rapidly — unwilling still   50
For you to try my dull, unlearned quill.
Nor should I now, but that I've known you long;
That you first taught me all the sweets of song:
The grand, the sweet, the terse, the free, the fine;
What swell'd with pathos, and what right divine:
Spenserian vowels that elope with ease,
And float along like birds o'er summer seas;
Miltonian storms, and more, Miltonian tenderness;
Michael in arms, and more, meek Eve's fair slenderness.
Who read for me the sonnet swelling loudly   60
Up to its climax and then dying proudly?
Who found for me the grandeur of the ode,
Growing, like Atlas, stronger from its load?
Who let me taste that more than cordial dram,
The sharp, the rapier-pointed epigram?
Shew'd me that epic was of all the king,
Round, vast, and spanning all like Saturn's ring?
You too upheld the veil from Clio's beauty,
And pointed out the patriot's stern duty;
The might of Alfred, and the shaft of Tell;   70
The hand of Brutus, that so grandly fell
Upon a tyrant's head. Ah! had I never seen,
Or known your kindness, what might I have been?
What my enjoyments in my youthful years,
Bereft of all that now my life endears?
And can I e'er these benefits forget?
And can I e'er repay the friendly debt?
No, doubly no; — yet should these rhymings please,
I shall roll on the grass with two-fold ease:
For I have long time been my fancy feeding   80
With hopes that you would one day think the reading
Of my rough verses not an hour misspent;
Should it e'er be so, what a rich content!

Some weeks have pass'd since last I saw the spires
In lucent Thames reflected: — warm desires
To see the sun o'er peep the eastern dimness,

And morning shadows streaking into slimness
Across the lawny fields, and pebbly water;
To mark the time as they grow broad, and shorter;
To feel the air that plays about the hills,   90
And sips its freshness from the little rills;
To see high, golden corn wave in the light
When Cynthia smiles upon a summer's night,
And peers among the cloudlets jet and white,
As though she were reclining in a bed
Of bean blossoms, in heaven freshly shed.
No sooner had I stepp'd into these pleasures
Than I began to think of rhymes and measures:
The air that floated by me seem'd to say
"Write! thou wilt never have a better day."   100
And so I did. When many lines I'd written,
Though with their grace I was not oversmitten,
Yet, as my hand was warm, I thought I'd better
Trust to my feelings, and write you a letter.
Such an attempt required an inspiration
Of a peculiar sort, — a consummation; —
Which, had I felt, these scribblings might have been
Verses from which the soul would never wean:
But many days have passed since last my heart
Was warm'd luxuriously by divine Mozart;   110
By Arne delighted, or by Handel madden'd;
Or by the song of Erin pierc'd and sadden'd.
What time you were before the music sitting,
And the rich notes to each sensation fitting.
Since I have walk'd with you through shady lanes
That freshly terminate in open plains,
And revel'd in a chat that ceased not
When at night-fall among your books we got:
No, nor when supper came, nor after that, —
Nor when reluctantly I took my hat;   120
No, nor till cordially you shook my hand
Mid-way between our homes: — your accents bland
Still sounded in my ears, when I no more
Could hear your footsteps touch the grav'ly floor.
Sometimes I lost them, and then found again;
You chang'd the footpath for the grassy plain.
In those still moments I have wish'd you joys
That well you know to honour: — "Life's very toys
With him," said I, "will take a pleasant charm;
It cannot be that aught will work him harm."   130
These thoughts now come o'er me with all their might: —
Again I shake your hand, — friend Charles, good night.

ON FIRST LOOKING INTO CHAPMAN'S HOMER

MUCH have I travell'd in the realms of gold,
  And many goodly states and kingdoms seen;
  Round many western islands have I been
Which bards in fealty to Apollo hold.
Oft of one wide expanse had I been told
  That deep-brow'd Homer ruled as his demesne;
  Yet did I never breathe its pure serene
Till I heard Chapman speak out loud and bold:
Then felt I like some watcher of the skies
  When a new planet swims into his ken;   10
Or like stout Cortez when with eagle eyes
  He star'd at the Pacific — and all his men
Look'd at each other with a wild surmise —
  Silent, upon a peak in Darien.

KEEN, FITFUL GUSTS

KEEN, fitful gusts are whisp'ring here and there
  Among the bushes half leafless, and dry;
  The stars look very cold about the sky,
And I have many miles on foot to fare.
Yet feel I little of the cool bleak air,
  Or of the dead leaves rustling drearily,
  Or of those silver lamps that burn on high,
Or of the distance from home's pleasant lair:
For I am brimfull of the friendliness
  That in a little cottage I have found;   10
Of fair-hair'd Milton's eloquent distress,
  And all his love for gentle Lycid drown'd;
Of lovely Laura in her light green dress,
  And faithful Petrarch gloriously crown'd.

TO MY BROTHERS

SMALL, busy flames play through the fresh laid coals,
  And their faint cracklings o'er our silence creep
  Like whispers of the household gods that keep
A gentle empire o'er fraternal souls.
And while, for rhymes, I search around the poles,
  Your eyes are fix'd, as in poetic sleep,

Upon the lore so voluble and deep,
That aye at fall of night our care condoles.
This is your birth-day Tom, and I rejoice
  That thus it passes smoothly, quietly.   10
Many such eves of gently whisp'ring noise
  May we together pass, and calmly try
What are this world's true joys, — ere the great voice,
  From its fair face, shall bid our spirits fly.

[SECOND SONNET TO HAYDON]

ADDRESSED TO THE SAME

GREAT spirits now on earth are sojourning;
  He of the cloud, the cataract, the lake,
  Who on Helvellyn's summit, wide awake,
Catches his freshness from Archangel's wing:
He of the rose, the violet, the spring,
  The social smile, the chain for Freedom's sake:
  And lo! — whose stedfastness would never take
A meaner sound than Raphael's whispering.
And other spirits there are standing apart
  Upon the forehead of the age to come;   10
These, these will give the world another heart,
  And other pulses. Hear ye not the hum
Of mighty workings? —
  Listen awhile ye nations, and be dumb.

ON THE GRASSHOPPER AND CRICKET

THE poetry of earth is never dead:
  When all the birds are faint with the hot sun,
  And hide in cooling trees, a voice will run
From hedge to hedge about the new-mown mead;
That is the Grasshopper's — he takes the lead
  In summer luxury, — he has never done
  With his delights; for when tired out with fun
He rests at ease beneath some pleasant weed.
The poetry of earth is ceasing never:
  On a lone winter evening, when the frost   10
  Has wrought a silence, from the stove there shrills
The Cricket's song, in warmth increasing ever,
  And seems to one in drowsiness half lost,
    The Grasshopper's among some grassy hills.

I STOOD TIP-TOE

"Places of nestling green for Poets made."
Story of Rimini.

I STOOD tip-toe upon a little hill,
The air was cooling, and so very still,
That the sweet buds which with a modest pride
Pull droopingly, in slanting curve aside,
Their scantly leaved, and finely tapering stems,
Had not yet lost those starry diadems
Caught from the early sobbing of the morn.
The clouds were pure and white as flocks new shorn,
And fresh from the clear brook; sweetly they slept
On the blue fields of heaven, and then there crept   10
A little noiseless noise among the leaves,
Born of the very sigh that silence heaves:
For not the faintest motion could be seen
Of all the shades that slanted o'er the green.
There was wide wand'ring for the greediest eye,
To peer about upon variety;
Far round the horizon's crystal air to skim,
And trace the dwindled edgings of its brim;
To picture out the quaint, and curious bending
Of a fresh woodland alley, never ending;   20
Or by the bowery clefts, and leafy shelves,
Guess where the jaunty streams refresh themselves.
I gazed awhile, and felt as light, and free
As though the fanning wings of Mercury
Had play'd upon my heels: I was light-hearted,
And many pleasures to my vision started;
So I straightway began to pluck a posey
Of luxuries bright, milky, soft and rosy.

A bush of May flowers with the bees about them;
Ah, sure no tasteful nook would be without them;   30
And let a lush laburnum oversweep them,
And let long grass grow round the roots to keep them
Moist, cool and green; and shade the violets,
That they may bind the moss in leafy nets.

A filbert hedge with wild briar overtwined,
And clumps of woodbine taking the soft wind

Upon their summer thrones; there too should be
The frequent chequer of a youngling tree,
That with a score of light green brethren shoots
From the quaint mossiness of aged roots: 40
Round which is heard a spring-head of clear waters
Babbling so wildly of its lovely daughters
The spreading bluebells: it may haply mourn
That such fair clusters should be rudely torn
From their fresh beds, and scattered thoughtlessly
By infant hands, left on the path to die.

Open afresh your round of starry folds,
Ye ardent marigolds!
Dry up the moisture from your golden lids,
For great Apollo bids   50
That in these days your praises should be sung
On many harps, which he has lately strung;
And when again your dewiness he kisses,
Tell him, I have you in my world of blisses:
So haply when I rove in some far vale,
His mighty voice may come upon the gale.

Here are sweet peas, on tip-toe for a flight:
With wings of gentle flush o'er delicate white,
And taper fingers catching at all things,
To bind them all about with tiny rings.   60

Linger awhile upon some bending planks
That lean against a streamlet's rushy banks,
And watch intently Nature's gentle doings:
They will be found softer than ring-dove's cooings.
How silent comes the water round that bend;
Not the minutest whisper does it send
To the o'erhanging sallows: blades of grass
Slowly across the chequer'd shadows pass.
Why, you might read two sonnets, ere they reach
To where the hurrying freshnesses aye preach   70
A natural sermon o'er their pebbly beds;
Where swarms of minnows show their little heads,
Staying their wavy bodies 'gainst the streams,
To taste the luxury of sunny beams
Temper'd with coolness. How they ever wrestle
With their own sweet delight, and ever nestle
Their silver bellies on the pebbly sand.
If you but scantily hold out the hand,
That very instant not one will remain;

But turn your eye, and they are there again.   80
The ripples seem right glad to reach those cresses,
And cool themselves among the em'rald tresses;
The while they cool themselves, they freshness give,
And moisture, that the bowery green may live:
So keeping up an interchange of favours,
Like good men in the truth of their behaviours.
Sometimes goldfinches one by one will drop
From low hung branches; little space they stop;
But sip, and twitter, and their feathers sleek;
Then off at once, as in a wanton freak: 90
Or perhaps, to show their black, and golden wings,
Pausing upon their yellow flutterings.
Were I in such a place, I sure should pray
That nought less sweet might call my thoughts away,
Than the soft rustle of a maiden's gown
Fanning away the dandelion's down;
Than the light music of her nimble toes
Patting against the sorrel as she goes.
How she would start, and blush, thus to be caught
Playing in all her innocence of thought.   100
O let me lead her gently o'er the brook,
Watch her half-smiling lips, and downward look;
O let me for one moment touch her wrist;
Let me one moment to her breathing list;
And as she leaves me may she often turn
Her fair eyes looking through her locks auburne.
What next? A tuft of evening primroses,
O'er which the mind may hover till it dozes;
O'er which it well might take a pleasant sleep,
But that 'tis ever startled by the leap   110
Of buds into ripe flowers; or by the flitting
Of diverse moths, that aye their rest are quitting;
Or by the moon lifting her silver rim
Above a cloud, and with a gradual swim
Coming into the blue with all her light.
O Maker of sweet poets, dear delight
Of this fair world, and all its gentle livers;
Spangler of clouds, halo of crystal rivers,
Mingler with leaves, and dew and tumbling streams,
Closer of lovely eyes to lovely dreams,   120
Lover of loneliness, and wandering,
Of upcast eye, and tender pondering!
Thee must I praise above all other glories
That smile us on to tell delightful stories.
For what has made the sage or poet write

But the fair paradise of Nature's light?
In the calm grandeur of a sober line,
We see the waving of the mountain pine;
And when a tale is beautifully staid,
We feel the safety of a hawthorn glade: 130
When it is moving on luxurious wings,
The soul is lost in pleasant smotherings:
Fair dewy roses brush against our faces,
And flowering laurels spring from diamond vases;
O'er head we see the jasmine and sweet briar,
And bloomy grapes laughing from green attire;
While at our feet, the voice of crystal bubbles
Charms us at once away from all our troubles:
So that we feel uplifted from the world,
Walking upon the white clouds wreath'd and curl'd. 140
So felt he, who first told, how Psyche went
On the smooth wind to realms of wonderment;
What Psyche felt, and Love, when their full lips
First touch'd; what amorous, and fondling nips
They gave each other's cheeks; with all their sighs,
And how they kist each other's tremulous eyes:
The silver lamp, — the ravishment, — the wonder —
The darkness, — loneliness, — the fearful thunder;
Their woes gone by, and both to heaven upflown,
To bow for gratitude before Jove's throne. 150
So did he feel, who pull'd the boughs aside,
That we might look into a forest wide,
To catch a glimpse of Fauns, and Dryades
Coming with softest rustle through the trees;
And garlands woven of flowers wild, and sweet,
Upheld on ivory wrists, or sporting feet:
Telling us how fair, trembling Syrinx fled
Arcadian Pan, with such a fearful dread.
Poor nymph,— poor Pan, — how he did weep to find,
Nought but a lovely sighing of the wind 160
Along the reedy stream; a half heard strain,
Full of sweet desolation — balmy pain.

What first inspired a bard of old to sing
Narcissus pining o'er the untainted spring?
In some delicious ramble, he had found
A little space, with boughs all woven round;
And in the midst of all, a clearer pool
Than e'er reflected in its pleasant cool,
The blue sky here, and there, serenely peeping
Through tendril wreaths fantastically creeping. 170

And on the bank a lonely flower he spied,
A meek and forlorn flower, with naught of pride,
Drooping its beauty o'er the watery clearness,
To woo its own sad image into nearness:
Deaf to light Zephyrus it would not move;
But still would seem to droop, to pine, to love.
So while the poet stood in this sweet spot,
Some fainter gleamings o'er his fancy shot;
Nor was it long ere he had told the tale
Of young Narcissus, and sad Echo's bale.   180

Where had he been, from whose warm head out-flew
That sweetest of all songs, that ever new,
That aye refreshing, pure deliciousness,
Coming ever to bless
The wanderer by moonlight? to him bringing
Shapes from the invisible world, unearthly singing
From out the middle air, from flowery nests,
And from the pillowy silkiness that rests
Full in the speculation of the stars.
Ah! surely he had burst our mortal bars;   190
Into some wond'rous region he had gone,
To search for thee, divine Endymion!

He was a Poet, sure a lover too,
Who stood on Latmus' top, what time there blew
Soft breezes from the myrtle vale below;
And brought in faintness solemn, sweet, and slow
A hymn from Dian's temple; while upswelling,
The incense went to her own starry dwelling.
But though her face was clear as infant's eyes,
Though she stood smiling o'er the sacrifice,   200
The Poet wept at her so piteous fate,
Wept that such beauty should be desolate:
So in fine wrath some golden sounds he won,
And gave meek Cynthia her Endymion.

Queen of the wide air; thou most lovely queen
Of all the brightness that mine eyes have seen!
As thou exceedest all things in thy shine,
So every tale, does this sweet tale of thine.
O for three words of honey, that I might
Tell but one wonder of thy bridal night!   210

Where distant ships do seem to show their keels,
Phoebus awhile delayed his mighty wheels,

And turned to smile upon thy bashful eyes,
Ere he his unseen pomp would solemnize.
The evening weather was so bright, and clear,
That men of health were of unusual cheer;
Stepping like Homer at the trumpet's call,
Or young Apollo on the pedestal:
And lovely women were as fair and warm,
As Venus looking sideways in alarm.   220
The breezes were ethereal, and pure,
And crept through half closed lattices to cure
The languid sick; it cool'd their fever'd sleep,
And soothed them into slumbers full and deep.
Soon they awoke clear eyed: nor burnt with thirsting,
Nor with hot fingers, nor with temples bursting:
And springing up, they met the wond'ring sight
Of their dear friends, nigh foolish with delight;
Who feel their arms, and breasts, and kiss and stare,
And on their placid foreheads part the hair.   230
Young men, and maidens at each other gaz'd
With hands held back, and motionless, amaz'd
To see the brightness in each other's eyes;
And so they stood, fill'd with a sweet surprise,
Until their tongues were loos'd in poesy.
Therefore no lover did of anguish die:
But the soft numbers, in that moment spoken,
Made silken ties, that never may be broken.
Cynthia! I cannot tell the greater blisses,
That follow'd thine, and thy dear shepherd's kisses: 240
Was there a Poet born? — but now no more,
My wand'ring spirit must no further soar. —

SLEEP AND POETRY

As I lay in my bed slepe full unmete
Was unto me, but why that I ne might
Rest I ne wist, for there n'as erthly wight
[As I suppose] had more of hertis ese
Than I, for I n'ad sicknesse nor disese.
                                        CHAUCER.

WHAT is more gentle than a wind in summer?
What is more soothing than the pretty hummer
That stays one moment in an open flower,
And buzzes cheerily from bower to bower?
What is more tranquil than a musk-rose blowing
In a green island, far from all men's knowing?
More healthful than the leafiness of dales?
More secret than a nest of nightingales?
More serene than Cordelia's countenance?
More full of visions than a high romance?   10
What, but thee Sleep? Soft closer of our eyes!
Low murmurer of tender lullabies!
Light hoverer around our happy pillows!
Wreather of poppy buds, and weeping willows!
Silent entangler of a beauty's tresses!
Most happy listener! when the morning blesses
Thee for enlivening all the cheerful eyes
That glance so brightly at the new sun-rise.

But what is higher beyond thought than thee?
Fresher than berries of a mountain tree?   20
More strange, more beautiful, more smooth, more regal,
Than wings of swans, than doves, than dim-seen eagle?
What is it? And to what shall I compare it?
It has a glory, and nought else can share it:
The thought thereof is awful, sweet, and holy,
Chacing away all worldliness and folly;
Coming sometimes like fearful claps of thunder,
Or the low rumblings earth's regions under;
And sometimes like a gentle whispering
Of all the secrets of some wond'rous thing   30
That breathes about us in the vacant air;
So that we look around with prying stare,
Perhaps to see shapes of light, aerial limning,
And catch soft floatings from a faint-heard hymning;

To see the laurel wreath, on high suspended,
That is to crown our name when life is ended.
Sometimes it gives a glory to the voice,
And from the heart upsprings "Rejoice! rejoice!"
Sounds which will reach the Framer of all things,
And die away in ardent mutterings.   40

No one who once the glorious sun has seen,
And all the clouds, and felt his bosom clean
For his great Maker's presence, but must know
What 'tis I mean, and feel his being glow:
Therefore no insult will I give his spirit,
By telling what he sees from native merit.

O Poesy! for thee I hold my pen
That am not yet a glorious denizen
Of thy wide heaven — Should I rather kneel
Upon some mountain-top until I feel   50
A glowing splendour round about me hung,
And echo back the voice of thine own tongue?
O Poesy! for thee I grasp my pen
That am not yet a glorious denizen
Of thy wide heaven; yet, to my ardent prayer,
Yield from thy sanctuary some clear air,
Smoothed for intoxication by the breath
Of flowering bays, that I may die a death
Of luxury, and my young spirit follow
The morning sun-beams to the great Apollo   60
Like a fresh sacrifice; or, if I can bear
The o'erwhelming sweets, 'twill bring to me the fair
Visions of all places: a bowery nook
Will be elysium — an eternal book
Whence I may copy many a lovely saying
About the leaves, and flowers — about the playing
Of nymphs in woods, and fountains; and the shade
Keeping a silence round a sleeping maid;
And many a verse from so strange influence
That we must ever wonder how, and whence   70
It came. Also imaginings will hover
Round my fire-side, and haply there discover
Vistas of solemn beauty, where I'd wander
In happy silence, like the clear Meander
Through its lone vales; and where I found a spot
Of awfuller shade, or an enchanted grot,
Or a green hill o'erspread with chequered dress
Of flowers, and fearful from its loveliness,

Write on my tablets all that was permitted,
All that was for our human senses fitted.   80
Then the events of this wide world I'd seize
Like a strong giant, and my spirit teaze
Till at its shoulders it should proudly see
Wings to find out an immortality.

Stop and consider! life is but a day;
A fragile dew-drop on its perilous way
From a tree's summit; a poor Indian's sleep
While his boat hastens to the monstrous steep
Of Montmorenci. Why so sad a moan?
Life is the rose's hope while yet unblown;   90
The reading of an ever-changing tale;
The light uplifting of a maiden's veil;
A pigeon tumbling in clear summer air;
A laughing school-boy, without grief or care,
Riding the springy branches of an elm.

O for ten years, that I may overwhelm
Myself in poesy; so I may do the deed
That my own soul has to itself decreed.
Then will I pass the countries that I see
In long perspective, and continually   100
Taste their pure fountains. First the realm I'll pass
Of Flora, and old Pan: sleep in the grass,
Feed upon apples red, and strawberries,
And choose each pleasure that my fancy sees;
Catch the white-handed nymphs in shady places,
To woo sweet kisses from averted faces, —
Play with their fingers, touch their shoulders white
Into a pretty shrinking with a bite
As hard as lips can make it: till agreed,
A lovely tale of human life we'll read.   110
And one will teach a tame dove how it best
May fan the cool air gently o'er my rest;
Another, bending o'er her nimble tread,
Will set a green robe floating round her head,
And still will dance with ever varied ease,
Smiling upon the flowers and the trees:
Another will entice me on, and on
Through almond blossoms and rich cinnamon;
Till in the bosom of a leafy world
We rest in silence, like two gems upcurl'd   120
In the recesses of a pearly shell.

And can I ever bid these joys farewell?
Yes, I must pass them for a nobler life,
Where I may find the agonies, the strife
Of human hearts: for lo! I see afar,
O'er sailing the blue cragginess, a car
And steeds with streamy manes — the charioteer
Looks out upon the winds with glorious fear:
And now the numerous tramplings quiver lightly
Along a huge cloud's ridge; and now with sprightly   130
Wheel downward come they into fresher skies,
Tipt round with silver from the sun's bright eyes.
Still downward with capacious whirl they glide;
And now I see them on the green-hill's side
In breezy rest among the nodding stalks.
The charioteer with wond'rous gesture talks
To the trees and mountains; and there soon appear
Shapes of delight, of mystery, and fear,
Passing along before a dusky space
Made by some mighty oaks: as they would chase   140
Some ever-fleeting music on they sweep.
Lo! how they murmur, laugh, and smile, and weep:
Some with upholden hand and mouth severe;
Some with their faces muffled to the ear
Between their arms; some, clear in youthful bloom,
Go glad and smilingly athwart the gloom;
Some looking back, and some with upward gaze;
Yes, thousands in a thousand different ways
Flit onward — now a lovely wreath of girls
Dancing their sleek hair into tangled curls;   150
And now broad wings. Most awfully intent
The driver of those steeds is forward bent,
And seems to listen: O that I might know
All that he writes with such a hurrying glow.

The visions all are fled — the car is fled
Into the light of heaven, and in their stead
A sense of real things comes doubly strong,
And, like a muddy stream, would bear along
My soul to nothingness: but I will strive
Against all doubtings, and will keep alive   160
The thought of that same chariot, and the strange
Journey it went.

                    Is there so small a range
In the present strength of manhood, that the high
Imagination cannot freely fly

As she was wont of old? prepare her steeds,
Paw up against the light, and do strange deeds
Upon the clouds? Has she not shewn us all?
From the clear space of ether, to the small
Breath of new buds unfolding? From the meaning
Of Jove's large eye-brow, to the tender greening   170
Of April meadows? Here her altar shone,
E'en in this isle; and who could paragon
The fervid choir that lifted up a noise
Of harmony, to where it aye will poise
Its mighty self of convoluting sound,
Huge as a planet, and like that roll round,
Eternally around a dizzy void?
Ay, in those days the Muses were nigh cloy'd
With honors; nor had any other care
Than to sing out and sooth their wavy hair.   180

Could all this be forgotten? Yes, a schism
Nurtured by foppery and barbarism,
Made great Apollo blush for this his land.
Men were thought wise who could not understand
His glories: with a puling infant's force
They sway'd about upon a rocking horse,
And thought it Pegasus. Ah dismal soul'd!
The winds of heaven blew, the ocean roll'd
Its gathering waves — ye felt it not. The blue
Bared its eternal bosom, and the dew   190
Of summer nights collected still to make
The morning precious: beauty was awake!
Why were ye not awake? But ye were dead
To things ye knew not of, — were closely wed
To musty laws lined out with wretched rule
And compass vile: so that ye taught a school
Of dolts to smooth, inlay, and clip, and fit,
Till, like the certain wands of Jacob's wit,
Their verses tallied. Easy was the task:
A thousand handicraftsmen wore the mask   200
Of Poesy. Ill-fated, impious race!
That blasphemed the bright Lyrist to his face,
And did not know it, — no, they went about,
Holding a poor, decrepid standard out
Mark'd with most flimsy mottos, and in large
The name of one Boileau!

                              O ye whose charge
It is to hover round our pleasant hills!

Whose congregated majesty so fills
My boundly reverence, that I cannot trace
Your hallowed names, in this unholy place, 210
So near those common folk; did not their shames
Affright you? Did our old lamenting Thames
Delight you? Did ye never cluster round
Delicious Avon, with a mournful sound,
And weep? Or did ye wholly bid adieu
To regions where no more the laurel grew?
Or did ye stay to give a welcoming
To some lone spirits who could proudly sing
Their youth away, and die? 'Twas even so:
But let me think away those times of woe: 220
Now 'tis a fairer season; ye have breathed
Rich benedictions o'er us; ye have wreathed
Fresh garlands: for sweet music has been heard
In many places; — some has been upstirr'd
From out its crystal dwelling in a lake,
By a swan's ebon bill; from a thick brake,
Nested and quiet in a valley mild,
Bubbles a pipe; fine sounds are floating wild
About the earth: happy are ye and glad.

These things are doubtless: yet in truth we've had 230
Strange thunders from the potency of song;
Mingled indeed with what is sweet and strong,
From majesty: but in clear truth the themes
Are ugly clubs, the Poets Polyphemes
Disturbing the grand sea. A drainless shower
Of light is poesy; 'tis the supreme of power;
'Tis might half slumb'ring on its own right arm.
The very archings of her eye-lids charm
A thousand willing agents to obey,
And still she governs with the mildest sway: 240
But strength alone though of the Muses born
Is like a fallen angel: trees uptorn,
Darkness, and worms, and shrouds, and sepulchres
Delight it; for it feeds upon the burrs,
And thorns of life; forgetting the great end
Of poesy, that it should be a friend
To sooth the cares, and lift the thoughts of man.

Yet I rejoice: a myrtle fairer than
E'er grew in Paphos, from the bitter weeds
Lifts its sweet head into the air, and feeds 250
A silent space with ever sprouting green.

All tenderest birds there find a pleasant screen,
Creep through the shade with jaunty fluttering,
Nibble the little cupped flowers and sing.
Then let us clear away the choking thorns
From round its gentle stem; let the young fawns,
Yeaned in after times, when we are flown,
Find a fresh sward beneath it, overgrown
With simple flowers: let there nothing be
More boisterous than a lover's bended knee;   260
Nought more ungentle than the placid look
Of one who leans upon a closed book;
Nought more untranquil than the grassy slopes
Between two hills. All hail delightful hopes!
As she was wont, th' imagination
Into most lovely labyrinths will be gone,
And they shall be accounted poet kings
Who simply tell the most heart-easing things.
O may these joys be ripe before I die.

Will not some say that I presumptuously   270
Have spoken? that from hastening disgrace
'Twere better far to hide my foolish face?
That whining boyhood should with reverence bow
Ere the dread thunderbolt could reach? How!
If I do hide myself, it sure shall be
In the very fane, the light of Poesy:
If I do fall, at least I will be laid
Beneath the silence of a poplar shade;
And over me the grass shall be smooth shaven;
And there shall be a kind memorial graven.   280
But off Despondence! miserable bane!
They should not know thee, who athirst to gain
A noble end, are thirsty every hour.
What though I am not wealthy in the dower
Of spanning wisdom; though I do not know
The shiftings of the mighty winds that blow
Hither and thither all the changing thoughts
Of man: though no great minist'ring reason sorts
Out the dark mysteries of human souls
To clear conceiving: yet there ever rolls   290
A vast idea before me, and I glean
Therefrom my liberty; thence too I've seen
The end and aim of Poesy. 'Tis clear
As any thing most true; as that the year
Is made of the four seasons — manifest
As a large cross, some old cathedral's crest,
Lifted to the white clouds. Therefore should I

Be but the essence of deformity,
A coward, did my very eye-lids wink
At speaking out what I have dared to think.   300
Ah! rather let me like a madman run
Over some precipice; let the hot sun
Melt my Dedalian wings, and drive me down
Convuls'd and headlong! Stay! an inward frown
Of conscience bids me be more calm awhile.
An ocean dim, sprinkled with many an isle,
Spreads awfully before me. How much toil!
How many days! what desperate turmoil!
Ere I can have explored its widenesses.
Ah, what a task! upon my bended knees,   310
I could unsay those — no, impossible!
Impossible!

       For sweet relief I'll dwell
On humbler thoughts, and let this strange assay
Begun in gentleness die so away.
E'en now all tumult from my bosom fades:
I turn full hearted to the friendly aids
That smooth the path of honour; brotherhood,
And friendliness the nurse of mutual good.
The hearty grasp that sends a pleasant sonnet
Into the brain ere one can think upon it;   320
The silence when some rhymes are coming out;
And when they're come, the very pleasant rout:
The message certain to be done to-morrow.
'Tis perhaps as well that it should be to borrow
Some precious book from out its snug retreat,
To cluster round it when we next shall meet.
Scarce can I scribble on; for lovely airs
Are fluttering round the room like doves in pairs;
Many delights of that glad day recalling,
When first my senses caught their tender falling.   330
And with these airs come forms of elegance
Stooping their shoulders o'er a horse's prance,
Careless, and grand — fingers soft and round
Parting luxuriant curls; — and the swift bound
Of Bacchus from his chariot, when his eye
Made Ariadne's cheek look blushingly.
Thus I remember all the pleasant flow
Of words at opening a portfolio.

Things such as these are ever harbingers
To trains of peaceful images: the stirs   340
Of a swan's neck unseen among the rushes:

A linnet starting all about the bushes:
A butterfly, with golden wings broad parted,
Nestling a rose, convuls'd as though it smarted
With over pleasure — many, many more,
Might I indulge at large in all my store
Of luxuries: yet I must not forget
Sleep, quiet with his poppy coronet:
For what there may be worthy in these rhymes
I partly owe to him: and thus, the chimes   350
Of friendly voices had just given place
To as sweet a silence, when I 'gan retrace
The pleasant day, upon a couch at ease.
It was a poet's house who keeps the keys
Of pleasure's temple. Round about were hung
The glorious features of the bards who sung
In other ages — cold and sacred busts
Smiled at each other. Happy he who trusts
To clear Futurity his darling fame!
Then there were fauns and satyrs taking aim   360
At swelling apples with a frisky leap
And reaching fingers, 'mid a luscious heap
Of vine leaves. Then there rose to view a fane
Of liny marble, and thereto a train
Of nymphs approaching fairly o'er the sward:
One, loveliest, holding her white hand toward
The dazzling sun-rise: two sisters sweet
Bending their graceful figures till they meet
Over the trippings of a little child:
And some are hearing, eagerly, the wild   370
Thrilling liquidity of dewy piping.
See, in another picture, nymphs are wiping
Cherishingly Diana's timorous limbs; —
A fold of lawny mantle dabbling swims
At the bath's edge, and keeps a gentle motion
With the subsiding crystal: as when ocean
Heaves calmly its broad swelling smoothness o'er
Its rocky marge, and balances once more
The patient weeds; that now unshent by foam
Feel all about their undulating home.   380

Sappho's meek head was there half smiling down
At nothing; just as though the earnest frown
Of over thinking had that moment gone
From off her brow, and left her all alone.

Great Alfred's too, with anxious, pitying eyes,
As if he always listened to the sighs

Of the goaded world; and Kosciusko's worn
By horrid suffrance — mightily forlorn.

Petrarch, outstepping from the shady green,   390
Starts at the sight of Laura; nor can wean
His eyes from her sweet face. Most happy they!
For over them was seen a free display
Of out-spread wings, and from between them shone
The face of Poesy; from off her throne
She overlook'd things that I scarce could tell.
The very sense of where I was might well
Keep Sleep aloof: but more than that there came
Thought after thought to nourish up the flame
Within my breast; so that the morning light
Surprised me even from a sleepless night;   400
And up I rose refresh'd, and glad, and gay,
Resolving to begin that very day
These lines; and howsoever they be done,
I leave them as a father does his son.

DEDICATION

TO LEIGH HUNT, ESQ.

GLORY and loveliness have passed away;
   For if we wander out in early morn,
   No wreathed incense do we see upborne
Into the east, to meet the smiling day:
No crowd of nymphs soft voic'd and young, and gay,
   In woven baskets bringing ears of corn,
   Roses, and pinks, and violets, to adorn
The shrine of Flora in her early May.
But there are left delights as high as these,
   And I shall ever bless my destiny,
That in a time, when under pleasant trees   10
   Pan is no longer sought, I feel a free,
A leafy luxury, seeing I could please
   With these poor offerings, a man like thee.

ON SEEING THE ELGIN MARBLES

MY SPIRIT is too weak; mortality
   Weighs heavily on me like unwilling sleep,
   And each imagined pinnacle and steep
Of godlike hardship tells me I must die
Like a sick eagle looking at the sky.
   Yet 'tis a gentle luxury to weep,
   That I have not the cloudy winds to keep
Fresh for the opening of the morning's eye.
Such dim-conceived glories of the brain
   Bring round the heart an indescribable feud;   10
So do these wonders a most dizzy pain,
   That mingles Grecian grandeur with the rude
Wasting of old Time — with a billowy main,
   A sun, a shadow of a magnitude.

ON AN ENGRAVED GEM OF LEANDER

COME hither all sweet maidens soberly,
   Down-looking aye, and with a chasten'd light
   Hid in the fringes of your eyelids white,
And meekly let your fair hands joined be;

As if so gentle that ye could not see,
    Untouch'd, a victim of your beauty bright,
    Sinking away to his young spirit's night,
Sinking bewilder'd 'mid the dreary sea:
'Tis young Leander toiling to his death;
    Nigh swooning, he doth purse his weary lips   10
      For Hero's cheek, and smiles against her smile.
    O horrid dream! see how his body dips,
      Dead-heavy; arms and shoulders gleam awhile:
He's gone; up bubbles all his amorous breath!

ON LEIGH HUNT'S POEM
"THE STORY OF RIMINI"

Who loves to peer up at the morning sun,
    With half-shut eyes and comfortable cheek,
    Let him, with this sweet tale, full often seek
For meadows where the little rivers run;
Who loves to linger with that brightest one
    Of Heaven — Hesperus — let him lowly speak
    These numbers to the night, and starlight meek,
Or moon, if that her hunting be begun.
He who knows these delights, and too is prone
    To moralise upon a smile or tear,   10
Will find at once a region of his own,
    A bower for his spirit, and will steer
To alleys where the fir-tree drops its cone,
    Where robins hop, and fallen leaves are sear.

ON THE SEA

It keeps eternal whisperings around
    Desolate shores, and with its mighty swell
    Gluts twice ten thousand caverns, till the spell
Of Hecate leaves them their old shadowy sound.
Often 'tis in such gentle temper found,
    That scarcely will the very smallest shell
    Be moved for days from where it sometime fell.
When last the winds of heaven were unbound.
Oh ye! who have your eye-balls vexed and tired,
    Feast them upon the wideness of the Sea;   10
      Oh ye! whose ears are dinn'd with uproar rude,
    Or fed too much with cloying melody —
      Sit ye near some old cavern's mouth, and brood
Until ye start, as if the sea-nymphs quired!

ENDYMION:

A POETIC ROMANCE.

"The stretched metre of an antique song"

INSCRIBED TO THE MEMORY OF THOMAS CHATTERTON

PREFACE

KNOWING WITHIN myself the manner in which this Poem has been produced, it is not without a feeling of regret that I make it public.

What manner I mean, will be quite clear to the reader, who must soon perceive great inexperience, immaturity, and every error denoting a feverish attempt, rather than a deed accomplished. The two first books, and indeed the two last, I feel sensible are not of such completion as to warrant their passing the press; nor should they if I thought a year's castigation would do them any good; — it will not: the foundations are too sandy. It is just that this youngster should die away: a sad thought for me, if I had not some hope that while it is dwindling I may be plotting, and fitting myself for verses fit to live.

This may be speaking too presumptuously, and may deserve a punishment: but no feeling man will be forward to inflict it: he will leave me alone, with the conviction that there is not a fiercer hell than the failure in a great object. This is not written with the least atom of purpose to forestall criticisms of course, but from the desire I have to conciliate men who are competent to look, and who do look with a zealous eye, to the honour of English literature.

The imagination of a boy is healthy, and the mature imagination of a man is healthy; but there is a space of life between, in which the soul is in a ferment, the character undecided, the way of life uncertain, the ambition thick-sighted: thence proceeds mawkishness, and all the thousand bitters which those men I speak of must necessarily taste in going over the following pages.

I hope I have not in too late a day touched the beautiful mythology of Greece, and dulled its brightness: for I wish to try once more, before I bid it farewel.

Teignmouth, April 10, 1818.

BOOK I

A THING of beauty is a joy for ever:
Its loveliness increases; it will never
Pass into nothingness; but still will keep
A bower quiet for us, and a sleep
Full of sweet dreams, and health, and quiet breathing.
Therefore, on every morrow, are we wreathing
A flowery band to bind us to the earth,
Spite of despondence, of the inhuman dearth
Of noble natures, of the gloomy days,
Of all the unhealthy and o'er-darkened ways   10
Made for our searching: yes, in spite of all,
Some shape of beauty moves away the pall
From our dark spirits. Such the sun, the moon,
Trees old and young, sprouting a shady boon
For simple sheep; and such are daffodils
With the green world they live in; and clear rills
That for themselves a cooling covert make
'Gainst the hot season; the mid forest brake,
Rich with a sprinkling of fair musk-rose blooms:
And such too is the grandeur of the dooms   20
We have imagined for the mighty dead;
All lovely tales that we have heard or read:
An endless fountain of immortal drink,
Pouring unto us from the heaven's brink.

Nor do we merely feel these essences
For one short hour; no, even as the trees
That whisper round a temple become soon
Dear as the temple's self, so does the moon,
The passion poesy, glories infinite,
Haunt us till they become a cheering light   30
Unto our souls, and bound to us so fast,
That, whether there be shine, or gloom o'ercast,
They alway must be with us, or we die.

Therefore, 'tis with full happiness that I
Will trace the story of Endymion.
The very music of the name has gone
Into my being, and each pleasant scene
Is growing fresh before me as the green
Of our own vallies: so I will begin
Now while I cannot hear the city's din;   40
Now while the early budders are just new,
And run in mazes of the youngest hue

About old forests; while the willow trails
Its delicate amber; and the dairy pails
Bring home increase of milk. And, as the year
Grows lush in juicy stalks, I'll smoothly steer
My little boat, for many quiet hours,
With streams that deepen freshly into bowers.
Many and many a verse I hope to write,
Before the daisies, vermeil rimm'd and white,   50
Hide in deep herbage; and ere yet the bees
Hum about globes of clover and sweet peas,
I must be near the middle of my story.
O may no wintry season, bare and hoary,
See it half finished: but let Autumn bold,
With universal tinge of sober gold,
Be all about me when I make an end.
And now at once, adventuresome, I send
My herald thought into a wilderness:
There let its trumpet blow, and quickly dress   60
My uncertain path with green, that I may speed
Easily onward, thorough flowers and weed.

Upon the sides of Latmos was outspread
A mighty forest; for the moist earth fed
So plenteously all weed-hidden roots
Into o'er-hanging boughs, and precious fruits.
And it had gloomy shades, sequestered deep,
Where no man went; and if from shepherd's keep
A lamb stray'd far a-down those inmost glens,
Never again saw he the happy pens   70
Whither his brethren, bleating with content,
Over the hills at every nightfall went.
Among the shepherds, 'twas believed ever,
That not one fleecy lamb which thus did sever
From the white flock, but pass'd unworried
By angry wolf, or pard with prying head,
Until it came to some unfooted plains
Where fed the herds of Pan: ay great his gains
Who thus one lamb did lose. Paths there were many,
Winding through palmy fern, and rushes fenny,   80
And ivy banks; all leading pleasantly
To a wide lawn, whence one could only see
Stems thronging all around between the swell
Of turf and slanting branches: who could tell
The freshness of the space of heaven above,
Edg'd round with dark tree tops? through which a **dove**
Would often beat its wings, and often too
A little cloud would move across the blue.

Full in the middle of this pleasantness
There stood a marble altar, with a tress   90
Of flowers budded newly; and the dew
Had taken fairy phantasies to strew
Daisies upon the sacred sward last eve,
And so the dawned light in pomp receive.
For 'twas the morn: Apollo's upward fire
Made every eastern cloud a silvery pyre
Of brightness so unsullied, that therein
A melancholy spirit well might win
Oblivion, and melt out his essence fine
Into the winds: rain-scented eglantine   100
Gave temperate sweets to that well-wooing sun;
The lark was lost in him; cold springs had run
To warm their chilliest bubbles in the grass;
Man's voice was on the mountains; and the mass
Of nature's lives and wonders puls'd tenfold,
To feel this sun-rise and its glories old.

Now while the silent workings of the dawn
Were busiest, into that self-same lawn
All suddenly, with joyful cries, there sped
A troop of little children garlanded;   110
Who gathering round the altar, seemed to pry
Earnestly round as wishing to espy
Some folk of holiday: nor had they waited
For many moments, ere their ears were sated
With a faint breath of music, which ev'n then
Fill'd out its voice, and died away again.
Within a little space again it gave
Its airy swellings, with a gentle wave,
To light-hung leaves, in smoothest echoes breaking
Through copse-clad vallies, — ere their death, o'ertaking 120
The surgy murmurs of the lonely sea.

And now, as deep into the wood as we
Might mark a lynx's eye, there glimmered light
Fair faces and a rush of garments white,
Plainer and plainer shewing, till at last
Into the widest alley they all past,
Making directly for the woodland altar.
O kindly muse! let not my weak tongue faulter
In telling of this goodly company,
Of their old piety, and of their glee: 130
But let a portion of ethereal dew
Fall on my head, and presently unmew

My soul; that I may dare, in wayfaring,
To stammer where old Chaucer used to sing.

Leading the way, young damsels danced along,
Bearing the burden of a shepherd song;
Each having a white wicker over brimm'd
With April's tender younglings: next, well trimm'd,
A crowd of shepherds with as sunburnt looks
As may be read of in Arcadian books;   140
Such as sat listening round Apollo's pipe,
When the great deity, for earth too ripe,
Let his divinity o'er-flowing die
In music, through the vales of Thessaly:
Some idly trailed their sheep-hooks on the ground,
And some kept up a shrilly mellow sound
With ebon-tipped flutes: close after these,
Now coming from beneath the forest trees,
A venerable priest full soberly,
Begirt with ministring looks: alway his eye   150
Stedfast upon the matted turf he kept,
And after him his sacred vestments swept.
From his right hand there swung a vase, milk-white,
Of mingled wine, out-sparkling generous light;
And in his left he held a basket full
Of all sweet herbs that searching eye could cull:
Wild thyme, and valley-lilies whiter still
Than Leda's love, and cresses from the rill.
His aged head, crowned with beechen wreath,
Seem'd like a poll of ivy in the teeth   160
Of winter hoar. Then came another crowd
Of shepherds, lifting in due time aloud
Their share of the ditty. After them appear'd,
Up-followed by a multitude that rear'd
Their voices to the clouds, a fair wrought car,
Easily rolling so as scarce to mar
The freedom of three steeds of dapple brown:
Who stood therein did seem of great renown
Among the throng. His youth was fully blown,
Shewing like Ganymede to manhood grown;   170
And, for those simple times, his garments were
A chieftain king's: beneath his breast, half bare,
Was hung a silver bugle, and between
His nervy knees there lay a boar-spear keen.
A smile was on his countenance; he seem'd,
To common lookers on, like one who dream'd
Of idleness in groves Elysian:

But there were some who feelingly could scan
A lurking trouble in his nether lip,
And see that oftentimes the reins would slip   180
Through his forgotten hands: then would they sigh,
And think of yellow leaves, of owlets' cry,
Of logs piled solemnly. — Ah, well-a-day,
Why should our young Endymion pine away!

   Soon the assembly, in a circle rang'd,
Stood silent round the shrine: each look was chang'd
To sudden veneration: women meek
Beckon'd their sons to silence; while each cheek
Of virgin bloom paled gently for slight fear.
Endymion too, without a forest peer,   190
Stood, wan, and pale, and with an awed face,
Among his brothers of the mountain chase.
In midst of all, the venerable priest
Eyed them with joy from greatest to the least,
And, after lifting up his aged hands,
Thus spake he: "Men of Latmos! shepherd bands!
Whose care it is to guard a thousand flocks:
Whether descended from beneath the rocks
That overtop your mountains; whether come
From vallies where the pipe is never dumb;   200
Or from your swelling downs, where sweet air stirs
Blue hare-bells lightly, and where prickly furze
Buds lavish gold; or ye, whose precious charge
Nibble their fill at ocean's very marge,
Whose mellow reeds are touch'd with sounds forlorn
By the dim echoes of old Triton's horn:
Mothers and wives! who day by day prepare
The scrip, with needments, for the mountain air;
And all ye gentle girls who foster up
Udderless lambs, and in a little cup   210
Will put choice honey for a favoured youth:
Yea, every one attend! for in good truth
Our vows are wanting to our great god Pan.
Are not our lowing heifers sleeker than
Night-swollen mushrooms? Are not our wide plains
Speckled with countless fleeces? Have not rains
Green'd over April's lap? No howling sad
Sickens our fearful ewes; and we have had
Great bounty from Endymion our lord.
The earth is glad: the merry lark has pour'd   220
His early song against yon breezy sky,
That spreads so clear o'er our solemnity."

Thus ending, on the shrine he heap'd a spire
Of teeming sweets, enkindling sacred fire;
Anon he stain'd the thick and spongy sod
With wine, in honour of the shepherd-god.
Now while the earth was drinking it, and while
Bay leaves were crackling in the fragrant pile,
And gummy frankincense was sparkling bright
'Neath smothering parsley, and a hazy light   230
Spread greyly eastward, thus a chorus sang:

"O THOU, whose mighty palace roof doth hang
From jagged trunks, and overshadoweth
Eternal whispers, glooms, the birth, life, death
Of unseen flowers in heavy peacefulness;
Who lov'st to see the hamadryads dress
Their ruffled locks where meeting hazels darken;
And through whole solemn hours dost sit, and hearken
The dreary melody of bedded reeds —
In desolate places, where dank moisture breeds   240
The pipy hemlock to strange overgrowth;
Bethinking thee, how melancholy loth
Thou wast to lose fair Syrinx — do thou now,
By thy love's milky brow!
By all the trembling mazes that she ran,
Hear us, great Pan!

"O thou, for whose soul-soothing quiet, turtles
Passion their voices cooingly 'mong myrtles,
What time thou wanderest at eventide
Through sunny meadows, that outskirt the side   250
Of thine enmossed realms: O thou, to whom
Broad leaved fig trees even now foredoom
Their ripen'd fruitage; yellow girted bees
Their golden honeycombs; our village leas
Their fairest blossom'd beans and poppied corn;
The chuckling linnet its five young unborn,
To sing for thee; low creeping strawberries
Their summer coolness; pent up butterflies
Their freckled wings; yea, the fresh budding year
All its completions — be quickly near,   260
By every wind that nods the mountain pine,
O forester divine!

"Thou, to whom every faun and satyr flies
For willing service; whether to surprise

The squatted hare while in half sleeping fit;
Or upward ragged precipices flit
To save poor lambkins from the eagle's maw;
Or by mysterious enticement draw
Bewildered shepherds to their path again;
Or to tread breathless round the frothy main,   270
And gather up all fancifullest shells
For thee to tumble into Naiads' cells,
And, being hidden, laugh at their out-peeping;
Or to delight thee with fantastic leaping,
The while they pelt each other on the crown
With silvery oak apples, and fir cones brown —
By all the echoes that about thee ring,
Hear us, O satyr king!

"O Hearkener to the loud clapping shears,
While ever and anon to his shorn peers   280
A ram goes bleating: Winder of the horn,
When snouted wild-boars routing tender corn
Anger our huntsmen: Breather round our farms,
To keep off mildews, and all weather harms:
Strange ministrant of undescribed sounds,
That come a-swooning over hollow grounds,
And wither drearily on barren moors:
Dread opener of the mysterious doors
Leading to universal knowledge — see,
Great son of Dryope,   290
The many that are come to pay their vows
With leaves about their brows!

"Be still the unimaginable lodge
For solitary thinkings; such as dodge
Conception to the very bourne of heaven,
Then leave the naked brain: be still the leaven,
That spreading in this dull and clodded earth
Gives it a touch ethereal — a new birth:
Be still a symbol of immensity;
A firmament reflected in a sea;   300
An element filling the space between;
An unknown — but no more: we humbly screen
With uplift hands our foreheads, lowly bending,
And giving out a shout most heaven rending,
Conjure thee to receive our humble Pæan,
Upon thy Mount Lycean!"

Even while they brought the burden to a close,
A shout from the whole multitude arose,
That lingered in the air like dying rolls
Of abrupt thunder, when Ionian shoals   310
Of dolphins bob their noses through the brine.
Meantime, on shady levels, mossy fine,
Young companies nimbly began dancing
To the swift treble pipe, and humming string.
Aye, those fair living forms swam heavenly
To tunes forgotten — out of memory:
Fair creatures! whose young children's children bred
Thermopylæ its heroes — not yet dead,
But in old marbles ever beautiful.
High genitors, unconscious did they cull   320
Time's sweet first-fruits — they danc'd to weariness,
And then in quiet circles did they press
The hillock turf, and caught the latter end
Of some strange history, potent to send
A young mind from its bodily tenement.
Or they might watch the quoit-pitchers, intent
On either side; pitying the sad death
Of Hyacinthus, when the cruel breath
Of Zephyr slew him, — Zephyr penitent,
Who now, ere Phœbus mounts the firmament,   330
Fondles the flower amid the sobbing rain.
The archers too, upon a wider plain,
Beside the feathery whizzing of the shaft,
And the dull twanging bowstring, and the raft
Branch down sweeping from a tall ash top,
Call'd up a thousand thoughts to envelope
Those who would watch. Perhaps, the trembling knee
And frantic gape of lonely Niobe,
Poor, lonely Niobe! when her lovely young
Were dead and gone, and her caressing tongue   340
Lay a lost thing upon her paly lip,
And very, very deadliness did nip
Her motherly cheeks. Arous'd from this sad mood
By one, who at a distance loud halloo'd,
Uplifting his strong bow into the air,
Many might after brighter visions stare:
After the Argonauts, in blind amaze
Tossing about on Neptune's restless ways,
Until, from the horizon's vaulted side,
There shot a golden splendour far and wide,   350
Spangling those million poutings of the brine
With quivering ore: 'twas even an awful shine

From the exaltation of Apollo's bow;
A heavenly beacon in their dreary woe.
Who thus were ripe for high contemplating,
Might turn their steps towards the sober ring
Where sat Endymion and the aged priest
'Mong shepherds gone in eld, whose looks increas'd
The silvery setting of their mortal star.
There they discours'd upon the fragile bar   360
That keeps us from our homes ethereal;
And what our duties there: to nightly call
Vesper, the beauty-crest of summer weather;
To summon all the downiest clouds together
For the sun's purple couch; to emulate
In ministring the potent rule of fate
With speed of fire-tailed exhalations;
To tint her pallid cheek with bloom, who cons
Sweet poesy by moonlight: besides these,
A world of other unguess'd offices.   370
Anon they wander'd, by divine converse,
Into Elysium; vieing to rehearse
Each one his own anticipated bliss.
One felt heart-certain that he could not miss
His quick gone love, among fair blossom'd boughs,
Where every zephyr-sigh pouts, and endows
Her lips with music for the welcoming.
Another wish'd, mid that eternal spring,
To meet his rosy child, with feathery sails,
Sweeping, eye-earnestly, through almond vales: 380
Who, suddenly, should stoop through the smooth wind,
And with the balmiest leaves his temples bind;
And, ever after, through those regions be
His messenger, his little Mercury.
Some were athirst in soul to see again
Their fellow huntsmen o'er the wide champaign
In times long past; to sit with them, and talk
Of all the chances in their earthly walk;
Comparing, joyfully, their plenteous stores
Of happiness, to when upon the moors,   390
Benighted, close they huddled from the cold,
And shar'd their famish'd scrips. Thus all out-told
Their fond imaginations, — saving him
Whose eyelids curtain'd up their jewels dim,
Endymion: yet hourly had he striven
To hide the cankering venom, that had riven
His fainting recollections. Now indeed
His senses had swoon'd off: he did not heed

The sudden silence, or the whispers low,
Or the old eyes dissolving at his woe, 400
Or anxious calls, or close of trembling palms,
Or maiden's sigh, that grief itself embalms:
But in the self-same fixed trance he kept,
Like one who on the earth had never stept.
Aye, even as dead-still as a marble man,
Frozen in that old tale Arabian.

Who whispers him so pantingly and close?
Peona, his sweet sister: of all those,
His friends, the dearest. Hushing signs she made,
And breath'd a sister's sorrow to persuade 410
A yielding up, a cradling on her care.
Her eloquence did breathe away the curse:
She led him, like some midnight spirit nurse
Of happy changes in emphatic dreams,
Along a path between two little streams, —
Guarding his forehead, with her round elbow,
From low-grown branches, and his footsteps slow
From stumbling over stumps and hillocks small;
Until they came to where these streamlets fall,
With mingled bubblings and a gentle rush, 420
Into a river, clear, brimful, and flush
With crystal mocking of the trees and sky.
A little shallop, floating there hard by,
Pointed its beak over the fringed bank;
And soon it lightly dipt, and rose, and sank,
And dipt again, with the young couple's weight, —
Peona guiding, through the water straight,
Towards a bowery island opposite;
Which gaining presently, she steered light
Into a shady, fresh, and ripply cove, 430
Where nested was an arbour, overwove
By many a summer's silent fingering;
To whose cool bosom she was used to bring
Her playmates, with their needle broidery,
And minstrel memories of times gone by.

So she was gently glad to see him laid
Under her favourite bower's quiet shade,
On her own couch, new made of flower leaves,
Dried carefully on the cooler side of sheaves
When last the sun his autumn tresses shook, 440
And the tann'd harvesters rich armfuls took.

Soon was he quieted to slumbrous rest:
But, ere it crept upon him, he had prest
Peona's busy hand against his lips,
And still, a-sleeping, held her finger-tips
In tender pressure. And as a willow keeps
A patient watch over the stream that creeps
Windingly by it, so the quiet maid
Held her in peace: so that a whispering blade
Of grass, a wailful gnat, a bee bustling   450
Down in the blue-bells, or a wren light rustling
Among sere leaves and twigs, might all be heard.

    O magic sleep! O comfortable bird,
That broodest o'er the troubled sea of the mind
Till it is hush'd and smooth! O unconfin'd
Restraint! imprisoned liberty! great key
To golden palaces, strange minstrelsy,
Fountains grotesque, new trees, bespangled caves,
Echoing grottos, full of tumbling waves
And moonlight; aye, to all the mazy world   460
Of silvery enchantment! — who, upfurl'd
Beneath thy drowsy wing a triple hour,
But renovates and lives? — Thus, in the bower,
Endymion was calm'd to life again.
Opening his eyelids with a healthier brain,
He said: "I feel this thine endearing love
All through my bosom: thou art as a dove
Trembling its closed eyes and sleeked wings
About me; and the pearliest dew not brings
Such morning incense from the fields of May,   470
As do those brighter drops that twinkling stray
From those kind eyes, — the very home and haunt
Of sisterly affection. Can I want
Aught else, aught nearer heaven, than such tears?
Yet dry them up, in bidding hence all fears
That, any longer, I will pass my days
Alone and sad. No, I will once more raise
My voice upon the mountain-heights; once more
Make my horn parley from their foreheads hoar:
Again my trooping hounds their tongues shall loll   480
Around the breathed boar: again I'll poll
The fair-grown yew tree, for a chosen bow,
And, when the pleasant sun is getting low,
Again I'll linger in a sloping mead
To hear the speckled thrushes, and see feed
Our idle sheep. So be thou cheered, sweet

And, if thy lute is here, softly intreat
My soul to keep in its resolved course."

Hereat Peona, in their silver source,
Shut her pure sorrow drops with glad exclaim,   490
And took a lute, from which there pulsing came
A lively prelude, fashioning the way
In which her voice should wander. 'Twas a lay
More subtle cadenced, more forest wild
Than Dryope's lone lulling of her child;
And nothing since has floated in the air
So mournful strange. Surely some influence rare
Went, spiritual, through the damsel's hand;
For still, with Delphic emphasis, she spann'd
The quick invisible strings, even though she saw   500
Endymion's spirit melt away and thaw
Before the deep intoxication.
But soon she came, with sudden burst, upon
Her self-possession — swung the lute aside,
And earnestly said: "Brother, 'tis vain to hide
That thou dost know of things mysterious,
Immortal, starry; such alone could thus
Weigh down thy nature. Hast thou sinn'd in aught
Offensive to the heavenly powers? Caught
A Paphian dove upon a message sent?   510
Thy deathful bow against some deer-herd bent,
Sacred to Dian? Haply, thou hast seen
Her naked limbs among the alders green;
And that, alas! is death. No, I can trace
Something more high-perplexing in thy face!"

Endymion look'd at her, and press'd her hand,
And said, "Art thou so pale, who wast so bland
And merry in our meadows? How is this?
Tell me thine ailment: tell me all amiss! —
Ah! thou hast been unhappy at the change   520
Wrought suddenly in me. What indeed more strange?
Or more complete to overwhelm surmise?
Ambition is no sluggard: 'tis no prize,
That toiling years would put within my grasp,
That I have sigh'd for: with so deadly gasp
No man e'er panted for a mortal love.
So all have set my heavier grief above
These things which happen. Rightly have they done:
I, who still saw the horizontal sun

Heave his broad shoulder o'er the edge of the world,   530
Out-facing Lucifer, and then had hurl'd
My spear aloft, as signal for the chace —
I, who, for very sport of heart, would race
With my own steed from Araby; pluck down
A vulture from his towery perching; frown
A lion into growling, loth retire —
To lose, at once, all my toil-breeding fire,
And sink thus low! but I will ease my breast
Of secret grief, here in this bowery nest.

  "This river does not see the naked sky,   540
Till it begins to progress silverly
Around the western border of the wood,
Whence, from a certain spot, its winding flood
Seems at the distance like a crescent moon:
And in that nook, the very pride of June,
Had I been used to pass my weary eves;
The rather for the sun unwilling leaves
So dear a picture of his sovereign power,
And I could witness his most kingly hour,
When he doth tighten up the golden reins,   550
And paces leisurely down amber plains
His snorting four. Now when his chariot last
Its beams against the zodiac-lion cast,
There blossom'd suddenly a magic bed
Of sacred ditamy, and poppies red:
At which I wondered greatly, knowing well
That but one night had wrought this flowery spell;
And, sitting down close by, began to muse
What it might mean. Perhaps, thought I, Morpheus,
In passing here, his owlet pinions shook;   560
Or, it may be, ere matron Night uptook
Her ebon urn, young Mercury, by stealth,
Had dipt his rod in it: such garland wealth
Came not by common growth. Thus on I thought,
Until my head was dizzy and distraught.
Moreover, through the dancing poppies stole
A breeze, most softly lulling to my soul;
And shaping visions all about my sight
Of colours, wings, and bursts of spangly light;
The which became more strange, and strange, and dim,   570
And then were gulph'd in a tumultuous swim:
And then I fell asleep. Ah, can I tell
The enchantment that afterwards befel?

Yet it was but a dream: yet such a dream
That never tongue, although it overteem
With mellow utterance, like a cavern spring,
Could figure out and to conception bring
All I beheld and felt. Methought I lay
Watching the zenith, where the milky way
Among the stars in virgin splendour pours;   580
And travelling my eye, until the doors
Of heaven appear'd to open for my flight,
I became loth and fearful to alight
From such high soaring by a downward glance:
So kept me stedfast in that airy trance,
Spreading imaginary pinions wide.
When, presently, the stars began to glide,
And faint away, before my eager view:
At which I sigh'd that I could not pursue,
And dropt my vision to the horizon's verge;   590
And lo! from opening clouds, I saw emerge
The loveliest moon, that ever silver'd o'er
A shell for Neptune's goblet: she did soar
So passionately bright, my dazzled soul
Commingling with her argent spheres did roll
Through clear and cloudy, even when she went
At last into a dark and vapoury tent —
Whereat, methought, the lidless-eyed train
Of planets all were in the blue again.
To commune with those orbs, once more I rais'd   600
My sight right upward: but it was quite dazed
By a bright something, sailing down apace,
Making me quickly veil my eyes and face:
Again I look'd, and, O ye deities,
Who from Olympus watch our destinies!
Whence that completed form of all completeness?
Whence came that high perfection of all sweetness?
Speak, stubborn earth, and tell me where, O where
Hast thou a symbol of her golden hair?
Not oat-sheaves drooping in the western sun;   610
Not — thy soft hand, fair sister! let me shun
Such follying before thee — yet she had,
Indeed, locks bright enough to make me mad;
And they were simply gordian'd up and braided,
Leaving, in naked comeliness, unshaded,
Her pearl round ears, white neck, and orbed brow;
The which were blended in, I know not how,
With such a paradise of lips and eyes,
Blush-tinted cheeks, half smiles, and faintest sighs.

That, when I think thereon, my spirit clings   620
And plays about its fancy, till the stings
Of human neighbourhood envenom all.
Unto what awful power shall I call?
To what high fane? — Ah! see her hovering feet,
More bluely vein'd, more soft, more whitely sweet
Than those of sea-born Venus, when she rose
From out her cradle shell. The wind out-blows
Her scarf into a fluttering pavilion;
'Tis blue, and over-spangled with a million
Of little eyes, as though thou wert to shed,   630
Over the darkest, lushest blue-bell bed,
Handfuls of daisies." — "Endymion, how strange!
Dream within dream!" — "She took an airy range,
And then, towards me, like a very maid,
Came blushing, waning, willing, and afraid,
And press'd me by the hand: Ah! 'twas too much;
Methought I fainted at the charmed touch,
Yet held my recollection, even as one
Who dives three fathoms where the waters run
Gurgling in beds of coral: for anon,   640
I felt upmounted in that region
Where falling stars dart their artillery forth,
And eagles struggle with the buffeting north
That balances the heavy meteor-stone; —
Felt too, I was not fearful, nor alone,
But lapp'd and lull'd along the dangerous sky.
Soon, as it seem'd, we left our journeying high,
And straightway into frightful eddies swoop'd;
Such as ay muster where grey time has scoop'd
Huge dens and caverns in a mountain's side: 650
There hollow sounds arous'd me, and I sigh'd
To faint once more by looking on my bliss —
I was distracted; madly did I kiss
The wooing arms which held me, and did give
My eyes at once to death: but 'twas to live,
To take in draughts of life from the gold fount
Of kind and passionate looks; to count, and count
The moments, by some greedy help that seem'd
A second self, that each might be redeem'd
And plunder'd of its load of blessedness.   660
Ah, desperate mortal! I e'en dar'd to press
Her very cheek against my crowned lip,
And, at that moment, felt my body dip
Into a warmer air: a moment more,
Our feet were soft in flowers. There was store

Of newest joys upon that alp. Sometimes
A scent of violets, and blossoming limes,
Loiter'd around us; then of honey cells,
Made delicate from all white-flower bells;
And once, above the edges of our nest,   670
An arch face peep'd, — an Oread as I guess'd.

 "Why did I dream that sleep o'er-power'd me
In midst of all this heaven? Why not see,
Far off, the shadows of his pinions dark,
And stare them from me? But no, like a spark
That needs must die, although its little beam
Reflects upon a diamond, my sweet dream
Fell into nothing — into stupid sleep.
And so it was, until a gentle creep,
A careful moving caught my waking ears,   680
And up I started: Ah! my sighs, my tears,
My clenched hands; — for lo! the poppies hung
Dew-dabbled on their stalks, the ouzel sung
A heavy ditty, and the sullen day
Had chidden herald Hesperus away,
With leaden looks: the solitary breeze
Bluster'd, and slept, and its wild self did teaze
With wayward melancholy; and I thought,
Mark me, Peona! that sometimes it brought
Faint fare-thee-wells, and sigh-shrilled adieus! — 690
Away I wander'd — all the pleasant hues
Of heaven and earth had faded: deepest shades
Were deepest dungeons; heaths and sunny glades
Were full of pestilent light; our taintless rills
Seem'd sooty, and o'er-spread with upturn'd gills
Of dying fish; the vermeil rose had blown
In frightful scarlet, and its thorns out-grown
Like spiked aloe. If an innocent bird
Before my heedless footsteps stirr'd, and stirr'd
In little journeys, I beheld in it   700
A disguis'd demon, missioned to knit
My soul with under darkness; to entice
My stumblings down some monstrous precipice:
Therefore I eager followed, and did curse
The disappointment. Time, that aged nurse,
Rock'd me to patience. Now, thank gentle heaven!
These things, with all their comfortings, are given
To my down-sunken hours, and with thee,
Sweet sister, help to stem the ebbing sea
Of weary life."

                    Thus ended he, and both   710
Sat silent: for the maid was very loth
To answer; feeling well that breathed words
Would all be lost, unheard, and vain as swords
Against the enchased crocodile, or leaps
Of grasshoppers against the sun. She weeps,
And wonders; struggles to devise some blame;
To put on such a look as would say, *Shame
On this poor weakness!* but, for all her strife,
She could as soon have crush'd away the life
From a sick dove. At length, to break the pause,   720
She said with trembling chance: "Is this the cause?
This all? Yet it is strange, and sad, alas!
That one who through this middle earth should pass
Most like a sojourning demi-god, and leave
His name upon the harp-string, should achieve
No higher bard than simple maidenhood,
Singing alone, and fearfully, — how the blood
Left his young cheek; and how he used to stray
He knew not where; and how he would say, *nay*,
If any said 'twas love: and yet 'twas love;   730
What could it be but love? How a ring-dove
Let fall a sprig of yew tree in his path;
And how he died: and then, that love doth scathe
The gentle heart, as northern blasts do roses;
And then the ballad of his sad life closes
With sighs, and an alas! — Endymion!
Be rather in the trumpet's mouth, — anon
Among the winds at large — that all may hearken!
Although, before the crystal heavens darken,
I watch and dote upon the silver lakes   740
Pictur'd in western cloudiness, that takes
The semblance of gold rocks and bright gold sands,
Islands, and creeks, and amber-fretted strands
With horses prancing o'er them, palaces
And towers of amethyst, — would I so tease
My pleasant days, because I could not mount
Into those regions? The Morphean fount
Of that fine element that visions, dreams,
And fitful whims of sleep are made of, streams
Into its airy channels with so subtle,   750
So thin a breathing, not the spider's shuttle,
Circled a million times within the space
Of a swallow's nest-door, could delay a trace,
A tinting of its quality: how light
Must dreams themselves be; seeing they're more slight

Than the mere nothing that engenders them!
Then wherefore sully the entrusted gem
Of high and noble life with thoughts so sick?
Why pierce high-fronted honour to the quick
For nothing but a dream?" Hereat the youth   760
Look'd up: a conflicting of shame and ruth
Was in his plaited brow: yet, his eyelids
Widened a little, as when Zephyr bids
A little breeze to creep between the fans
Of careless butterflies: amid his pains
He seem'd to taste a drop of manna-dew,
Full palatable; and a colour grew
Upon his cheek, while thus he lifeful spake.

    "Peona! ever have I long'd to slake
My thirst for the world's praises: nothing base,   770
No merely slumberous phantasm, could unlace
The stubborn canvas for my voyage prepar'd —
Though now 'tis tatter'd; leaving my bark bar'd
And sullenly drifting: yet my higher hope
Is of too wide, too rainbow-large a scope,
To fret at myriads of earthly wrecks.
Wherein lies happiness? In that which becks
Our ready minds to fellowship divine,
A fellowship with essence; till we shine,
Full alchemiz'd, and free of space. Behold   780
The clear religion of heaven! Fold
A rose leaf round thy finger's taperness,
And soothe thy lips: hist, when the airy stress
Of music's kiss impregnates the free winds,
And with a sympathetic touch unbinds
Eolian magic from their lucid wombs:
Then old songs waken from enclouded tombs;
Old ditties sigh above their father's grave;
Ghosts of melodious prophecyings rave
Round every spot where trod Apollo's foot;   790
Bronze clarions awake, and faintly bruit,
Where long ago a giant battle was;
And, from the turf, a lullaby doth pass
In every place where infant Orpheus slept.
Feel we these things? — that moment have we stept
Into a sort of oneness, and our state
Is like a floating spirit's. But there are
Richer entanglements, enthralments far
More self-destroying, leading, by degrees,
To the chief intensity: the crown of these   800

Is made of love and friendship, and sits high
Upon the forehead of humanity.
All its more ponderous and bulky worth
Is friendship, whence there ever issues forth
A steady splendour; but at the tip-top,
There hangs by unseen film, an orbed drop
Of light, and that is love: its influence,
Thrown in our eyes, genders a novel sense,
At which we start and fret; till in the end,
Melting into its radiance, we blend,   810
Mingle, and so become a part of it, —
Nor with aught else can our souls interknit
So wingedly: when we combine therewith,
Life's self is nourish'd by its proper pith,
And we are nurtured like a pelican brood.
Aye, so delicious is the unsating food,
That men, who might have tower'd in the van
Of all the congregated world, to fan
And winnow from the coming step of time
All chaff of custom, wipe away all slime   820
Left by men-slugs and human serpentry,
Have been content to let occasion die,
Whilst they did sleep in love's elysium.
And, truly, I would rather be struck dumb,
Than speak against this ardent listlessness:
For I have ever thought that it might bless
The world with benefits unknowingly;
As does the nightingale, upperched high,
And cloister'd among cool and bunched leaves —
She sings but to her love, nor e'er conceives   830
How tiptoe Night holds back her dark-grey hood.
Just so may love, although 'tis understood
The mere commingling of passionate breath,
Produce more than our searching witnesseth:
What I know not: but who, of men, can tell
That flowers would bloom, or that green fruit would swell
To melting pulp, that fish would have bright mail,
The earth its dower of river, wood, and vale,
The meadows runnels, runnels pebble-stones,
The seed its harvest, or the lute its tones,   840
Tones ravishment, or ravishment its sweet,
If human souls did never kiss and greet?

    "Now, if this earthly love has power to make
Men's being mortal, immortal; to shake

Ambition from their memories, and brim
Their measure of content: what merest whim
Seems all this poor endeavour after fame,
To one, who keeps within his stedfast aim
A love immortal, an immortal too.
Look not so wilder'd; for these things are true, 850
And never can be born of atomies
That buzz about our slumbers, like brain-flies,
Leaving us fancy-sick. No, no, I'm sure,
My restless spirit never could endure
To brood so long upon one luxury,
Unless it did, though fearfully, espy
A hope beyond the shadow of a dream.
My sayings will the less obscured seem,
When I have told thee how my waking sight
Has made me scruple whether that same night 860
Was pass'd in dreaming. Hearken, sweet Peona!
Beyond the matron-temple of Latona,
Which we should see but for these darkening boughs,
Lies a deep hollow, from whose ragged brows
Bushes and trees do lean all round athwart
And meet so nearly, that with wings outraught,
And spreaded tail, a vulture could not glide
Past them, but he must brush on every side.
Some moulder'd steps lead into this cool cell,
Far as the slabbed margin of a well, 870
Whose patient level peeps its crystal eye
Right upward, through the bushes, to the sky.
Oft have I brought thee flowers, on their stalks set
Like vestal primroses, but dark velvet
Edges them round, and they have golden pits:
'Twas there I got them, from the gaps and slits
In a mossy stone, that sometimes was my seat,
When all above was faint with mid-day heat.
And there in strife no burning thoughts to heed,
I'd bubble up the water through a reed; 880
So reaching back to boy-hood: make me ships
Of moulted feathers, touchwood, alder chips,
With leaves stuck in them; and the Neptune be
Of their petty ocean. Oftener, heavily,
When love-lorn hours had left me less a child,
I sat contemplating the figures wild
Of o'er-head clouds melting the mirror through.
Upon a day, while thus I watch'd, by flew
A cloudy Cupid, with his bow and quiver;
So plainly character'd, no breeze would shiver 890

The happy chance: so happy, I was fain
To follow it upon the open plain,
And, therefore, was just going; when, behold!
A wonder, fair as any I have told —
The same bright face I tasted in my sleep,
Smiling in the clear well. My heart did leap
Through the cool depth. — It moved as if to flee —
I started up, when lo! refreshfully,
There came upon my face in plenteous showers
Dew-drops, and dewy buds, and leaves, and flowers,
Wrapping all objects from my smothered sight,
Bathing my spirit in a new delight.
Aye, such a breathless honey-feel of bliss
Alone preserved me from the drear abyss
Of death, for the fair form had gone again.
Pleasure is oft a visitant; but pain
Clings cruelly to us, like the gnawing sloth
On the deer's tender haunches: late, and loth,
'Tis scar'd away by slow returning pleasure.
How sickening, how dark the dreadful leisure   910
Of weary days, made deeper exquisite,
By a fore-knowledge of unslumbrous night!
Like sorrow came upon me, heavier still,
Than when I wander'd from the poppy hill:
And a whole age of lingering moments crept
Sluggishly by, ere more contentment swept
Away at once the deadly yellow spleen.
Yes, thrice have I this fair enchantment seen;
Once more been tortured with renewed life.
When last the wintry gusts gave over strife   920
With the conquering sun of spring, and left the skies
Warm and serene, but yet with moistened eyes
In pity of the shatter'd infant buds, —
That time thou didst adorn, with amber studs,
My hunting cap, because I laugh'd and smil'd,
Chatted with thee, and many days exil'd
All torment from my breast; — 'twas even then,
Straying about, yet, coop'd up in the den
Of helpless discontent, — hurling my lance
From place to place, and following at chance,   930
At last, by hap, through some young trees it struck,
And, plashing among bedded pebbles, stuck
In the middle of a brook, — whose silver ramble
Down twenty little falls, through reeds and bramble,
Tracing along, it brought me to a cave,
Whence it ran brightly forth, and white did lave

The nether sides of mossy stones and rock, —
'Mong which it gurgled blythe adieus, to mock
Its own sweet grief at parting. Overhead,
Hung a lush screen of drooping weeds, and spread   940
Thick, as to curtain up some wood-nymph's home.
'Ah! impious mortal, whither do I roam?'
Said I, low voic'd: 'Ah, whither! 'Tis the grot
Of Proserpine, when Hell, obscure and hot,
Doth her resign; and where her tender hands
She dabbles, on the cool and sluicy sands:
Or 'tis the cell of Echo, where she sits,
And babbles thorough silence, till her wits
Are gone in tender madness, and anon,
Faints into sleep, with many a dying tone   950
Of sadness. O that she would take my vows,
And breathe them sighingly among the boughs,
To sue her gentle ears for whose fair head,
Daily, I pluck sweet flowerets from their bed,
And weave them dyingly — send honey-whispers
Round every leaf, that all those gentle lispers
May sigh my love unto her pitying!
O charitable Echo! hear, and sing
This ditty to her! — tell her' — so I stay'd
My foolish tongue, and listening, half afraid,   960
Stood stupefied with my own empty folly,
And blushing for the freaks of melancholy.
Salt tears were coming, when I heard my name
Most fondly lipp'd, and then these accents came:
'Endymion! the cave is secreter
Than the isle of Delos. Echo hence shall stir
No sighs but sigh-warm kisses, or light noise
Of thy combing hand, the while it travelling cloys
And trembles through my labyrinthine hair.'
At that oppress'd I hurried in. — Ah! where   970
Are those swift moments? Whither are they fled?
I'll smile no more, Peona; nor will wed
Sorrow the way to death; but patiently
Bear up against it: so farewel, sad sigh;
And come instead demurest meditation,
To occupy me wholly, and to fashion
My pilgrimage for the world's dusky brink.
No more will I count over, link by link,
My chain of grief: no longer strive to find
A half-forgetfulness in mountain wind   980
Blustering about my ears: aye, thou shalt see
Dearest of sisters, what my life shall be;

What a calm round of hours shall make my days.
There is a paly flame of hope that plays
Where'er I look: but yet, I'll say 'tis naught —
And here I bid it die. Have not I caught,
Already, a more healthy countenance?
By this the sun is setting; we may chance
Meet some of our near-dwellers with my car."

This said, he rose, faint-smiling like a star   990
Through autumn mists, and took Peona's hand:
They stept into the boat, and launch'd from land.

BOOK II

O SOVEREIGN power of love! O grief! O balm!
All records, saving thine, come cool, and calm,
And shadowy, through the mist of passed years:
For others, good or bad, hatred and tears
Have become indolent; but touching thine,
One sigh doth echo, one poor sob doth pine,
One kiss brings honey-dew from buried days.
The woes of Troy, towers smothering o'er their blaze,
Stiff-holden shields, far-piercing spears, keen blades,
Struggling, and blood, and shrieks — all dimly fades   10
Into some backward corner of the brain;
Yet, in our very souls, we feel amain
The close of Troilus and Cressid sweet.
Hence, pageant history! hence, gilded cheat!
Swart planet in the universe of deeds!
Wide sea, that one continuous murmur breeds
Along the pebbled shore of memory!
Many old rotten-timber'd boats there be
Upon thy vaporous bosom, magnified
To goodly vessels; many a sail of pride,   20
And golden keel'd, is left unlaunch'd and dry.
But wherefore this? What care, though owl did fly
About the great Athenian admiral's mast?
What care, though striding Alexander past
The Indus with his Macedonian numbers?
Though old Ulysses tortured from his slumbers
The glutted Cyclops, what care? — Juliet leaning
Amid her window-flowers, — sighing, — weaning
Tenderly her fancy from its maiden snow,
Doth more avail than these: the silver flow   30

Of Hero's tears, the swoon of Imogen,
Fair Pastorella in the bandit's den,
Are things to brood on with more ardency
Than the death-day of empires. Fearfully
Must such conviction come upon his head,
Who, thus far, discontent, has dared to tread,
Without one muse's smile, or kind behest,
The path of love and poesy. But rest,
In chaffing restlessness, is yet more drear
Than to be crush'd, in striving to uprear   40
Love's standard on the battlements of song.
So once more days and nights aid me along,
Like legion'd soldiers.

              Brain-sick shepherd-prince,
What promise hast thou faithful guarded since
The day of sacrifice? Or, have new sorrows
Come with the constant dawn upon thy morrows?
Alas! 'tis his old grief. For many days,
Has he been wandering in uncertain ways:
Through wilderness, and woods of mossed oaks;
Counting his woe-worn minutes, by the strokes   50
Of the lone woodcutter; and listening still,
Hour after hour, to each lush-leav'd rill.
Now he is sitting by a shady spring,
And elbow-deep with feverous fingering
Stems the upbursting cold: a wild rose tree
Pavilions him in bloom, and he doth see
A bud which snares his fancy: lo! but now
He plucks it, dips its stalk in the water: how!
It swells, it buds, it flowers beneath his sight;
And, in the middle, there is softly pight   60
A golden butterfly; upon whose wings
There must be surely character'd strange things,
For with wide eye he wonders, and smiles oft.

   Lightly this little herald flew aloft,
Follow'd by glad Endymion's clasped hands:
Onward it flies. From languor's sullen bands
His limbs are loos'd, and eager, on he hies
Dazzled to trace it in the sunny skies.
It seem'd he flew, the way so easy was;
And like a new-born spirit did he pass   70
Through the green evening quiet in the sun,
O'er many a heath, through many a woodland dun,

Through buried paths, where sleepy twilight dreams
The summer time away. One track unseams
A wooded cleft, and, far away, the blue
Of ocean fades upon him; then, anew,
He sinks adown a solitary glen,
Where there was never sound of mortal men,
Saving, perhaps, some snow-light cadences
Melting to silence, when upon the breeze   80
Some holy bark let forth an anthem sweet,
To cheer itself to Delphi. Still his feet
Went swift beneath the merry-winged guide,
Until it reached a splashing fountain's side
That, near a cavern's mouth, for ever pour'd
Unto the temperate air: then high it soar'd,
And, downward, suddenly began to dip,
As if, athirst with so much toil, 'twould sip
The crystal spout-head: so it did, with touch
Most delicate, as though afraid to smutch   90
Even with mealy gold the waters clear.
But, at that very touch, to disappear
So fairy-quick, was strange! Bewildered,
Endymion sought around, and shook each bed
Of covert flowers in vain; and then he flung
Himself along the grass. What gentle tongue,
What whisperer disturb'd his gloomy rest?
It was a nymph uprisen to the breast
In the fountain's pebbly margin, and she stood
'Mong lilies, like the youngest of the brood.   100
To him her dripping hand she softly kist,
And anxiously began to plait and twist
Her ringlets round her fingers, saying: "Youth!
Too long, alas, hast thou starv'd on the ruth,
The bitterness of love: too long indeed,
Seeing thou art so gentle. Could I weed
Thy soul of care, by heavens, I would offer
All the bright riches of my crystal coffer
To Amphitrite; all my clear-eyed fish,
Golden, or rainbow-sided, or purplish,   110
Vermilion-tail'd, or finn'd with silvery gauze;
Yea, or my veined pebble-floor, that draws
A virgin light to the deep; my grotto-sands
Tawny and gold, ooz'd slowly from far lands
By my diligent springs; my level lilies, shells,
My charming rod, my potent river spells;
Yes, every thing, even to the pearly cup
Meander gave me. — for I bubbled up

To fainting creatures in a desert wild.
But woe is me, I am but as a child   120
To gladden thee; and all I dare to say,
Is, that I pity thee; that on this day
I've been thy guide; that thou must wander far
In other regions, past the scanty bar
To mortal steps, before thou canst be ta'en
From every wasting sigh, from every pain,
Into the gentle bosom of thy love.
Why it is thus, one knows in heaven above:
But, a poor Naiad, I guess not. Farewel!
I have a ditty for my hollow cell."   130

    Hereat, she vanished from Endymion's gaze,
Who brooded o'er the water in amaze:
The dashing fount pour'd on, and where its pool
Lay, half asleep, in grass and rushes cool,
Quick waterflies and gnats were sporting still,
And fish were dimpling, as if good nor ill
Had fallen out that hour. The wanderer,
Holding his forehead, to keep off the burr
Of smothering fancies, patiently sat down;
And, while beneath the evening's sleepy frown   140
Glow-worms began to trim their starry lamps,
Thus breath'd he to himself: "Whoso encamps
To take a fancied city of delight,
O what a wretch is he! and when 'tis his,
After long toil and travelling, to miss
The kernel of his hopes, how more than vile:
Yet, for him there's refreshment even in toil;
Another city doth he set about,
Free from the smallest pebble-bead of doubt
That he will seize on trickling honey-combs: 150
Alas, he finds them dry; and then he foams,
And onward to another city speeds.
But this is human life: the war, the deeds,
The disappointment, the anxiety,
Imagination's struggles, far and nigh,
All human; bearing in themselves this good,
That they are still the air, the subtle food,
To make us feel existence, and to shew
How quiet death is. Where soil is men grow,
Whether to weeds or flowers; but for me,   160
There is no depth to strike in: I can see
Nought earthly worth my compassing; so stand
Upon a misty, jutting head of land —

Alone? No, no; and by the Orphean lute,
When mad Eurydice is listening to't;
I'd rather stand upon this misty peak,
With not a thing to sigh for, or to seek,
But the soft shadow of my thrice-seen love,
Than be — I care not what. O meekest dove
Of heaven! O Cynthia, ten-times bright and fair!   170
From thy blue throne, now filling all the air,
Glance but one little beam of temper'd light
Into my bosom, that the dreadful might
And tyranny of love be somewhat scar'd!
Yet do not so, sweet queen; one torment spar'd,
Would give a pang to jealous misery,
Worse than the torment's self: but rather tie
Large wings upon my shoulders, and point out
My love's far dwelling. Though the playful rout
Of Cupids shun thee, too divine art thou,   180
Too keen in beauty, for thy silver prow
Not to have dipp'd in love's most gentle stream.
O be propitious, nor severely deem
My madness impious; for, by all the stars
That tend thy bidding, I do think the bars
That kept my spirit in are burst — that I
Am sailing with thee through the dizzy sky!
How beautiful thou art! The world how deep!
How tremulous-dazzlingly the wheels sweep
Around their axle! Then these gleaming reins,   190
How lithe! When this thy chariot attains
Its airy goal, haply some bower veils
Those twilight eyes? Those eyes! — my spirit fails —
Dear goddess, help! or the wide-gaping air
Will gulph me — help!" — At this with madden'd stare,
And lifted hands, and trembling lips he stood;
Like old Deucalion mountain'd o'er the flood,
Or blind Orion hungry for the morn.
And, but from the deep cavern there was borne
A voice, he had been froze to senseless stone;   200
Nor sigh of his, nor plaint, nor passion'd moan
Had more been heard. Thus swell'd it forth: "Descend,
Young mountaineer! descend where alleys bend
Into the sparry hollows of the world!
Oft hast thou seen bolts of the thunder hurl'd
As from thy threshold; day by day hast been
A little lower than the chilly sheen
Of icy pinnacles, and dipp'dst thine arms
Into the deadening ether that still charms

Their marble being: now, as deep profound   210
As those are high, descend! He ne'er is crown'd
With immortality, who fears to follow
Where airy voices lead: so through the hollow,
The silent mysteries of earth, descend!"

He heard but the last words, nor could contend
One moment in reflection: for he fled
Into the fearful deep, to hide his head
From the clear moon, the trees, and coming madness.

'Twas far too strange, and wonderful for sadness;
Sharpening, by degrees, his appetite   220
To dive into the deepest. Dark, nor light,
The region; nor bright, nor sombre wholly,
But mingled up; a gleaming melancholy;
A dusky empire and its diadems;
One faint eternal eventide of gems.
Aye, millions sparkled on a vein of gold,
Along whose track the prince quick footsteps told,
With all its lines abrupt and angular:
Out-shooting sometimes, like a meteor-star,
Through a vast antre; then the metal woof,   230
Like Vulcan's rainbow, with some monstrous roof
Curves hugely: now, far in the deep abyss,
It seems an angry lightning, and doth hiss
Fancy into belief: anon it leads
Through winding passages, where sameness breeds
Vexing conceptions of some sudden change,
Whether to silver grots, or giant range
Of sapphire columns, or fantastic bridge
Athwart a flood of crystal. On a ridge
Now fareth he, that o'er the vast beneath   240
Towers like an ocean-cliff, and whence he seeth
A hundred waterfalls, whose voices come
But as the murmuring surge. Chilly and numb
His bosom grew, when first he, far away,
Descried an orbed diamond, set to fray
Old darkness from his throne:'twas like the sun
Uprisen o'er chaos: and with such a stun
Came the amazement, that, absorb'd in it,
He saw not fiercer wonders — past the wit
Of any spirit to tell, but one of those   250
Who, when this planet's sphering time doth close,
Will be its high remembrancers: who they?
The mighty ones who have made eternal day

For Greece and England. While astonishment
With deep-drawn sighs was quieting, he went
Into a marble gallery, passing through
A mimic temple, so complete and true
In sacred custom, that he well nigh fear'd
To search it inwards; whence far off appear'd,   260
Through a long pillar'd vista, a fair shrine,
And just beyond, on light tiptoe divine,
A quiver'd Dian. Stepping awfully,
The youth approach'd; oft turning his veil'd eye
Down sidelong aisles, and into niches old.
And when, more near against the marble cold
He had touch'd his forehead, he began to thread
All courts and passages, where silence dead
Rous'd by his whispering footsteps murmured faint:
And long he travers'd to and fro, to acquaint
Himself with every mystery, and awe;   270
Till, weary, he sat down before the maw
Of a wide outlet, fathomless and dim,
To wild uncertainty and shadows grim.
There, when new wonders ceas'd to float before,
And thoughts of self came on, how crude and sore
The journey homeward to habitual self!
A mad-pursuing of the fog-born elf,
Whose flitting lantern, through rude nettle-briar,
Cheats us into a swamp, into a fire,
Into the bosom of a hated thing.   280

    What misery most drowningly doth sing
In lone Endymion's ear, now he has caught
The goal of consciousness? Ah, 'tis the thought,
The deadly feel of solitude: for lo!
He cannot see the heavens, nor the flow
Of rivers, nor hill-flowers running wild
In pink and purple chequer, nor, up-pil'd,
The cloudy rack slow journeying in the west,
Like herded elephants; nor felt, nor prest
Cool grass, nor tasted the fresh slumberous air;   290
But far from such companionship to wear
An unknown time, surcharg'd with grief, away,
Was now his lot. And must he patient stay,
Tracing fantastic figures with his spear?
"No!" exclaimed he, "why should I tarry here?"
No! loudly echoed times innumerable.
At which he straightway started, and 'gan tell

His paces back into the temple's chief;
Warming and glowing strong in the belief
Of help from Dian: so that when again   300
He caught her airy form, thus did he plain,
Moving more near the while: "O Haunter chaste
Of river sides, and woods, and heathy waste,
Where with thy silver bow and arrows keen
Art thou now forested? O woodland Queen,
What smoothest air thy smoother forehead woos?
Where dost thou listen to the wide halloos
Of thy disparted nymphs? Through what dark tree
Glimmers thy crescent? Wheresoe'er it be,
'Tis in the breath of heaven: thou dost taste   310
Freedom as none can taste it, nor dost waste
Thy loveliness in dismal elements;
But, finding in our green earth sweet contents,
There livest blissfully. Ah, if to thee
It feels Elysian, how rich to me,
An exil'd mortal, sounds its pleasant name!
Within my breast there lives a choking flame —
O let me cool it the zephyr-boughs among!
A homeward fever parches up my tongue —
O let me slake it at the running springs!   320
Upon my ear a noisy nothing rings —
O let me once more hear the linnet's note!
Before mine eyes thick films and shadows float —
O let me 'noint them with the heaven's light!
Dost thou now lave thy feet and ankles white?
O think how sweet to me the freshening sluice!
Dost thou now please thy thirst with berry-juice?
O think how this dry palate would rejoice!
If in soft slumber thou dost hear my voice,
O think how I should love a bed of flowers! —   330
Young goddess! let me see my native bowers!
Deliver me from this rapacious deep!"

Thus ending loudly, as he would o'erleap
His destiny, alert he stood: but when
Obstinate silence came heavily again,
Feeling about for its old couch of space
And airy cradle, lowly bow'd his face
Desponding, o'er the marble floor's cold thrill.
But 'twas not long; for, sweeter than the rill
To its old channel, or a swollen tide   340
To margin sallows, were the leaves he spied,
And flowers, and wreaths, and ready myrtle crowns
Up heaping through the slab: refreshment drowns

Itself, and strives its own delights to hide —
Nor in one spot alone; the floral pride
In a long whispering birth enchanted grew
Before his footsteps; as when heav'd anew
Old ocean rolls a lengthened wave to the shore,
Down whose green back the short-liv'd foam, **all hoar,**
Bursts gradual, with a wayward indolence.   350

   Increasing still in heart, and pleasant sense,
Upon his fairy journey on he hastes;
So anxious for the end, he scarcely wastes
One moment with his hand among the sweets:
Onward he goes — he stops — his bosom beats
As plainly in his ear, as the faint charm
Of which the throbs were born. This still alarm,
This sleepy music, forc'd him walk tiptoe:
For it came more softly than the east could blow
Arion's magic to the Atlantic isles;   360
Or than the west, made jealous by the smiles
Of thron'd Apollo, could breathe back the lyre
To seas Ionian and Tyrian.

   O did he ever live, that lonely man,
Who lov'd — and music slew not? 'Tis the pest
Of love, that fairest joys give most unrest;
That things of delicate and tenderest worth
Are swallow'd all, and made a seared dearth,
By one consuming flame: it doth immerse
And suffocate true blessings in a curse.   370
Half-happy, by comparison of bliss,
Is miserable. 'Twas even so with this
Dew-dropping melody, in the Carian's ear;
First heaven, then hell, and then forgotten clear,
Vanish'd in elemental passion.

   And down some swart abysm he had gone,
Had not a heavenly guide benignant led
To where thick myrtle branches, 'gainst his head
Brushing, awakened: then the sounds again
Went noiseless as a passing noontide rain   380
Over a bower, where little space he stood;
For as the sunset peeps into a wood
So saw he panting light, and towards it went
Through winding alleys; and lo, wonderment!
Upon soft verdure saw, one here, one there,
Cupids a-slumbering on their pinions fair.

After a thousand mazes overgone,
At last, with sudden step, he came upon
A chamber, myrtle wall'd, embowered high,
Full of light, incense, tender minstrelsy,   390
And more of beautiful and strange beside:
For on a silken couch of rosy pride,
In midst of all, there lay a sleeping youth
Of fondest beauty; fonder, in fair sooth,
Than sighs could fathom, or contentment reach:
And coverlids gold-tinted like the peach,
Or ripe October's faded marigolds,
Fell sleek about him in a thousand folds —
Not hiding up an Apollonian curve
Of neck and shoulder, nor the tenting swerve   400
Of knee from knee, nor ankles pointing light;
But rather, giving them to the filled sight
Officiously. Sideway his face repos'd
On one white arm, and tenderly unclos'd,
By tenderest pressure, a faint damask mouth
To slumbery pout; just as the morning south
Disparts a dew-lipp'd rose. Above his head,
Four lily stalks did their white honours wed
To make a coronal; and round him grew
All tendrils green, of every bloom and hue,   410
Together intertwin'd and trammel'd fresh:
The vine of glossy sprout; the ivy mesh,
Shading its Ethiop berries; and woodbine,
Of velvet leaves and bugle-blooms divine;
Convolvulus in streaked vases flush;
The creeper, mellowing for an autumn blush;
And virgin's bower, trailing airily;
With others of the sisterhood. Hard by,
Stood serene Cupids watching silently.
One, kneeling to a lyre, touch'd the strings,   420
Muffling to death the pathos with his wings;
And, ever and anon, uprose to look
At the youth's slumber; while another took
A willow-bough, distilling odorous dew,
And shook it on his hair; another flew
In through the woven roof, and fluttering-wise
Rain'd violets upon his sleeping eyes.

At these enchantments, and yet many more,
The breathless Latmian wonder'd o'er and o'er;
Until, impatient in embarrassment,   430
He forthright pass'd, and lightly treading went

To that same feather'd lyrist, who straightway,
Smiling, thus whisper'd: "Though from upper day
Thou art a wanderer, and thy presence here
Might seem unholy, be of happy cheer!
For 'tis the nicest touch of human honour,
When some ethereal and high-favouring donor
Presents immortal bowers to mortal sense;
As now 'tis done to thee, Endymion. Hence
Was I in no wise startled. So recline   440
Upon these living flowers. Here is wine,
Alive with sparkles — never, I aver,
Since Ariadne was a vintager,
So cool a purple: taste these juicy pears,
Sent me by sad Vertumnus, when his fears
Were high about Pomona: here is cream,
Deepening to richness from a snowy gleam;
Sweeter than that nurse Amalthea skimm'd
For the boy Jupiter: and here, undimm'd
By any touch, a bunch of blooming plums   450
Ready to melt between an infant's gums:
And here is manna pick'd from Syrian trees,
In starlight, by the three Hesperides.
Feast on, and meanwhile I will let thee know
Of all these things around us." He did so,
Still brooding o'er the cadence of his lyre;
And thus: "I need not any hearing tire
By telling how the sea-born goddess pin'd
For a mortal youth, and how she strove to bind
Him all in all unto her doting self.   460
Who would not be so prison'd? but, fond elf,
He was content to let her amorous plea
Faint through his careless arms; content to see
An unseiz'd heaven dying at his feet;
Content, O fool! to make a cold retreat,
When on the pleasant grass such love, lovelorn,
Lay sorrowing; when every tear was born
Of diverse passion; when her lips and eyes
Were clos'd in sullen moisture, and quick sighs
Came vex'd and pettish through her nostrils small.   470
Hush! no exclaim — yet, justly mightst thou call
Curses upon his head. — I was half glad,
But my poor mistress went distract and mad,
When the boar tusk'd him: so away she flew
To Jove's high throne, and by her plainings drew
Immortal tear-drops down the thunderer's beard;
Whereon, it was decreed he should be rear'd

Each summer time to life. Lo! this is he,
That same Adonis, safe in the privacy
Of this still region all his winter-sleep.   480
Aye, sleep; for when our love-sick queen did weep
Over his waned corse, the tremulous shower
Heal'd up the wound, and, with a balmy power,
Medicined death to a lengthened drowsiness:
The which she fills with visions, and doth dress
In all this quiet luxury; and hath set
Us young immortals, without any let,
To watch his slumber through. 'Tis well nigh pass'd,
Even to a moment's filling up, and fast
She scuds with summer breezes, to pant through   490
The first long kiss, warm firstling, to renew
Embower'd sports in Cytherea's isle.
Look! how those winged listeners all this while
Stand anxious: see! behold!" — This clamant word
Broke through the careful silence; for they heard
A rustling noise of leaves, and out there flutter'd
Pigeons and doves: Adonis something mutter'd
The while one hand, that erst upon his thigh
Lay dormant, mov'd convuls'd and gradually
Up to his forehead. Then there was a hum   500
Of sudden voices, echoing, "Come! come!
Arise! awake! Clear summer has forth walk'd
Unto the clover-sward, and she has talk'd
Full soothingly to every nested finch:
Rise, Cupids! or we'll give the blue-bell pinch
To your dimpled arms. Once more sweet life begin!"
At this, from every side they hurried in,
Rubbing their sleepy eyes with lazy wrists,
And doubling over head their little fists
In backward yawns. But all were soon alive: 510
For as delicious wine doth, sparkling, dive
In nectar'd clouds and curls through water fair,
So from the arbour roof down swell'd an air
Odorous and enlivening; making all
To laugh, and play, and sing, and loudly call
For their sweet queen: when lo! the wreathed green
Disparted, and far upward could be seen
Blue heaven, and a silver car, air-borne,
Whose silent wheels, fresh wet from clouds of morn,
Spun off a drizzling dew, — which falling chill   520
On soft Adonis' shoulders, made him still
Nestle and turn uneasily about.
Soon were the white doves plain, with necks stretch'd out,

And silken traces tighten'd in descent;
And soon, returning from love's banishment,
Queen Venus leaning downward open arm'd:
Her shadow fell upon his breast, and charm'd
A tumult to his heart, and a new life
Into his eyes. Ah, miserable strife,
But for her comforting! unhappy sight,   530
But meeting her blue orbs! Who, who can write
Of these first minutes? The unchariest muse
To embracements warm as theirs makes coy excuse.

    O it has ruffled every spirit there,
Saving Love's self, who stands superb to share
The general gladness: awfully he stands;
A sovereign quell is in his waving hands;
No sight can bear the lightning of his bow;
His quiver is mysterious, none can know
What themselves think of it; from forth his eyes   540
There darts strange light of varied hues and dyes:
A scowl is sometimes on his brow, but who
Look full upon it feel anon the blue
Of his fair eyes run liquid through their souls.
Endymion feels it, and no more controls
The burning prayer within him; so, bent low,
He had begun a plaining of his woe.
But Venus, bending forward, said: "My child,
Favour this gentle youth; his days are wild
With love — he — but alas! too well I see   550
Thou know'st the deepness of his misery.
Ah, smile not so, my son: I tell thee true,
That when through heavy hours I used to rue
The endless sleep of this new-born Adon',
This stranger ay I pitied. For upon
A dreary morning once I fled away
Into the breezy clouds, to weep and pray
For this my love: for vexing Mars had teaz'd
Me even to tears: thence, when a little eas'd,
Down-looking, vacant, through a hazy wood,   560
I saw this youth as he despairing stood:
Those same dark curls blown vagrant in the wind;
Those same full fringed lids a constant blind
Over his sullen eyes: I saw him throw
Himself on wither'd leaves, even as though
Death had come sudden; for no jot he mov'd,
Yet mutter'd wildly. I could hear he lov'd

Some fair immortal, and that his embrace
Had zoned her through the night. There is no trace
Of this in heaven: I have mark'd each cheek,   570
And find it is the vainest thing to seek;
And that of all things 'tis kept secretest.
Endymion! one day thou wilt be blest:
So still obey the guiding hand that fends
Thee safely through these wonders for sweet ends.
'Tis a concealment needful in extreme;
And if I guess'd not so, the sunny beam
Thou shouldst mount up to with me. Now adieu!
Here must we leave thee." — At these words up flew
The impatient doves, up rose the floating car,   580
Up went the hum celestial. High afar
The Latmian saw them minish into nought;
And, when all were clear vanish'd, still he caught
A vivid lightning from that dreadful bow.
When all was darkened, with Etnean throe
The earth clos'd — gave a solitary moan —
And left him once again in twilight lone.

He did not rave, he did not stare aghast,
For all those visions were o'ergone, and past,
And he in loneliness: he felt assur'd   590
Of happy times, when all he had endur'd
Would seem a feather to the mighty prize.
So, with unusual gladness, on he hies
Through caves, and palaces of mottled ore,
Gold dome, and crystal wall, and turquois floor,
Black polish'd porticos of awful shade,
And, at the last, a diamond balustrade,
Leading afar past wild magnificence,
Spiral through ruggedest loopholes, and thence
Stretching across a void, then guiding o'er   600
Enormous chasms, where, all foam and roar,
Streams subterranean tease their granite beds;
Then heighten'd just above the silvery heads
Of a thousand fountains, so that he could dash
The waters with his spear; but at the splash,
Done heedlessly, those spouting columns rose
Sudden a poplar's height, and 'gan to enclose
His diamond path with fretwork, streaming round
Alive, and dazzling cool, and with a sound,
Haply, like dolphin tumults, when sweet shells   610
Welcome the float of Thetis. Long he dwells
On this delight; for, every minute's space,

The streams with changed magic interlace:
Sometimes like delicatest lattices,
Cover'd with crystal vines; then weeping trees,
Moving about as in a gentle wind,
Which, in a wink, to watery gauze refin'd,
Pour'd into shapes of curtain'd canopies,
Spangled, and rich with liquid broideries
Of flowers, peacocks, swans, and naiads fair.   620
Swifter than lightning went these wonders rare;
And then the water, into stubborn streams
Collecting, mimick'd the wrought oaken beams,
Pillars, and frieze, and high fantastic roof,
Of those dusk places in times far aloof
Cathedrals call'd. He bade a loth farewel
To these founts Protean, passing gulph, and dell,
And torrent, and ten thousand jutting shapes,
Half seen through deepest gloom, and griesly gapes,
Blackening on every side, and overhead   630
A vaulted dome like Heaven's, far bespread
With starlight gems: aye, all so huge and strange,
The solitary felt a hurried change
Working within him into something dreary, —
Vex'd like a morning eagle, lost, and weary,
And purblind amid foggy, midnight wolds.
But he revives at once: for who beholds
New sudden things, nor casts his mental slough?
Forth from a rugged arch, in the dusk below,
Came mother Cybele! alone — alone —   640
In sombre chariot; dark foldings thrown
About her majesty, and front death-pale,
With turrets crown'd. Four maned lions hale
The sluggish wheels; solemn their toothed maws,
Their surly eyes brow-hidden, heavy paws
Uplifted drowsily, and nervy tails
Cowering their tawny brushes. Silent sails
This shadowy queen athwart, and faints away
In another gloomy arch.
                         Wherefore delay,
Young traveller, in such a mournful place?   650
Art thou wayworn, or canst not further trace
The diamond path? And does it indeed end
Abrupt in middle air? Yet earthward bend
Thy forehead, and to Jupiter cloud-borne
Call ardently! He was indeed wayworn;
Abrupt, in middle air, his way was lost;
To cloud-borne Jove he bowed, and there crost

Towards him a large eagle, 'twixt whose wings,
Without one impious word, himself he flings,
Committed to the darkness and the gloom: 660
Down, down, uncertain to what pleasant doom,
Swift as a fathoming plummet down he fell
Through unknown things; till exhaled asphodel,
And rose, with spicy fannings interbreath'd,
Came swelling forth where little caves were wreath'd
So thick with leaves and mosses, that they seem'd
Large honey-combs of green, and freshly teem'd
With airs delicious. In the greenest nook
The eagle landed him, and farewel took.

    It was a jasmine bower, all bestrown   670
With golden moss. His every sense had grown
Ethereal for pleasure; 'bove his head
Flew a delight half-graspable; his tread
Was Hesperean; to his capable ears
Silence was music from the holy spheres;
A dewy luxury was in his eyes;
The little flowers felt his pleasant sighs
And stirr'd them faintly. Verdant cave and cell
He wander'd through, oft wondering at such swell
Of sudden exaltation: but, "Alas!"   680
Said he, "will all this gush of feeling pass
Away in solitude? And must they wane,
Like melodies upon a sandy plain,
Without an echo? Then shall I be left
So sad, so melancholy, so bereft!
Yet still I feel immortal! O my love,
My breath of life, where art thou? High above,
Dancing before the morning gates of heaven?
Or keeping watch among those starry seven,
Old Atlas' children? Art a maid of the waters,   690
One of shell-winding Triton's bright-hair'd daughters?
Or art, impossible! a nymph of Dian's,
Weaving a coronal of tender scions
For very idleness? Where'er thou art,
Methinks it now is at my will to start
Into thine arms; to scare Aurora's train,
And snatch thee from the morning; o'er the main
To scud like a wild bird, and take thee off
From thy sea-foamy cradle; or to doff
Thy shepherd vest, and woo thee mid fresh leaves.   700
No, no, too eagerly my soul deceives
Its powerless self: I know this cannot be.

O let me then by some sweet dreaming flee
To her entrancements: hither, sleep, awhile!
Hither, most gentle sleep! and soothing foil
For some few hours the coming solitude."

    Thus spake he, and that moment felt endued
With power to dream deliciously; so wound
Through a dim passage, searching till he found
The smoothest mossy bed and deepest, where   710
He threw himself, and just into the air
Stretching his indolent arms, he took, O bliss!
A naked waist: "Fair Cupid, whence is this?"
A well-known voice sigh'd, "Sweetest, here am I!"
At which soft ravishment, with doating cry
They trembled to each other. — Helicon!
O fountain'd hill! Old Homer's Helicon!
That thou wouldst spout a little streamlet o'er
These sorry pages; then the verse would soar
And sing above this gentle pair, like lark   720
Over his nested young: but all is dark
Around thine aged top, and thy clear fount
Exhales in mists to heaven. Aye, the count
Of mighty Poets is made up; the scroll
Is folded by the Muses; the bright roll
Is in Apollo's hand: our dazed eyes
Have seen a new tinge in the western skies:
The world has done its duty. Yet, oh yet,
Although the sun of poesy is set,
These lovers did embrace, and we must weep   730
That there is no old power left to steep
A quill immortal in their joyous tears.
Long time in silence did their anxious fears
Question that thus it was; long time they lay
Fondling and kissing every doubt away;
Long time ere soft caressing sobs began
To mellow into words, and then there ran
Two bubbling springs of talk from their sweet lips.
"O known Unknown! from whom my being sips
Such darling essence, wherefore may I not   740
Be ever in these arms? in this sweet spot
Pillow my chin for ever? ever press
These toying hands and kiss their smooth excess?
Why not for ever and for ever feel
That breath about my eyes? Ah, thou wilt steal
Away from me again, indeed, indeed —
Thou wilt be gone away, and wilt not heed

My lonely madness. Speak, my kindest fair!
Is — is it to be so? No! Who will dare
To pluck thee from me? And, of thine own will,   750
Full well I feel thou wouldst not leave me. Still
Let me entwine thee surer, surer — now
How can we part? Elysium! who art thou?
Who, that thou canst not be for ever here,
Or lift me with thee to some starry sphere?
Enchantress! tell me by this soft embrace,
By the most soft completion of thy face,
Those lips, O slippery blisses, twinkling eyes,
And by these tenderest, milky sovereignties —
These tenderest, and by the nectar-wine,   760
The passion" ——— "O lov'd Ida the divine!
Endymion! dearest! Ah, unhappy me!
His soul will 'scape us — O felicity!
How he does love me! His poor temples beat
To the very tune of love — how sweet, sweet, sweet.
Revive, dear youth, or I shall faint and die;
Revive, or these soft hours will hurry by
In tranced dulness; speak, and let that spell
Affright this lethargy! I cannot quell
Its heavy pressure, and will press at least   770
My lips to thine, that they may richly feast
Until we taste the life of love again.
What! dost thou move? dost kiss? O bliss! O pain!
I love thee, youth, more than I can conceive;
And so long absence from thee doth bereave
My soul of any rest: yet must I hence:
Yet, can I not to starry eminence
Uplift thee; nor for very shame can own
Myself to thee. Ah, dearest, do not groan
Or thou wilt force me from this secrecy,   780
And I must blush in heaven. O that I
Had done it already; that the dreadful smiles
At my lost brightness, my impassion'd wiles,
Had waned from Olympus' solemn height,
And from all serious Gods; that our delight
Was quite forgotten, save of us alone!
And wherefore so ashamed? 'Tis but to atone
For endless pleasure, by some coward blushes:
Yet must I be a coward! — Horror rushes
Too palpable before me — the sad look   790
Of Jove — Minerva's start — no bosom shook
With awe of purity — no Cupid pinion
In reverence veiled — my crystaline dominion

Half lost, and all old hymns made nullity!
But what is this to love? O I could fly
With thee into the ken of heavenly powers,
So thou wouldst thus, for many sequent hours,
Press me so sweetly. Now I swear at once
That I am wise, that Pallas is a dunce —
Perhaps her love like mine is but unknown —   800
O I do think that I have been alone
In chastity: yes, Pallas has been sighing,
While every eve saw me my hair uptying
With fingers cool as aspen leaves. Sweet love,
I was as vague as solitary dove,
Nor knew that nests were built. Now a soft kiss —
Aye, by that kiss, I vow an endless bliss,
An immortality of passion's thine:
Ere long I will exalt thee to the shine
Of heaven ambrosial; and we will shade   810
Ourselves whole summers by a river glade;
And I will tell thee stories of the sky,
And breathe thee whispers of its minstrelsy.
My happy love will overwing all bounds!
O let me melt into thee; let the sounds
Of our close voices marry at their birth;
Let us entwine hoveringly — O dearth
Of human words! roughness of mortal speech!
Lispings empyrean will I sometime teach
Thine honied tongue — lute-breathings, which I gasp   820
To have thee understand, now while I clasp
Thee thus, and weep for fondness — I am pain'd,
Endymion: woe! woe! is grief contain'd
In the very deeps of pleasure, my sole life?" —
Hereat, with many sobs, her gentle strife
Melted into a languor. He return'd
Entranced vows and tears.

                          Ye who have yearn'd
With too much passion, will here stay and pity,
For the mere sake of truth; as 'tis a ditty
Not of these days, but long ago 'twas told   830
By a cavern wind unto a forest old;
And then the forest told it in a dream
To a sleeping lake, whose cool and level gleam
A poet caught as he was journeying
To Phœbus' shrine; and in it he did fling
His weary limbs, bathing an hour's space,
And after, straight in that inspired place

He sang the story up into the air,
Giving it universal freedom. There
Has it been ever sounding for those ears   840
Whose tips are glowing hot. The legend cheers
Yon centinel stars; and he who listens to it
Must surely be self-doomed or he will rue it:
For quenchless burnings come upon the heart,
Made fiercer by a fear lest any part
Should be engulphed in the eddying wind.
As much as here is penn'd doth always find
A resting place, thus much comes clear and plain;
Anon the strange voice is upon the wane —
And 'tis but echo'd from departing sound,   850
That the fair visitant at last unwound
Her gentle limbs, and left the youth asleep. —
Thus the tradition of the gusty deep.

Now turn we to our former chroniclers. —
Endymion awoke, that grief of hers
Sweet paining on his ear: he sickly guess'd
How lone he was once more, and sadly press'd
His empty arms together, hung his head,
And most forlorn upon that widow'd bed
Sat silently. Love's madness he had known: 860
Often with more than tortured lion's groan
Moanings had burst from him; but now that rage
Had pass'd away: no longer did he wage
A rough-voic'd war against the dooming stars.
No, he had felt too much for such harsh jars:
The lyre of his soul Eolian tun'd
Forgot all violence, and but commun'd
With melancholy thought: O he had swoon'd
Drunken from pleasure's nipple; and his love
Henceforth was dove-like. — Loth was he to move   870
From the imprinted couch, and when he did,
'Twas with slow, languid paces, and face hid
In muffling hands. So temper'd, out he stray'd
Half seeing visions that might have dismay'd
Alecto's serpents; ravishments more keen
Than Hermes' pipe, when anxious he did lean
Over eclipsing eyes: and at the last
It was a sounding grotto, vaulted, vast,
O'er studded with a thousand, thousand pearls,
And crimson mouthed shells with stubborn curls,   880
Of every shape and size, even to the bulk
In which whales arbour close, to brood and sulk

Against an endless storm. Moreover too,
Fish-semblances, of green and azure hue,
Ready to snort their streams. In this cool wonder
Endymion sat down, and 'gan to ponder
On all his life: his youth, up to the day
When 'mid acclaim, and feasts, and garlands gay,
He stept upon his shepherd throne: the look
Of his white palace in wild forest nook,   890
And all the revels he had lorded there:
Each tender maiden whom he once thought fair,
With every friend and fellow-woodlander —
Pass'd like a dream before him. Then the spur
Of the old bards to mighty deeds: his plans
To nurse the golden age 'mong shepherd clans:
That wondrous night: the great Pan-festival:
His sister's sorrow; and his wanderings all,
Until into the earth's deep maw he rush'd:
Then all its buried magic, till it flush'd   900
High with excessive love. "And now," thought he,
"How long must I remain in jeopardy
Of blank amazements that amaze no more?
Now I have tasted her sweet soul to the core
All other depths are shallow: essences,
Once spiritual, are like muddy lees,
Meant but to fertilize my earthly root,
And make my branches lift a golden fruit
Into the bloom of heaven: other light,
Though it be quick and sharp enough to blight   910
The Olympian eagle's vision, is dark,
Dark as the parentage of chaos. Hark!
My silent thoughts are echoing from these shells;
Or they are but the ghosts, the dying swells
Of noises far away? — list!" — Hereupon
He kept an anxious ear. The humming tone
Came louder, and behold, there as he lay,
On either side outgush'd, with misty spray,
A copious spring; and both together dash'd
Swift, mad, fantastic round the rocks, and lash'd   920
Among the conchs and shells of the lofty grot,
Leaving a trickling dew. At last they shot
Down from the ceiling's height, pouring a noise
As of some breathless racers whose hopes poize
Upon the last few steps, and with spent force
Along the ground they took a winding course.
Endymion follow'd — for it seem'd that one
Ever pursued, the other strove to shun —

Follow'd their languid mazes, till well nigh
He had left thinking of the mystery, —   930
And was now rapt in tender hoverings
Over the vanish'd bliss. Ah! what is it sings
His dream away? What melodies are these?
They sound as through the whispering of trees,
Not native in such barren vaults. Give ear!

"O Arethusa, peerless nymph! why fear
Such tenderness as mine? Great Dian, why,
Why didst thou hear her prayer? O that I
Were rippling round her dainty fairness now,
Circling about her waist, and striving how   940
To entice her to a dive! then stealing in
Between her luscious lips and eyelids thin.
O that her shining hair was in the sun,
And I distilling from it thence to run
In amorous rillets down her shrinking form!
To linger on her lily shoulders, warm
Between her kissing breasts, and every charm
Touch raptur'd! — See how painfully I flow:
Fair maid, be pitiful to my great woe.
Stay, stay thy weary course, and let me lead,   950
A happy wooer, to the flowery mead
Where all that beauty snar'd me." — "Cruel god,
Desist! or my offended mistress' nod
Will stagnate all thy fountains: — tease me not
With syren words — Ah, have I really got
Such power to madden thee? And is it true —
Away, away, or I shall dearly rue
My very thoughts: in mercy then away,
Kindest Alpheus, for should I obey
My own dear will, 'twould be a deadly bane. —   960
O, Oread-Queen! would that thou hadst a pain
Like this of mine, then would I fearless turn
And be a criminal. — Alas, I burn,
I shudder — gentle river, get thee hence.
Alpheus! thou enchanter! every sense
Of mine was once made perfect in these woods.
Fresh breezes, bowery lawns, and innocent floods.
Ripe fruits, and lonely couch, contentment gave;
But ever since I heedlessly did lave
In thy deceitful stream, a panting glow   970
Grew strong within me: wherefore serve me so,
And call it love? Alas, 'twas cruelty.
Not once more did I close my happy eyes
Amid the thrush's song. Away! Avaunt!

O 'twas a cruel thing." — "Now thou dost taunt
So softly, Arethusa, that I think
If thou wast playing on my shady brink,
Thou wouldst bathe once again. Innocent maid!
Stifle thine heart no more; — nor be afraid
Of angry powers: there are deities   980
Will shade us with their wings. Those fitful sighs
'Tis almost death to hear: O let me pour
A dewy balm upon them! — fear no more,
Sweet Arethusa! Dian's self must feel
Sometimes these very pangs. Dear maiden, steal
Blushing into my soul, and let us fly
These dreary caverns for the open sky.
I will delight thee all my winding course,
From the green sea up to my hidden source
About Arcadian forests; and will shew   990
The channels where my coolest waters flow
Through mossy rocks; where, 'mid exuberant green,
I roam in pleasant darkness, more unseen
Than Saturn in his exile; where I brim
Round flowery islands, and take thence a skim
Of mealy sweets, which myriads of bees
Buzz from their honied wings: and thou shouldst please
Thyself to choose the richest, where we might
Be incense-pillow'd every summer night.
Doff all sad fears, thou white deliciousness,   1000
And let us be thus comforted; unless
Thou couldst rejoice to see my hopeless stream
Hurry distracted from Sol's temperate beam,
And pour to death along some hungry sands." —
"What can I do, Alpheus? Dian stands
Severe before me: persecuting fate!
Unhappy Arethusa! thou wast late
A huntress free in" — At this, sudden fell
Those two sad streams adown a fearful dell.
The Latmian listen'd, but he heard no more,   1010
Save echo, faint repeating o'er and o'er
The name of Arethusa. On the verge
Of that dark gulph he wept, and said: "I urge
Thee, gentle Goddess of my pilgrimage,
By our eternal hopes, to soothe, to assuage,
If thou art powerful, these lovers' pains;
And make them happy in some happy plains."

He turn'd — there was a whelming sound — he stept,
There was a cooler light; and so he kept
Towards it by a sandy path, and lo!   1020

More suddenly than doth a moment go,
The visions of the earth were gone and fled —
He saw the giant sea above his head.

BOOK III

THERE are who lord it o'er their fellow-men
With most prevailing tinsel: who unpen
Their baaing vanities, to browse away
The comfortable green and juicy hay
From human pastures; or, O torturing fact!
Who, through an idiot blink, will see unpack'd
Fire-branded foxes to sear up and singe
Our gold and ripe-ear'd hopes. With not one tinge
Of sanctuary splendour, not a sight
Able to face an owl's, they still are dight   10
By the blear-eyed nations in empurpled vests,
And crowns, and turbans. With unladen breasts,
Save of blown self-applause, they proudly mount
To their spirit's perch, their being's high account,
Their tiptop nothings, their dull skies, their thrones —
Amid the fierce intoxicating tones
Of trumpets, shoutings, and belabour'd drums,
And sudden cannon. Ah! how all this hums,
In wakeful ears, like uproar past and gone —
Like thunder clouds that spake to Babylon,   20
And set those old Chaldeans to their tasks. —
Are then regalities all gilded masks?
No, there are throned seats unscalable
But by a patient wing, a constant spell,
Or by ethereal things that, unconfin'd,
Can make a ladder of the eternal wind,
And poise about in cloudy thunder-tents
To watch the abysm-birth of elements.
Aye, 'bove the withering of old-lipp'd Fate
A thousand Powers keep religious state,   30
In water, fiery realm, and airy bourne;
And, silent as a consecrated urn,
Hold sphery sessions for a season due.
Yet few of these far majesties, ah, few!
Have bared their operations to this globe —
Few, who with gorgeous pageantry enrobe
Our piece of heaven — whose benevolence
Shakes hand with our own Ceres; every sense
Filling with spiritual sweets to plenitude,

As bees gorge full their cells. And, by the feud   40
'Twixt Nothing and Creation, I here swear,
Eterne Apollo! that thy Sister fair
Is of all these the gentlier-mightiest.
When thy gold breath is misting in the west,
She unobserved steals unto her throne,
And there she sits most meek and most alone;
As if she had not pomp subservient;
As if thine eye, high Poet! was not bent
Towards her with the Muses in thine heart;
As if the ministring stars kept not apart,   50
Waiting for silver-footed messages.
O Moon! the oldest shades 'mong oldest trees
Feel palpitations when thou lookest in:
O Moon! old boughs lisp forth a holier din
The while they feel thine airy fellowship.
Thou dost bless every where, with silver lip
Kissing dead things to life. The sleeping kine,
Couched in thy brightness, dream of fields divine:
Innumerable mountains rise, and rise,
Ambitious for the hallowing of thine eyes;   60
And yet thy benediction passeth not
One obscure hiding-place, one little spot
Where pleasure may be sent: the nested wren
Has thy fair face within its tranquil ken,
And from beneath a sheltering ivy leaf
Takes glimpses of thee; thou art a relief
To the poor patient oyster, where it sleeps
Within its pearly house. — The mighty deeps,
The monstrous sea is thine — the myriad sea!
O Moon! far-spooming Ocean bows to thee,   70
And Tellus feels his forehead's cumbrous load.

    Cynthia! where art thou now? What far abode
Of green or silvery bower doth enshrine
Such utmost beauty? Alas, thou dost pine
For one as sorrowful: thy cheek is pale
For one whose cheek is pale: thou dost bewail
His tears, who weeps for thee. Where dost thou sigh?
Ah! surely that light peeps from Vesper's eye,
Or what a thing is love! 'Tis She, but lc'
How chang'd, how full of ache, how gone in woe!   80
She dies at the thinnest cloud; her loveliness
Is wan on Neptune's blue: yet there's a stress
Of love-spangles, just off yon cape of trees,
Dancing upon the waves, as if to please

The curly foam with amorous influence.
O, not so idle: for down-glancing thence
She fathoms eddies, and runs wild about
O'erwhelming water-courses; scaring out
The thorny sharks from hiding-holes, and fright'ning
Their savage eyes with unaccustomed lightning.   90
Where will the splendor be content to reach?
O love! how potent hast thou been to teach
Strange journeyings! Wherever beauty dwells,
In gulf or aerie, mountains or deep dells,
In light, in gloom, in star or blazing sun,
Thou pointest out the way, and straight 'tis won.
Amid his toil thou gav'st Leander breath;
Thou leddest Orpheus through the gleams of death;
Thou madest Pluto bear thin element;
And now, O winged Chieftain! thou hast sent   100
A moon-beam to the deep, deep water-world,
To find Endymion.

On gold sand impearl'd
With lily shells, and pebbles milky white,
Poor Cynthia greeted him, and sooth'd her light
Against his pallid face: he felt the charm
To breathlessness, and suddenly a warm
Of his heart's blood: 'twas very sweet; he stay'd
His wandering steps, and half-entranced laid
His head upon a tuft of straggling weeds,
To taste the gentle moon, and freshening beads,   110
Lashed from the crystal roof by fishes' tails.
And so he kept, until the rosy veils
Mantling the east, by Aurora's peering hand
Were lifted from the water's breast, and fann'd
Into sweet air; and sober'd morning came
Meekly through billows: — when like taper-flame
Left sudden by a dallying breath of air,
He rose in silence, and once more 'gan fare
Along his fated way.

Far had he roam'd,
With nothing save the hollow vast, that foam'd   120
Above, around, and at his feet; save things
More dead than Morpheus' imaginings;
Old rusted anchors, helmets, breast-plates large
Of gone sea-warriors; brazen beaks and targe;
Rudders that for a hundred years had lost
The sway of human hand; gold vase emboss'd

With long-forgotten story, and wherein
No reveller had ever dipp'd a chin
But those of Saturn's vintage; mouldering scrolls,
Writ in the tongue of heaven, by those souls   130
Who first were on the earth; and sculptures rude
In ponderous stone, developing the mood
Of ancient Nox; — then skeletons of man,
Of beast, behemoth, and leviathan,
And elephant, and eagle, and huge jaw
Of nameless monster. A cold leaden awe
These secrets struck into him; and unless
Dian had chaced away that heaviness,
He might have died: but now, with cheered feel,
He onward kept; wooing these thoughts to steal   140
About the labyrinth in his soul of love.

"What is there in thee, Moon! that thou shouldst move
My heart so potently! When yet a child
I oft have dried my tears when thou hast smil'd.
Thou seem'dst my sister: hand in hand we went
From eve to morn across the firmament.
No apples would I gather from the tree,
Till thou hadst cool'd their cheeks deliciously:
No tumbling water ever spake romance,
But when my eyes with thine thereon could dance: 150
No woods were green enough, no bower divine,
Until thou liftedst up thine eyelids fine:
In sowing time ne'er would I dibble take,
Or drop a seed, till thou wast wide awake;
And, in the summer tide of blossoming,
No one but thee hath heard me blithly sing
And mesh my dewy flowers all the night.
No melody was like a passing spright
If it went not to solemnize thy reign.
Yes, in my boyhood, every joy and pain   160
By thee were fashion'd to the self-same end;
And as I grew in years, still didst thou blend
With all my ardours: thou wast the deep glen;
Thou wast the mountain-top — the sage's pen —
The poet's harp — the voice of friends — the sun;
Thou wast the river — thou wast glory won;
Thou wast my clarion's blast — thou wast my steed —
My goblet full of wine — my topmost deed: —
Thou wast the charm of women, lovely Moon!
O what a wild and harmonized tune   170
My spirit struck from all the beautiful!

On some bright essence could I lean, and lull
Myself to immortality: I prest
Nature's soft pillow in a wakeful rest.
But, gentle Orb! there came a nearer bliss —
My strange love came — Felicity's abyss!
She came, and thou didst fade, and fade away —
Yet not entirely; no, thy starry sway
Has been an under-passion to this hour.
Now I begin to feel thine orby power   180
Is coming fresh upon me: O be kind,
Keep back thine influence, and do not blind
My sovereign vision. — Dearest love, forgive
That I can think away from thee and live! —
Pardon me, airy planet, that I prize
One thought beyond thine argent luxuries!
How far beyond!" At this a surpris'd start
Frosted the springing verdure of his heart;
For as he lifted up his eyes to swear
How his own goddess was past all things fair,   190
He saw far in the concave green of the sea
An old man sitting calm and peacefully.
Upon a weeded rock this old man sat,
And his white hair was awful, and a mat
Of weeds were cold beneath his cold thin feet;
And, ample as the largest winding-sheet,
A cloak of blue wrapp'd up his aged bones,
O'erwrought with symbols by the deepest groans
Of ambitious magic: every ocean-form
Was woven in with black distinctness; storm,   200
And calm, and whispering, and hideous roar,
Quicksand, and whirlpool, and deserted shore,
Were emblem'd in the woof; with every shape
That skims, or dives, or sleeps, 'twixt cape and cape.
The gulphing whale was like a dot in the spell,
Yet look upon it, and 'twould size and swell
To its huge self; and the minutest fish
Would pass the very hardest gazer's wish,
And shew his little eye's anatomy.
Then there was pictur'd the regality   210
Of Neptune; and the sea nymphs round his state,
In beauteous vassalage, look up and wait.
Beside this old man lay a pearly wand,
And in his lap a book, the which he conn'd
So stedfastly, that the new denizen
Had time to keep him in amazed ken,
To mark these shadowings, and stand in awe.

The old man rais'd his hoary head and saw
The wilder'd stranger — seeming not to see,
His features were so lifeless. Suddenly   220
He woke as from a trance; his snow-white brows
Went arching up, and like two magic ploughs
Furrow'd deep wrinkles in his forehead large,
Which kept as fixedly as rocky marge,
Till round his wither'd lips had gone a smile.
Then up he rose, like one whose tedious toil
Had watch'd for years in forlorn hermitage,
Who had not from mid-life to utmost age
Eas'd in one accent his o'er-burden'd soul,
Even to the trees. He rose: he grasp'd his stole,   230
With convuls'd clenches waving it abroad,
And in a voice of solemn joy, that aw'd
Echo into oblivion, he said: —

"Thou art the man! Now shall I lay my head
In peace upon my watery pillow: now
Sleep will come smoothly to my weary brow.
O Jove! I shall be young again, be young!
O shell-borne Neptune, I am pierc'd and stung
With new-born life! What shall I do? Where go,
When I have cast this serpent-skin of woe? —   240
I'll swim to the syrens, and one moment listen
Their melodies, and see their long hair glisten;
Anon upon that giant's arm I'll be,
That writhes about the roots of Sicily:
To northern seas I'll in a twinkling sail,
And mount upon the snortings of a whale
To some black cloud; thence down I'll madly sweep
On forked lightning, to the deepest deep,
Where through some sucking pool I will be hurl'd
With rapture to the other side of the world!   250
O, I am full of gladness! Sisters three,
I bow full hearted to your old decree!
Yes, every god be thank'd, and power benign,
For I no more shall wither, droop, and pine.
Thou art the man!" Endymion started back
Dismay'd; and, like a wretch from whom the rack
Tortures hot breath, and speech of agony,
Mutter'd: "What lonely death am I to die
In this cold region? Will he let me freeze,
And float my brittle limbs o'er polar seas?   260
Or will he touch me with his searing hand,
And leave a black memorial on the sand?

Or tear me piece-meal with a bony saw,
And keep me as a chosen food to draw
His magian fish through hated fire and flame?
O misery of hell! resistless, tame,
Am I to be burnt up? No, I will shout,
Until the gods through heaven's blue look out! —
O Tartarus! but some few days agone
Her soft arms were entwining me, and on   270
Her voice I hung like fruit among green leaves:
Her lips were all my own, and — ah, ripe sheaves
Of happiness! ye on the stubble droop,
But never may be garner'd. I must stoop
My head, and kiss death's foot. Love! love, farewell!
Is there no hope from thee? This horrid spell
Would melt at thy sweet breath. — By Dian's hind
Feeding from her white fingers, on the wind
I see thy streaming hair! and now, by Pan,
I care not for this old mysterious man!"   280

He spake, and walking to that aged form,
Look'd high defiance. Lo! his heart 'gan warm
With pity, for the grey-hair'd creature wept.
Had he then wrong'd a heart where sorrow kept?
Had he, though blindly contumelious, brought
Rheum to kind eyes, a sting to human thought,
Convulsion to a mouth of many years?
He had in truth; and he was ripe for tears.
The penitent shower fell, as down he knelt
Before that care-worn sage, who trembling felt   290
About his large dark locks, and faultering spake:

"Arise, good youth, for sacred Phœbus' sake!
I know thine inmost bosom, and I feel
A very brother's yearning for thee steal
Into mine own: for why? thou openest
The prison gates that have so long opprest
My weary watching. Though thou know'st it not,
Thou art commission'd to this fated spot
For great enfranchisement. O weep no more;
I am a friend to love, to loves of yore: 300
Aye, hadst thou never lov'd an unknown power,
I had been grieving at this joyous hour.
But even now most miserable old,
I saw thee, and my blood no longer cold
Gave mighty pulses: in this tottering case
Grew a new heart, which at this moment plays

As dancingly as thine. Be not afraid,
For thou shalt hear this secret all display'd,
Now as we speed towards our joyous task."

   So saying, this young soul in age's mask   310
Went forward with the Carian side by side:
Resuming quickly thus; while ocean's tide
Hung swollen at their backs, and jewel'd sands
Took silently their foot-prints.
                    "My soul stands
Now past the midway from mortality,
And so I can prepare without a sigh
To tell thee briefly all my joy and pain.
I was a fisher once, upon this main,
And my boat danc'd in every creek and bay;
Rough billows were my home by night and day, —   320
The sea-gulls not more constant; for I had
No housing from the storm and tempests mad,
But hollow rocks, — and they were palaces
Of silent happiness, of slumberous ease:
Long years of misery have told me so.
Aye, thus it was one thousand years ago.
One thousand years! — Is it then possible
To look so plainly through them? to dispel
A thousand years with backward glance sublime?
To breathe away as 'twere all scummy slime   330
From off a crystal pool, to see its deep,
And one's own image from the bottom peep?
Yes: now I am no longer wretched thrall,
My long captivity and moanings all
Are but a slime, a thin-pervading scum,
The which I breathe away, and thronging come
Like things of yesterday my youthful pleasures.

   "I touch'd no lute, I sang not, trod no measures:
I was a lonely youth on desert shores.
My sports were lonely, 'mid continuous roars,   340
And craggy isles, and sea-mew's plaintive cry
Plaining discrepant between sea and sky.
Dolphins were still my playmates; shapes unseen
Would let me feel their scales of gold and green,
Nor be my desolation; and, full oft,
When a dread waterspout had rear'd aloft
Its hungry hugeness, seeming ready ripe
To burst with hoarsest thunderings, and wipe

My life away like a vast sponge of fate,
Some friendly monster, pitying my sad state,   350
Has dived to its foundations, gulph'd it down,
And left me tossing safely. But the crown
Of all my life was utmost quietude:
More did I love to lie in cavern rude,
Keeping in wait whole days for Neptune's voice,
And if it came at last, hark, and rejoice!
There blush'd no summer eve but I would steer
My skiff along green shelving coasts, to hear
The shepherd's pipe come clear from aery steep,
Mingled with ceaseless bleatings of his sheep: 360
And never was a day of summer shine,
But I beheld its birth upon the brine:
For I would watch all night to see unfold
Heaven's gates, and Æthon snort his morning gold
Wide o'er the swelling streams: and constantly
At brim of day-tide, on some grassy lea,
My nets would be spread out, and I at rest.
The poor folk of the sea-country I blest
With daily boon of fish most delicate:
They knew not whence this bounty, and elate   370
Would strew sweet flowers on a sterile beach.

     "Why was I not contented? Wherefore reach
At things which, but for thee, O Latmian!
Had been my dreary death? Fool! I began
To feel distemper'd longings: to desire
The utmost privilege that ocean's sire
Could grant in benediction: to be free
Of all his kingdom. Long in misery
I wasted, ere in one extremest fit
I plung'd for life or death. To interknit   380
One's senses with so dense a breathing stuff
Might seem a work of pain; so not enough
Can I admire how crystal-smooth it felt,
And buoyant round my limbs. At first I dwelt
Whole days and days in sheer astonishment;
Forgetful utterly of self-intent;
Moving but with the mighty ebb and flow.
Then, like a new fledg'd bird that first doth shew
His spreaded feathers to the morrow chill,
I tried in fear the pinions of my will.   390
'Twas freedom! and at once I visited
The ceaseless wonders of this ocean-bed.
No need to tell thee of them, for I see

That thou hast been a witness — it must be —
For these I know thou canst not feel a drouth,
By the melancholy corners of that mouth.
So I will in my story straightway pass
To more immediate matter. Woe, alas!
That love should be my bane! Ah, Scylla fair!
Why did poor Glaucus ever — ever dare   400
To sue thee to his heart? Kind stranger-youth!
I lov'd her to the very white of truth,
And she would not conceive it. Timid thing!
She fled me swift as sea-bird on the wing,
Round every isle, and point, and promontory,
From where large Hercules wound up his story
Far as Egyptian Nile. My passion grew
The more, the more I saw her dainty hue
Gleam delicately through the azure clear:
Until 'twas too fierce agony to bear;   410
And in that agony, across my grief
It flash'd, that Circe might find some relief —
Cruel enchantress! So above the water
I rear'd my head, and look'd for Phœbus' daughter.
Æææa's isle was wondering at the moon: —
It seem'd to whirl around me, and a swoon
Left me dead-drifting to that fatal power.

    "When I awoke, 'twas in a twilight bower;
Just when the light of morn, with hum of bees,
Stole through its verdurous matting of fresh trees.   420
How sweet, and sweeter! for I heard a lyre,
And over it a sighing voice expire.
It ceased — I caught light footsteps; and anon
The fairest face that morn e'er look'd upon
Push'd through a screen of roses. Starry Jove!
With tears, and smiles, and honey-words she wove
A net whose thraldom was more bliss than all
The range of flower'd Elysium. Thus did fall
The dew of her rich speech: 'Ah! Art awake?
O let me hear thee speak, for Cupid's sake!   430
I am so oppress'd with joy! Why, I have shed
An urn of tears, as though thou wert cold dead;
And now I find thee living, I will pour
From these devoted eyes their silver store,
Until exhausted of the latest drop,
So it will pleasure thee, and force thee stop
Here, that I too may live: but if beyond
Such cool and sorrowful offerings, thou art fond

Of soothing warmth, of dalliance supreme;
If thou art ripe to taste a long love dream;   440
If smiles, if dimples, tongues for ardour mute,
Hang in thy vision like a tempting fruit,
O let me pluck it for thee.' Thus she link'd
Her charming syllables, till indistinct
Their music came to my o'er-sweeten'd soul;
And then she hover'd over me, and stole
So near, that if no nearer it had been
This furrow'd visage thou hadst never seen.

"Young man of Latmos! thus particular
Am I, that thou may'st plainly see how far   450
This fierce temptation went: and thou may'st not
Exclaim, How then, was Scylla quite forgot?

"Who could resist? Who in this universe?
She did so breathe ambrosia; so immerse
My fine existence in a golden clime.
She took me like a child of suckling time,
And cradled me in roses. Thus condemn'd,
The current of my former life was stemm'd,
And to this arbitrary queen of sense
I bow'd a tranced vassal: nor would thence   460
Have mov'd, even though Amphion's harp had woo'd
Me back to Scylla o'er the billows rude.
For as Apollo each eve doth devise
A new appareling for western skies;
So every eve, nay every spendthrift hour
Shed balmy consciousness within that bower.
And I was free of haunts umbrageous;
Could wander in the mazy forest-house
Of squirrels, foxes shy, and antler'd deer,
And birds from coverts innermost and drear   470
Warbling for very joy mellifluous sorrow —
To me new born delights!

                                        "Now let me borrow,
For moments few, a temperament as stern
As Pluto's sceptre, that my words not burn
These uttering lips, while I in calm speech tell
How specious heaven was changed to real hell.

"One morn she left me sleeping: half awake
I sought for her smooth arms and lips, to slake
My greedy thirst with nectarous camel-draughts;
But she was gone. Whereat the barbed shafts·   480

Of disappointment stuck in me so sore,
That out I ran and search'd the forest o'er.
Wandering about in pine and cedar gloom
Damp awe assail'd me; for there 'gan to boom
A sound of moan, an agony of sound,
Sepulchral from the distance all around.
Then came a conquering earth-thunder, and rumbled
That fierce complain to silence: while I stumbled
Down a precipitous path, as if impell'd.
I came to a dark valley. — Groanings swell'd   490
Poisonous about my ears, and louder grew,
The nearer I approach'd a flame's gaunt blue,
That glar'd before me through a thorny brake.
This fire, like the eye of gordian snake,
Bewitch'd me towards; and I soon was near
A sight too fearful for the feel of fear:
In thicket hid I curs'd the haggard scene —
The banquet of my arms, my arbour queen,
Seated upon an uptorn forest root;
And all around her shapes, wizard and brute,   500
Laughing, and wailing, groveling, serpenting,
Showing tooth, tusk, and venom-bag, and sting!
O such deformities! Old Charon's self,
Should he give up awhile his penny pelf,
And take a dream 'mong rushes Stygian,
It could not be so phantasied. Fierce, wan,
And tyrannizing was the lady's look,
As over them a gnarled staff she shook.
Oft-times upon the sudden she laugh'd out,
And from a basket emptied to the rout   510
Clusters of grapes, the which they raven'd quick
And roar'd for more; with many a hungry lick
About their shaggy jaws. Avenging, slow,
Anon she took a branch of mistletoe,
And emptied on't a black dull-gurgling phial:
Groan'd one and all, as if some piercing trial
Was sharpening for their pitiable bones.
She lifted up the charm: appealing groans
From their poor breasts went sueing to her ear
In vain; remorseless as an infant's bier   520
She whisk'd against their eyes the sooty oil.
Whereat was heard a noise of painful toil,
Increasing gradual to a tempest rage,
Shrieks, yells, and groans of torture-pilgrimage;
Until their grieved bodies 'gan to bloat
And puff from the tail's end to stifled throat:

Then was appalling silence: then a sight
More wildering than all that hoarse affright;
For the whole herd, as by a whirlwind writhen,
Went through the dismal air like one huge Python   530
Antagonizing Boreas, — and so vanish'd.
Yet there was not a breath of wind: she banish'd
These phantoms with a nod. Lo! from the dark
Came waggish fauns, and nymphs, and satyrs stark,
With dancing and loud revelry, — and went
Swifter than centaurs after rapine bent. —
Sighing an elephant appear'd and bow'd
Before the fierce witch, speaking thus aloud
In human accent: 'Potent goddess! chief
Of pains resistless! make my being brief,   540
Or let me from this heavy prison fly:
Or give me to the air, or let me die!
I sue not for my happy crown again;
I sue not for my phalanx on the plain;
I sue not for my lone, my widow'd wife;
I sue not for my ruddy drops of life,
My children fair, my lovely girls and boys!
I will forget them; I will pass these joys;
Ask nought so heavenward, so too — too high:
Only I pray, as fairest boon, to die,   550
Or be deliver'd from this cumbrous flesh,
From this gross, detestable, filthy mesh,
And merely given to the cold bleak air.
Have mercy, Goddess! Circe, feel my prayer!"

    "That curst magician's name fell icy numb
Upon my wild conjecturing: truth had come
Naked and sabre-like against my heart.
I saw a fury whetting a death-dart;
And my slain spirit, overwrought with fright,
Fainted away in that dark lair of night.   560
Think, my deliverer, how desolate
My waking must have been! disgust, and hate,
And terrors manifold divided me
A spoil amongst them. I prepar'd to flee
Into the dungeon core of that wild wood:
I fled three days — wher lo! before me stood
Glaring the angry witch. O Dis, even now,
A clammy dew is beading on my brow,
At mere remembering her pale laugh, and curse.
'Ha! ha! Sir Dainty! there must be a nurse   570
Made of rose leaves and thistledown, express,

To cradle thee my sweet, and lull thee: yes,
I am too flinty-hard for thy nice touch:
My tenderest squeeze is but a giant's clutch.
So, fairy-thing, it shall have lullabies
Unheard of yet: and it shall still its cries
Upon some breast more lily-feminine.
Oh, no — it shall not pine, and pine, and pine
More than one pretty, trifling thousand years;
And then 'twere pity, but fate's gentle shears   580
Cut short its immortality. Sea-flirt!
Young dove of the waters! truly I'll not hurt
One hair of thine: see how I weep and sigh,
That our heart-broken parting is so nigh.
And must we part? Ah, yes, it must be so.
Yet ere thou leavest me in utter woe,
Let me sob over thee my last adieus,
And speak a blessing: Mark me! Thou hast thews
Immortal, for thou art of heavenly race:
But such a love is mine, that here I chase   590
Eternally away from thee all bloom
Of youth, and destine thee towards a tomb.
Hence shalt thou quickly to the watery vast;
And there, ere many days be overpast,
Disabled age shall seize thee; and even then
Thou shalt not go the way of aged men;
But live and wither, cripple and still breathe
Ten hundred years: which gone, I then bequeath
Thy fragile bones to unknown burial.
Adieu, sweet love, adieu!' — As shot stars fall,   600
She fled ere I could groan for mercy. Stung
And poison'd was my spirit: despair sung
A war-song of defiance 'gainst all hell.
A hand was at my shoulder to compel
My sullen steps; another 'fore my eyes
Moved on with pointed finger. In this guise
Enforced, at the last by ocean's foam
I found me; by my fresh, my native home.
Its tempering coolness, to my life akin,
Came salutary as I waded in;   610
And, with a blind voluptuous rage, I gave
Battle to the swollen billow-ridge, and drave
Large froth before me, while there yet remain'd
Hale strength, nor from my bones all marrow drain'd.

  "Young lover, I must weep — such hellish spite
With dry cheek who can tell? While thus my might

Proving upon this element, dismay'd,
Upon a dead thing's face my hand I laid;
I look'd — 'twas Scylla! Cursed, cursed Circe!
O vulture-witch, hast never heard of mercy?   620
Could not thy harshest vengeance be content,
But thou must nip this tender innocent
Because I lov'd her? — Cold, O cold indeed
Were her fair limbs, and like a common weed
The sea-swell took her hair. Dead as she was
I clung about her waist, nor ceas'd to pass
Fleet as an arrow through unfathom'd brine,
Until there shone a fabric crystalline,
Ribb'd and inlaid with coral, pebble, and pearl.
Headlong I darted; at one eager swirl   630
Gain'd its bright portal, enter'd, and behold!
'Twas vast, and desolate, and icy-cold;
And all around — But wherefore this to thee
Who in few minutes more thyself shalt see?   —
I left poor Scylla in a niche and fled.
My fever'd parchings up, my scathing dread
Met palsy half way: soon these limbs became
Gaunt, wither'd, sapless, feeble, cramp'd, and lame.

"Now let me pass a cruel, cruel space,
Without one hope, without one faintest trace   640
Of mitigation, or redeeming bubble
Of colour'd phantasy; for I fear 'twould trouble
Thy brain to loss of reason: and next tell
How a restoring chance came down to quell
One half of the witch in me.

                    "On a day,
Sitting upon a rock above the spray,
I saw grow up from the horizon's brink
A gallant vessel: soon she seem'd to sink
Away from me again, as though her course
Had been resum'd in spite of hindering force —   650
So vanish'd: and not long, before arose
Dark clouds, and muttering of winds morose.
Old Eolus would stifle his mad spleen,
But could not: therefore all the billows green
Toss'd up the silver spume against the clouds.
The tempest came: I saw that vessel's shrouds
In perilous bustle; while upon the deck
Stood trembling creatures. I beheld the wreck;

The final gulphing; the poor struggling souls:
I heard their cries amid loud thunder-rolls.   660
O they had all been sav'd but crazed eld
Annull'd my vigorous cravings: and thus quell'd
And curb'd, think on't, O Latmian! did I sit
Writhing with pity, and a cursing fit
Against that hell-born Circe. The crew had gone,
By one and one, to pale oblivion;
And I was gazing on the surges prone,
With many a scalding tear and many a groan,
When at my feet emerg'd an old man's hand,
Grasping this scroll, and this same slender wand.   670
I knelt with pain — reached out my hand — had grasp'd
These treasures — touch'd the knuckles — they unclasp'd —
I caught a finger: but the downward weight
O'erpowered me — it sank. Then 'gan abate
The storm, and through chill aguish gloom outburst
The comfortable sun. I was athirst
To search the book, and in the warming air
Parted its dripping leaves with eager care.
Strange matters did it treat of, and drew on
My soul page after page, till well-nigh won   680
Into forgetfulness; when, stupefied,
I read these words, and read again, and tried
My eyes against the heavens, and read again.
O what a load of misery and pain
Each Atlas-line bore off! — a shine of hope
Came gold around me, cheering me to cope
Strenuous with hellish tyranny. Attend!
For thou hast brought their promise to an end.

"In the wide sea there lives a forlorn wretch,
Doom'd with enfeebled carcase to outstretch   690
His loath'd existence through ten centuries,
And then to die alone. Who can devise
A total opposition? No one. So
One million times ocean must ebb and flow,
And he oppressed. Yet he shall not die,
These things accomplish'd: — If he utterly
Scans all the depths of magic, and expounds
The meanings of all motions, shapes and sounds;
If he explores all forms and substances
Straight homeward to their symbol-essences;   700
He shall not die. Moreover, and in chief,
He must pursue this task of joy and grief

Most piously; — all lovers tempest-tost,
And in the savage overwhelming lost,
He shall deposit side by side, until
Time's creeping shall the dreary space fulfil:
Which done, and all these labours ripened,
A youth, by heavenly power lov'd and led,
Shall stand before him; whom he shall direct
How to consummate all. The youth elect   710
Must do the thing, or both will be destroy'd." —

"Then," cried the young Endymion, overjoy'd,
"We are twin brothers in this destiny!
Say, I intreat thee, what achievement high
Is, in this restless world, for me reserv'd.
What! if from thee my wandering feet had swerv'd,
Had we both perish'd?" — "Look!" the sage replied,
"Dost thou not mark a gleaming through the tide,
Of divers brilliances? 'tis the edifice
I told thee, of, where lovely Scylla lies;   720
And where I have enshrined piously
All lovers, whom fell storms have doom'd to die
Throughout my bondage." Thus discoursing, on
They went till unobscur'd the porches shone;
Which hurryingly they gain'd, and enter'd straight.
Sure never since king Neptune held his state
Was seen such wonder underneath the stars.
Turn to some level plain where haughty Mars
Has legion'd all his battle; and behold
How every soldier, with firm foot, doth hold   730
His even breast: see, many steeled squares,
And rigid ranks of iron — whence who dares
One step? Imagine further, line by line,
These warrior thousands on the field supine: —
So in that crystal place, in silent rows,
Poor lovers lay at rest from joys and woes. —
The stranger from the mountains, breathless, trac'd
Such thousands of shut eyes in order plac'd;
Such ranges of white feet, and patient lips
All ruddy, — for here death no blossom nips.   740
He mark'd their brows and foreheads; saw their hair
Put sleekly on one side with nicest care;
And each one's gentle wrists, with reverence,
Put cross-wise to its heart.
                "Let us commence,"
Whisper'd the guide, stuttering with joy, "even now."
He spake, and, trembling like an aspen-bough,

Began to tear his scroll in pieces small,
Uttering the while some mumblings funeral.
He tore it into pieces small as snow
That drifts unfeather'd when bleak northerns blow;   750
And having done it, took his dark blue cloak
And bound it round Endymion: then struck
His wand against the empty air times nine. —
"What more there is to do, young man, is thine:
But first a little patience; first undo
This tangled thread, and wind it to a clue.
Ah, gentle! 'tis as weak as spider's skein;
And shouldst thou break it — What, is it done so clean?
A power overshadows thee! Oh, brave!
The spite of hell is tumbling to its grave.   760
Here is a shell; 'tis pearly blank to me,
Nor mark'd with any sign or charactery —
Canst thou read aught? O read for pity's sake!
Olympus! we are safe! Now, Carian, break
This wand against yon lyre on the pedestal."

'Twas done: and straight with sudden swell and fall
Sweet music breath'd her soul away, and sigh'd
A lullaby to silence. — "Youth! now strew
These minced leaves on me, and passing through
Those files of dead, scatter the same around,   770
And thou wilt see the issue." — 'Mid the sound
Of flutes and viols, ravishing his heart,
Endymion from Glaucus stood apart,
And scatter'd in his face some fragments light.
How lightning-swift the change! a youthful wight
Smiling beneath a coral diadem,
Out-sparkling sudden like an upturn'd gem,
Appear'd, and, stepping to a beauteous corse,
Kneel'd down beside it, and with tenderest force
Press'd its cold hand, and wept — and Scylla sigh'd!   780
Endymion, with quick hand, the charm applied —
The nymph arose: he left them to their joy,
And onward went upon his high employ,
Showering those powerful fragments on the dead.
And, as he pass'd, each lifted up its head,
As doth a flower at Apollo's touch.
Death felt it to his inwards: 'twas too much:
Death fell a-weeping in his charnel-house.
The Latmian persever'd along, and thus
All were re-animated. There arose   790
A noise of harmony, pulses and throes

Of gladness in the air — while many, who
Had died in mutual arms devout and true,
Sprang to each other madly; and the rest
Felt a high certainty of being blest.
They gaz'd upon Endymion. Enchantment
Grew drunken, and would have its head and bent.
Delicious symphonies, like airy flowers,
Budded, and swell'd, and, full-blown, shed full showers
Of light, soft, unseen leaves of sounds divine.   800
The two deliverers tasted a pure wine
Of happiness, from fairy-press ooz'd out.
Speechless they eyed each other, and about
The fair assembly wander'd to and fro,
Distracted with the richest overflow
Of joy that ever pour'd from heaven.

                                        —— "Away!"
Shouted the new born god; "Follow, and pay
Our piety to Neptunus supreme!" —
Then Scylla, blushing sweetly from her dream,
They led on first, bent to her meek surprise,   810
Through portal columns of a giant size,
Into the vaulted, boundless emerald.
Joyous all follow'd as the leader call'd,
Down marble steps; pouring as easily
As hour-glass sand, — and fast, as you might see
Swallows obeying the south summer's call,
Or swans upon a gentle waterfall.

    Thus went that beautiful multitude, nor far,
Ere from among some rocks of glittering spar,
Just within ken, they saw descending thick   820
Another multitude. Whereat more quick
Moved either host. On a wide sand they met,
And of those numbers every eye was wet;
For each their old love found. A murmuring rose,
Like what was never heard in all the throes
Of wind and waters: 'tis past human wit
To tell; 'tis dizziness to think of it.

    This mighty consummation made, the host
Mov'd on for many a league; and gain'd, and lost
Huge sea-marks; vanward swelling in array,   830
And from the rear diminishing away, —
Till a faint dawn surpris'd them. Glaucus cried,
"Behold! behold, the palace of his pride!

God Neptune's palaces!" With noise increas'd,
They shoulder'd on towards that brightening east.
At every onward step proud domes arose
In prospect, — diamond gleams, and golden glows
Of amber 'gainst their faces levelling.
Joyous, and many as the leaves in spring,
Still onward; still the splendour gradual swell'd.   840
Rich opal domes were seen, on high upheld
By jasper pillars, letting through their shafts
A blush of coral. Copious wonder-draughts
Each gazer drank; and deeper drank more near:
For what poor mortals fragment up, as mere
As marble was there lavish, to the vast
Of one fair palace, that far far surpass'd,
Even for common bulk, those olden three,
Memphis, and Babylon, and Nineveh.

    As large, as bright, as colour'd as the bow   850
Of Iris, when unfading it doth shew
Beyond a silvery shower, was the arch
Through which this Paphian army took its march,
Into the outer courts of Neptune's state:
Whence could be seen, direct, a golden gate,
To which the leaders sped; but not half raught
Ere it burst open swift as fairy thought,
And made those dazzled thousands veil their eyes
Like callow eagles at the first sunrise.
Soon with an eagle nativeness their gaze   860
Ripe from hue-golden swoons took all the blaze,
And then, behold! large Neptune on his throne
Of emerald deep: yet not exalt alone;
At his right hand stood winged Love, and on
His left sat smiling Beauty's paragon.

    Far as the mariner on highest mast
Can see all round upon the calmed vast,
So wide was Neptune's hall: and as the blue
Doth vault the waters, so the waters drew
Their doming curtains, high, magnificent,   870
Aw'd from the throne aloof; — and when storm-rent
Disclos'd the thunder-gloomings in Jove's air;
But sooth'd as now, flash'd sudden everywhere,
Noiseless, sub-marine cloudlets, glittering
Death to a human eye: for there did spring
From natural west, and east, and south, and north,
A light as of four sunsets, blazing forth

A gold-green zenith 'bove the Sea-God's head.
Of lucid depth the floor, and far outspread
As breezeless lake, on which the slim canoe   880
Of feather'd Indian darts about, as through
The delicatest air: air verily,
But for the portraiture of clouds and sky:
This palace floor breath-air, — but for the amaze
Of deep-seen wonders motionless, — and blaze
Of the dome pomp, reflected in extremes,
Globing a golden sphere.

                They stood in dreams
Till Triton blew his horn. The palace rang;
The Nereids danc'd; the Syrens faintly sang;
And the great Sea-King bow'd his dripping head.   890
Then Love took wing, and from his pinions shed
On all the multitude a nectarous dew.
The ooze-born Goddess beckoned and drew
Fair Scylla and her guides to conference;
And when they reach'd the throned eminence
She kist the sea-nymph's cheek, — who sat her down
A-toying with the doves. Then, — "Mighty crown
And sceptre of this kingdom!" Venus said,
"Thy vows were on a time to Nais paid:
Behold!" — Two copious tear-drops instant fell   900
From the God's large eyes; he smil'd delectable,
And over Glaucus held his blessing hands. —
"Endymion! Ah! still wandering in the bands
Of love? Now this is cruel. Since the hour
I met thee in earth's bosom, all my power
Have I put forth to serve thee. What, not yet
Escap'd from dull mortality's harsh net?
A little patience, youth! 'twill not be long,
Or I am skilless quite: an idle tongue,
A humid eye, and steps luxurious,   910
Where these are new and strange, are ominous.
Aye, I have seen these signs in one of heaven,
When others were all blind: and were I given
To utter secrets, haply I might say
Some pleasant words: — but Love will have his day.
So wait awhile expectant. Pr'ythee soon,
Even in the passing of thine honey-moon,
Visit thou my Cythera: thou wilt find
Cupid well-natured, my Adonis kind;
And pray persuade with thee — Ah, I have done,   920
All blisses be upon thee, my sweet son!" —

Thus the fair goddess: while Endymion
Knelt to receive those accents halycon.

Meantime a glorious revelry began
Before the Water-Monarch. Nectar ran
In courteous fountains to all cups outreach'd;
And plunder'd vines, teeming exhaustless, pleach'd
New growth about each shell and pendent lyre;
The which, in disentangling for their fire,
Pull'd down fresh foliage and coverture   930
For dainty toying. Cupid, empire-sure,
Flutter'd and laugh'd, and oft-times through the throng
Made a delighted way. Then dance, and song,
And garlanding grew wild; and pleasure reign'd.
In harmless tendril they each other chain'd,
And strove who should be smother'd deepest in
Fresh crush of leaves.

                    O 'tis a very sin
For one so weak to venture his poor verse
In such a place as this. O do not curse,
High Muses! let him hurry to the ending.   940

All suddenly were silent. A soft blending
Of dulcet instruments came charmingly;
And then a hymn.
                    "KING of the stormy sea!
Brother of Jove, and co-inheritor
Of elements! Eternally before
Thee the waves awful bow. Fast, stubborn rock,
At thy fear'd trident shrinking, doth unlock
Its deep foundations, hissing into foam.
All mountain-rivers lost, in the wide home
Of thy capacious bosom ever flow.   950
Thou frownest, and old Eolus thy foe
Skulks to his cavern, 'mid the gruff complaint
Of all his rebel tempests. Dark clouds faint
When, from thy diadem, a silver gleam
Slants over blue dominion. Thy bright team
Gulphs in the morning light, and scuds along
To bring thee nearer to that golden song
Apollo singeth, while his chariot
Waits at the doors of heaven. Thou art not
For scenes like this: an empire stern hast thou;   960
And it hath furrow'd that large front: yet now,

As newly come of heaven, dost thou sit
To blend and interknit
Subdued majesty with this glad time.
O shell-borne King sublime;
We lay our hearts before thee evermore —
We sing, and we adore!

   "Breathe softly, flutes;
Be tender of your strings, ye soothing lutes;
Nor be the trumpet heard! O vain, O vain;   970
Not flowers budding in an April rain,
Nor breath of sleeping dove, nor river's flow, —
No, nor the Eolian twang of Love's own bow,
Can mingle music fit for the soft ear
Of goddess Cytherea!
Yet deign, white Queen of Beauty, thy fair eyes
On our souls' sacrifice.

   "Bright-winged Child!
Who has another care when thou hast smil'd?
Unfortunates on earth, we see at last   980
All death-shadows, and glooms that overcast
Our spirits, fann'd away by thy light pinions.
O sweetest essence! sweetest of all minions!
God of warm pulses, and dishevell'd hair,
And panting bosoms bare!
Dear unseen light in darkness! eclipser
Of light in light! delicious poisoner!
Thy venom'd goblet will we quaff until
We fill — we fill!
And by thy Mother's lips ———— "

                  Was heard no more   990
For clamour, when the golden palace door
Opened again, and from without, in shone
A new magnificence. On oozy throne
Smooth-moving came Oceanus the old,
To take a latest glimpse at his sheep-fold,
Before he went into his quiet cave
To muse for ever — Then a lucid wave,
Scoop'd from its trembling sisters of mid-sea,
Afloat, and pillowing up the majesty
Of Doris, and the Egean seer, her spouse —   1000
Next, on a dolphin, clad in laurel boughs,
Theban Amphion leaning on his lute:
His fingers went across it — All were mute

To gaze on Amphitrite, queen of pearls,
And Thetis pearly too. —

     The palace whirls
Around giddy Endymion; seeing he
Was there far strayed from mortality.
He could not bear it — shut his eyes in vain;
Imagination gave a dizzier pain.
"O I shall die! sweet Venus, be my stay!   1010
Where is my lovely mistress? Well-away!
I die — I hear her voice — I feel my wing — "
At Neptune's feet he sank. A sudden ring
Of Nereids were about him, in kind strife
To usher back his spirit into life:
But still he slept. At last they interwove
Their cradling arms, and purpos'd to convey
Towards a crystal bower far away.

 Lo! while slow carried through the pitying crowd,
To his inward senses these words spake aloud;   1020
Written in star-light on the dark above:
Dearest Endymion! my entire love!
How have I dwelt in fear of fate: 'tis done —
Immortal bliss for me too hast thou won.
Arise then! for the hen-dove shall not hatch
Her ready eggs, before I'll kissing snatch
Thee into endless heaven. Awake! Awake!

 The youth at once arose: a placid lake
Came quiet to his eyes; and forest green,
Cooler than all the wonders he had seen,   1030
Lull'd with its simple song his fluttering breast.
How happy once again in grassy nest!

BOOK IV

MUSE of my native land! loftiest Muse!
O first-born on the mountains! by the hues
Of heaven on the spiritual air begot:
Long didst thou sit alone in northern grot,
While yet our England was a wolfish den;
Before our forests heard the talk of men;
Before the first of Druids was a child; —
Long didst thou sit amid our regions wild
Rapt in a deep prophetic solitude.

There came an eastern voice of solemn mood: — 10
Yet wast thou patient. Then sang forth the Nine,
Apollo's garland: — yet didst thou divine
Such home-bred glory, that they cry'd in vain,
"Come hither, Sister of the Island!" Plain
Spake fair Ausonia; and once more she spake
A higher summons: — still didst thou betake
Thee to thy native hopes. O thou hast won
A full accomplishment! The thing is done,
Which undone, these our latter days had risen
On barren souls. Great Muse, thou know'st what prison 20
Of flesh and bone curbs, and confines, and frets
Our spirit's wings; despondency besets
Our pillows; and the fresh to-morrow morn
Seems to give forth its light in very scorn
Of our dull, uninspired, snail-paced lives.
Long have I said, how happy he who shrives
To thee! But then I thought on poets gone,
And could not pray; — nor could I now — so on
I move to the end in lowliness of heart. ——

"Ah, woe is me! that I should fondly part 30
From my dear native land! Ah, foolish maid!
Glad was the hour, when, with thee, myriads bade
Adieu to Ganges and their pleasant fields!
To one so friendless the clear freshet yields
A bitter coolness; the ripe grape is sour:
Yet I would have, great gods! but one short hour
Of native air — let me but die at home."

Endymion to heaven's airy dome
Was offering up a hecatomb of vows,
When these words reach'd him. Whereupon he bows 40
His head through thorny-green entanglement
Of underwood, and to the sound is bent,
Anxious as hind towards her hidden fawn.

"Is no one near to help me? No fair dawn
Of life from charitable voice? No sweet saying
To set my dull and sadden'd spirit playing?
No hand to toy with mine? No lips so sweet
That I may worship them? No eyelids meet
To twinkle on my bosom? No one dies
Before me, till from these enslaving eyes 50
Redemption sparkles! — I am sad and lost."

    Thou, Carian lord, hadst better have been tost
Into a whirlpool. Vanish into air,
Warm mountaineer! for canst thou only bear
A woman's sigh alone and in distress?
See not her charms! Is Phœbe passionless?
Phœbe is fairer far — O gaze no more: —
Yet if thou wilt behold all beauty's store,
Behold her panting in the forest grass!
Do not those curls of glossy jet surpass   60
For tenderness the arms so idly lain
Amongst them? Feelest not a kindred pain,
To see such lovely eyes in swimming search
After some warm delight, that seems to perch
Dovelike in the dim cell lying beyond
Their upper lids? — Hist!

              "O for Hermes' wand,
To touch this flower into human shape!
That woodland Hyacinthus could escape
From his green prison, and here kneeling down
Call me his queen, his second life's fair crown!   70
Ah me, how I could love! — My soul doth melt
For the unhappy youth — Love! I have felt
So faint a kindness, such a meek surrender
To what my own full thoughts had made too tender,
That but for tears my life had fled away! —
Ye deaf and senseless minutes of the day,
And thou, old forest, hold ye this for true,
There is no lightning, no authentic dew
But in the eye of love: there's not a sound,
Melodious howsoever, can confound   80
The heavens and earth in one to such a death
As doth the voice of love: there's not a breath
Will mingle kindly with the meadow air,
Till it has panted round, and stolen a share
Of passion from the heart!" —

                Upon a bough
He leant, wretched. He surely cannot now
Thirst for another love: O impious,
That he can ever dream upon it thus! —
Thought he, "Why am I not as are the dead,
Since to a woe like this I have been led   90
Through the dark earth, and through the wondrous sea?
Goddess! I love thee not the less: from thee

By Juno's smile I turn not — no, no, no —
While the great waters are at ebb and flow. —
I have a triple soul! O fond pretence —
For both, for both my love is so immense,
I feel my heart is cut for them in twain."

And so he groan'd, as one by beauty slain.
The lady's heart beat quick, and he could see
Her gentle bosom heave tumultuously.   100
He sprang from his green covert: there she lay,
Sweet as a muskrose upon new-made hay:
With all her limbs on tremble, and her eyes
Shut softly up alive. To speak he tries.
"Fair damsel, pity me! forgive that I
Thus violate thy bower's sanctity!
O pardon me, for I am full of grief —
Grief born of thee, young angel! fairest thief!
Who stolen hast away the wings wherewith
I was to top the heavens. Dear maid, sith   110
Thou art my executioner, and I feel
Loving and hatred, misery and weal,
Will in a few short hours be nothing to me,
And all my story that much passion slew me;
Do smile upon the evening of my days:
And, for my tortur'd brain begins to craze,
Be thou my nurse; and let me understand
How dying I shall kiss that lily hand. —
Dost weep for me? Then should I be content.
Scowl on, ye fates! until the firmament   120
Outblackens Erebus, and the full-cavern'd earth
Crumbles into itself. By the cloud girth
Of Jove, those tears have given me a thirst
To meet oblivion." — As her heart would burst
The maiden sobb'd awhile, and then replied:
"Why must such desolation betide
As that thou speakest of? Are not these green nooks
Empty of all misfortune? Do the brooks
Utter a gorgon voice? Does yonder thrush,
Schooling its half-fledg'd little ones to brush   130
About the dewy forest, whisper tales? —
Speak not of grief, young stranger, or cold snails
Will slime the rose to-night. Though if thou wilt,
Methinks 'twould be a guilt — a very guilt —
Not to companion thee, and sigh away
The light — the dusk — the dark — till break of day!"
"Dear lady," said Endymion, " 'tis past:

I love thee! and my days can never last.
That I may pass in patience still speak:
Let me have music dying, and I seek   140
No more delight — I bid adieu to all.
Didst thou not after other climates call,
And murmur about Indian streams?" — Then she,
Sitting beneath the midmost forest tree,
For pity sang this roundelay ——

     "O Sorrow,
      Why dost borrow
The natural hue of health, from vermeil lips? —
      To give maiden blushes
      To the white rose bushes?   150
Or is it thy dewy hand the daisy tips?

     "O Sorrow,
      Why dost borrow
The lustrous passion from a falcon-eye? —
      To give the glow-worm light?
      Or, on a moonless night,
To tinge, on syren shores, the salt sea-spry?

     "O Sorrow,
      Why dost borrow
The mellow ditties from a mourning tongue? —   160
      To give at evening pale
      Unto the nightingale,
That thou mayst listen the cold dews among?

     "O Sorrow,
      Why dost borrow
Heart's lightness from the merriment of May? —
      A lover would not tread
      A cowslip on the head,
Though he should dance from eve till peep of day —
      Nor any drooping flower   170
      Held sacred for thy bower,
Wherever he may sport himself and play.

     "To Sorrow,
      I bade good-morrow,
And thought to leave her far away behind;
      But cheerly, cheerly,
      She loves me dearly;
She is so constant to me, and so kind·

I would deceive her
And so leave her, 180
But ah! she is so constant and so kind.

"Beneath my palm trees, by the river side
I sat a-weeping: in the whole world wide
There was no one to ask me why I wept. —
And so I kept
Brimming the water-lily cups with tears
Cold as my fears.

"Beneath my palm trees, by the river side,
I sat a-weeping: what enamour'd bride,
Cheated by shadowy wooer from the clouds, 190
But hides and shrouds
Beneath dark palm trees by a river side?

"And as I sat, over the light blue hills
There came a noise of revellers: the rills
Into the wide stream came of purple hue —
'Twas Bacchus and his crew!
The earnest trumpet spake, and silver thrills
From kissing cymbals made a merry din —
'Twas Bacchus and his kin!
Like to a moving vintage down they came, 200
Crown'd with green leaves, and faces all on flame;
All madly dancing through the pleasant valley,
To scare thee, Melancholy!
O then, O then, thou wast a simple name!
And I forgot thee, as the berried holly
By shepherds is forgotten, when, in June,
Tall chestnuts keep away the sun and moon: —
I rush'd into the folly!

"Within his car, aloft, young Bacchus stood,
Trifling his ivy-dart, in dancing mood, 210
With sidelong laughing;
And little rills of crimson wine imbrued
His plump white arms, and shoulders, enough white
For Venus' pearly bite:
And near him rode Silenus on his ass,
Pelted with flowers as he on did pass
Tipsily quaffing.

"Whence came ye, merry Damsels! whence came ye!
So many, and so many, and such glee?

Why have ye left your bowers desolate,   220
    Your lutes, and gentler fate? —
'We follow Bacchus! Bacchus on the wing,
    A-conquering!
Bacchus, young Bacchus! good or ill betide,
We dance before him thorough kingdoms wide: —
Come hither, lady fair, and joined be
    To our wild minstrelsy!'

"Whence came ye, jolly Satyrs! whence came ye!
So many, and so many, and such glee?
Why have ye left your forest haunts, why left   230
    Your nuts in oak-tree cleft? —
'For wine, for wine we left our kernel tree;
For wine we left our heath, and yellow brooms,
    And cold mushrooms;
For wine we follow Bacchus through the earth;
Great God of breathless cups and chirping mirth! —
Come hither, lady fair, and joined be
    To our mad minstrelsy!'

"Over wide streams and mountains great we went,
And, save when Bacchus kept his ivy tent,   240
Onward the tiger and the leopard pants,
    With Asian elephants:
Onward these myriads — with song and dance,
With zebras striped, and sleek Arabians' prance,
Web-footed alligators, crocodiles,
Bearing upon their scaly backs, in files,
Plump infant laughers mimicking the coil
Of seamen, and stout galley-rowers' toil:
With toying oars and silken sails they glide,
    Nor care for wind and tide.   250

"Mounted on panthers' furs and lions' manes,
From rear to van they scour about the plains;
A three days' journey in a moment done:
And always, at the rising of the sun,
About the wilds they hunt with spear and horn,
    On spleenful unicorn.

"I saw Osirian Egypt kneel adown
    Before the vine-wreath crown!
I saw parch'd Abyssinia rouse and sing
    To the silver cymbals' ring!   260

I saw the whelming vintage hotly pierce
   Old Tartary the fierce!
The kings of Inde their jewel-sceptres vail,
And from their treasures scatter pearled hail;
Great Brahma from his mystic heaven groans,
   And all his priesthood moans;
Before young Bacchus' eye-wink turning pale. —
Into these regions came I following him,
Sick hearted, weary — so I took a whim
To stray away into these forests drear   270
   Alone, without a peer:
And I have told thee all thou mayest hear.

   "Young stranger!
   I've been a ranger
In search of pleasure throughout every clime:
   Alas, 'tis not for me!
   Bewitch'd I sure must be,
To lose in grieving all my maiden prime.

   "Come then, Sorrow!
   Sweetest Sorrow!   280
Like an own babe I nurse thee on my breast:
   I thought to leave thee
   And deceive thee,
But now of all the world I love thee best.

   "There is not one,
   No, no, not one
But thee to comfort a poor lonely maid:
   Thou art her mother,
   And her brother,
Her playmate, and her wooer in the shade."   290

 O what a sigh she gave in finishing,
And look, quite dead to every worldly thing!
Endymion could not speak, but gazed on her;
And listened to the wind that now did stir
About the crisped oaks full drearily,
Yet with as sweet a softness as might be
Remember'd from its velvet summer song.
At last he said: "Poor lady, how thus long
Have I been able to endure that voice?
Fair Melody! kind Syren! I've no choice;   300
I must be thy sad servant evermore:
I cannot choose but kneel here and adore.

Alas, I must not think — by Phœbe, no!
Let me not think, soft Angel! shall it be so?
Say, beautifullest, shall I never think?
O thou could'st foster me beyond the brink
Of recollection! make my watchful care
Close up its bloodshot eyes, nor see despair!
Do gently murder half my soul, and I
Shall feel the other half so utterly! —   310
I'm giddy at that cheek so fair and smooth;
O let it blush so ever! let it soothe
My madness! let it mantle rosy-warm
With the tinge of love, panting in safe alarm. —
This cannot be thy hand, and yet it is;
And this is sure thine other softling — this
Thine own fair bosom, and I am so near!
Wilt fall asleep? O let me sip that tear!
And whisper one sweet word that I may know
This is this world — sweet dewy blossom!" — *Woe!*   320
Woe! — Woe to that Endymion! Where is he? —
Even these words went echoing dismally
Through the wide forest — a most fearful tone,
Like one repenting in his latest moan;
And while it died away a shade pass'd by,
As of a thunder cloud. When arrows fly
Through the thick branches, poor ring-doves **sleek forth**
Their timid necks and tremble; so these both
Leant to each other trembling, and sat so
Waiting for some destruction — when lo,   330
Foot-feather'd Mercury appear'd sublime
Beyond the tall tree tops; and in less time
Than shoots the slanted hail-storm, down he dropt
Towards the ground; but rested not, nor stopt
One moment from his home: only the sward
He with his wand light touch'd, and heavenward
Swifter than sight was gone — even before
The teeming earth a sudden witness bore
Of his swift magic. Diving swans appear
Above the crystal circlings white and clear;   340
And catch the cheated eye in wide surprise,
How they can dive in sight and unseen rise —
So from the turf outsprang two steeds jet-black,
Each with large dark blue wings upon his back.
The youth of Caria plac'd the lovely dame
On one, and felt himself in spleen to tame
The other's fierceness. Through the air they flew,
High as the eagles. Like two drops of dew

Exhal'd to Phœbus' lips, away they are gone,
Far from the earth away — unseen, alone,   350
Among cool clouds and winds, but that the free,
The buoyant life of song can floating be
Above their heads, and follow them untir'd. —
Muse of my native land, am I inspir'd?
This is the giddy air, and I must spread
Wide pinions to keep here; nor do I dread
Or height, or depth, or width, or any chance
Precipitous: I have beneath my glance
Those towering horses and their mournful freight.
Could I thus sail, and see, and thus await   360
Fearless for power of thought, without thine aid? —
There is a sleepy dusk, an odorous shade
From some approaching wonder, and behold
Those winged steeds, with snorting nostrils bold
Snuff at its faint extreme, and seem to tire,
Dying to embers from their native fire!

    There curl'd a purple mist around them; soon,
It seem'd as when around the pale new moon
Sad Zephyr droops the clouds like weeping willow:
'Twas Sleep slow journeying with head on pillow.   370
For the first time, since he came nigh dead born
From the old womb of night, his cave forlorn
Had he left more forlorn; for the first time,
He felt aloof the day and morning's prime —
Because into his depth Cimmerian
There came a dream, shewing how a young man,
Ere a lean bat could plump its wintery skin,
Would at high Jove's empyreal footstool win
An immortality, and how espouse
Jove's daughter, and be reckon'd of his house.   380
Now was he slumbering towards heaven's gate,
That he might at the threshold one hour wait
To hear the marriage melodies, and then
Sink downward to his dusky cave again.
His litter of smooth semilucent mist,
Diversely ting'd with rose and amethyst,
Puzzled those eyes that for the centre sought;
And scarcely for one moment could be caught
His sluggish form reposing motionless.
Those two on winged steeds, with all the stress   390
Of vision search'd for him, as one would look
Athwart the sallows of a river nook
To catch a glance at silver-throated eels, —

Or from old Skiddaw's top, when fog conceals
His rugged forehead in a mantle pale,
With an eye-guess towards some pleasant vale
Descry a favourite hamlet faint and far.

These raven horses, though they foster'd are
Of earth's splenetic fire, dully drop
Their full-veined ears, nostrils blood wide, and stop;   400
Upon the spiritless mist have they outspread
Their ample feathers, are in slumber dead, —
And on those pinions, level in mid air,
Endymion sleepeth and the lady fair.
Slowly they sail, slowly as icy isle
Upon a calm sea drifting: and meanwhile
The mournful wanderer dreams. Behold! he walks
On heaven's pavement; brotherly he talks
To divine powers: from his hand full fain
Juno's proud birds are pecking pearly grain: 410
He tries the nerve of Phœbus' golden bow,
And asketh where the golden apples grow:
Upon his arm he braces Pallas' shield,
And strives in vain to unsettle and wield
A Jovian thunderbolt: arch Hebe brings
A full-brimm'd goblet, dances lightly, sings
And tantalizes long; at last he drinks,
And lost in pleasure at her feet he sinks,
Touching with dazzled lips her starlight hand.
He blows a bugle, — an ethereal band   420
Are visible above: the Seasons four, —
Green-kyrtled Spring, flush Summer, golden store
In Autumn's sickle, Winter frosty hoar,
Join dance with shadowy Hours; while still the blast
In swells unmitigated, still doth last
To sway their floating morris. "Whose is this?
Whose bugle?" he inquires; they smile — "O Dis!
Why is this mortal here? Dost thou not know
Its mistress' lips? Not thou? — 'Tis Dian's: lo!
She rises crescented!" He looks, 'tis she,   430
His very goddess: good-bye earth, and sea,
And air, and pains, and care, and suffering;
Good-bye to all but love! Then doth he spring
Towards her, and awakes — and, strange, o'erhead.
Of those same fragrant exhalations bred,
Beheld awake his very dream: the gods
Stood smiling; merry Hebe laughs and nods;
And Phœbe bends towards him crescented.

O state perplexing! On the pinion bed,
Too well awake, he feels the panting side   440
Of his delicious lady. He who died
For soaring too audacious in the sun,
When that same treacherous wax began to run,
Felt not more tongue-tied than Endymion.
His heart leapt up as to its rightful throne,
To that fair shadow'd passion puls'd its way —
Ah, what perplexity! Ah, well a day!
So fond, so beauteous was his bed-fellow,
He could not help but kiss her: then he grew
Awhile forgetful of all beauty save   450
Young Phœbe's, golden hair'd; and so 'gan crave
Forgiveness: yet he turn'd once more to look
At the sweet sleeper, — all his soul was shook, —
She press'd his hand in slumber; so once more
He could not help but kiss her and adore.
At this the shadow wept, melting away.
The Latmian started up: "Bright goddess, stay!
Search my most hidden breast! By truth's own tongue,
I have no dædale heart: why is it wrung
To desperation? Is there nought for me,   460
Upon the bourne of bliss, but misery?"

These words awoke the stranger of dark tresses:
Her dawning love-look rapt Endymion blesses
With 'haviour soft. Sleep yawned from underneath.
"Thou swan of Ganges, let us no more breathe
This murky phantasm! thou contented seem'st
Pillow'd in lovely idleness, nor dream'st
What horrors may discomfort thee and me.
Ah, shouldst thou die from my heart-treachery! —
Yet did she merely weep — her gentle soul   470
Hath no revenge in it: as it is whole
In tenderness, would I were whole in love!
Can I prize thee, fair maid, all price above,
Even when I feel as true as innocence?
I do, I do. — What is this soul then? Whence
Came it? It does not seem my own, and I
Have no self-passion or identity.
Some fearful end must be: where, where is it?
By Nemesis, I see my spirit flit
Alone about the dark — Forgive me, sweet: 480
Shall we away?" He rous'd the steeds: they beat
Their wings chivalrous into the clear air,
Leaving old Sleep within his vapoury lair.

The good-night blush of eve was waning slow,
And Vesper, risen star, began to throe
In the dusk heavens silverly, when they
Thus sprang direct towards the Galaxy.
Nor did speed hinder converse soft and strange —
Eternal oaths and vows they interchange,
In such wise, in such temper, so aloof   490
Up in the winds, beneath a starry roof,
So witless of their doom, that verily
'Tis well nigh past man's search their hearts to see;
Whether they wept, or laugh'd, or griev'd, or toy'd —
Most like with joy gone mad, with sorrow cloy'd.

Full facing their swift flight, from ebon streak,
The moon put forth a little diamond peak,
No bigger than an unobserved star,
Or tiny point of fairy scymetar;
Bright signal that she only stoop'd to tie   500
Her silver sandals, ere deliciously
She bow'd into the heavens her timid head.
Slowly she rose, as though she would have fled,
While to his lady meek the Carian turn'd,
To mark if her dark eyes had yet discern'd
This beauty in its birth — Despair! despair!
He saw her body fading gaunt and spare
In the cold moonshine. Straight he seiz'd her wrist;
It melted from his grasp: her hand he kiss'd,
And, horror! kiss'd his own — he was alone.   510
Her steed a little higher soar'd, and then
Dropt hawkwise to the earth.

                                    There lies a den,
Beyond the seeming confines of the space
Made for the soul to wander in and trace
Its own existence, of remotest glooms.
Dark regions are around it, where the tombs
Of buried griefs the spirit sees, but scarce
One hour doth linger weeping, for the pierce
Of new-born woe it feels more inly smart:
And in these regions many a venom'd dart   520
At random flies; they are the proper home
Of every ill: the man is yet to come
Who hath not journeyed in this native hell.
But few have ever felt how calm and well
Sleep may be had in that deep den of all.
There anguish does not sting; nor pleasure pall:

Woe-hurricanes beat ever at the gate,
Yet all is still within and desolate.
Beset with painful gusts, within ye hear
No sound so loud as when on curtain'd bier   530
The death-watch tick is stifled. Enter none
Who strive therefore: on the sudden it is won.
Just when the sufferer begins to burn,
Then it is free to him; and from an urn,
Still fed by melting ice, he takes a draught —
Young Semele such richness never quaft
In her maternal longing. Happy gloom!
Dark Paradise! where pale becomes the bloom
Of health by due; where silence dreariest
Is most articulate; where hopes infest;   540
Where those eyes are the brightest far that keep
Their lids shut longest in a dreamless sleep.
O happy spirit-home! O wondrous soul!
Pregnant with such a den to save the whole
In thine own depth. Hail, gentle Carian!
For, never since thy griefs and woes began,
Hast thou felt so content: a grievous feud
Hath led thee to this Cave of Quietude.
Aye, his lull'd soul was there, although upborne
With dangerous speed: and so he did not mourn   550
Because he knew not whither he was going.
So happy was he, not the aerial blowing
Of trumpets at clear parley from the east
Could rouse from that fine relish, that high feast.
They stung the feather'd horse: with fierce alarm
He flapp'd towards the sound. Alas, no charm
Could lift Endymion's head, or he had view'd
A skyey mask, a pinion'd multitude, —
And silvery was its passing: voices sweet
Warbling the while as if to lull and greet   560
The wanderer in his path. Thus warbled they,
While past the vision went in bright array.

"Who, who from Dian's feast would be away?
For all the golden bowers of the day
Are empty left? Who, who away would be
From Cynthia's wedding and festivity?
Not Hesperus: lo! upon his silver wings
He leans away for highest heaven and sings,
Snapping his lucid fingers merrily! —
Ah, Zephyrus! art here, and Flora too!   570
Ye tender bibbers of the rain and dew,
Young playmates of the rose and daffodil.

Be careful, ere ye enter in, to fill
      Your baskets high
With fennel green, and balm, and golden pines,
Savory, latter-mint, and columbines,
Cool parsley, basil sweet, and sunny thyme;
Yea, every flower and leaf of every clime,
All gather'd in the dewy morning: hie
      Away! fly, fly! —   580
Crystalline brother of the belt of heaven,
Aquarius! to whom king Jove has given
Two liquid pulse-streams 'stead of feather'd wings,
Two fan-like fountains, — thine illuminings
      For Dian play:
Dissolve the frozen purity of air;
Let thy white shoulders silvery and bare
Shew cold through watery pinions; make more bright
The Star-Queen's crescent on her marriage night:
      Haste, haste away! —   590
Castor has tamed the planet Lion, see!
And of the Bear has Pollux mastery:
A third is in the race! who is the third
Speeding away swift as the eagle bird?
      The ramping Centaur!
The Lion's mane's on end: the Bear how fierce!
The Centaur's arrow ready seems to pierce
Some enemy: far forth his bow is bent
Into the blue of heaven. He'll he shent,
      Pale unrelentor,   600
When he shall hear the wedding lutes a-playing. —
Andromeda! sweet woman! why delaying
So timidly among the stars: come hither!
Join this bright throng, and nimbly follow whither
      They all are going.
Danae's Son, before Jove newly bow'd,
Has wept for thee, calling to Jove aloud.
Thee, gentle lady, did he disenthral:
Ye shall for ever live and love, for all
      Thy tears are flowing. —   610
By Daphne's fright, behold Apollo! — "

                     More
Endymion heard not: down his steed him bore,
Prone to the green head of a misty hill.

   His first touch of the earth went nigh to kill.
"Alas!" said he, "were I but always borne
Through dangerous winds, had but my footsteps worn

A path in hell, for ever would I bless
Horrors which nourish an uneasiness
For my own sullen conquering: to him
Who lives beyond earth's boundary, grief is dim,   620
Sorrow is but a shadow: now I see
The grass; I feel the solid ground — Ah, me!
It is thy voice — divinest! Where? — who? who
Left thee so quiet on this bed of dew?
Behold upon this happy earth we are;
Let us ay love each other; let us fare
On forest-fruits, and never, never go
Among the abodes of mortals here below,
Or be by phantoms duped. O destiny!
Into a labyrinth now my soul would fly,   630
But with thy beauty will I deaden it.
Where didst thou melt to? By thee will I sit
For ever: let our fate stop here — a kid
I on this spot will offer: Pan will bid
Us live in peace, in love and peace among
His forest wildernesses. I have clung
To nothing, lov'd a nothing, nothing seen
Or felt but a great dream! O I have been
Presumptuous against love, against the sky,
Against all elements, against the tie   640
Of mortals each to each, against the blooms
Of flowers, rush of rivers, and the tombs
Of heroes gone! Against his proper glory
Has my own soul conspired: so my story
Will I to children utter, and repent.
There never liv'd a mortal man, who bent
His appetite beyond his natural sphere,
But starv'd and died. My sweetest Indian, here,
Here will I kneel, for thou redeemed hast
My life from too thin breathing: gone and past   650
Are cloudy phantasms. Caverns lone, farewell!
And air of visions, and the monstrous swell
Of visionary seas! No, never more
Shall airy voices cheat me to the shore
Of tangled wonder, breathless and aghast.
Adieu, my daintiest Dream! although so vast
My love is still for thee. The hour may come
When we shall meet in pure elysium.
On earth I may not love thee; and therefore
Doves will I offer up, and sweetest store   660
All through the teeming year: so thou wilt shine
On me, and on this damsel fair of mine,

And bless our simple lives. My Indian bliss!
My river-lily bud! one human kiss!
One sigh of real breath — one gentle squeeze,
Warm as a dove's nest among summer trees,
And warm with dew at ooze from living blood!
Whither didst melt? Ah, what of that! — all good
We'll talk about — no more of dreaming. — Now,
Where shall our dwelling be? Under the brow   670
Of some steep mossy hill, where ivy dun
Would hide us up, although spring leaves were none;
And where dark yew trees, as we rustle through,
Will drop their scarlet berry cups of dew?
O thou wouldst joy to live in such a place;
Dusk for our loves, yet light enough to grace
Those gentle limbs on mossy bed reclin'd:
For by one step the blue sky shouldst thou find,
And by another, in deep dell below,
See, through the trees, a little river go   680
All in its mid-day gold and glimmering.
Honey from out the gnarled hive I'll bring,
And apples, wan with sweetness, gather thee, —
Cresses that grow where no man may them see,
And sorrel untorn by the dew-claw'd stag:
Pipes will I fashion of the syrinx flag,
That thou mayst always know whither I roam,
When it shall please thee in our quiet home
To listen and think of love. Still let me speak;
Still let me dive into the joy I seek, —   690
For yet the past doth prison me. The rill,
Thou haply mayst delight in, will I fill
With fairy fishes from the mountain tarn,
And thou shalt feed them from the squirrel's barn.
Its bottom will I strew with amber shells,
And pebbles blue from deep enchanted wells.
Its sides I'll plant with dew-sweet eglantine,
And honeysuckles full of clear bee-wine.
I will entice this crystal rill to trace
Love's silver name upon the meadow's face.   700
I'll kneel to Vesta, for a flame of fire;
And to god Phœbus, for a golden lyre;
To Empress Dian, for a hunting spear;
To Vesper, for a taper silver-clear,
That I may see thy beauty through the night;
To Flora, and a nightingale shall light
Tame on thy finger; to the River-gods,
And they shall bring thee taper fishing-rods

Of gold, and lines of Naiads' long bright tress.
Heaven shield thee for thine utter loveliness!   710
Thy mossy footstool shall the altar be
'Fore which I'll bend, bending, dear love, to thee:
Those lips shall be my Delphos, and shall speak
Laws to my footsteps, colour to my cheek,
Trembling or stedfastness to this same voice,
And of three sweetest pleasurings the choice:
And that affectionate light, those diamond things,
Those eyes, those passions, those supreme pearl springs,
Shall be my grief, or twinkle me to pleasure.
Say, is not bliss within our perfect seisure?   720
O that I could not doubt!"

            The mountaineer
Thus strove by fancies vain and crude to clear
His briar'd path to some tranquillity.
It gave bright gladness to his lady's eye,
And yet the tears she wept were tears of sorrow;
Answering thus, just as the golden morrow
Beam'd upward from the vallies of the east:
"O that the flutter of this heart had ceas'd,
Or the sweet name of love had pass'd away.
Young feather'd tyrant! by a swift decay   730
Wilt thou devote this body to the earth:
And I do think that at my very birth
I lisp'd thy blooming titles inwardly;
For at the first, first dawn and thought of thee,
With uplift hands I blest the stars of heaven.
Art thou not cruel? Ever have I striven
To think thee kind, but ah, it will not do!
When yet a child, I heard that kisses drew
Favour from thee, and so I kisses gave
To the void air, bidding them find out love: 740
But when I came to feel how far above
All fancy, pride, and fickle maidenhood,
All earthly pleasure, all imagin'd good,
Was the warm tremble of a devout kiss, —
Even then, that moment, at the thought of this,
Fainting I fell into a bed of flowers,
And languish'd there three days. Ye milder powers,
Am I not cruelly wrong'd? Believe, believe
Me, dear Endymion, were I to weave
With my own fancies garlands of sweet life,   750
Thou shouldst be one of all. Ah, bitter strife!
I may not be thy love: I am forbidden —

Indeed I am — thwarted, affrighted, chidden,
By things I trembled at, and gorgon wrath.
Twice hast thou ask'd whither I went: henceforth
Ask me no more! I may not utter it,
Nor may I be thy love. We might commit
Ourselves at once to vengeance; we might die;
We might embrace and die; voluptuous thought!
Enlarge not to my hunger, or I'm caught   760
In trammels of perverse deliciousness.
No, no, that shall not be: thee will I bless,
And bid a long adieu."

             The Carian
No word return'd: both lovelorn, silent, wan,
Into the vallies green together went.
Far wandering, they were perforce content
To sit beneath a fair lone beechen tree;
Nor at each other gaz'd, but heavily
Por'd on its hazle cirque of shedded leaves.

     Endymion! unhappy! it nigh grieves   770
Me to behold thee thus in last extreme:
Ensky'd ere this, but truly that I deem
Truth the best music in a first-born song.
Thy lute-voic'd brother will I sing ere long,
And thou shalt aid — hast thou not aided me?
Yes, moonlight Emperor! felicity
Has been thy meed for many thousand years;
Yet often have I, on the brink of tears,
Mourn'd as if yet thou wert a forester; —
Forgetting the old tale.

            He did not stir   780
His eyes from the dead leaves, or one small pulse
Of joy he might have felt. The spirit culls
Unfaded amaranth, when wild it strays
Through the old garden-ground of boyish days.
A little onward ran the very stream
By which he took his first soft poppy dream;
And on the very bark 'gainst which he leant
A crescent he had carv'd, and round it spent
His skill in little stars. The teeming tree
Had swollen and green'd the pious charactery,   790
But not ta'en out. Why, there was not a slope
Up which he had not fear'd the antelope;

And not a tree, beneath whose rooty shade
He had not with his tamed leopards play'd:
Nor could an arrow light, or javelin,
Fly in the air where his had never been —
And yet he knew it not.

O treachery!
Why does his lady smile, pleasing her eye
With all his sorrowing? He sees her not.
But who so stares on him? His sister sure!   800
Peona of the woods! — Can she endure —
Impossible — how dearly they embrace!
His lady smiles; delight is in her face;
It is no treachery.

"Dear brother mine!
Endymion, weep not so! Why shouldst thou pine
When all great Latmos so exalt will be?
Thank the great gods, and look not bitterly;
And speak not one pale word, and sigh no more.
Sure I will not believe thou hast such store
Of grief, to last thee to my kiss again.   810
Thou surely canst not bear a mind in pain,
Come hand in hand with one so beautiful.
Be happy both of you! for I will pull
The flowers of autumn for your coronals.
Pan's holy priest for young Endymion calls;
And when he is restor'd, thou, fairest dame,
Shalt be our queen. Now, is it not a shame
To see ye thus, — not very, very sad?
Perhaps ye are too happy to be glad:
O feel as if it were a common day;   820
Free-voic'd as one who never was away.
No tongue shall ask, whence come ye? but ye shall
Be gods of your own rest imperial.
Not even I, for one whole month, will pry
Into the hours that have pass'd us by,
Since in my arbour I did sing to thee.
O Hermes! on this very night will be
A hymning up to Cynthia, queen of light;
For the soothsayers old saw yesternight
Good visions in the air, — whence will befal,   830
As say these sages, health perpetual
To shepherds and their flocks; and furthermore,
In Dian's face they read the gentle lore:

Therefore for her these vesper-carols are.
Our friends will all be there from nigh and far.
Many upon thy death have ditties made;
And many, even now, their foreheads shade
With cypress, on a day of sacrifice.
New singing for our maids shalt thou devise,
And pluck the sorrow from our huntsmen's brows.   840
Tell me, my lady-queen, how to espouse
This wayward brother to his rightful joys!
His eyes are on thee bent, as thou didst poise
His fate most goddess-like. Help me, I pray,
To lure — Endymion, dear brother, say
What ails thee?" He could bear no more, and so
Bent his soul fiercely like a spiritual bow,
And twang'd it inwardly, and calmly said:
"I would have thee my only friend, sweet maid!
My only visitor! not ignorant though,   850
That those deceptions which for pleasure go
'Mong men, are pleasures real as real may be:
But there are higher ones I may not see,
If impiously an earthly realm I take.
Since I saw thee, I have been wide awake
Night after night, and day by day, until
Of the empyrean I have drunk my fill.
Let it content thee, Sister, seeing me
More happy than betides mortality.
A hermit young, I'll live in mossy cave,   860
Where thou alone shalt come to me, and lave
Thy spirit in the wonders I shall tell.
Through me the shepherd realm shall prosper well;
For to thy tongue will I all health confide.
And, for my sake, let this young maid abide
With thee as a dear sister. Thou alone,
Peona, mayst return to me. I own
This may sound strangely: but when, dearest girl,
Thou seest it for my happiness, no pearl
Will trespass down those cheeks. Companion fair!   870
Wilt be content to dwell with her, to share
This sister's love with me?" Like one resign'd
And bent by circumstance, and thereby blind
In self-commitment, thus that meek unknown:
"Aye, but a buzzing by my ears has flown,
Of jubilee to Dian: — truth I heard!
Well then, I see there is no little bird,
Tender soever, but is Jove's own care.
Long have I sought for rest, and, unaware,

Behold I find it! so exalted too! 880
So after my own heart! I knew, I knew
There was a place untenanted in it:
In that same void white Chastity shall sit,
And monitor me nightly to lone slumber.
With sanest lips I vow me to the number
Of Dian's sisterhood; and, kind lady,
With thy good help, this very night shall see
My future days to her fane consecrate."

    As feels a dreamer what doth most create
His own particular fright, so these three felt: 890
Or like one who, in after ages, knelt
To Lucifer or Baal, when he'd pine
After a little sleep: or when in mine
Far under-ground, a sleeper meets his friends
Who know him not. Each diligently bends
Towards common thoughts and things for very fear;
Striving their ghastly malady to cheer,
By thinking it a thing of yes and no,
That housewives talk of. But the spirit-blow
Was struck, and all were dreamers. At the last 900
Endymion said: "Are not our fates all cast?
Why stand we here? Adieu, ye tender pair!
Adieu!" Whereat those maidens, with wild stare,
Walk'd dizzily away. Pained and hot
His eyes went after them, until they got
Near to a cypress grove, whose deadly maw,
In one swift moment, would what then he saw
Engulph for ever. "Stay!" he cried, "ah, stay!
Turn, damsels! hist! one word I have to say:
Sweet Indian, I would see thee once again. 910
It is a thing I dote on: so I'd fain,
Peona, ye should hand in hand repair
Into those holy groves, that silent are
Behind great Dian's temple. I'll be yon,
At vesper's earliest twinkle — they are gone —
But once, once, once again — " At this he press'd
His hands against his face, and then did rest
His head upon a mossy hillock green,
And so remain'd as he a corpse had been
All the long day; save when he scantly lifted 920
His eyes abroad, to see how shadows shifted
With the slow move of time, — sluggish and weary
Until the poplar tops, in journey dreary,
Had reach'd the river's brim. Then up he rose,

And, slowly as that very river flows,
Walk'd towards the temple grove with this lament:
"Why such a golden eve? The breeze is sent
Careful and soft, that not a leaf may fall
Before the serene father of them all
Bows down his summer head below the west.   930
Now am I of breath, speech, and speed possest,
But at the setting I must bid adieu
To her for the last time. Night will strew
On the damp grass myriads of lingering leaves,
And with them shall I die; nor much it grieves
To die, when summer dies on the cold sward.
Why, I have been a butterfly, a lord
Of flowers, garlands, love-knots, silly posies,
Groves, meadows, melodies, and arbour roses;
My kingdom's at its death, and just it is   940
That I should die with it: so in all this
We miscall grief, bale, sorrow, heartbreak, woe,
What is there to plain of? By Titan's foe
I am but rightly serv'd." So saying, he
Tripp'd lightly on, in sort of deathful glee
Laughing at the clear stream and setting sun,
As though they jests had been: nor had he done
His laugh at nature's holy countenance,
Until that grove appear'd, as if perchance,
And then his tongue with sober seemlihed   950
Gave utterance as he entered: "Ha! I said,
King of the butterflies; but by this gloom,
And by old Rhadamanthus' tongue of doom,
This dusk religion, pomp of solitude,
And the Promethean clay by thief endued,
By old Saturnus' forelock, by his head
Shook with eternal palsy, I did wed
Myself to things of light from infancy;
And thus to be cast out, thus lorn to die,
Is sure enough to make a mortal man   960
Grow impious." So he inwardly began
On things for which no wording can be found;
Deeper and deeper sinking, until drown'd
Beyond the reach of music: for the choir
Of Cynthia he heard not, though rough briar
Nor muffling thicket interpos'd to dull
The vesper hymn, far swollen, soft and full,
Through the dark pillars of those sylvan aisles.
He saw not the two maidens, nor their smiles,
Wan as primroses gather'd at midnight   970

By chilly finger'd spring. "Unhappy wight!
Endymion!" said Peona, "we are here!
What wouldst thou ere we all are laid on bier?"
Then he embrac'd her, and his lady's hand
Press'd, saying: "Sister, I would have command,
If it were heaven's will, on our sad fate."
At which that dark-eyed stranger stood elate
And said, in a new voice, but sweet as love,
To Endymion's amaze: "By Cupid's dove,
And so thou shalt! and by the lily truth   980
Of my own breast thou shalt, beloved youth!"
And as she spake, into her face there came
Light, as reflected from a silver flame:
Her long black hair swell'd ampler, in display
Full golden; in her eyes a brighter day
Dawn'd blue and full of love. Aye, he beheld
Phœbe, his passion! joyous she upheld
Her lucid bow, continuing thus: "Drear, drear
Has our delaying been; but foolish fear
Withheld me first; and then decrees of fate;   990
And then 'twas fit that from this mortal state
Thou shouldst, my love, by some unlook'd for change
Be spiritualiz'd. Peona, we shall range
These forests, and to thee they safe shall be
As was thy cradle; hither shalt thou flee
To meet us many a time." Next Cynthia bright
Peona kiss'd, and bless'd with fair good night:
Her brother kiss'd her too, and knelt adown
Before his goddess, in a blissful swoon.
She gave her fair hands to him, and behold,   1000
Before three swiftest kisses he had told,
They vanish'd far away! — Peona went
Home through the gloomy wood in wonderment.

THE END

IN DREAR-NIGHTED DECEMBER

I.

In drear-nighted December,
 Too happy, happy tree,
Thy branches ne'er remember
 Their green felicity:
The north cannot undo them
With a sleety whistle through them;
Nor frozen thawings glue them
 From budding at the prime.

II.

In drear-nighted December,
 Too happy, happy brook,   10
Thy bubblings ne'er remember
 Apollo's summer look;
But with a sweet forgetting,
They stay their crystal fretting,
Never, never petting
 About the frozen time.

III.

Ah! would 'twere so with many
 A gentle girl and boy!
But were there ever any
 Writh'd not of passed joy?   20
The feel of not to feel it,
When there is none to heal it,
Nor numbed sense to steel it,
 Was never said in rhyme.

ON SEEING A LOCK OF MILTON'S HAIR

Chief of organic numbers!
 Old Scholar of the Spheres!
Thy spirit never slumbers,
 But rolls about our ears
For ever and for ever!
O what a mad endeavour

Worketh he,
Who to thy sacred and ennobled hearse
Would offer a burnt sacrifice of verse
And melody.   10

How heavenward thou soundest!
Live Temple of sweet noise,
And Discord unconfoundest,
Giving Delight new joys,
And Pleasure nobler pinions:
O where are thy dominions?
Lend thine ear
To a young Delian oath, — aye, by thy soul,
By all that from thy mortal lips did roll,
And by the kernel of thine earthly love,   20
Beauty in things on earth and things above,
I swear!

When every childish fashion
Has vanished from my rhyme,
Will I, grey-gone in passion,
Leave to an after-time,
Hymning and harmony
Of thee and of thy works, and of thy life;
But vain is now the burning and the strife;
Pangs are in vain, until I grow high-rife
With old Philosophy,
And mad with glimpses of futurity.

For many years my offerings must be hushed;
When I do speak, I'll think upon this hour,
Because I feel my forehead hot and flushed,
Even at the simplest vassal of thy power,
A lock of thy bright hair, —
Sudden it came,
And I was startled, when I caught thy name
Coupled so unaware;   40
Yet at the moment temperate was my blood —
I thought I had beheld it from the flood!

ON SITTING DOWN TO READ *KING LEAR* ONCE AGAIN

O GOLDEN-TONGUED Romance with serene lute!
Fair plumed Syren! Queen of far away!

Leave melodizing on this wintry day,
Shut up thine olden pages, and be mute:
Adieu! for once again the fierce dispute
  Betwixt damnation and impassion'd clay
  Must I burn through; once more humbly **assay**
The bitter-sweet of this Shakespearian fruit.
Chief Poet! and ye clouds of Albion,
  Begetters of our deep eternal theme,
When through the old oak forest I am gone,
  Let me not wander in a barren dream,
But when I am consumed in the fire,
Give me new Phœnix wings to fly at my desire.

WHEN I HAVE FEARS

WHEN I have fears that I may cease to be
  Before my pen has glean'd my teeming brain,
Before high-piled books, in charact'ry,
  Hold like rich garners the full-ripen'd grain;
When I behold, upon the night's starr'd face,
  Huge cloudy symbols of a high romance,
And think that I may never live to trace
  Their shadows, with the magic hand of chance;
And when I feel, fair creature of an hour!
  That I shall never look upon thee more,   10
Never have relish in the faery power
  Of unreflecting love! — then on the shore
Of the wide world I stand alone, and think
Till Love and Fame to nothingness do sink.

GOD OF THE MERIDIAN

God of the Meridian,
    And of the East and West,
To thee my soul is flown,
    And my body is earthward press'd. —
It is an awful mission,
A terrible division;
And leaves a gulph austere
To be fill'd with worldly fear.
Aye, when the soul is fled
To high above our head,   10
Affrighted do we gaze
After its airy maze,

As doth a mother wild,
When her young infant child
Is in an eagle's claws —
And is not this the cause
Of madness? — God of Song,
Thou bearest me along
Through sights I scarce can bear:
O let me, let me share,   20
With the hot lyre and thee,
The staid Philosophy.
Temper my lonely hours,
And let me see thy bowers
More unalarm'd!

LINES ON THE MERMAID TAVERN

SOULS of Poets dead and gone,
What Elysium have ye known,
Happy field or mossy cavern,
Choicer than the Mermaid Tavern?
Have ye tippled drink more fine
Than mine host's Canary wine?
Or are fruits of Paradise
Sweeter than those dainty pies
Of venison? O generous food!
Drest as though bold Robin Hood   10
Would, with his maid Marian,
Sup and bowse from horn and can.

I have heard that on a day
Mine host's sign-board flew away,
Nobody knew whither, till
An astrologer's old quill
To a sheepskin gave the story,
Said he saw you in your glory,
Underneath a new old sign
Sipping beverage divine,   20
And pledging with contented smack
The Mermaid in the Zodiac.

Souls of Poets dead and gone,
What Elysium have ye known,
Happy field or mossy cavern,
Choicer than the Mermaid Tavern?

ROBIN HOOD

TO A FRIEND

No! THOSE days are gone away,
And their hours are old and gray,
And their minutes buried all
Under the down-trodden pall
Of the leaves of many years:
Many times have winter's shears,
Frozen North, and chilling East,
Sounded tempests to the feast
Of the forest's whispering fleeces,
Since men knew nor rent nor leases.   10

No, the bugle sounds no more,
And the twanging bow no more;
Silent is the ivory shrill
Past the heath and up the hill;
There is no mid-forest laugh,
Where lone Echo gives the half
To some wight, amaz'd to hear
Jesting, deep in forest drear.

On the fairest time of June
You may go, with sun or moon,   20
Or the seven stars to light you,
Or the polar ray to right you;
But you never may behold
Little John, or Robin bold;
Never one, of all the clan,
Thrumming on an empty can
Some old hunting ditty, while
He doth his green way beguile
To fair hostess Merriment,
Down beside the pasture Trent;   30
For he left the merry tale
Messenger for spicy ale.

Gone, the merry morris din;
Gone, the song of Gamelyn;
Gone, the tough-belted outlaw
Idling in the "grenè shawe";
All are gone away and past!

And if Robin should be cast
Sudden from his turfed grave,
And if Marian should have   **40**
Once again her forest days,
She would weep, and he would craze:
He would swear, for all his oaks,
Fall'n beneath the dockyard strokes,
Have rotted on the briny seas;
She would weep that her wild bees
Sang not to her — strange! that honey
Can't be got without hard money!

So it is: yet let us sing,
Honour to the old bow-string!   **50**
Honour to the bugle-horn!
Honour to the woods unshorn!
Honour to the Lincoln green!
Honour to the archer keen!
Honour to tight little John,
And the horse he rode upon!
Honour to bold Robin Hood,
Sleeping in the underwood!
Honour to maid Marian,
And to all the Sherwood-clan!   **60**
Though their days have hurried by
Let us two a burden try.

TO A LADY SEEN FOR A FEW MOMENTS
AT VAUXHALL

Time's sea hath been five years at its slow ebb;
   Long hours have to and fro let creep the sand;
Since I was tangled in thy beauty's web,
   And snared by the ungloving of thine hand.
And yet I never look on midnight sky,
   But I behold thine eyes' well memoried light;
I cannot look upon the rose's dye,
   But to thy cheek my soul doth take its flight;
I cannot look on any budding flower,
   But my fond ear, in fancy at thy lips   **10**
And hearkening for a love-sound, doth devour
   Its sweets in the wrong sense: — Thou dost eclipse
Every delight with sweet remembering,
And grief unto my darling joys dost bring.

WHAT THE THRUSH SAID

LINES FROM A LETTER TO JOHN HAMILTON REYNOLDS

O THOU whose face hath felt the Winter's wind,
    Whose eye has seen the snow-clouds hung in mist,
    And the black elm-tops 'mong the freezing stars,
    To thee the Spring will be a harvest-time.
O thou, whose only book has been the light
    Of supreme darkness, which thou feddest on
    Night after night, when Phœbus was away,
    To thee the Spring shall be a triple morn.
O fret not after knowledge — I have none,
    And yet my song comes native with the warmth.   **10**
O fret not after knowledge — I have none,
    And yet the evening listens. He who saddens
At thought of idleness cannot be idle,
And he's awake who thinks himself asleep.

THE HUMAN SEASONS

FOUR seasons fill the measure of the year;
    There are four seasons in the mind of man:
He has his lusty Spring, when fancy clear
    Takes in all beauty with an easy span:
He has his Summer, when luxuriously
    Spring's honied cud of youthful thought he loves
To ruminate, and by such dreaming nigh
    His nearest unto heaven: quiet coves
His soul has in its Autumn, when his wings
    He furleth close; contented so to look   **10**
On mists in idleness — to let fair things
    Pass by unheeded as a threshold brook.
He has his Winter too of pale misfeature,
Or else he would forgo his mortal nature.

EPISTLE TO JOHN HAMILTON REYNOLDS

DEAR Reynolds! as last night I lay in bed,
There came before my eyes that wonted thread
Of shapes, and shadows, and remembrances,
That every other minute vex and please:
Things all disjointed come from north and south, —
Two witch's eyes above a cherub's mouth,
Voltaire with casque and shield and habergeon,
And Alexander with his nightcap on;
Old Socrates a-tying his cravat,
And Hazlitt playing with Miss Edgeworth's cat;   10
And Junius Brutus, pretty well so so,
Making the best of's way towards Soho.

Few are there who escape these visitings, —
Perhaps one or two whose lives have patent wings,
And thro' whose curtains peeps no hellish nose,
No wild-boar tushes, and no mermaid's toes;
But flowers bursting out with lusty pride,
And young Æolian harps personified;
Some, Titian colours touch'd into real life, —
The sacrifice goes on; the pontiff knife   20
Gleams in the sun, the milk-white heifer lows,
The pipes go shrilly, the libation flows:
A white sail shows above the green-head cliff,
Moves round the point, and throws her anchor stiff;
The mariners join hymn with those on land.

You know the Enchanted Castle, — it doth **stand**
Upon a rock, on the border of a lake,
Nested in trees, which all do seem to shake
From some old magic like Urganda's sword.
O Phœbus! that I had thy sacred word   30
To show this Castle, in fair dreaming wise,
Unto my friend, while sick and ill he lies!

You know it well enough, where it doth seem
A mossy place, a Merlin's Hall, a dream;
You know the clear lake, and the little isles,
The mountains blue, and cold near neighbour rills,
All which elsewhere are but half animate;
There do they look alive to love and hate,

To smiles and frowns; they seem a lifted mound
Above some giant, pulsing underground.   40

    Part of the building was a chosen See,
Built by a banish'd Santon of Chaldee;
The other part, two thousand years from him,
Was built by Cuthbert de Saint Aldebrim;
Then there's a little wing, far from the sun,
Built by a Lapland witch turn'd maudlin nun;
And many other juts of aged stone
Founded with many a mason-devil's groan.

    The doors all look as if they oped themselves,
The windows as if latched by fays and elves,   50
And from them comes a silver flash of light,
As from the westward of a summer's night;
Or like a beauteous woman's large blue eyes
Gone mad thro' olden songs and poesies.

    See! what is coming from the distance dim!
A golden galley all in silken trim!
Three rows of oars are lightening, moment whiles,
Into the verd'rous bosoms of those isles;
Towards the shade, under the Castle wall,
It comes in silence, — now 'tis hidden all.   60
The clarion sounds, and from a postern-gate
An echo of sweet music doth create
A fear in the poor herdsman, who doth bring
His beasts to trouble the enchanted spring, —
He tells of the sweet music, and the spot,
To all his friends, and they believe him not.

    O that our dreamings all, of sleep or wake,
Would all their colours from the sunset take:
From something of material sublime,
Rather than shadow our own soul's day-time   70
In the dark void of night. For in the world
We jostle, — but my flag is not unfurl'd
On the admiral-staff, — and to philosophise
I dare not yet! Oh, never will the prize,
High reason, and the lore of good and ill,
Be my award! Things cannot to the will
Be settled, but they tease us out of thought;
Or is it that imagination brought
Beyond its proper bound, yet still confin'd,
Lost in a sort of Purgatory blind,   80

Cannot refer to any standard law
Of either earth or heaven? It is a flaw
In happiness, to see beyond our bourn, —
It forces us in summer skies to mourn,
It spoils the singing of the nightingale.

   Dear Reynolds! I have a mysterious tale,
And cannot speak it: the first page I read
Upon a lampit rock of green sea-weed
Among the breakers; 'twas a quiet eve,
The rocks were silent, the wide sea did weave
An untumultuous fringe of silver foam
Along the flat brown sand; I was at home
And should have been most happy, — but I saw
Too far into the sea, where every maw
The greater on the less feeds evermore. —
But I saw too distinct into the core
Of an eternal fierce destruction,
And so from happiness I far was gone.
Still am I sick of it, and tho', to-day,
I've gather'd young spring-leaves, and flowers gay   100
Of periwinkle and wild strawberry,
Still do I that most fierce destruction see, —
The shark at savage prey, — the hawk at pounce, —
The gentle robin, like a pard or ounce,
Ravening a worm, — Away, ye horrid moods!
Moods of one's mind! You know I hate them well.
You know I'd sooner be a clapping bell
To some Kamschatkan missionary church,
Than with these horrid moods be left i' the lurch. —
Do you get health — and Tom the same — I'll **dance,**   110
And from detested moods in new romance
Take refuge — Of bad lines a centaine dose
Is sure enough — and so "here follows prose". —

ISABELLA;

OR, THE POT OF BASIL

A Story from Boccaccio.

I.

FAIR Isabel, poor simple Isabel!
  Lorenzo, a young palmer in Love's eye!
They could not in the self-same mansion dwell
  Without some stir of heart, some malady;
They could not sit at meals but feel how well
  It soothed each to be the other by;
They could not, sure, beneath the same roof sleep
But to each other dream, and nightly weep.

II.

With every morn their love grew tenderer,
  With every eve deeper and tenderer still;   10
He might not in house, field, or garden stir,
  But her full shape would all his seeing fill;
And his continual voice was pleasanter
  To her, than noise of trees or hidden rill;
Her lute-string gave an echo of his name,
She spoilt her half-done broidery with the same.

III.

He knew whose gentle hand was at the latch,
  Before the door had given her to his eyes;
And from her chamber-window he would catch
  Her beauty farther than the falcon spies;   20
And constant as her vespers would he watch,
  Because her face was turn'd to the same skies;
And with sick longing all the night outwear,
To hear her morning-step upon the stair.

IV

A whole long month of May in this sad plight
  Made their cheeks paler by the break of June:
"To-morrow will I bow to my delight,
  To-morrow will I ask my lady's boon." —

"O may I never see another night,
    Lorenzo, if thy lips breathe not love's tune." —   30
So spake they to their pillows; but, alas,
Honeyless days and days did he let pass;

v.

Until sweet Isabella's untouch'd cheek
    Fell sick within the rose's just domain,
Fell thin as a young mother's, who doth seek
    By every lull to cool her infant's pain:
"How ill she is," said he, "I may not speak,
    And yet I will, and tell my love all plain:
If looks speak love-laws, I will drink her tears,
And at the least 'twill startle off her cares."   40

vi.

So said he one fair morning, and all day
    His heart beat awfully against his side;
And to his heart he inwardly did pray
    For power to speak; but still the ruddy tide
Stifled his voice, and puls'd resolve away —
    Fever'd his high conceit of such a bride,
Yet brought him to the meekness of a child:
Alas! when passion is both meek and wild!

vii.

So once more he had wak'd and anguished
    A dreary night of love and misery,   50
If Isabel's quick eye had not been wed
    To every symbol on his forehead high;
She saw it waxing very pale and dead,
    And straight all flush'd; so, lisped tenderly,
"Lorenzo!" — here she ceas'd her timid quest,
But in her tone and look he read the rest.

viii.

"O Isabella, I can half perceive
    That I may speak my grief into thine ear;
If thou didst ever any thing believe,
    Believe how I love thee, believe how near   60
My soul is to its doom: I would not grieve
    Thy hand by unwelcome pressing, would not fear

Thine eyes by gazing; but I cannot live
Another night, and not my passion shrive.

IX.

"Love! thou art leading me from wintry cold,
   Lady! thou leadest me to summer clime,
And I must taste the blossoms that unfold
   In its ripe warmth this gracious morning time."
So said, his erewhile timid lips grew bold,
   And poesied with hers in dewy rhyme: 70
Great bliss was with them, and great happiness
Grew, like a lusty flower in June's caress.

X.

Parting they seem'd to tread upon the air,
   Twin roses by the zephyr blown apart
Only to meet again more close, and share
   The inward fragrance of each other's heart.
She, to her chamber gone, a ditty fair
   Sang, of delicious love and honey'd dart;
He with light steps went up a western hill,
And bade the sun farewell, and joy'd his fill.   80

XI.

All close they met again, before the dusk
   Had taken from the stars its pleasant veil,
All close they met, all eves, before the dusk
   Had taken from the stars its pleasant veil,
Close in a bower of hyacinth and musk,
   Unknown of any, free from whispering tale.
Ah! better had it been for ever so,
Than idle ears should pleasure in their woe.

XII.

Were they unhappy then? — It cannot be —
   Too many tears for lovers have been shed,   90
Too many sighs give we to them in fee,
   Too much of pity after they are dead,
Too many doleful stories do we see,
   Whose matter in bright gold were best be read;
Except in such a page where Theseus' spouse
Over the pathless waves towards him bows.

XIII.

But, for the general award of love,
 The little sweet doth kill much bitterness;
Though Dido silent is in under-grove,
 And Isabella's was a great distress,   100
Though young Lorenzo in warm Indian clove
 Was not embalm'd, this truth is not the less —
Even bees, the little almsmen of spring-bowers,
Know there is richest juice in poison-flowers.

XIV.

With her two brothers this fair lady dwelt,
 Enriched from ancestral merchandize,
And for them many a weary hand did swelt
 In torched mines and noisy factories,
And many once proud-quiver'd loins did melt
 In blood from stinging whip; — with hollow eyes   110
Many all day in dazzling river stood,
To take the rich-ored driftings of the flood.

XV.

For them the Ceylon diver held his breath,
 And went all naked to the hungry shark;
For them his ears gush'd blood; for them in death
 The seal on the cold ice with piteous bark
Lay full of darts; for them alone did seethe
 A thousand men in troubles wide and dark:
Half-ignorant, they turn'd an easy wheel,
That set sharp racks at work, to pinch and peel.   120

XVI.

Why were they proud? Because their marble founts
 Gush'd with more pride than do a wretch's tears? —
Why were they proud? Because fair orange-mounts
 Were of more soft ascent than lazar stairs? —
Why were they proud? Because red-lin'd accounts
 Were richer than the songs of Grecian years? —
Why were they proud? again we ask aloud,
Why in the name of Glory were they proud?

XVII.

Yet were these Florentines as self-retired
 In hungry pride and gainful cowardice,   130

As two close Hebrews in that land inspired,
    Paled in and vineyarded from beggar-spies;
The hawks of ship-mast forests — the untired
    And pannier'd mules for ducats and old lies —
Quick cat's-paws on the generous stray-away, —
Great wits in Spanish, Tuscan, and Malay.

XVIII.

How was it these same ledger-men could spy
    Fair Isabella in her downy nest?
How could they find out in Lorenzo's eye
    A straying from his toil? Hot Egypt's pest   140
Into their vision covetous and sly!
    How could these money-bags see east and west? —
Yet so they did — and every dealer fair
Must see behind, as doth the hunted hare.

XIX.

O eloquent and famed Boccaccio!
    Of thee we now should ask forgiving boon,
And of thy spicy myrtles as they blow,
    And of thy roses amorous of the moon,
And of thy lilies, that do paler grow
    Now they can no more hear thy ghittern's tune,   150
For venturing syllables that ill beseem
The quiet glooms of such a piteous theme.

XX.

Grant thou a pardon here, and then the tale
    Shall move on soberly, as it is meet;
There is no other crime, no mad assail
    To make old prose in modern rhyme more sweet:
But it is done — succeed the verse or fail —
    To honour thee, and thy gone spirit greet;
To stead thee as a verse in English tongue,
An echo of thee in the north-wind sung.   160

XXI.

These brethren having found by many signs
    What love Lorenzo for their sister had,
And how she lov'd him too, each unconfines
    His bitter thoughts to other, well nigh mad

That he, the servant of their trade designs,
   Should in their sister's love be blithe and glad,
When 'twas their plan to coax her by degrees
To some high noble and his olive-trees.

XXII.

And many a jealous conference had they,
   And many times they bit their lips alone,   170
Before they fix'd upon a surest way
   To make the youngster for his crime atone;
And at the last, these men of cruel clay
   Cut Mercy with a sharp knife to the bone;
For they resolved in some forest dim
To kill Lorenzo, and there bury him.

XXIII.

So on a pleasant morning, as he leant
   Into the sun-rise, o'er the balustrade
Of the garden-terrace, towards him they bent
   Their footing through the dews; and to him said,   180
"You seem there in the quiet of content,
   Lorenzo, and we are most loth to invade
Calm speculation; but if you are wise,
Bestride your steed while cold is in the skies.

XXIV.

"To-day we purpose, ay, this hour we mount
   To spur three leagues towards the Apennine;
Come down, we pray thee, ere the hot sun count
   His dewy rosary on the eglantine."
Lorenzo, courteously as he was wont,
   Bow'd a fair greeting to these serpents' whine;   190
And went in haste, to get in readiness,
With belt, and spur, and bracing huntsman's dress.

XXV.

And as he to the court-yard pass'd along,
   Each third step did he pause, and listen'd oft
If he could hear his lady's matin-song,
   Or the light whisper of her footstep soft;
And as he thus over his passion hung,
   He heard a laugh full musical aloft;

When, looking up, he saw her features bright
Smile through an in-door lattice, all delight.   200

XXVI.

"Love, Isabel!" said he, "I was in pain
    Lest I should miss to bid thee a good morrow:
Ah! what if I should lose thee, when so fain
    I am to stifle all the heavy sorrow
Of a poor three hours' absence? but we'll gain
    Out of the amorous dark what day doth borrow.
Good bye! I'll soon be back." — "Good bye!" said she: —
And as he went she chanted merrily.

XXVII.

So the two brothers and their murder'd man
    Rode past fair Florence, to where Arno's stream   210
Gurgles through straiten'd banks, and still doth fan
    Itself with dancing bulrush, and the bream
Keeps head against the freshets. Sick and wan
    The brothers' faces in the ford did seem,
Lorenzo's flush with love. — They pass'd the water
Into a forest quiet for the slaughter.

XXVIII.

There was Lorenzo slain and buried in,
    There in that forest did his great love cease;
Ah! when a soul doth thus its freedom win,
    It aches in loneliness — is ill at peace   220
As the break-covert blood-hounds of such sin:
    They dipp'd their swords in the water, and did tease
Their horses homeward, with convulsed spur,
Each richer by his being a murderer.

XXIX.

They told their sister how, with sudden speed,
    Lorenzo had ta'en ship for foreign lands,
Because of some great urgency and need
    In their affairs, requiring trusty hands.
Poor Girl! put on thy stifling widow's weed,
    And 'scape at once from Hope's accursed bands;   230
To-day thou wilt not see him, nor to-morrow,
And the next day will be a day of sorrow.

XXX.

She weeps alone for pleasures not to be;
  Sorely she wept until the night came on,
And then, instead of love, O misery!
  She brooded o'er the luxury alone:
His image in the dusk she seem'd to see,
  And to the silence made a gentle moan,
Spreading her perfect arms upon the air,
And on her couch low murmuring, "Where? O where?"   240

XXXI.

But Selfishness, Love's cousin, held not long
  Its fiery vigil in her single breast;
She fretted for the golden hour, and hung
  Upon the time with feverish unrest —
Not long — for soon into her heart a throng
  Of higher occupants, a richer zest,
Came tragic; passion not to be subdued,
And sorrow for her love in travels rude.

XXXII.

In the mid days of autumn, on their eves
  The breath of Winter comes from far away,   250
And the sick west continually bereaves
  Of some gold tinge, and plays a roundelay
Of death among the bushes and the leaves,
  To make all bare before he dares to stray
From his north cavern. So sweet Isabel
By gradual decay from beauty fell,

XXXIII.

Because Lorenzo came not. Oftentimes
  She ask'd her brothers, with an eye all pale,
Striving to be itself, what dungeon climes
  Could keep him off so long? They spake a tale   260
Time after time, to quiet her. Their crimes
  Came on them, like a smoke from Hinnom's vale;
And every night in dreams they groan'd aloud,
To see their sister in her snowy shroud.

XXXIV.

And she had died in drowsy ignorance,
  But for a thing more deadly dark than all;
It came like a fierce potion, drunk by chance,
  Which saves a sick man from the feather'd pall
For some few gasping moments; like a lance,
  Waking an Indian from his cloudy hall   270
With cruel pierce, and bringing him again
Sense of the gnawing fire at heart and brain.

XXXV.

It was a vision. — In the drowsy gloom,
  The dull of midnight, at her couch's foot
Lorenzo stood, and wept: the forest tomb
  Had marr'd his glossy hair which once could shoot
Lustre into the sun, and put cold doom
  Upon his lips, and taken the soft lute
From his lorn voice, and past his loamed ears
Had made a miry channel for his tears.   280

XXXVI.

Strange sound it was, when the pale shadow spake;
  For there was striving, in its piteous tongue,
To speak as when on earth it was awake,
  And Isabella on its music hung:
Languor there was in it, and tremulous shake,
  As in a palsied Druid's harp unstrung;
And through it moan'd a ghostly under-song,
Like hoarse night-gusts sepulchral briars among.

XXXVII.

Its eyes, though wild, were still all dewy bright
  With love, and kept all phantom fear aloof   290
From the poor girl by magic of their light,
  The while it did unthread the horrid woof
Of the late darken'd time, — the murderous spite
  Of pride and avarice, — the dark pine roof
In the forest, — and the sodden turfed dell,
Where, without any word, from stabs he fell.

XXXVIII.

Saying moreover, "Isabel, my sweet!
  Red whortle-berries droop above my head,
And a large flint-stone weighs upon my feet;
  Around me beeches and high chestnuts shed   300
Their leaves and prickly nuts; a sheep-fold bleat
  Comes from beyond the river to my bed:
Go, shed one tear upon my heather-bloom,
And it shall comfort me within the tomb.

XXXIX.

"I am a shadow now, alas! alas!
  Upon the skirts of human-nature dwelling
Alone: I chant alone the holy mass,
  While little sounds of life are round me knelling,
And glossy bees at noon do fieldward pass,
  And many a chapel bell the hour is telling,   310
Paining me through: those sounds grow strange to me,
And thou art distant in Humanity.

XL.

"I know what was, I feel full well what is,
  And I should rage, if spirits could go mad;
Though I forget the taste of earthly bliss,
  That paleness warms my grave, as though I had
A Seraph chosen from the bright abyss
  To be my spouse: thy paleness makes me glad;
Thy beauty grows upon me, and I feel
A greater love through all my essence steal."   320

XLI.

The Spirit mourn'd "Adieu!" — dissolv'd, and left
  The atom darkness in a slow turmoil;
As when of healthful midnight sleep bereft,
  Thinking on rugged hours and fruitless toil,
We put our eyes into a pillowy cleft,
  And see the spangly gloom froth up and boil:
It made sad Isabella's eyelids ache,
And in the dawn she started up awake;

XLII.

"Ha! ha!" said she, "I knew not this hard life,
   I thought the worst was simple misery;   330
I thought some Fate with pleasure or with strife
   Portion'd us — happy days, or else to die;
But there is crime — a brother's bloody knife!
   Sweet Spirit, thou hast school'd my infancy:
I'll visit thee for this, and kiss thine eyes,
And greet thee morn and even in the skies."

XLIII.

When the full morning came, she had devised
   How she might secret to the forest hie;
How she might find the clay, so dearly prized,
   And sing to it one latest lullaby;   340
How her short absence might be unsurmised,
   While she the inmost of the dream would try.
Resolv'd, she took with her an aged nurse,
And went into that dismal forest-hearse.

XLIV.

See, as they creep along the river side,
   How she doth whisper to that aged Dame,
And, after looking round the champaign wide,
   Shows her a knife. — "What feverous hectic flame
Burns in thee, child? — What good can thee betide,
   That thou should'st smile again?" — The evening came, 350
And they had found Lorenzo's earthy bed;
The flint was there, the berries at his head.

XLV.

Who hath not loiter'd in a green church-yard,
   And let his spirit, like a demon-mole,
Work through the clayey soil and gravel hard,
   To see scull, coffin'd bones, and funeral stole;
Pitying each form that hungry Death hath marr'd,
   And filling it once more with human soul?
Ah! this is holiday to what was felt
When Isabella by Lorenzo knelt.   360

XLVI.

She gaz'd into the fresh-thrown mould, as though
    One glance did fully all its secrets tell;
Clearly she saw, as other eyes would know
    Pale limbs at bottom of a crystal well;
Upon the murderous spot she seem'd to grow,
    Like to a native lily of the dell:
Then with her knife, all sudden, she began
To dig more fervently than misers can.

XLVII.

Soon she turn'd up a soiled glove, whereon
    Her silk had play'd in purple phantasies,   370
She kiss'd it with a lip more chill than stone,
    And put it in her bosom, where it dries
And freezes utterly unto the bone
    Those dainties made to still an infant's cries:
Then 'gan she work again; nor stay'd her care,
But to throw back at times her veiling hair.

XLVIII.

That old nurse stood beside her wondering,
    Until her heart felt pity to the core
At sight of such a dismal labouring,
    And so she kneeled, with her locks all hoar,   380
And put her lean hands to the horrid thing:
    Three hours they labour'd at this travail sore;
At last they felt the kernel of the grave,
And Isabella did not stamp and rave.

XLIX.

Ah! wherefore all this wormy circumstance?
    Why linger at the yawning tomb so long?
O for the gentleness of old Romance,
    The simple plaining of a minstrel's song!
Fair reader, at the old tale take a glance,
    For here, in truth, it doth not well belong   390
To speak: — O turn thee to the very tale,
And taste the music of that vision pale.

L.

With duller steel than the Perséan sword
    They cut away no formless monster's head,
But one, whose gentleness did well accord
    With death, as life. The ancient harps have said,
Love never dies, but lives, immortal Lord:
    If Love impersonate was ever dead,
Pale Isabella kiss'd it, and low moan'd.
'Twas love; cold, — dead indeed, but not dethroned.   **400**

LI.

In anxious secrecy they took it home,
    And then the prize was all for Isabel:
She calm'd its wild hair with a golden comb,
    And all around each eye's sepulchral cell
Pointed each fringed lash; the smeared loam
    With tears, as chilly as a dripping well,
She drench'd away: — and still she comb'd, and kept
Sighing all day — and still she kiss'd, and wept.

LII.

Then in a silken scarf, — sweet with the dews
    Of precious flowers pluck'd in Araby,   **410**
And divine liquids come with odorous ooze
    Through the cold serpent-pipe refreshfully, —
She wrapp'd it up; and for its tomb did choose
    A garden-pot, wherein she laid it by,
And cover'd it with mould, and o'er it set
Sweet Basil, which her tears kept ever wet.

LIII.

And she forgot the stars, the moon, and sun,
    And she forgot the blue above the trees,
And she forgot the dells where waters run,
    And she forgot the chilly autumn breeze;
She had no knowledge when the day was done,
    And the new morn she saw not: but in peace
Hung over her sweet Basil evermore,
And moisten'd it with tears unto the core.

LIV.

And so she ever fed it with thin tears,
  Whence thick, and green, and beautiful it grew,
So that it smelt more balmy than its peers
  Of Basil-tufts in Florence; for it drew
Nurture besides, and life, from human fears,
  From the fast mouldering head there shut from view: 430
So that the jewel, safely casketed,
Came forth, and in perfumed leafits spread.

LV.

O Melancholy, linger here awhile!
  O Music, Music, breathe despondingly!
O Echo, Echo, from some sombre isle,
  Unknown, Lethean, sigh to us — O sigh!
Spirits in grief, lift up your heads, and smile;
  Lift up your heads, sweet Spirits, heavily,
And make a pale light in your cypress glooms,
Tinting with silver wan your marble tombs.   440

LVI.

Moan hither, all ye syllables of woe,
  From the deep throat of sad Melpomene!
Through bronzed lyre in tragic order go,
  And touch the strings into a mystery;
Sound mournfully upon the winds and low;
  For simple Isabel is soon to be
Among the dead: She withers, like a palm
Cut by an Indian for its juicy balm.

LVII.

O leave the palm to wither by itself;
  Let not quick Winter chill its dying hour! —   450
It may not be — those Baälites of pelf,
  Her brethren, noted the continual shower
From her dead eyes: and many a curious elf,
  Among her kindred, wonder'd that such dower
Of youth and beauty should be thrown aside
By one mark'd out to be a Noble's bride.

LVIII.

And, furthermore, her brethren wonder'd much
    Why she sat drooping by the Basil green,
And why it flourish'd, as by magic touch;
    Greatly they wonder'd what the thing might mean: 460
They could not surely give belief, that such
    A very nothing would have power to wean
Her from her own fair youth, and pleasures gay,
And even remembrance of her love's delay.

LIX.

Therefore they watch'd a time when they might sift
    This hidden whim; and long they watch'd in vain;
For seldom did she go to chapel-shrift,
    And seldom felt she any hunger-pain;
And when she left, she hurried back, as swift
    As bird on wing to breast its eggs again;   470
And, patient as a hen-bird, sat her there
Beside her Basil, weeping through her hair.

LX.

Yet they contriv'd to steal the Basil-pot,
And to examine it in secret place:
The thing was vile with green and livid spot,
    And yet they knew it was Lorenzo's face:
The guerdon of their murder they had got,
    And so left Florence in a moment's space,
Never to turn again. — Away they went,
With blood upon their heads, to banishment.   480

LXI.

O Melancholy, turn thine eyes away!
    O Music, Music, breathe despondingly!
O Echo, Echo, on some other day,
    From isles Lethean, sigh to us — O sigh!
Spirits of grief, sing not your "Well-a-way!"
    For Isabel, sweet Isabel, will die;
Will die a death too lone and incomplete,
Now they have ta'en away her Basil sweet.

LXII.

Piteous she look'd on dead and senseless things,
    Asking for her lost Basil amorously;   490
And with melodious chuckle in the strings
    Of her lorn voice, she oftentimes would cry
After the Pilgrim in his wanderings,
    To ask him where her Basil was; and why
'Twas hid from her: "For cruel 'tis," said she,
"To steal my Basil-pot away from me."

LXIII.

And so she pined, and so she died forlorn,
    Imploring for her Basil to the last.
No heart was there in Florence but did mourn
    In pity of her love, so overcast.   500
And a sad ditty of this story born
    From mouth to mouth through all the country pass'd:
Still is the burthen sung — "O cruelty,
To steal my Basil-pot away from me!"

TO HOMER

STANDING aloof in giant ignorance,
    Of thee I hear and of the Cyclades,
As one who sits ashore and longs perchance
    To visit dolphin-coral in deep seas.
So thou wast blind! — but then the veil was rent;
    For Jove uncurtain'd Heaven to let thee live,
And Neptune made for thee a spumy tent,
    And Pan made sing for thee his forest-hive;
Aye, on the shores of darkness there is light,
    And precipices show untrodden green;   **10**
There is a budding morrow in midnight;
    There is a triple sight in blindness keen;
Such seeing hadst thou, as it once befel
To Dian, Queen of Earth, and Heaven, and Hell.

FRAGMENT OF AN ODE TO MAIA

MOTHER of Hermes! and still youthful Maia!
        May I sing to thee
As thou wast hymned on the shores of Baiæ?
        Or may I woo thee
In earlier Sicilian? or thy smiles
Seek as they once were sought, in Grecian isles,
By bards who died content on pleasant sward,
    Leaving great verse unto a little clan?
O, give me their old vigour, and unheard
    Save of the quiet primrose, and the span   **10**
        Of heaven and few ears,
Rounded by thee, my song should die away
        Content as theirs,
Rich in the simple worship of a day.

ON VISITING THE TOMB OF BURNS

THE town, the churchyard, and the setting sun,
    The clouds, the trees, the rounded hills all seem,
    Though beautiful, cold — strange — as in a dream,
I dreamed long ago, now new begun.
The short-liv'd, paly Summer is but won
    From Winter's ague, for one hour's gleam;
    Though sapphire-warm, their stars do never beam:

All is cold Beauty; pain is never done:
For who has mind to relish, Minos-wise,
    The Real of Beauty, free from that dead hue   10
      Sickly imagination and sick pride
   Cast wan upon it? Burns! with honour due
      I oft have honour'd thee. Great shadow, hide
Thy face; I sin against thy native skies.

MEG MERRILIES

OLD MEG she was a gipsy,
   And lived upon the moors;
Her bed it was the brown heath-turf,
   And her house was out of doors.

Her apples were swart blackberries,
   Her currants, pods o' broom;
Her wine was dew of the wild white rose,
   Her book a churchyard tomb.

Her brothers were the craggy hills,
   Her sisters larchen trees;   10
Alone with her great family
   She lived as she did please.

No breakfast had she many a morn,
   No dinner many a noon,
And, 'stead of supper, she would stare
   Full hard against the moon!

But every morn, of woodbine fresh
   She made her garlanding;
And every night, the dark glen yew
   She wove, and she would sing.   20

And with her fingers, old and brown,
   She plaited mats o' rushes,
And gave them to the cottagers
   She met among the bushes.

Old Meg was brave as Margaret Queen
   And tall as Amazon;
An old red blanket cloak she wore;
   A chip hat had she on.
God rest her aged bones somewhere!
   She died full long agone.   30

STAFFA

Not Aladdin magian
Ever such a work began;
Not the wizard of the Dee
Ever such a dream could see;
Not St. John, in Patmos' Isle,
In the passion of his toil,
When he saw the churches seven,
Golden aisled, built up in heaven,
Gaz'd at such a rugged wonder.
As I stood its roofing under,   10
Lo! I saw one sleeping there,
On the marble cold and bare.
While the surges wash'd his feet,
And his garments white did beat
Drench'd about the sombre rocks,
On his neck his well-grown locks,
Lifted dry above the main,
Were upon the curl again.
"What is this? and what art thou?"
Whisper'd I, and touch'd his brow;   20
"What art thou? and what is this?"
Whisper'd I, and strove to kiss
The spirit's hand, to wake his eyes;
Up he started in a trice:
"I am Lycidas," said he,
"Fam'd in funeral minstrelsy!
This was architected thus
By the great Oceanus! —
Here his mighty waters play
Hollow organs all the day;   30
Here by turns his dolphins all,
Finny palmers great and small,
Come to pay devotion due —
Each a mouth of pearls must strew.
Many a mortal of these days,
Dares to pass our sacred ways,
Dares to touch audaciously
This Cathedral of the Sea!
I have been the pontiff-priest
Where the waters never rest,   40
Where a fledgy sea-bird choir
Soars for ever; holy fire

I have hid from mortal man;
Proteus is my Sacristan.
But the stupid eye of mortal
Hath pass'd beyond the rocky portal;
So for ever will I leave
Such a taint, and soon unweave
All the magic of the place.
'Tis now free to stupid face, 50
To cutters, and to fashion boats,
To cravats and to petticoats: —
The great sea shall war it down,
For its fame shall not be blown
At each farthing quadrille dance."
So saying, with a Spirit's glance
He dived!

WRITTEN UPON THE TOP OF BEN NEVIS

READ me a lesson, Muse, and speak it loud
    Upon the top of Nevis, blind in mist!
I look into the chasms, and a shroud
    Vaporous doth hide them, — just so much I wist
Mankind do know of hell; I look o'erhead,
    And there is sullen mist, — even so much
Mankind can tell of heaven; mist is spread
    Before the earth, beneath me, — even such,
Even so vague is man's sight of himself!
    Here are the craggy stones beneath my feet, — 10
Thus much I know that, a poor witless elf,
    I tread on them, — that all my eye doth meet
Is mist and crag, not only on this height,
But in the world of thought and mental might!

HYPERION

A FRAGMENT

BOOK I

DEEP in the shady sadness of a vale
Far sunken from the healthy breath of morn,
Far from the fiery noon, and eve's one star,
Sat gray-hair'd Saturn, quiet as a stone,
Still as the silence round about his lair;
Forest on forest hung about his head
Like cloud on cloud. No stir of air was there,
Not so much life as on a summer's day
Robs not one light seed from the feather'd grass,
But where the dead leaf fell, there did it rest.   10
A stream went voiceless by, still deadened more
By reason of his fallen divinity
Spreading a shade: the Naiad 'mid her reeds
Press'd her cold finger closer to her lips.

　　Along the margin-sand large foot-marks went,
No further than to where his feet had stray'd,
And slept there since. Upon the sodden ground
His old right hand lay nerveless, listless, dead,
Unsceptred; and his realmless eyes were closed;
While his bow'd head seem'd list'ning to the Earth,   20
His ancient mother, for some comfort yet.

　　It seem'd no force could wake him from his place;
But there came one, who with a kindred hand
Touch'd his wide shoulders, after bending low
With reverence, though to one who knew it not.
She was a Goddess of the infant world;
By her in stature the tall Amazon
Had stood a pigmy's height: she would have ta'en
Achilles by the hair and bent his neck;
Or with a finger stay'd Ixion's wheel.   30
Her face was large as that of Memphian sphinx,
Pedestal'd haply in a palace court,
When sages look'd to Egypt for their lore.
But oh! how unlike marble was that face:
How beautiful, if sorrow had not made

Sorrow more beautiful than Beauty's self.
There was a listening fear in her regard,
As if calamity had but begun;
As if the vanward clouds of evil days
Had spent their malice, and the sullen rear   40
Was with its stored thunder labouring up.
One hand she press'd upon that aching spot
Where beats the human heart, as if just there,
Though an immortal, she felt cruel pain:
The other upon Saturn's bended neck
She laid, and to the level of his ear
Leaning with parted lips, some words she spake
In solemn tenour and deep organ tone:
Some mourning words, which in our feeble tongue
Would come in these like accents; O how frail   50
To that large utterance of the early Gods!
"Saturn, look up! — though wherefore, poor old King?
I have no comfort for thee, no not one:
I cannot say, 'O wherefore sleepest thou?'
For heaven is parted from thee, and the earth
Knows thee not, thus afflicted, for a God;
And ocean too, with all its solemn noise,
Has from thy sceptre pass'd; and all the air
Is emptied of thine hoary majesty.
Thy thunder, conscious of the new command,   60
Rumbles reluctant o'er our fallen house;
And thy sharp lightning in unpractised hands
Scorches and burns our once serene domain.
O aching time! O moments big as years!
All as ye pass swell out the monstrous truth,
And press it so upon our weary griefs
That unbelief has not a space to breathe.
Saturn, sleep on: — O thoughtless, why did I
Thus violate thy slumbrous solitude?
Why should I ope thy melancholy eyes?   70
Saturn, sleep on! while at thy feet I weep."

      As when, upon a tranced summer-night,
Those green-rob'd senators of mighty woods,
Tall oaks, branch-charmed by the earnest stars,
Dream, and so dream all night without a stir,
Save from one gradual solitary gust
Which comes upon the silence, and dies off,
As if the ebbing air had but one wave;
So came these words and went; the while in tears
She touch'd her fair large forehead to the ground,   80

Just where her falling hair might be outspread
A soft and silken mat for Saturn's feet.
One moon, with alteration slow, had shed
Her silver seasons four upon the night,
And still these two were postured motionless,
Like natural sculpture in cathedral cavern;
The frozen God still couchant on the earth,
And the sad Goddess weeping at his feet:
Until at length old Saturn lifted up
His faded eyes, and saw his kingdom gone,   90
And all the gloom and sorrow of the place,
And that fair kneeling Goddess; and then spake,
As with a palsied tongue, and while his beard
Shook horrid with such aspen-malady:
"O tender spouse of gold Hyperion,
Thea, I feel thee ere I see thy face;
Look up, and let me see our doom in it;
Look up, and tell me if this feeble shape
Is Saturn's; tell me, if thou hear'st the voice
Of Saturn; tell me, if this wrinkling brow,   100
Naked and bare of its great diadem,
Peers like the front of Saturn. Who had power
To make me desolate? whence came the strength?
How was it nurtur'd to such bursting forth,
While Fate seem'd strangled in my nervous grasp?
But it is so; and I am smother'd up,
And buried from all godlike exercise
Of influence benign on planets pale,
Of admonitions to the winds and seas,
Of peaceful sway above man's harvesting,   110
And all those acts which Deity supreme
Doth ease its heart of love in. — I am gone
Away from my own bosom: I have left
My strong identity, my real self,
Somewhere between the throne, and where I sit
Here on this spot of earth. Search, Thea, search!
Open thine eyes eterne, and sphere them round
Upon all space: space starr'd, and lorn of light;
Space region'd with life-air; and barren void;
Spaces of fire, and all the yawn of hell. —   120
Search, Thea, search! and tell me, if thou seest
A certain shape or shadow, making way
With wings or chariot fierce to repossess
A heaven he lost erewhile: it must — it must
Be of ripe progress — Saturn must be King.
Yes, there must be a golden victory;

There must be Gods thrown down, and trumpets blown
Of triumph calm, and hymns of festival
Upon the gold clouds metropolitan,
Voices of soft proclaim, and silver stir   130
Of strings in hollow shells; and there shall be
Beautiful things made new, for the surprise
Of the sky-children; I will give command:
Thea! Thea! Thea! where is Saturn?"

    This passion lifted him upon his feet,
And made his hands to struggle in the air,
His Druid locks to shake and ooze with sweat,
His eyes to fever out, his voice to cease.
He stood, and heard not Thea's sobbing deep;
A little time, and then again he snatch'd   140
Utterance thus. — "But cannot I create?
Cannot I form? Cannot I fashion forth
Another world, another universe,
To overbear and crumble this to nought?
Where is another chaos? Where?" — That word
Found way unto Olympus, and made quake
The rebel three. — Thea was startled up,
And in her bearing was a sort of hope,
As thus she quick-voic'd spake, yet full of awe.

    "This cheers our fallen house: come to our friends,   150
O Saturn! come away, and give them heart;
I know the covert, for thence came I hither."
Thus brief; then with beseeching eyes she went
With backward footing through the shade a space:
He follow'd, and she turn'd to lead the way
Through aged boughs, that yielded like the mist
Which eagles cleave upmounting from their nest.

    Meanwhile in other realms big tears were shed,
More sorrow like to this, and such like woe,
Too huge for mortal tongue or pen of scribe: 160
The Titans fierce, self-hid, or prison-bound,
Groan'd for the old allegiance once more,
And listen'd in sharp pain for Saturn's voice.
But one of the whole mammoth-brood still kept
His sov'reignty, and rule, and majesty; —
Blazing Hyperion on his orbed fire
Still sat, still snuff'd the incense, teeming up
From man to the sun's God; yet unsecure:
For as among us mortals omens drear

Fright and perplex, so also shuddered he —   170
Not at dog's howl, or gloom-bird's hated screech,
Or the familiar visiting of one
Upon the first toll of his passing-bell,
Or prophesyings of the midnight lamp;
But horrors, portion'd to a giant nerve,
Oft made Hyperion ache. His palace bright
Bastion'd with pyramids of glowing gold,
And touch'd with shade of bronzed obelisks,
Glar'd a blood-red through all its thousand courts,
Arches, and domes, and fiery galleries;   180
And all its curtains of Aurorian clouds
Flush'd angerly: while sometimes eagle's wings,
Unseen before by Gods or wondering men,
Darken'd the place; and neighing steeds were heard,
Not heard before by Gods or wondering men.
Also, when he would taste the spicy wreaths
Of incense, breath'd aloft from sacred hills,
Instead of sweets, his ample palate took
Savour of poisonous brass and metal sick:
And so, when harbour'd in the sleepy west,   190
After the full completion of fair day, —
For rest divine upon exalted couch
And slumber in the arms of melody,
He pac'd away the pleasant hours of ease
With stride colossal, on from hall to hall;
While far within each aisle and deep recess,
His winged minions in close clusters stood,
Amaz'd and full of fear; like anxious men
Who on wide plains gather in panting troops,
When earthquakes jar their battlements and towers.   200
Even now, while Saturn, rous'd from icy trance,
Went step for step with Thea through the woods,
Hyperion, leaving twilight in the rear,
Came slope upon the threshold of the west;
Then, as was wont, his palace-door flew ope
In smoothest silence, save what solemn tubes,
Blown by the serious Zephyrs, gave of sweet
And wandering sounds, slow-breathed melodies;
And like a rose in vermeil tint and shape,
In fragrance soft, and coolness to the eye,   210
That inlet to severe magnificence
Stood full blown, for the God to enter in.

He enter'd, but he enter'd full of wrath;
His flaming robes stream'd out beyond his heels,

And gave a roar, as if of earthly fire,
That scar'd away the meek ethereal Hours
And made their dove-wings tremble. On he flared,
From stately nave to nave, from vault to vault,
Through bowers of fragrant and enwreathed light,
And diamond-paved lus rous long arcades,   220
Until he reach'd the great main cupola;
There standing fierce beneath, he stampt his foot,
And from the basements deep to the high towers
Jarr'd his own golden region; and before
The quavering thunder thereupon had ceas'd,
His voice leapt out, despite of godlike curb,
To this result: "O dreams of day and night!
O monstrous forms! O effigies of pain!
O spectres busy in a cold, cold gloom!
O lank-eared Phantoms of black-weeded pools!   230
Why do I know ye? why have I seen ye? why
Is my eternal essence thus distraught
To see and to behold these horrors new?
Saturn is fallen, am I too to fall?
Am I to leave this haven of my rest,
This cradle of my glory, this soft clime,
This calm luxuriance of blissful light,
These crystalline pavilions, and pure fanes,
Of all my lucent empire? It is left
Deserted, void, nor any haunt of mine.   240
The blaze, the splendor, and the symmetry,
I cannot see — but darkness, death and darkness.
Even here, into my centre of repose,
The shady visions come to domineer,
Insult, and blind, and stifle up my pomp. —
Fall! — No, by Tellus and her briny robes!
Over the fiery frontier of my realms
I will advance a terrible right arm
Shall scare that infant thunderer, rebel Jove,
And bid old Saturn take his throne again." —   250
He spake, and ceas'd, the while a heavier threat
Held struggle with his throat but came not forth;
For as in theatres of crowded men
Hubbub increases more they call out "Hush!"
So at Hyperion's words the Phantoms pale
Bestirr'd themselves, thrice horrible and cold;
And from the mirror'd level where he stood
A mist arose, as from a scummy marsh.
At this, through all his bulk an agony
Crept gradual, from the feet unto the crown,   260

Like a lithe serpent vast and muscular
Making slow way, with head and neck convuls'd
From over-strained might. Releas'd, he fled
To the eastern gates, and full six dewy hours
Before the dawn in season due should blush,
He breath'd fierce breath against the sleepy portals,
Clear'd them of heavy vapours, burst them wide
Suddenly on the ocean's chilly streams.
The planet orb of fire, whereon he rode
Each day from east to west the heavens through,   270
Spun round in sable curtaining of clouds;
Not therefore veiled quite, blindfold, and hid,
But ever and anon the glancing spheres,
Circles, and arcs, and broad-belting colure,
Glow'd through, and wrought upon the muffling dark
Sweet-shaped lightnings from the nadir deep
Up to the zenith, — hieroglyphics old
Which sages and keen-eyed astrologers
Then living on the earth, with labouring thought
Won from the gaze of many centuries: 280
Now lost, save what we find on remnants huge
Of stone, or marble swart; their import gone,
Their wisdom long since fled. — Two wings this orb
Possess'd for glory, two fair argent wings,
Ever exalted at the God's approach:
And now, from forth the gloom their plumes immense
Rose, one by one, till all outspreaded were;
While still the dazzling globe maintain'd eclipse,
Awaiting for Hyperion's command.
Fain would he have commanded, fain took throne   290
And bid the day begin, if but for change.
He might not: — No, though a primeval God:
The sacred seasons might not be disturb'd.
Therefore the operations of the dawn
Stay'd in their birth, even as here 'tis told.
Those silver wings expanded sisterly,
Eager to sail their orb; the porches wide
Open'd upon the dusk demesnes of night;
And the bright Titan, phrenzied with new woes,
Unus'd to bend, by hard compulsion bent   300
His spirit to the sorrow of the time;
And all along a dismal rack of clouds,
Upon the boundaries of day and night,
He stretch'd himself in grief and radiance faint.
There as he lay, the Heaven with its stars
Look'd down on him with pity, and the voice

Of Cœlus, from the universal space,
Thus whisper'd low and solemn in his ear.
"O brightest of my children dear, earth-born
And sky-engendered, Son of Mysteries   310
All unrevealed even to the powers
Which met at thy creating; at whose joys
And palpitations sweet, and pleasures soft,
I, Cœlus, wonder, how they came and whence;
And at the fruits thereof what shapes they be,
Distinct, and visible; symbols divine,
Manifestations of that beauteous life
Diffus'd unseen throughout eternal space:
Of these new-form'd art thou, oh brightest child!
Of these, thy brethren and the Goddesses!   320
There is sad feud among ye, and rebellion
Of son against his sire. I saw him fall,
I saw my first-born tumbled from his throne!
To me his arms were spread, to me his voice
Found way from forth the thunders round his head!
Pale wox I, and in vapours hid my face.
Art thou, too, near such doom? vague fear there is:
For I have seen my sons most unlike Gods.
Divine ye were created, and divine
In sad demeanour, solemn, undisturb'd,   330
Unruffled, like high Gods, ye liv'd and ruled:
Now I behold in you fear, hope, and wrath;
Actions of rage and passion; even as
I see them, on the mortal world beneath,
In men who die. — This is the grief, O Son!
Sad sign of ruin, sudden dismay, and fall!
Yet do thou strive; as thou art capable,
As thou canst move about, an evident God;
And canst oppose to each malignant hour
Ethereal presence: — I am but a voice;   340
My life is but the life of winds and tides,
No more than winds and tides can I avail: —
But thou canst. Be thou therefore in the van
Of circumstance; yea, seize the arrow's barb
Before the tense string murmur. — To the earth!
For there thou wilt find Saturn, and his woes.
Meantime I will keep watch on thy bright sun,
And of thy seasons be a careful nurse." —
Ere half this region-whisper had come down,
Hyperion arose, and on the stars   350
Lifted his curved lids, and kept them wide
Until it ceas'd; and still he kept them wide:

And still they were the same bright, patient stars.
Then with a slow incline of his broad breast,
Like to a diver in the pearly seas,
Forward he stoop'd over the airy shore,
And plung'd all noiseless into the deep night.

BOOK II

JUST at the self-same beat of Time's wide wings
Hyperion slid into the rustled air,
And Saturn gain'd with Thea that sad place
Where Cybele and the bruised Titans mourn'd.
It was a den where no insulting light
Could glimmer on their tears; where their own groans
They felt, but heard not, for the solid roar
Of thunderous waterfalls and torrents hoarse,
Pouring a constant bulk, uncertain where.
Crag jutting forth to crag, and rocks that seem'd   10
Ever as if just rising from a sleep,
Forehead to forehead held their monstrous horns:
And thus in thousand hugest phantasies
Made a fit roofing to this nest of woe.
Instead of thrones, hard flint they sat upon,
Couches of rugged stone, and slaty ridge
Stubborn'd with iron. All were not assembled:
Some chain'd in torture, and some wandering.
Cœus, and Gyges, and Briareüs,
Typhon, and Dolor, and Porphyrion,   20
With many more, the brawniest in assault,
Were pent in regions of laborious breath;
Dungeon'd in opaque element, to keep
Their clenched teeth still clench'd, and all their limbs
Lock'd up like veins of metal, crampt and screw'd;
Without a motion, save of their big hearts
Heaving in pain, and horribly convuls'd
With sanguine feverous boiling gurge of pulse.
Mnemosyne was straying in the world;
Far from her moon had Phœbe wandered;   30
And many else were free to roam abroad,
But for the main, here found they covert drear.
Scarce images of life, one here, one there,
Lay vast and edgeways; like a dismal cirque
Of Druid stones, upon a forlorn moor,
When the chill rain begins at shut of eve,

In dull November, and their chancel vault,
The Heaven itself, is blinded throughout night.
Each one kept shroud, nor to his neighbour gave
Or word, or look, or action of despair.   40
Creüs was one; his ponderous iron mace
Lay by him, and a shatter'd rib of rock
Told of his rage, ere he thus sank and pined.
Iäpetus another; in his grasp,
A serpent's plashy neck; its barbed tongue
Squeez'd from the gorge, and all its uncurl'd length
Dead; and because the creature could not spit
Its poison in the eyes of conquering Jove.
Next Cottus: prone he lay, chin uppermost,
As though in pain; for still upon the flint   50
He ground severe his skull, with open mouth
And eyes at horrid working. Nearest him
Asia, born of most enormous Caf,
Who cost her mother Tellus keener pangs,
Though feminine, than any of her sons:
More thought than woe was in her dusky face,
For she was prophesying of her glory;
And in her wide imagination stood
Palm-shaded temples, and high rival fanes,
By Oxus or in Ganges' sacred isles.   60
Even as Hope upon her anchor leans,
So leant she, not so fair, upon a tusk
Shed from the broadest of her elephants.
Above her, on a crag's uneasy shelve,
Upon his elbow rais'd, all prostrate else,
Shadow'd Enceladus; once tame and mild
As grazing ox unworried in the meads;
Now tiger-passion'd, lion-thoughted, wroth,
He meditated, plotted, and even now
Was hurling mountains in that second war,   70
Not long delay'd, that scar'd the younger Gods
To hide themselves in forms of beast and bird.
Not far hence Atlas; and beside him prone
Phorcus, the sire of Gorgons. Neighbour'd close
Oceanus, and Tethys, in whose lap
Sobb'd Clymene among her tangled hair.
In midst of all lay Themis, at the feet
Of Ops the queen all clouded round from sight;
No shape distinguishable, more than when
Thick night confounds the pine-tops with the clouds: 80
And many else whose names may not be told.
For when the Muse's wings are air-ward spread,

Who shall delay her flight? And she must chaunt
Of Saturn, and his guide, who now had climb'd
With damp and slippery footing from a depth
More horrid still. Above a sombre cliff
Their heads appear'd, and up their stature grew
Till on the level height their steps found ease:
Then Thea spread abroad her trembling arms
Upon the precincts of this nest of pain,   90
And sidelong fix'd her eye on Saturn's face;
There saw she direst strife; the supreme God
At war with all the frailty of grief,
Of rage, of fear, anxiety, revenge,
Remorse, spleen, hope, but most of all despair.
Against these plagues he strove in vain; for Fate
Had pour'd a mortal oil upon his head,
A disanointing poison: so that Thea,
Affrighted, kept her still, and let him pass
First onwards in, among the fallen tribe.   100

      As with us mortal men, the laden heart
Is persecuted more, and fever'd more,
When it is nighing to the mournful house
Where other hearts are sick of the same bruise;
So Saturn, as he walk'd into the midst,
Felt faint, and would have sunk among the rest,
But that he met Enceladus's eye,
Whose mightiness, and awe of him, at once
Came like an inspiration; and he shouted,
"Titans, behold your God!" at which some groan'd;   110
Some started on their feet; some also shouted;
Some wept, some wail'd, all bow'd with reverence;
And Ops, uplifting her black folded veil,
Show'd her pale cheeks, and all her forehead wan,
Her eye-brows thin and jet, and hollow eyes.
There is a roaring in the bleak-grown pines
When Winter lifts his voice; there is a noise
Among immortals when a God gives sign,
With hushing finger, how he means to load
His tongue with the full weight of utterless thought,   120
With thunder, and with music, and with pomp:
Such noise is like the roar of bleak-grown pines:
Which, when it ceases in this mountain'd world,
No other sound succeeds; but ceasing here,
Among these fallen, Saturn's voice therefrom
Grew up like organ, that begins anew
Its strain, when other harmonies, stopt short,

Leave the dinn'd air vibrating silverly.
Thus grew it up — "Not in my own sad breast,
Which is its own great judge and searcher out, 130
Can I find reason why ye should be thus:
Not in the legends of the first of days,
Studied from that old spirit-leaved book
Which starry Uranus with finger bright
Sav'd from the shores of darkness, when the waves
Low-ebb'd still hid it up in shallow gloom; —
And the which book ye know I ever kept
For my firm-based footstool: — Ah, infirm!
Not there, nor in sign, symbol, or portent
Of element, earth, water, air, and fire, — 140
At war, at peace, or inter-quarreling
One against one, or two, or three, or all
Each several one against the other three,
As fire with air loud warring when rain-floods
Drown both, and press them both against earth's face,
Where, finding sulphur, a quadruple wrath
Unhinges the poor world; — not in that strife,
Wherefrom I take strange lore, and read it deep,
Can I find reason why ye should be thus:
No, no-where can unriddle, though I search, 150
And pore on Nature's universal scroll
Even to swooning, why ye, Divinities,
The first-born of all shap'd and palpable Gods,
Should cower beneath what, in comparison,
Is untremendous might. Yet ye are here,
O'erwhelm'd, and spurn'd, and batter'd, ye are here!
O Titans, shall I say 'Arise!' — Ye groan:
Shall I say 'Crouch!' — Ye groan. What can I then?
O Heaven wide! O unseen parent dear!
What can I? Tell me, all ye brethren Gods, 160
How we can war, how engine our great wrath!
O speak your counsel now, for Saturn's ear
Is all a-hunger'd. Thou, Oceanus,
Ponderest high and deep; and in thy face
I see, astonied, that severe content
Which comes of thought and musing: give us help!"

So ended Saturn; and the God of the Sea,
Sophist and sage, from no Athenian grove,
But cogitation in his watery shades,
Arose, with locks not oozy, and began, 170
In murmurs, which his first-endeavouring tongue
Caught infant-like from the far-foamed sands.

"O ye, whom wrath consumes! who, passion-stung,
Writhe at defeat, and nurse your agonies!
Shut up your senses, stifle up your ears,
My voice is not a bellows unto ire.
Yet listen, ye who will, whilst I bring proof
How ye, perforce, must be content to stoop:
And in the proof much comfort will I give,
If ye will take that comfort in its truth.   180
We fall by course of Nature's law, not force
Of thunder, or of Jove. Great·Saturn, thou
Hast sifted well the atom-universe;
But for this reason, that thou art the King,
And only·blind from sheer supremacy,
One avenue was shaded from thine eyes,
Through which I wandered to eternal truth.
And first, as thou wast not the first of powers,
So art thou not the last; it cannot be:
Thou art not the beginning nor the end.   190
From Chaos and parental Darkness came
Light, the first fruits of that intestine broil,
That sullen ferment, which for wondrous ends
Was ripening in itself. The ripe hour came,
And with it Light, and Light, engendering
Upon its own producer, forthwith touch'd
The whole enormous matter into life.
Upon that very hour, our parentage,
The Heavens and the Earth, were manifest:
Then thou first-born, and we the giant-race,   200
Found ourselves ruling new and beauteous realms.
Now comes the pain of truth, to whom 'tis pain;
O folly! for to bear all naked truths,
And to envisage circumstance, all calm,
That is the top of sovereignty. Mark well!
As Heaven and Earth are fairer, fairer far
Than Chaos and blank Darkness, though once chiefs;
And as we show beyond that Heaven and Earth
In form and shape compact and beautiful,
In will, in action free, companionship,   210
And thousand other signs of purer life;
So on our heels a fresh perfection treads,
A power more strong in beauty, born of us
And fated to excel us, as we pass
In glory that old Darkness: nor are we
. Thereby more conquer'd, than by us the rule
Of shapeless Chaos. Say, doth the dull soil .
Quarrel with the proud forests it hath fed,

And feedeth still, more comely than itself?
Can it deny the chiefdom of green groves?   220
Or shall the tree be envious of the dove
Because it cooeth, and hath snowy wings
To wander wherewithal and find its joys?
We are such forest-trees, and our fair boughs
Have bred forth, not pale solitary doves,
But eagles golden-feather'd, who do tower
Above us in their beauty, and must reign
In right thereof; for 'tis the eternal law
That first in beauty should be first in might:
Yea, by that law, another race may drive   230
Our conquerors to mourn as we do now.
Have ye beheld the young God of the Seas,
My dispossessor? Have ye seen his face?
Have ye beheld his chariot, foam'd along
By noble winged creatures he hath made?
I saw him on the calmed waters scud,
With such a glow of beauty in his eyes,
That it enforc'd me to bid sad farewell
To all my empire: farewell sad I took,
And hither came, to see how dolorous fate   240
Had wrought upon ye; and how I might best
Give consolation in this woe extreme.
Receive the truth, and let it be your balm."

Whether through poz'd conviction, or disdain,
They guarded silence, when Oceanus
Left murmuring, what deepest thought can tell?
But so it was, none answer'd for a space,
Save one whom none regarded, Clymene;
And yet she answer'd not, only complain'd,
With hectic lips, and eyes up-looking mild,   250
Thus wording timidly among the fierce:
"O Father, I am here the simplest voice,
And all my knowledge is that joy is gone,
And this thing woe crept in among our hearts,
There to remain for ever, as I fear:
I would not bode of evil, if I thought
So weak a creature could turn off the help
Which by just right should come of mighty Gods;
Yet let me tell my sorrow, let me tell
Of what I heard, and how it made me weep,   260
And know that we had parted from all hope.
I stood upon a shore, a pleasant shore,
Where a sweet clime was breathed from a land

Of fragrance, quietness, and trees, and flowers.
Full of calm joy it was, as I of grief;
Too full of joy and soft delicious warmth;
So that I felt a movement in my heart
To chide, and to reproach that solitude
With songs of misery, music of our woes;
And sat me down, and took a mouthed shell   270
And murmur'd into it, and made melody —
O melody no more! for while I sang,
And with poor skill let pass into the breeze
The dull shell's echo, from a bowery strand
Just opposite, an island of the sea,
There came enchantment with the shifting wind,
That did both drown and keep alive my ears.
I threw my shell away upon the sand,
And a wave fill'd it, as my sense was fill'd
With that new blissful golden melody.   280
A living death was in each gush of sounds,
Each family of rapturous hurried notes,
That fell, one after one, yet all at once,
Like pearl beads dropping sudden from their string:
And then another, then another strain,
Each like a dove leaving its olive perch,
With music wing'd instead of silent plumes,
To hover round my head, and make me sick
Of joy and grief at once. Grief overcame,
And I was stopping up my frantic ears,   290
When, past all hindrance of my trembling hands,
A voice came sweeter, sweeter than all tune,
And still it cried, 'Apollo! young Apollo!
The morning-bright Apollo! young Apollo!'
I fled, it follow'd me, and cried 'Apollo!'
O Father, and O Brethren, had ye felt
Those pains of mine; O Saturn, hadst thou felt,
Ye would not call this too indulged tongue
Presumptuous, in thus venturing to be heard."

So far her voice flow'd on, like timorous brook   300
That, lingering along a pebbled coast,
Doth fear to meet the sea: but sea it met,
And shudder'd; for the overwhelming voice
Of huge Enceladus swallow'd it in wrath:
The ponderous syllables, like sullen waves
In the half-glutted hollows of reef-rocks,
Came booming thus, while still upon his arm
He lean'd; not rising, from supreme contempt.

"Or shall we listen to the over-wise,
Or to the over-foolish, Giant-Gods? 310
Not thunderbolt on thunderbolt, till all
That rebel Jove's whole armoury were spent,
Not world on world upon these shoulders piled,
Could agonize me more than baby-words
In midst of this dethronement horrible.
Speak! roar! shout! yell! ye sleepy Titans all.
Do ye forget the blows, the buffets vile?
Are ye not smitten by a youngling arm?
Dost thou forget, sham Monarch of the Waves,
Thy scalding in the seas? What, have I rous'd 320
Your spleens with so few simple words as these?
O joy! for now I see ye are not lost:
O joy! for now I see a thousand eyes
Wide glaring for revenge!" — As this he said,
He lifted up his stature vast, and stood,
Still without intermission speaking thus:
"Now ye are flames, I'll tell you how to burn,
And purge the ether of our enemies;
How to feed fierce the crooked stings of fire,
And singe away the swollen clouds of Jove, 330
Stifling that puny essence in its tent.
O let him feel the evil he hath done;
For though I scorn Oceanus's lore,
Much pain have I for more than loss of realms:
The days of peace and slumberous calm are fled;
Those days, all innocent of scathing war,
When all the fair Existences of heaven
Came open-eyed to guess what we would speak: —
That was before our brows were taught to frown,
Before our lips knew else but solemn sounds; 340
That was before we knew the winged thing,
Victory, might be lost, or might be won.
And be ye mindful that Hyperion,
Our brightest brother, still is undisgraced —
Hyperion, lo! his radiance is here!"

All eyes were on Enceladus's face,
And they beheld, while still Hyperion's name
Flew from his lips up to the vaulted rocks,
A pallid gleam across his features stern:
Not savage, for he saw full many a God 350
Wroth as himself. He look'd upon them all,
And in each face he saw a gleam of light,
But splendider in Saturn's, whose hoar locks

Shone like the bubbling foam about a keel
When the prow sweeps into a midnight cove.
In pale and silver silence they remain'd,
Till suddenly a splendour, like the morn,
Pervaded all the beetling gloomy steeps,
All the sad spaces of oblivion,
And every gulf, and every chasm old,　　　　　　　　360
And every height, and every sullen depth,
Voiceless, or hoarse with loud tormented streams:
And all the everlasting cataracts,
And all the headlong torrents far and near,
Mantled before in darkness and huge shade,
Now saw the light and made it terrible.
It was Hyperion: — a granite peak
His bright feet touch'd, and there he stay'd to view
The misery his brilliance had betray'd
To the most hateful seeing of itself.　　　　　　　370
Golden his hair of short Numidian curl,
Regal his shape majestic, a vast shade
In midst of his own brightness, like the bulk
Of Memnon's image at the set of sun
To one who travels from the dusking East:
Sighs, too, as mournful as that Memnon's harp
He utter'd, while his hands contemplative
He press'd together, and in silence stood.
Despondence seiz'd again the fallen Gods
At sight of the dejected King of Day,　　　　　　　380
And many hid their faces from the light:
But fierce Enceladus sent forth his eyes
Among the brotherhood; and, at their glare,
Uprose Iäpetus, and Creüs too,
And Phorcus, sea-born, and together strode
To where he towered on his eminence.
There those four shouted forth old Saturn's name;
Hyperion from the peak loud answered, "Saturn!"
Saturn sat near the Mother of the Gods,
In whose face was no joy, though all the Gods　　　390
Gave from their hollow throats the name of "Saturn!"

BOOK III

THUS in alternate uproar and sad peace,
Amazed were those Titans utterly.
O leave them, Muse! O leave them to their woes;
For thou art weak to sing such tumults dire:

A solitary sorrow best befits
Thy lips, and antheming a lonely grief.
Leave them, O Muse! for thou anon wilt find
Many a fallen old Divinity
Wandering in vain about bewildered shores.
Meantime touch piously the Delphic harp,   10
And not a wind of heaven but will breathe
In aid soft warble from the Dorian flute;
For lo! 'tis for the Father of all verse.
Flush every thing that hath a vermeil hue,
Let the rose glow intense and warm the air,
And let the clouds of even and of morn
Float in voluptuous fleeces o'er the hills;
Let the red wine within the goblet boil,
Cold as a bubbling well; let faint-lipp'd shells,
On sands, or in great deeps, vermilion turn   20
Through all their labyrinths; and let the maid
Blush keenly, as with some warm kiss surpris'd.
Chief isle of the embowered Cyclades,
Rejoice, O Delos, with thine olives green,
And poplars, and lawn-shading palms, and beech,
In which the Zephyr breathes the loudest song,
And hazels thick, dark-stemm'd beneath the shade:
Apollo is once more the golden theme!
Where was he, when the Giant of the Sun
Stood bright, amid the sorrow of his peers?   30
Together had he left his mother fair
And his twin-sister sleeping in their bower,
And in the morning twilight wandered forth
Beside the osiers of a rivulet,
Full ankle-deep in lilies of the vale.
The nightingale had ceas'd, and a few stars
Were lingering in the heavens, while the thrush
Began calm-throated. Throughout all the isle
There was no covert, no retired cave
Unhaunted by the murmurous noise of waves,   40
Though scarcely heard in many a green recess.
He listen'd, and he wept, and his bright tears
Went trickling down the golden bow he held.
Thus with half-shut suffused eyes he stood,
While from beneath some cumbrous boughs hard by
With solemn step an awful Goddess came,
And there was purport in her looks for him,
Which he with eager guess began to read
Perplex'd, the while melodiously he said:
"How cam'st thou over the unfooted sea?   50

Or hath that antique mien and robed form
Mov'd in these vales invisible till now?
Sure I have heard those vestments sweeping o'er
The fallen leaves, when I have sat alone
In cool mid-forest. Surely I have traced
The rustle of those ample skirts about
These grassy solitudes, and seen the flowers
Lift up their heads, as still the whisper pass'd.
Goddess! I have beheld those eyes before,
And their eternal calm, and all that face,   60
Or I have dream'd." — "Yes," said the supreme shape,
"Thou hast dream'd of me; and awaking up
Didst find a lyre all golden by thy side,
Whose strings touch'd by thy fingers, all the vast
Unwearied ear of the whole universe
Listen'd in pain and pleasure at the birth
Of such new tuneful wonder. Is't not strange
That thou shouldst weep, so gifted? Tell me, youth,
What sorrow thou canst feel; for I am sad
When thou dost shed a tear: explain thy griefs   70
To one who in this lonely isle hath been
The watcher of thy sleep and hours of life,
From the young day when first thy infant hand
Pluck'd witless the weak flowers, till thine arm
Could bend that bow heroic to all times.
Show thy heart's secret to an ancient Power
Who hath forsaken old and sacred thrones
For prophecies of thee, and for the sake
Of loveliness new born." — Apollo then,
With sudden scrutiny and gloomless eyes,   80
Thus answer'd, while his white melodious throat
Throbb'd with the syllables. — "Mnemosyne!
Thy name is on my tongue, I know not how;
Why should I tell thee what thou so well seest?
Why should I strive to show what from thy lips
Would come no mystery? For me, dark, dark,
And painful vile oblivion seals my eyes:
I strive to search wherefore I am so sad,
Until a melancholy numbs my limbs;
And then upon the grass I sit, and moan,   90
Like one who once had wings. — O why should I
Feel curs'd and thwarted, when the liegeless air
Yields to my step aspirant? why should I
Spurn the green turf as hateful to my feet?
Goddess benign, point forth some unknown thing:
Are there not other regions than this isle?

What are the stars? There is the sun, the sun!
And the most patient brilliance of the moon!
And stars by thousands! Point me out the way
To any one particular beauteous star,   100
And I will flit into it with my lyre,
And make its silvery splendour pant with bliss.
I have heard the cloudy thunder: Where is power?
Whose hand, whose essence, what divinity
Makes this alarum in the elements,
While I here idle listen on the shores
In fearless yet in aching ignorance?
O tell me, lonely Goddess, by thy harp,
That waileth every morn and eventide,
Tell me why thus I rave, about these groves!   110
Mute thou remainest — Mute! yet I can read
A wondrous lesson in thy silent face:
Knowledge enormous makes a God of me.
Names, deeds, gray legends, dire events, rebellions,
Majesties, sovran voices, agonies,
Creations and destroyings, all at once
Pour into the wide hollows of my brain,
And deify me, as if some blithe wine
Or bright elixir peerless I had drunk,
And so become immortal." — Thus the God,   120
While his enkindled eyes, with level glance
Beneath his white soft temples, stedfast kept
Trembling with light upon Mnemosyne.
Soon wild commotions shook him, and made flush
All the immortal fairness of his limbs;
Most like the struggle at the gate of death;
Or liker still to one who should take leave
Of pale immortal death, and with a pang
As hot as death's is chill, with fierce convulse
Die into life: so young Apollo anguish'd: 130
His very hair, his golden tresses famed
Kept undulation round his eager neck.
During the pain Mnemosyne upheld
Her arms as one who prophesied. — At length
Apollo shriek'd; — and lo! from all his limbs
Celestial   *   *   *   *   *   *

FANCY

EVER let the Fancy roam,
Pleasure never is at home:
At a touch sweet Pleasure melteth,
Like to bubbles when rain pelteth;
Then let winged Fancy wander
Through the thought still spread beyond her:
Open wide the mind's cage-door,
She'll dart forth, and cloudward soar.
O sweet Fancy! let her loose;
Summer's joys are spoilt by use,   10
And the enjoying of the Spring
Fades as does its blossoming;
Autumn's red-lipp'd fruitage too,
Blushing through the mist and dew,
Cloys with tasting: What do then?
Sit thee by the ingle, when
The sear faggot blazes bright,
Spirit of a winter's night;
When the soundless earth is muffled,
And the caked snow is shuffled   20
From the ploughboy's heavy shoon;
When the Night doth meet the Noon
In a dark conspiracy
To banish Even from her sky.
Sit thee there, and send abroad,
With a mind self-overaw'd,
Fancy, high-commission'd: — send her!
She has vassals to attend her:
She will bring, in spite of frost,
Beauties that the earth hath lost;   30
She will bring thee, all together,
All delights of summer weather;
All the buds and bells of May,
From dewy sward or thorny spray;
All the heaped Autumn's wealth,
With a still, mysterious stealth:
She will mix these pleasures up
Like three fit wines in a cup,
And thou shalt quaff it: — thou shalt hear
Distant harvest-carols clear;   40
Rustle of the reaped corn;
Sweet birds antheming the morn:

And, in the same moment — hark!
'Tis the early April lark,
Or the rooks, with busy caw,
Foraging for sticks and straw.
Thou shalt, at one glance, behold
The daisy and the marigold;
White-plum'd lilies, and the first
Hedge-grown primrose that hath burst;   50
Shaded hyacinth, alway
Sapphire queen of the mid-May;
And every leaf, and every flower
Pearled with the self-same shower.
Thou shalt see the field-mouse peep
Meagre from its celled sleep;
And the snake all winter-thin
Cast on sunny bank its skin;
Freckled nest-eggs thou shalt see
Hatching in the hawthorn-tree,   60
When the hen-bird's wing doth rest
Quiet on her mossy nest;
Then the hurry and alarm
When the bee-hive casts its swarm;
Acorns ripe down-pattering,
While the autumn breezes sing.

Oh, sweet Fancy! let her loose;
Every thing is spoilt by use:
Where's the cheek that doth not fade,
Too much gaz'd at? Where's the maid   70
Whose lip mature is ever new?
Where's the eye, however blue,
Doth not weary? Where's the face
One would meet in every place?
Where's the voice, however soft,
One would hear so very oft?
At a touch sweet Pleasure melteth
Like the bubbles when rain pelteth.
Let, then, winged Fancy find
Thee a mistress to thy mind: 80
Dulcet-eyed as Ceres' daughter,
Ere the God of Torment taught her
How to frown and how to chide;
With a waïst and with a side
White as Hebe's, when her zone
Slipt its golden clasp, and down
Fell her kirtle to her feet,

While she held the goblet sweet,
And Jove grew languid. — Break the mesh
Of the Fancy's silken leash;   90
Quickly break her prison-string
And such joys as these she'll bring. —
Let the winged Fancy roam,
Pleasure never is at home.

ODE
["BARDS OF PASSION"]

BARDS of Passion and of Mirth,
Ye have left your souls on earth!
Have ye souls in heaven too,
Double-lived in regions new?
Yes, and those of heaven commune
With the spheres of sun and moon;
With the noise of fountains wond'rous,
And the parle of voices thund'rous;
With the whisper of heaven's trees
And one another, in soft ease   10
Seated on Elysian lawns
Brows'd by none but Dian's fawns;
Underneath large blue-bells tented,
Where the daisies are rose-scented,
And the rose herself has got
Perfume which on earth is not;
Where the nightingale doth sing
Not a senseless, tranced thing,
But divine melodious truth;
Philosophic numbers smooth;   20
Tales and golden histories
Of heaven and its mysteries.

Thus ye live on high, and then
On the earth ye live again;
And the souls ye left behind you
Teach us, here, the way to find you,
Where your other souls are joying,
Never slumber'd, never cloying.
Here, your earth-born souls still speak
To mortals, of their little week;   30
Of their sorrows and delights;
Of their passions and their spites;
Of their glory and their shame;
What doth strengthen and what maim.

Thus ye teach us, every day,
Wisdom, though fled far away.

Bards of Passion and of Mirth,
Ye have left your souls on earth!
Ye have souls in heaven too,
Double-lived in regions new!   40

THE EVE OF ST. AGNES

I.

St. Agnes' Eve — Ah, bitter chill it was!
The owl, for all his feathers, was a-cold;
The hare limp'd trembling through the frozen grass,
And silent was the flock in woolly fold:
Numb were the Beadsman's fingers, while he told
His rosary, and while his frosted breath,
Like pious incense from a censer old,
Seem'd taking flight for heaven, without a death,
Past the sweet Virgin's picture, while his prayer he saith.

II.

His prayer he saith, this patient, holy man;   10
Then takes his lamp, and riseth from his knees,
And back returneth, meagre, barefoot, wan,
Along the chapel aisle by slow degrees:
The sculptur'd dead, on each side, seem to freeze,
Emprison'd in black, purgatorial rails:
Knights, ladies, praying in dumb orat'ries,
He passeth by; and his weak spirit fails
To think how they may ache in icy hoods and mails.

III.

Northward he turneth through a little door,
And scarce three steps, ere Music's golden tongue   20
Flatter'd to tears this aged man and poor;
But no — already had his deathbell rung:
The joys of all his life were said and sung:
His was harsh penance on St. Agnes' Eve:
Another way he went, and soon among
Rough ashes sat he for his soul's reprieve,
And all night kept awake, for sinners' sake to grieve.

IV.

That ancient Beadsman heard the prelude soft;
And so it chanc'd, for many a door was wide,
From hurry to and fro. Soon, up aloft,   30
The silver, snarling trumpets 'gan to chide:
The level chambers, ready with their pride,
Were glowing to receive a thousand guests:
The carved angels, ever eager-eyed,
Star'd, where upon their heads the cornice rests,
With hair blown back, and wings put cross-wise on their breasts.

V.

At length burst in the argent revelry,
With plume, tiara, and all rich array,
Numerous as shadows haunting fairily
The brain, new stuff'd, in youth, with triumphs gay   40
Of old romance. These let us wish away,
And turn, sole-thoughted, to one Lady there,
Whose heart had brooded, all that wintry day,
On love, and wing'd St. Agnes' saintly care,
As she had heard old dames full many times declare.

VI.

They told her how, upon St. Agnes' Eve,
Young virgins might have visions of delight,
And soft adorings from their loves receive
Upon the honey'd middle of the night,
If ceremonies due they did aright;   50
As, supperless to bed they must retire,
And couch supine their beauties, lily white;
Nor look behind, nor sideways, but require
Of Heaven with upward eyes for all that they desire.

VII.

Full of this whim was thoughtful Madeline:
The music, yearning like a God in pain,
She scarcely heard: her maiden eyes divine,
Fix'd on the floor, saw many a sweeping train
Pass by — she heeded not at all: in vain
Came many a tiptoe, amorous cavalier,   60
And back retir'd; not cool'd by high disdain,
But she saw not: her heart was otherwhere:
She sigh'd for Agnes' dreams, the sweetest of the year.

VIII.

She danc'd along with vague, regardless eyes,
Anxious her lips, her breathing quick and short:
The hallow'd hour was near at hand: she sighs
Amid the timbrels, and the throng'd resort
Of whisperers in anger, or in sport;
'Mid looks of love, defiance, hate, and scorn,
Hoodwink'd with faery fancy; all amort,
Save to St. Agnes and her lambs unshorn,
And all the bliss to be before to-morrow morn.

70

IX.

So, purposing each moment to retire,
She linger'd still. Meantime, across the moors,
Had come young Porphyro, with heart on fire
For Madeline. Beside the portal doors,
Buttress'd from moonlight, stands he, and implores
All saints to give him sight of Madeline,
But for one moment in the tedious hours,
That he might gaze and worship all unseen;
Perchance speak, kneel, touch, kiss — in sooth such things have
been.

X.

He ventures in: let no buzz'd whisper tell:
All eyes be muffled, or a hundred swords
Will storm his heart, Love's fev'rous citadel:
For him, those chambers held barbarian hordes,
Hyena foemen, and hot-blooded lords,
Whose very dogs would execrations howl
Against his lineage: not one breast affords
Him any mercy, in that mansion foul,
Save one old beldame, weak in body and in soul.

90

XI.

Ah, happy chance! the aged creature came,
Shuffling along with ivory-headed wand,
To where he stood, hid from the torch's flame,
Behind a broad hall-pillar, far beyond
The sound of merriment and chorus bland:
He startled her; but soon she knew his face,
And grasp'd his fingers in her palsied hand,

Saying, "Mercy, Porphyro! hie thee from this place;
They are all here to-night, the whole blood-thirsty race!

XII.

"Get hence! get hence! there's dwarfish Hildebrand;   100
He had a fever late, and in the fit
He cursed thee and thine, both house and land:
Then there's that old Lord Maurice, not a whit
More tame for his gray hairs — Alas me! flit!
Flit like a ghost away." — "Ah, Gossip dear,
We're safe enough; here in this arm-chair sit,
And tell me how" — "Good Saints! not here, not here;
Follow me, child, or else these stones will be thy bier."

XIII.

He follow'd through a lowly arched way,
Brushing the cobwebs with his lofty plume,   110
And as she mutter'd "Well-a — well-a-day!"
He found him in a little moonlight room,
Pale, lattic'd, chill, and silent as a tomb.
"Now tell me where is Madeline," said he,
"O tell me, Angela, by the holy loom
Which none but secret sisterhood may see,
When they St. Agnes' wool are weaving piously."

XIV.

"St. Agnes! Ah! it is St. Agnes' Eve —
Yet men will murder upon holy days:
Thou must hold water in a witch's sieve,   120
And be liege-lord of all the Elves and Fays,
To venture so: it fills me with amaze
To see thee, Porphyro! — St. Agnes' Eve!
God's help! my lady fair the conjuror plays
This very night: good angels her deceive!
But let me laugh awhile, I've mickle time to grieve."

XV.

Feebly she laugheth in the languid moon,
While Porphyro upon her face doth look,
Like puzzled urchin on an aged crone
Who keepeth clos'd a wond'rous riddle-book,   130
As spectacled she sits in chimney nook.

But soon his eyes grew brilliant, when she told
His lady's purpose; and he scarce could brook
Tears, at the thought of those enchantments cold
And Madeline asleep in lap of legends old.

XVI.

Sudden a thought came like a full-blown rose,
Flushing his brow, and in his pained heart
Made purple riot: then doth he propose
A stratagem, that makes the beldame start:
"A cruel man and impious thou art: 140
Sweet lady, let her pray, and sleep, and dream
Alone with her good angels, far apart
From wicked men like thee. Go, go! — I deem
Thou canst not surely be the same that thou didst seem."

XVII.

"I will not harm her, by all saints I swear,"
Quoth Porphyro: "O may I ne'er find grace
When my weak voice shall whisper its last prayer,
If one of her soft ringlets I displace,
Or look with ruffian passion in her face:
Good Angela, believe me by these tears;   150
Or I will, even in a moment's space,
Awake, with horrid shout, my foemen's ears,
And beard them, though they be more fang'd than wolves and bears."

XVIII.

"Ah! why wilt thou affright a feeble soul?
A poor, weak, palsy-stricken, churchyard thing,
Whose passing-bell may ere the midnight toll;
Whose prayers for thee, each morn and evening,
Were never miss'd." — Thus plaining, doth she bring
A gentler speech from burning Porphyro;
So woful, and of such deep sorrowing,   160
That Angela gives promise she will do
Whatever he shall wish, betide her weal or woe.

XIX.

Which was, to lead him, in close secrecy,
Even to Madeline's chamber, and there hide

Him in a closet, of such privacy
That he might see her beauty unespied,
And win perhaps that night a peerless bride,
While legion'd fairies pac'd the coverlet,
And pale enchantment held her sleepy-eyed.
Never on such a night have lovers met,   170
Since Merlin paid his Demon all the monstrous debt.

xx.

"It shall be as thou wishest," said the Dame:
"All cates and dainties shall be stored there
Quickly on this feast-night: by the tambour frame
Her own lute thou wilt see: no time to spare,
For I am slow and feeble, and scarce dare
On such a catering trust my dizzy head.
Wait here, my child, with patience; kneel in prayer
The while: Ah! thou must needs the lady wed,
Or may I never leave my grave among the dead."   180

xxi.

So saying, she hobbled off with busy fear.
The lover's endless minutes slowly pass'd:
The dame return'd, and whisper'd in his ear
To follow her; with aged eyes aghast
From fright of dim espial. Safe at last,
Through many a dusky gallery, they gain
The maiden's chamber, silken, hush'd, and chaste;
Where Porphyro took covert, pleas'd amain.
His poor guide hurried back with agues in her brain.

xxii.

Her falt'ring hand upon the balustrade,   190
Old Angela was feeling for the stair,
When Madeline, St. Agnes' charmed maid,
Rose, like a mission'd spirit, unaware:
With silver taper's light, and pious care,
She turn'd, and down the aged gossip led
To a safe level matting. Now prepare,
Young Porphyro, for gazing on that bed;
She comes, she comes again, like ring-dove fray'd and fled.

xxiii.

Out went the taper as she hurried in;
Its little smoke, in pallid moonshine, died: 200

She clos'd the door, she panted, all akin
To spirits of the air, and visions wide:
No uttered syllable, or, woe betide!
But to her heart, her heart was voluble,
Paining with eloquence her balmy side;
As though a tongueless nightingale should swell
Her throat in vain, and die, heart-stifled, in her dell.

xxiv.

A casement high and triple-arch'd there was,
All garlanded with carven imag'ries
Of fruits, and flowers, and bunches of knot-grass,   210
And diamonded with panes of quaint device,
Innumerable of stains and splendid dyes,
As are the tiger-moth's deep-damask'd wings;
And in the midst, 'mong thousand heraldries,
And twilight saints, and dim emblazonings,
A shielded scutcheon blush'd with blood of queens and kings.

xxv.

Full on this casement shone the wintry moon,
And threw warm gules on Madeline's fair breast,
As down she knelt for heaven's grace and boon;
Rose-bloom fell on her hands, together prest,   220
And on her silver cross soft amethyst,
And on her hair a glory, like a saint:
She seem'd a splendid angel, newly drest,
Save wings, for heaven: — Porphyro grew faint:
She knelt, so pure a thing, so free from mortal taint

xxvi.

Anon his heart revives: her vespers done,
Of all its wreathed pearls her hair she frees;
Unclasps her warmed jewels one by one;
Loosens her fragrant boddice; by degrees
Her rich attire creeps rustling to her knees: 230
Half-hidden, like a mermaid in sea-weed,
Pensive awhile she dreams awake, and sees,
In fancy, fair St. Agnes in her bed,
But dares not look behind, or all the charm is fled.

xxvii.

Soon, trembling in her soft and chilly nest,
In sort of wakeful swoon, perplex'd she lay,

Until the poppied warmth of sleep oppress'd
Her soothed limbs, and soul fatigued away;
Flown, like a thought, until the morrow-day;
Blissfully haven'd both from joy and pain;   240
Clasp'd like a missal where swart Paynims pray;
Blinded alike from sunshine and from rain,
As though a rose should shut, and be a bud again.

XXVIII.

Stol'n to this paradise, and so entranced,
Porphyro gazed upon her empty dress,
And listen'd to her breathing, if it chanced
To wake into a slumberous tenderness;
Which when he heard, that minute did he bless,
And breath'd himself: then from the closet crept,
Noiseless as fear in a wide wilderness,   250
And over the hush'd carpet, silent, stept,
And 'tween the curtains peep'd, where, lo! — how fast she slept.

XXIX.

Then by the bed-side, where the faded moon
Made a dim, silver twilight, soft he set
A table, and, half anguish'd, threw thereon
A cloth of woven crimson, gold, and jet: —
O for some drowsy Morphean amulet!
The boisterous, midnight, festive clarion,
The kettle-drum, and far-heard clarinet,
Affray his ears, though but in dying tone: —   260
The hall door shuts again, and all the noise is gone.

XXX.

And still she slept an azure-lidded sleep,
In blanched linen, smooth, and lavender'd,
While he from forth the closet brought a heap
Of candied apple, quince, and plum, and gourd;
With jellies soother than the creamy curd,
And lucent syrops, tinct with cinnamon;
Manna and dates, in argosy transferr'd
From Fez; and spiced dainties, every one,
From silken Samarcand to cedar'd Lebanon.   270

XXXI.

These delicates he heap'd with glowing hand
On golden dishes and in baskets bright

Of wreathed silver: sumptuous they stand
In the retired quiet of the night,
Filling the chilly room with perfume light. —
"And now, my love, my seraph fair, awake!
Thou art my heaven, and I thine eremite:
Open thine eyes, for meek St. Agnes' sake,
Or I shall drowse beside thee, so my soul doth ache."

XXXII.

Thus whispering, his warm, unnerved arm   280
Sank in her pillow, Shaded was her dream
By the dusk curtains: — 'twas a midnight charm
Impossible to melt as iced stream:
The lustrous salvers in the moonlight gleam;
Broad golden fringe upon the carpet lies:
It seem'd he never, never could redeem
From such a stedfast spell his lady's eyes;
So mus'd awhile, entoil'd in woofed phantasies.

XXXIII.

Awakening up, he took her hollow lute, —
Tumultuous, — and, in chords that tenderest be.   290
He play'd an ancient ditty, long since mute,
In Provence call'd, "La belle dame sans mercy:"
Close to her ear touching the melody; —
Wherewith disturb'd, she utter'd a soft moan:
He ceased — she panted quick — and suddenly
Her blue affrayed eyes wide open shone:
Upon his knees he sank, pale as smooth-sculptured stone.

XXXIV.

Her eyes were open, but she still beheld,
Now wide awake, the vision of her sleep:
There was a painful change, that nigh expell'd   300
The blisses of her dream so pure and deep,
At which fair Madeline began to weep,
And moan forth witless words with many a sigh;
While still her gaze on Porphyro would keep;
Who knelt, with joined hands and piteous eye,
Fearing to move or speak, she look'd so dreamingly.

XXXV.

"Ah, Porphyro!" said she, "but even now
Thy voice was at sweet tremble in mine ear,

Made tuneable with every sweetest vow;
And those sad eyes were spiritual and clear: 310
How chang'd thou art! how pallid, chill, and drear!
Give me that voice again, my Porphyro,
Those looks immortal, those complainings dear!
    Oh leave me not in this eternal woe,
For if thou diest, my Love, I know not where to go."

XXXVI.

Beyond a mortal man impassion'd far
At these voluptuous accents, he arose,
Ethereal, flush'd, and like a throbbing star
Seen mid the sapphire heaven's deep repose;
Into her dream he melted, as the rose 320
Blendeth its odour with the violet, —
Solution sweet: meantime the frost-wind blows
    Like Love's alarum pattering the sharp sleet
Against the window-panes; St. Agnes' moon hath set.

XXXVII.

'Tis dark: quick pattereth the flaw-blown sleet:
"This is no dream, my bride, my Madeline!"
'Tis dark: the iced gusts still rave and beat:
"No dream, alas! alas! and woe is mine!
Porphyro will leave me here to fade and pine. —
Cruel! what traitor could thee hither bring? 330
I curse not, for my heart is lost in thine,
    Though thou forsakest a deceived thing; —
A dove forlorn and lost with sick unpruned wing."

XXXVIII.

"My Madeline! sweet dreamer! lovely bride!
Say, may I be for aye thy vassal blest?
Thy beauty's shield, heart-shap'd and vermeil dyed?
Ah, silver shrine, here will I take my rest
After so many hours of toil and quest,
A famish'd pilgrim, — saved by miracle.
Though I have found, I will not rob thy nest 340
Saving of thy sweet self; if thou think'st well
    To trust, fair Madeline, to no rude infidel.

XXXIX.

"Hark! 'tis an elfin-storm from faery land,
Of haggard seeming, but a boon indeed:

Arise — arise! the morning is at hand; —
The bloated wassaillers will never heed: —
Let us away, my love, with happy speed;
There are no ears to hear, or eyes to see, —
Drown'd all in Rhenish and the sleepy mead:
Awake! arise! my love, and fearless be,   350
For o'er the southern moors I have a home for thee."

XL.

She hurried at his words, beset with fears,
For there were sleeping dragons all around,
At glaring watch, perhaps, with ready spears —
Down the wide stairs a darkling way they found. —
In all the house was heard no human sound.
A chain-droop'd lamp was flickering by each door;
The arras, rich with horseman, hawk, and hound,
Flutter'd in the besieging wind's uproar;
And the long carpets rose along the gusty floor.   360

XLI.

They glide, like phantoms, into the wide hall;
Like phantoms, to the iron porch, they glide;
Where lay the Porter, in uneasy sprawl,
With a huge empty flaggon by his side:
The wakeful bloodhound rose, and shook his hide,
But his sagacious eye an inmate owns:
By one, and one, the bolts full easy slide: —
The chains lie silent on the footworn stones; —
The key turns, and the door upon its hinges groans.

XLII.

And they are gone: ay, ages long ago   370
These lovers fled away into the storm.
That night the Baron dreamt of many a woe,
And all his warrior-guests, with shade and form
Of witch, and demon, and large coffin-worm,
Were long be-nightmar'd. Angela the old
Died palsy-twitch'd, with meagre face deform;
The Beadsman, after thousand aves told,
For aye unsought for slept among his ashes cold.

THE EVE OF SAINT MARK

Upon a Sabbath-day it fell;
Twice holy was the Sabbath-bell,
That call'd the folk to evening prayer;
The city streets were clean and fair
From wholesome drench of April rains;
And, on the western window-panes,
The chilly sunset faintly told
Of unmatur'd green vallies cold,
Of the green thorny bloomless hedge,
Of rivers new with spring-tide sedge,   10
Of primroses by shelter'd rills,
And daisies on the aguish hills.
Twice holy was the Sabbath-bell:
The silent streets were crowded well
With staid and pious companies,
Warm from their fire-side orat'ries;
And moving, with demurest air,
To even-song, and vesper prayer.
Each arched porch, and entry low,
Was fill'd with patient folk and slow,   20
With whispers hush, and shuffling feet,
While play'd the organ loud and sweet.

The bells had ceased, the prayers begun,
And Bertha had not yet half done
A curious volume, patch'd and torn,
That all day long, from earliest morn,
Had taken captive her two eyes,
Among its golden broideries;
Perplex'd her with a thousand things, —
The stars of Heaven, and angels' wings,   30
Martyrs in a fiery blaze,
Azure saints in silver rays,
Aaron's breastplate, and the seven
Candlesticks John saw in Heaven,
The winged Lion of Saint Mark,
And the Covenantal Ark,
With its many mysteries,
Cherubim and golden mice.

Bertha was a maiden fair,
Dwelling in th' old Minster-square;   40

From her fire-side she could see,
Sidelong, its rich antiquity,
Far as the Bishop's garden-wall;
Where sycamores and elm-trees tall,
Full-leav'd, the forest had outstript,
By no sharp north-wind ever nipt,
So shelter'd by the mighty pile.
Bertha arose, and read awhile,
With forehead 'gainst the window-pane.
Again she tried, and then again,   50
Until the dusk eve left her dark
Upon the legend of St. Mark.
From plaited lawn-frill, fine and thin,
She lifted up her soft warm chin,
With aching neck and swimming eyes,
And daz'd with saintly imageries.

All was gloom, and silent all,
Save now and then the still foot-fall
Of one returning homewards late,
Past the echoing minster-gate.   60
The clamorous daws, that all the day
Above tree-tops and towers play,
Pair by pair had gone to rest,
Each in its ancient belfry-nest,
Where asleep they fall betimes,
To music of the drowsy chimes.

All was silent, all was gloom,
Abroad and in the homely room;
Down she sat, poor cheated soul!
And struck a lamp from the dismal coal;   70
Leaned forward, with bright drooping hair
And slant book, full against the glare.
Her shadow, in uneasy guise,
Hover'd about, a giant size,
On ceiling-beam and old oak chair,
The parrot's cage, and panel square;
And the warm angled winter screen,
On which were many monsters seen,
Call'd doves of Siam, Lima mice,
And legless birds of Paradise,   80
Macaw, and tender Av'davat,
And silken-furr'd Angora cat.
Untir'd she read, her shadow still
Glower'd about, as it would fill

The room with wildest forms and shades,
As though some ghostly queen of spades
Had come to mock behind her back,
And dance, and ruffle her garments black.
Untir'd she read the legend page,
Of holy Mark, from youth to age,   90
On land, on sea, in pagan chains,
Rejoicing for his many pains.
Sometimes the learned eremite,
With golden star, or dagger bright,
Referr'd to pious poesies
Written in smallest crow-quill size
Beneath the text; and thus the rhyme
Was parcell'd out from time to time:
—— "Als writith he of swevenis,
Men han beforne they wake in bliss,   100
Whanne that hir friendes thinke hem bound
In crimped shroude farre under grounde:
And how a litling child mote be
A saint er its nativitie,
Gif that the modre (God her blesse!)
Kepen in solitarinesse,
And kissen devoute the holy croce.
Of Goddes love, and Sathan's force, —
He writith; and thinges many mo:
Of swiche thinges I may not show.   110
Bot I must tellen verilie
Somdel of Saintè Cicilie,
And chieflie what he auctorethe
Of Saintè Markis life and dethe:"

At length her constant eyelids come
Upon the fervent martyrdom;
Then lastly to his holy shrine,
Exalt amid the tapers' shine
At Venice, — [1]

---

[1] The following lines, which Keats did not incorporate in the unfinished poem, are commented upon in the note attached to the introduction below.

> Gif ye wol standen hardie wight —
> Amiddes of the blacke night —
> Righte in the churchè porch, pardie
> Ye wol behold a companie
> Approchen thee full dolourouse
> For sooth to sain from everich house
> Be it in City or village
> Wol come the Phantom and image

Of ilka gent and ilka carle
Whom coldè Deathè hath in parle   10
And wol some day that very year
Touchen with foulè venime spear
And sadly do them all to die —
Hem all shalt thou see verilie —
And everichon shall by thee pass
All who must die that year Alas.

BRIGHT STAR [1]

BRIGHT star, would I were steadfast as thou art —
  Not in lone splendour hung aloft the night
And watching, with eternal lids apart,
  Like nature's patient, sleepless Eremite,
The moving waters at their priestlike task
  Of pure ablution round earth's human shores,
Or gazing on the new soft fallen mask
  Of snow upon the mountains and the moors —
No — yet still steadfast, still unchangeable,
  Pillow'd upon my fair love's ripening breast,   10
To feel for ever its soft fall and swell,
  Awake for ever in a sweet unrest,
Still, still to hear her tender-taken breath,
And so live ever — or else swoon to death.

WHY DID I LAUGH TO-NIGHT?

WHY did I laugh to-night? No voice will tell:
  No God, no Demon of severe response,
Deigns to reply from Heaven or from Hell.

---

[1] The following is the original version of this sonnet (see the notes):

Bright Star! would I were steadfast as thou art!
  Not in lone splendour hung amid the night;
Not watching, with eternal lids apart,
  Like Nature's devout sleepless Eremite,
The morning waters at their priestlike task
  Of pure ablution round earth's human shores;
Or, gazing on the new soft fallen mask
  Of snow upon the mountains and the moors: —
No; — yet still steadfast, still unchangeable,
  Cheek-pillow'd on my Love's white ripening breast,   10
To touch, for ever, its warm sink and swell,
  Awake, for ever, in a sweet unrest;
To hear, to feel her tender-taken breath,
  Half passionless, and so swoon on to death.

Then to my human heart I turn at once.
Heart! Thou and I are here sad and alone;
  I say, why did I laugh? O mortal pain!
O Darkness! Darkness! ever must I moan,
  To question Heaven and Hell and Heart in vain.
Why did I laugh? I know this Being's lease,
  My fancy to its utmost blisses spreads;   10
Yet would I on this very midnight cease,
  And the world's gaudy ensigns see in shreds;
Verse, Fame, and Beauty are intense indeed,
But Death intenser — Death is Life's high meed.

ON A DREAM

As HERMES once took to his feathers light,
  When lulled Argus, baffled, swoon'd and slept,
So on a Delphic reed, my idle spright
  So play'd, so charm'd, so conquer'd, so bereft
The dragon-world of all its hundred eyes;
  And seeing it asleep, so fled away,
Not to pure Ida with its snow-cold skies,
  Nor unto Tempe, where Jove griev'd a day;
But to that second circle of sad Hell,
  Where in the gust, the whirlwind, and the flaw   10
Of rain and hail-stones, lovers need not tell
  Their sorrows — pale were the sweet lips I saw,
Pale were the lips I kiss'd, and fair the form
I floated with, about that melancholy storm.

LA BELLE DAME SANS MERCI

(ORIGINAL VERSION)

O WHAT can ail thee, knight-at-arms,
  Alone and palely loitering?
The sedge has wither'd from the lake,
  And no birds sing.

O what can ail thee, knight-at-arms,
  So haggard, and so woe-begone?
The squirrel's granary is full,
  And the harvest's done.

I see a lily on thy brow,
  With anguish moist and fever dew,   10

And on thy cheeks a fading rose
  Fast withereth too.

I met a lady in the meads,
  Full beautiful — a faery's child,
Her hair was long, her foot was light,
  And her eyes were wild.

I made a garland for her head,
  And bracelets too, and fragrant zone;
She look'd at me as she did love,
  And made sweet moan.   20

I set her on my pacing steed,
  And nothing else saw all day long,
For sidelong would she bend and sing
  A faery's song.

She found me roots of relish sweet,
  And honey wild, and manna dew,
And sure in language strange she said
  "I love thee true."

She took me to her elfin grot,
  And there she wept and sigh'd full sore,   30
And there I shut her wild wild eyes
  With kisses four.

And there she lulled me asleep,
  And there I dream'd — Ah! woe betide!
The latest dream I ever dream'd
  On the cold hill side.

I saw pale kings and princes too,
  Pale warriors, death-pale were they all;
They cried, "La Belle Dame sans Merci
  Hath thee in thrall!"   40

I saw their starved lips in the gloam,
  With horrid warning gaped wide,
And I awoke, and found me here,
  On the cold hill's side.

And this is why I sojourn here,
  Alone and palely loitering,
Though the sedge is wither'd from the lake,
  And no birds sing.

LA BELLE DAME SANS MERCI

(REVISED VERSION)

AH, WHAT can ail thee, wretched wight,
   Alone and palely loitering;
The sedge is wither'd from the lake,
   And no birds sing.

Ah, what can ail thee, wretched wight,
   So haggard and so woe-begone?
The squirrel's granary is full,
   And the harvest's done.

I see a lily on thy brow,
   With anguish moist and fever dew;   **10**
And on thy cheek a fading rose
   Fast withereth too.

I met a lady in the meads
   Full beautiful, a fairy's child;
Her hair was long, her foot was light,
   And her eyes were wild.

I set her on my pacing steed,
   And nothing else saw all day long;
For sideways would she lean, and sing
   A fairy's song.   **20**

I made a garland for her head,
   And bracelets too, and fragrant zone:
She look'd at me as she did love,
   And made sweet moan.

She found me roots of relish sweet,
   And honey wild, and manna dew;
And sure in language strange she said,
   "I love thee true."

She took me to her elfin grot,
   And there she gaz'd and sighed deep,   **30**
And there I shut her wild sad eyes —
   So kiss'd to sleep.

And there we slumber'd on the moss,
    And there I dream'd, ah woe betide,
The latest dream I ever dream'd
    On the cold hill side.

I saw pale kings, and princes too,
    Pale warriors, death-pale were they all;
Who cry'd — "La belle Dame sans mercy
    Hath thee in thrall!"   **40**

I saw their starv'd lips in the gloom
    With horrid warning gaped wide,
And I awoke, and found me here
    On the cold hill side.

And this is why I sojourn here
    Alone and palely loitering,
Though the sedge is wither'd from the lake,
    And no birds sing.

TO SLEEP

O soft embalmer of the still midnight,
    Shutting, with careful fingers and benign,
Our gloom-pleased eyes, embower'd from the light,
    Enshaded in forgetfulness divine;
O soothest Sleep! if so it please thee, close,
    In midst of this thine hymn, my willing eyes,
Or wait the amen, ere thy poppy throws
    Around my bed its lulling charities;
Then save me, or the passed day will shine
Upon my pillow, breeding many woes;   **10**
    Save me from curious conscience, that still lords
Its strength for darkness, burrowing like a mole;
    Turn the key deftly in the oiled wards,
And seal the hushed casket of my soul.

ON FAME

II

"You cannot eat your cake and have it too." — *Proverb*

How fever'd is the man, who cannot look
    Upon his mortal days with temperate blood,

Who vexes all the leaves of his life's book,
    And robs his fair name of its maidenhood;
It is as if the rose should pluck herself,
    Or the ripe plum finger its misty bloom,
As if a Naiad, like a meddling elf,
    Should darken her pure grot with muddy gloom;
But the rose leaves herself upon the briar,
    For winds to kiss and grateful bees to feed,   10
And the ripe plum still wears its dim attire;
      The undisturbed lake has crystal space;
      Why then should man, teasing the world for grace,
Spoil his salvation for a fierce miscreed?

ON THE SONNET

IF BY dull rhymes our English must be chain'd,
    And, like Andromeda, the Sonnet sweet
Fetter'd, in spite of pained loveliness;
Let us find out, if we must be constrain'd,
    Sandals more interwoven and complete
To fit the naked foot of poesy;
Let us inspect the lyre, and weigh the stress
Of every chord, and see what may be gain'd
    By ear industrious, and attention meet;
Misers of sound and syllable, no less   10
Than Midas of his coinage, let us be
    Jealous of dead leaves in the bay-wreath crown;
So, if we may not let the Muse be free,
    She will be bound with garlands of her own.

ODE TO PSYCHE

O GODDESS! hear these tuneless numbers, wrung
    By sweet enforcement and remembrance dear,
And pardon that thy secrets should be sung
    Even into thine own soft-conched ear:
Surely I dreamt to-day, or did I see
    The winged Psyche with awaken'd eyes?
I wander'd in a forest thoughtlessly,
    And, on the sudden, fainting with surprise,
Saw two fair creatures, couched side by side
    In deepest grass, beneath the whisp'ring roof   10
    Of leaves and trembled blossoms, where there ran
      A brooklet, scarce espied:

'Mid hush'd, cool-rooted flowers, fragrant-eyed,
    Blue, silver-white, and budded Tyrian,
They lay calm-breathing on the bedded grass;
    Their arms embraced, and their pinions too;
    Their lips touch'd not, but had not bade adieu,
As if disjoined by soft-handed slumber,
And ready still past kisses to outnumber
    At tender eye-dawn of aurorean love: 20
        The winged boy I knew;
    But who wast thou, O happy, happy dove?
        His Psyche true!

O latest born and loveliest vision far
    Of all Olympus' faded hierarchy!
Fairer than Phœbe's sapphire-region'd star,
    Or Vesper, amorous glow-worm of the sky;
Fairer than these, though temple thou hast none,
      Nor altar heap'd with flowers;
Nor virgin-choir to make delicious moan   30
      Upon the midnight hours;
No voice, no lute, no pipe, no incense sweet
    From chain-swung censer teeming;
No shrine, no grove, no oracle, no heat
    Of pale-mouth'd prophet dreaming.

O brightest! though too late for antique vows,
    Too, too late for the fond believing lyre,
When holy were the haunted forest boughs,
    Holy the air, the water, and the fire;
Yet even in these days so far retir'd   40
    From happy pieties, thy lucent fans,
    Fluttering among the faint Olympians,
I see, and sing, by my own eyes inspired.
So let me be thy choir, and make a moan
      Upon the midnight hours;
Thy voice, thy lute, thy pipe, thy incense sweet
    From swinged censer teeming;
Thy shrine, thy grove, thy oracle, thy heat
    Of pale-mouth'd prophet dreaming.

Yes, I will be thy priest, and build a fane   50
    In some untrodden region of my mind,
Where branched thoughts, new grown with pleasant pain,
    Instead of pines shall murmur in the wind:
Far, far around shall those dark-cluster'd trees
    Fledge the wild-ridged mountains steep by steep;

And there by zephyrs, streams, and birds, and bees,
   The moss-lain Dryads shall be lull'd to sleep;
And in the midst of this wide quietness
A rosy sanctuary will I dress
With the wreath'd trellis of a working brain,   60
   With buds, and bells, and stars without a name,
With all the gardener Fancy e'er could feign,
   Who breeding flowers, will never breed the same:
And there shall be for thee all soft delight
   That shadowy thought can win,
A bright torch, and a casement ope at night,
   To let the warm Love in!

ODE TO A NIGHTINGALE — *source of loss and pain*

I.

MY HEART aches, and a drowsy numbness pains
   My sense, as though of hemlock I had drunk,
Or emptied some dull opiate to the drains
   One minute past, and Lethe-wards had sunk:
'Tis not through envy of thy happy lot,
   But being too happy in thine happiness, —
      That thou, light-winged Dryad of the trees,
        In some melodious plot
Of beechen green, and shadows numberless,
      Singest of summer in full-throated ease.   10

II.

O, for a draught of vintage! that hath been
   Cool'd a long age in the deep-delved earth,
Tasting of Flora and the country green,
   Dance, and Provençal song, and sunburnt mirth!
O for a beaker full of the warm South,
   Full of the true, the blushful Hippocrene,
      With beaded bubbles winking at the brim,
        And purple-stained mouth;
That I might drink, and leave the world unseen,
      And with thee fade away into the forest dim: 20

III.

Fade far away, dissolve, and quite forget
   What thou among the leaves hast never known,

The weariness, the fever, and the fret
  Here, where men sit and hear each other groan;
Where palsy shakes a few, sad, last gray hairs,
  Where youth grows pale, and spectre-thin, and dies;
    Where but to think is to be full of sorrow
      And leaden-eyed despairs,
Where Beauty cannot keep her lustrous eyes,
  Or new Love pine at them beyond to-morrow.   30

IV.

Away! away! for I will fly to thee,
  Not charioted by Bacchus and his pards,
But on the viewless wings of Poesy, —poetry
  Though the dull brain perplexes and retards:
Already with thee! tender is the night,
  And haply the Queen-Moon is on her throne,
    Cluster'd around by all her starry Fays;
      But here there is no light,
Save what from heaven is with the breezes blown
  Through verdurous glooms and winding mossy ways.   40

V.

I cannot see what flowers are at my feet,
  Nor what soft incense hangs upon the boughs,
But, in embalmed darkness, guess each sweet
  Wherewith the seasonable month endows
The grass, the thicket, and the fruit-tree wild;
  White hawthorn, and the pastoral eglantine;
    Fast fading violets cover'd up in leaves;
      And mid-May's eldest child,
The coming musk-rose, full of dewy wine,
  The murmurous haunt of flies on summer eves.   50

VI.

Darkling I listen; and, for many a time
  I have been half in love with easeful Death,
Call'd him soft names in many a mused rhyme,
  To take into the air my quiet breath;
Now more than ever seems it rich to die,
  To cease upon the midnight with no pain,
    While thou art pouring forth thy soul abroad
      In such an ecstasy!
Still wouldst thou sing, and I have ears in vain —
  To thy high requiem become a sod.   60

VII.

Thou wast not born for death, immortal Bird!
  No hungry generations tread thee down;
The voice I hear this passing night was heard
  In ancient days by emperor and clown:
Perhaps the self-same song that found a path
    Through the sad heart of Ruth, when, sick for home,
      She stood in tears amid the alien corn;
        The same that oft-times hath
Charm'd magic casements, opening on the foam
    Of perilous seas, in faery lands forlorn.   70

VIII.

Forlorn! the very word is like a bell
  To toll me back from thee to my sole self!
Adieu! the fancy cannot cheat so well
  As she is fam'd to do, deceiving elf.
Adieu! adieu! thy plaintive anthem fades
    Past the near meadows, over the still stream,
      Up the hill-side; and now 'tis buried deep
        In the next valley-glades:
Was it a vision, or a waking dream?
  Fled is that music: — Do I wake or sleep?   80

ODE ON A GRECIAN URN

I.

Thou still unravish'd bride of quietness,
  Thou foster-child of silence and slow time,
Sylvan historian, who canst thus express
  A flowery tale more sweetly than our rhyme:
What leaf-fring'd legend haunts about thy shape
  Of deities or mortals, or of both,
    In Tempe or the dales of Arcady?
  What men or gods are these? What maidens loth?
What mad pursuit? What struggle to escape?
    What pipes and timbrels? What wild ecstasy?   10

II.

Heard melodies are sweet, but those unheard
  Are sweeter; therefore, ye soft pipes, play on;

Not to the sensual ear, but, more endear'd,
  Pipe to the spirit ditties of no tone:
Fair youth, beneath the trees, thou canst not leave
  Thy song, nor ever can those trees be bare;
    Bold Lover, never, never canst thou kiss,
Though winning near the goal — yet, do not grieve;
  She cannot fade, though thou hast not thy bliss,
    For ever wilt thou love, and she be fair!   20

III.

Ah, happy, happy boughs! that cannot shed
  Your leaves, nor ever bid the Spring adieu;
And, happy melodist, unwearied,
  For ever piping songs for ever new;
More happy love! more happy, happy love!
  For ever warm and still to be enjoy'd,
    For ever panting, and for ever young;
All breathing human passion far above,
  That leaves a heart high-sorrowful and cloy'd,
    A burning forehead, and a parching tongue.   30

IV.

Who are these coming to the sacrifice?
  To what green altar, O mysterious priest,
Lead'st thou that heifer lowing at the skies,
  And all her silken flanks with garlands drest?
What little town by river or sea shore,
  Or mountain-built with peaceful citadel,
    Is emptied of this folk, this pious morn?
And, little town, thy streets for evermore
  Will silent be; and not a soul to tell
    Why thou art desolate, can e'er return.   40

V.

O Attic shape! Fair attitude! with brede
  Of marble men and maidens overwrought,
With forest branches and the trodden weed;
  Thou, silent form, dost tease us out of thought
As doth eternity: Cold Pastoral!
  When old age shall this generation waste,
    Thou shalt remain, in midst of other woe
Than ours, a friend to man, to whom thou say'st,
  "Beauty is truth, truth beauty, — that is all
    Ye know on earth, and all ye need to know."   50

ODE ON MELANCHOLY[1]

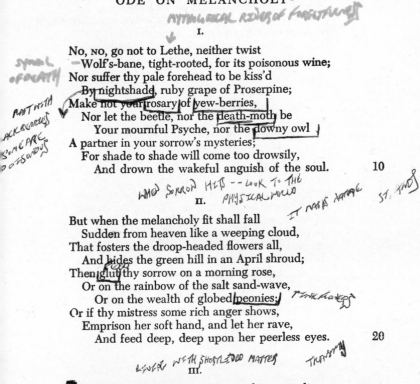

I.

No, NO, go not to Lethe, neither twist
 Wolf's-bane, tight-rooted, for its poisonous **wine**;
Nor suffer thy pale forehead to be kiss'd
 By nightshade, ruby grape of Proserpine;
Make not your rosary of yew-berries,
 Nor let the beetle, nor the death-moth be
 Your mournful Psyche, nor the downy owl
A partner in your sorrow's mysteries;
 For shade to shade will come too drowsily,
 And drown the wakeful anguish of the soul. 10

II.

But when the melancholy fit shall fall
 Sudden from heaven like a weeping cloud,
That fosters the droop-headed flowers all,
 And hides the green hill in an April shroud;
Then glut thy sorrow on a morning rose,
 Or on the rainbow of the salt sand-wave,
 Or on the wealth of globed peonies;
Or if thy mistress some rich anger shows,
 Emprison her soft hand, and let her rave,
 And feed deep, deep upon her peerless eyes. 20

III.

She dwells with Beauty — Beauty that must die;
 And Joy, whose hand is ever at his lips
Bidding adieu; and aching Pleasure nigh,

---

[1] The ode originally opened with the following stanza, which Keats later
cancelled:

> Though you should build a bark of dead men's bones,
> And rear a phantom gibbet for a mast,
> Stitch creeds together for a sail, with groans
> To fill it out, blood-stained and aghast;
> Although your rudder be a dragon's tail
> Long sever'd, yet still hard with agony,
> Your cordage large uprootings from the skull
> Of bald Medusa, certes you would fail
> To find the Melancholy — whether she
> Dreameth in any isle of Lethe dull. 10

Turning to poison while the bee-mouth sips:
Ay, in the very temple of Delight
   Veil'd Melancholy has her sovran shrine,
      Though seen of none save him whose strenuous tongue
Can burst Joy's grape against his palate fine;
   His soul shall taste the sadness of her might,
      And be among her cloudy trophies hung.   30

ODE ON INDOLENCE

"They toil not, neither do they spin."

I.

ONE morn before me were three figures seen,
   With bowed necks, and joined hands, side-faced;
And one behind the other stepp'd serene,
   In placid sandals, and in white robes graced;
They pass'd, like figures on a marble urn,
   When shifted round to see the other side;
      They came again; as when the urn once more
Is shifted round, the first seen shades return;
   And they were strange to me, as may betide
      With vases, to one deep in Phidian lore.   10

II.

How is it, Shadows! that I knew ye not?
   How came ye muffled in so hush a mask?
Was it a silent deep-disguised plot
   To steal away, and leave without a task
My idle days? Ripe was the drowsy hour;
   The blissful cloud of summer-indolence
      Benumb'd my eyes; my pulse grew less and less;
Pain had no sting, and pleasure's wreath no flower:
   O, why did ye not melt, and leave my sense
      Unhaunted quite of all but — nothingness?   20

III.

A third time came they by; — alas! wherefore?
   My sleep had been embroider'd with dim dreams;
My soul had been a lawn besprinkled o'er
   With flowers, and stirring shades, and baffled beams:

The morn was clouded, but no shower fell,
   Tho' in her lids hung the sweet tears of May;
     The open casement press'd a new-leav'd vine,
Let in the budding warmth and throstle's lay;
   O Shadows! 'twas a time to bid farewell!
     Upon your skirts had fallen no tears of mine.   30

IV.

A third time pass'd they by, and, passing, turn'd
   Each one the face a moment whiles to me;
Then faded, and to follow them I burn'd
   And ached for wings because I knew the three;
The first was a fair Maid, and Love her name;
   The second was Ambition, pale of cheek,
     And ever watchful with fatigued eye;
The last, whom I love more, the more of blame
   Is heap'd upon her, maiden most unmeek, —
     I knew to be my demon Poesy.   40

V.

They faded, and, forsooth! I wanted wings:
   O folly! What is Love! and where is it?
And for that poor Ambition! it springs
   From a man's little heart's short fever-fit;
For Poesy! — no, — she has not a joy, —
   At least for me, — so sweet as drowsy noons,
     And evenings steep'd in honied indolence;
O, for an age so shelter'd from annoy,
   That I may never know how change the moons,
     Or hear the voice of busy common-sense!   50

VI.

So, ye three Ghosts, adieu! Ye cannot raise
   My head cool-bedded in the flowery grass;
For I would not be dieted with praise,
   A pet-lamb in a sentimental farce!
Fade softly from my eyes, and be once more
   In masque-like figures on the dreamy urn;
     Farewell! I yet have visions for the night,
And for the day faint visions there is store;
   Vanish, ye Phantoms! from my idle spright,
     Into the clouds, and never more return!   60

LAMIA

PART I

U<small>PON</small> a time, before the faery broods
Drove Nymph and Satyr from the prosperous woods,
Before King Oberon's bright diadem,
Sceptre, and mantle, clasp'd with dewy gem,
Frighted away the Dryads and the Fauns
From rushes green, and brakes, and cowslip'd lawns,
The ever-smitten Hermes empty left
His golden throne, bent warm on amorous theft:
From high Olympus had he stolen light,
On this side of Jove's clouds, to escape the sight   10
Of his great summoner, and made retreat
Into a forest on the shores of Crete.
For somewhere in that sacred island dwelt
A nymph, to whom all hoofed Satyrs knelt;
At whose white feet the languid Tritons poured
Pearls, while on land they wither'd and adored.
Fast by the springs where she to bathe was wont,
And in those meads where sometime she might haunt,
Were strewn rich gifts, unknown to any Muse,
Though Fancy's casket were unlock'd to choose.   20
Ah, what a world of love was at her feet!
So Hermes thought, and a celestial heat
Burnt from his winged heels to either ear,
That from a whiteness, as the lily clear,
Blush'd into roses 'mid his golden hair,
Fallen in jealous curls about his shoulders bare.
From vale to vale, from wood to wood, he flew,
Breathing upon the flowers his passion new,
And wound with many a river to its head,
To find where this sweet nymph prepar'd her secret bed: 30
In vain; the sweet nymph might nowhere be found,
And so he rested, on the lonely ground,
Pensive, and full of painful jealousies
Of the Wood-Gods, and even the very trees.
There as he stood, he heard a mournful voice,
Such as once heard, in gentle heart, destroys
All pain but pity: thus the lone voice spake:
"When from this wreathed tomb shall I awake!
When move in a sweet body fit for life,
And love, and pleasure, and the ruddy strife   40

Of hearts and lips! Ah, miserable me!"
The God, dove-footed, glided silently
Round bush and tree, soft-brushing, in his speed,
The taller grasses and full-flowering weed,
Until he found a palpitating snake,
Bright, and cirque-couchant in a dusky brake.

She was a gordian shape of dazzling hue,
Vermilion-spotted, golden, green, and blue;
Striped like a zebra, freckled like a pard,
Eyed like a peacock, and all crimson barr'd;   50
And full of silver moons, that, as she breathed,
Dissolv'd, or brighter shone, or interwreathed
Their lustres with the gloomier tapestries —
So rainbow-sided, touch'd with miseries,
She seem'd, at once, some penanced lady elf,
Some demon's mistress, or the demon's self.
Upon her crest she wore a wannish fire
Sprinkled with stars, like Ariadne's tiar:
Her head was serpent, but ah, bitter-sweet!
She had a woman's mouth with all its pearls complete: 60
And for her eyes: what could such eyes do there
But weep, and weep, that they were born so fair?
As Proserpine still weeps for her Sicilian air.
Her throat was serpent, but the words she spake
Came, as through bubbling honey, for Love's sake,
And thus; while Hermes on his pinions lay,
Like a stoop'd falcon ere he takes his prey.

"Fair Hermes, crown'd with feathers, fluttering light,
I had a splendid dream of thee last night:
I saw thee sitting, on a throne of gold,   70
Among the Gods, upon Olympus old,
The only sad one; for thou didst not hear
The soft, lute-finger'd Muses chaunting clear,
Nor even Apollo when he sang alone,
Deaf to his throbbing throat's long, long melodious moan.
I dreamt I saw thee, robed in purple flakes,
Break amorous through the clouds, as morning breaks,
And, swiftly as a bright Phœbean dart,
Strike for the Cretan isle; and here thou art!
Too gentle Hermes, hast thou found the maid?"   80
Whereat the star of Lethe not delay'd
His rosy eloquence, and thus inquired:
"Thou smooth-lipp'd serpent, surely high inspired!
Thou beauteous wreath, with melancholy eyes,

Possess whatever bliss thou canst devise,
Telling me only where my nymph is fled, —
Where she doth breathe!" "Bright planet, thou hast said,"
Return'd the snake, "but seal with oaths, fair God!"
"I swear," said Hermes, "by my serpent rod,
And by thine eyes, and by thy starry crown!"   90
Light flew his earnest words, among the blossoms blown.
Then thus again the brilliance feminine:
"Too frail of heart! for this lost nymph of thine,
Free as the air, invisibly, she strays
About these thornless wilds; her pleasant days
She tastes unseen; unseen her nimble feet
Leave traces in the grass and flowers sweet;
From weary tendrils, and bow'd branches green,
She plucks the fruit unseen, she bathes unseen:
And by my power is her beauty veil'd   100
To keep it unaffronted, unassail'd
By the love-glances of unlovely eyes,
Of Satyrs, Fauns, and blear'd Silenus' sighs.
Pale grew her immortality, for woe
Of all these lovers, and she grieved so
I took compassion on her, bade her steep
Her hair in weïrd syrops, that would keep
Her loveliness invisible, yet free
To wander as she loves, in liberty.
Thou shalt behold her, Hermes, thou alone,   110
If thou wilt, as thou swearest, grant my boon!"
Then, once again, the charmed God began
An oath, and through the serpent's ears it ran
Warm, tremulous, devout, psalterian.
Ravish'd, she lifted her Circean head,
Blush'd a live damask, and swift-lisping said,
"I was a woman, let me have once more
A woman's shape, and charming as before.
I love a youth of Corinth — O the bliss!
Give me my woman's form, and place me where he is.   120
Stoop, Hermes, let me breathe upon thy brow,
And thou shalt see thy sweet nymph even now."
The God on half-shut feathers sank serene,
She breath'd upon his eyes, and swift was seen
Of both the guarded nymph near-smiling on the green.
It was no dream; or say a dream it was,
Real are the dreams of Gods, and smoothly pass
Their pleasures in a long immortal dream.
One warm, flush'd moment, hovering, it might seem
Dash'd by the wood-nymph's beauty, so he burn'd;   130

Then, lighting on the printless verdure, turn'd
To the swoon'd serpent, and with languid arm,
Delicate, put to proof the lythe Caducean charm.
So done, upon the nymph his eyes he bent
Full of adoring tears and blandishment,
And towards her stept: she, like a moon in wane,
Faded before him, cower'd, nor could restrain
Her fearful sobs, self-folding like a flower
That faints into itself at evening hour:
But the God fostering her chilled hand,   140
She felt the warmth, her eyelids open'd bland,
And, like new flowers at morning song of bees,
Bloom'd, and gave up her honey to the lees.
Into the green-recessed woods they flew;
Nor grew they pale, as mortal lovers do.

    Left to herself, the serpent now began
To change; her elfin blood in madness ran,
Her mouth foam'd, and the grass, therewith besprent,
Wither'd at dew so sweet and virulent;
Her eyes in torture fix'd, and anguish drear,   150
Hot, glaz'd, and wide, with lid-lashes all sear,
Flash'd phosphor and sharp sparks, without one cooling tear.
The colours all inflam'd throughout her train,
She writh'd about, convuls'd with scarlet pain:
A deep volcanian yellow took the place
Of all her milder-mooned body's grace;
And, as the lava ravishes the mead,
Spoilt all her silver mail, and golden brede;
Made gloom of all her frecklings, streaks and bars,
Eclips'd her crescents, and lick'd up her stars: 160
So that, in moments few, she was undrest
Of all her sapphires, greens, and amethyst,
And rubious-argent: of all these bereft,
Nothing but pain and ugliness were left.
Still shone her crown; that vanish'd, also she
Melted and disappear'd as suddenly;
And in the air, her new voice luting soft,
Cried, "Lycius! gentle Lycius!" — Borne aloft
With the bright mists about the mountains hoar
These words dissolv'd: Crete's forests heard no more.   170

    Whither fled Lamia, now a lady bright,
A full-born beauty new and exquisite?
She fled into that valley they pass o'er
Who go to Corinth from Cenchreas' shore;

And rested at the foot of those wild hills,
The rugged founts of the Peræan rills,
And of that other ridge whose barren back
Stretches, with all its mist and cloudy rack,
South-westward to Cleone. There she stood
About a young bird's flutter from a wood,   180
Fair, on a sloping green of mossy tread,
By a clear pool, wherein she passioned
To see herself escap'd from so sore ills,
While her robes flaunted with the daffodils.

    Ah, happy Lycius! — for she was a maid
More beautiful than ever twisted braid,
Or sigh'd, or blush'd, or on spring-flowered lea
Spread a green kirtle to the minstrelsy:
A virgin purest lipp'd, yet in the lore
Of love deep learned to the red heart's core: 190
Not one hour old, yet of sciential brain
To unperplex bliss from its neighbour pain;
Define their pettish limits, and estrange
Their points of contact, and swift counterchange;
Intrigue with the specious chaos, and dispart
Its most ambiguous atoms with sure art;
As though in Cupid's college she had spent
Sweet days a lovely graduate, still unshent,
And kept his rosy terms in idle languishment.

    Why this fair creature chose so fairily   200
By the wayside to linger, we shall see;
But first 'tis fit to tell how she could muse
And dream, when in the serpent prison-house,
Of all she list, strange or magnificent:
How, ever, where she will'd, her spirit went;
Whether to faint Elysium, or where
Down through tress-lifting waves the Nereids fair
Wind into Thetis' bower by many a pearly stair;
Or where God Bacchus drains his cups divine,
Stretch'd out, at ease, beneath a glutinous pine; 210
Or where in Pluto's gardens palatine
Mulciber's columns gleam in far piazzian line.
And sometimes into cities she would send
Her dream, with feast and rioting to blend;
And once, while among mortals dreaming thus,
She saw the young Corinthian Lycius
Charioting foremost in the envious race,
Like a young Jove with calm uneager face,

And fell into a swooning love of him.
Now on the moth-time of that evening dim   220
He would return that way, as well she knew,
To Corinth from the shore; for freshly blew
The eastern soft wind, and his galley now
Grated the quaystones with her brazen prow
In port Cenchreas, from Egina isle
Fresh anchor'd; whither he had been awhile
To sacrifice to Jove, whose temple there
Waits with high marble doors for blood and incense rare.
Jove heard his vows, and better'd his desire;
For by some freakful chance he made retire   230
From his companions, and set forth to walk,
Perhaps grown wearied of their Corinth talk:
Over the solitary hills he fared,
Thoughtless at first, but ere eve's star appeared
His phantasy was lost, where reason fades,
In the calm'd twilight of Platonic shades.
Lamia beheld him coming, near, more near —
Close to her passing, in indifference drear,
His silent sandals swept the mossy green;
So neighbour'd to him, and yet so unseen   240
She stood: he pass'd, shut up in mysteries,
His mind wrapp'd like his mantle, while her eyes
Follow'd his steps, and her neck regal white
Turn'd — syllabling thus, "Ah, Lycius bright,
And will you leave me on the hills alone?
Lycius, look back! and be some pity shown."
He did; not with cold wonder fearingly,
But Orpheus-like at an Eurydice;
For so delicious were the words she sung,
It seem'd he had lov'd them a whole summer long: 250
And soon his eyes had drunk her beauty up,
Leaving no drop in the bewildering cup,
And still the cup was full, — while he, afraid
Lest she should vanish ere his lip had paid
Due adoration, thus began to adore;
Her soft look growing coy, she saw his chain so sure:
"Leave thee alone! Look back! Ah, Goddess, see
Whether my eyes can ever turn from thee!
For pity do not this sad heart belie —
Even as thou vanishest so I shall die.   260
Stay! though a Naiad of the rivers, stay!
To thy far wishes will thy streams obey:
Stay! though the greenest woods be thy domain,
Alone they can drink up the morning rain:

Though a descended Pleiad, will not one
Of thine harmonious sisters keep in tune
Thy spheres, and as thy silver proxy shine?
So sweetly to these ravish'd ears of mine
Came thy sweet greeting, that if thou shouldst fade
Thy memory will waste me to a shade: —   270
For pity do not melt!" — "If I should stay,"
Said Lamia, "here, upon this floor of clay,
And pain my steps upon these flowers too rough,
What canst thou say or do of charm enough
To dull the nice remembrance of my home?
Thou canst not ask me with thee here to roam
Over these hills and vales, where no joy is, —
Empty of immortality and bliss!
Thou art a scholar, Lycius, and must know
That finer spirits cannot breathe below   280
In human climes, and live: Alas! poor youth,
What taste of purer air hast thou to soothe
My essence? What serener palaces,
Where I may all my many senses please,
And by mysterious sleights a hundred thirsts appease?
It cannot be — Adieu!" So said, she rose
Tiptoe with white arms spread. He, sick to lose
The amorous promise of her lone complain,
Swoon'd, murmuring of love, and pale with pain.
The cruel lady, without any show   290
Of sorrow for her tender favourite's woe,
But rather, if her eyes could brighter be,
With brighter eyes and slow amenity,
Put her new lips to his, and gave afresh
The life she had so tangled in her mesh:
And as he from one trance was wakening
Into another, she began to sing,
Happy in beauty, life, and love, and every thing,
A song of love, too sweet for earthly lyres,
While, like held breath, the stars drew in their panting fires. 300
And then she whisper'd in such trembling tone,
As those who, safe together met alone
For the first time through many anguish'd days,
Use other speech than looks; bidding him raise
His drooping head, and clear his soul of doubt,
For that she was a woman, and without
Any more subtle fluid in her veins
Than throbbing blood, and that the self-same pains
Inhabited her frail-strung heart as his.
And next she wonder'd how his eyes could miss   310

Her face so long in Corinth, where, she said,
She dwelt but half retir'd, and there had led
Days happy as the gold coin could invent
Without the aid of love; yet in content
Till she saw him, as once she pass'd him by,
Where 'gainst a column he leant thoughtfully
At Venus' temple porch, 'mid baskets heap'd
Of amorous herbs and flowers, newly reap'd
Late on that eve, as 'twas the night before
The Adonian feast; whereof she saw no more,   320
But wept alone those days, for why should she adore?
Lycius from death awoke into amaze,
To see her still, and singing so sweet lays;
Then from amaze into delight he fell
To hear her whisper woman's lore so well;
And every word she spake entic'd him on
To unperplex'd delight and pleasure known.
Let the mad poets say whate'er they please
Of the sweets of Fairies, Peris, Goddesses,
There is not such a treat among them all,   330
Haunters of cavern, lake, and waterfall,
As a real woman, lineal indeed
From Pyrrha's pebbles or old Adam's seed.
Thus gentle Lamia judg'd, and judg'd aright,
That Lycius could not love in half a fright,
So threw the goddess off, and won his heart
More pleasantly by playing woman's part,
With no more awe than what her beauty gave,
That, while it smote, still guaranteed to save.
Lycius to all made eloquent reply,   340
Marrying to every word a twinborn sigh;
And last, pointing to Corinth, ask'd her sweet,
If 'twas too far that night for her soft feet.
The way was short, for Lamia's eagerness
Made, by a spell, the triple league decrease
To a few paces; not at all surmised
By blinded Lycius, so in her comprized.
They pass'd the city gates, he knew not how,
So noiseless, and he never thought to know.

As men talk in a dream, so Corinth all,   350
Throughout her palaces imperial,
And all her populous streets and temples lewd,
Mutter'd, like tempest in the distance brew'd,
To the wide-spreaded night above her towers.
Men, women, rich and poor, in the cool hours,

Shuffled their sandals o'er the pavement white,
Companion'd or alone; while many a light
Flared, here and there, from wealthy festivals,
And threw their moving shadows on the walls,
Or found them cluster'd in the corniced shade   360
Of some arch'd temple door, or dusky colonnade.

Muffling his face, of greeting friends in fear,
Her fingers he press'd hard, as one came near
With curl'd gray beard, sharp eyes, and smooth bald crown,
Slow-stepp'd, and robed in philosophic gown:
Lycius shrank closer, as they met and past,
Into his mantle, adding wings to haste,
While hurried Lamia trembled: "Ah," said he,
"Why do you shudder, love, so ruefully?
Why does your tender palm dissolve in dew?"   370
"I'm wearied," said fair Lamia: "tell me who
Is that old man? I cannot bring to mind
His features: — Lycius! wherefore did you blind
Yourself from his quick eyes?" Lycius replied,
" 'Tis Apollonius sage, my trusty guide
And good instructor; but to-night he seems
The ghost of folly haunting my sweet dreams."

While yet he spake they had arrived before
A pillar'd porch, with lofty portal door,
Where hung a silver lamp, whose phosphor glow   380
Reflected in the slabbed steps below,
Mild as a star in water; for so new,
And so unsullied was the marble hue,
So through the crystal polish, liquid fine,
Ran the dark veins, that none but feet divine
Could e'er have touch'd there. Sounds Æolian
Breath'd from the hinges, as the ample span
Of the wide doors disclos'd a place unknown
Some time to any, but those two alone,
And a few Persian mutes, who that same year   390
Were seen about the markets: none knew where
They could inhabit; the most curious
Were foil'd, who watch'd to trace them to their house:
And but the flitter-winged verse must tell,
For truth's sake, what woe afterwards befel,
'Twould humour many a heart to leave them thus,
Shut from the busy world of more incredulous.

PART II

Love in a hut, with water and a crust,
Is — Love, forgive us! — cinders, ashes, dust;
Love in a palace is perhaps at last
More grievous torment than a hermit's fast: —
That is a doubtful tale from faery land,
Hard for the non-elect to understand.
Had Lycius liv'd to hand his story down,
He might have given the moral a fresh frown,
Or clench'd it quite: but too short was their bliss
To breed distrust and hate, that make the soft voice hiss.   10
Besides, there, nightly, with terrific glare,
Love, jealous grown of so complete a pair,
Hover'd and buzz'd his wings, with fearful roar,
Above the lintel of their chamber door,
And down the passage cast a glow upon the floor.

    For all this came a ruin: side by side
They were enthroned, in the even tide,
Upon a couch, near to a curtaining
Whose airy texture, from a golden string,
Floated into the room, and let appear   20
Unveil'd the summer heaven, blue and clear,
Betwixt two marble shafts: — there they reposed,
Where use had made it sweet, with eyelids closed,
Saving a tythe which love still open kept,
That they might see each other while they almost slept;
When from the slope side of a suburb hill,
Deafening the swallow's twitter, came a thrill
Of trumpets — Lycius started — the sounds fled,
But left a thought, a buzzing in his head.
For the first time, since first he harbour'd in   30
That purple-lined palace of sweet sin,
His spirit pass'd beyond its golden bourn
Into the noisy world almost forsworn.
The lady, ever watchful, penetrant,
Saw this with pain, so arguing a want
Of something more, more than her empery
Of joys; and she began to moan and sigh
Because he mused beyond her, knowing well
That but a moment's thought is passion's passing bell.
"Why do you sigh, fair creature?" whisper'd he: 40
"Why do you think?" return'd she tenderly:

"You have deserted me; — where am I now?
Not in your heart while care weighs on your brow:
No, no, you have dismiss'd me; and I go
From your breast houseless: ay, it must be so."
He answer'd, bending to her open eyes,
Where he was mirror'd small in paradise,
"My silver planet, both of eve and morn!
Why will you plead yourself so sad forlorn,
While I am striving how to fill my heart   50
With deeper crimson, and a double smart?
How to entangle, trammel up and snare
Your soul in mine, and labyrinth you there
Like the hid scent in an unbudded rose?
Ay, a sweet kiss — you see your mighty woes.
My thoughts! shall I unveil them? Listen then!
What mortal hath a prize, that other men
May be confounded and abash'd withal,
But lets it sometimes pace abroad majestical,
And triumph, as in thee I should rejoice   60
Amid the hoarse alarm of Corinth's voice.
Let my foes choke, and my friends shout afar,
While through the thronged streets your bridal car
Wheels round its dazzling spokes." — The lady's cheek
Trembled; she nothing said, but, pale and meek,
Arose and knelt before him, wept a rain
Of sorrows at his words; at last with pain
Beseeching him, the while his hand she wrung,
To change his purpose. He thereat was stung,
Perverse, with stronger fancy to reclaim   70
Her wild and timid nature to his aim:
Besides, for all his love, in self despite,
Against his better self, he took delight
Luxurious in her sorrows, soft and new.
His passion, cruel grown, took on a hue
Fierce and sanguineous as 'twas possible
In one whose brow had no dark veins to swell.
Fine was the mitigated fury, like
Apollo's presence when in act to strike
The serpent — Ha, the serpent! certes, she   80
Was none. She burnt, she lov'd the tyranny,
And, all subdued, consented to the hour
When to the bridal he should lead his paramour.
Whispering in midnight silence, said the youth,
"Sure some sweet name thou hast, though, by my truth,
I have not ask'd it, ever thinking thee
Not mortal, but of heavenly progeny,

As still I do. Hast any mortal name,
Fit appellation for this dazzling frame?
Or friends or kinsfolk on the citied earth,   90
To share our marriage feast and nuptial mirth?"
"I have no friends," said Lamia, "no, not one;
My presence in wide Corinth hardly known:
My parents' bones are in their dusty urns
Sepulchred, where no kindled incense burns,
Seeing all their luckless race are dead, save me,
And I neglect the holy rite for thee.
Even as you list invite your many guests;
But if, as now it seems, your vision rests
With any pleasure on me, do not bid   100
Old Apollonius — from him keep me hid."
Lycius, perplex'd at words so blind and blank,
Made close inquiry; from whose touch she shrank,
Feigning a sleep; and he to the dull shade
Of deep sleep in a moment was betray'd.

It was the custom then to bring away
The bride from home at blushing shut of day,
Veiled, in a chariot, heralded along
By strewn flowers, torches, and a marriage song,
With other pageants: but this fair unknown   110
Had not a friend. So being left alone,
(Lycius was gone to summon all his kin)
And knowing surely she could never win
His foolish heart from its mad pompousness,
She set herself, high-thoughted, how to dress
The misery in fit magnificence.
She did so, but 'tis doubtful how and whence
Came, and who were her subtle servitors.
About the halls, and to and from the doors,
There was a noise of wings, till in short space   120
The glowing banquet-room shone with wide-arched grace.
A haunting music, sole perhaps and lone
Supportress of the faery-roof, made moan
Throughout, as fearful the whole charm might fade.
Fresh carved cedar, mimicking a glade
Of palm and plantain, met from either side,
High in the midst, in honour of the bride:
Two palms and then two plantains, and so on,
From either side their stems branch'd one to one
All down the aisled place; and beneath all   130
There ran a stream of lamps straight on from wall to wall.
So canopied, lay an untasted feast

Teeming with odours. Lamia, regal drest,
Silently paced about, and as she went,
In pale contented sort of discontent,
Mission'd her viewless servants to enrich
The fretted splendour of each nook and niche.
Between the tree-stems, marbled plain at first,
Came jasper pannels; then, anon, there burst
Forth creeping imagery of slighter trees,   140
And with the larger wove in small intricacies.
Approving all, she faded at self-will,
And shut the chamber up, close, hush'd and still,
Complete and ready for the revels rude,
When dreadful guests would come to spoil her solitude.

    The day appear'd, and all the gossip rout.
O senseless Lycius! Madman! wherefore flout
The silent-blessing fate, warm cloister'd hours,
And show to common eyes these secret bowers?
The herd approach'd; each guest, with busy brain,   150
Arriving at the portal, gaz'd amain,
And enter'd marveling: for they knew the street,
Remember'd it from childhood all complete
Without a gap, yet ne'er before had seen
That royal porch, that high-built fair demesne;
So in they hurried all, maz'd, curious and keen:
Save one, who look'd thereon with eye severe,
And with calm-planted steps walk'd in austere;
'Twas Apollonius: something too he laugh'd,
As though some knotty problem, that had daft   160
His patient thought, had now begun to thaw,
And solve and melt: — 'twas just as he foresaw.

    He met within the murmurous vestibule
His young disciple. " 'Tis no common rule,
Lycius," said he, "for uninvited guest
To force himself upon you, and infest
With an unbidden presence the bright throng
Of younger friends; yet must I do this wrong,
And you forgive me." Lycius blush'd, and led
The old man through the inner doors broad-spread;   170
With reconciling words and courteous mien
Turning into sweet milk the sophist's spleen.

    Of wealthy lustre was the banquet-room,
Fill'd with pervading brilliance and perfume:
Before each lucid pannel fuming stood

A censer fed with myrrh and spiced wood,
Each by a sacred tripod held aloft,
Whose slender feet wide-swerv'd upon the soft
Wool-woofed carpets: fifty wreaths of smoke
From fifty censers their light voyage took   180
To the high roof, still mimick'd as they rose
Along the mirror'd walls by twin-clouds odorous.
Twelve sphered tables, by silk seats insphered,
High as the level of a man's breast rear'd
On libbard's paws, upheld the heavy gold
Of cups and goblets, and the store thrice told
Of Ceres' horn, and, in huge vessels, wine
Come from the gloomy tun with merry shine.
Thus loaded with a feast the tables stood,
Each shrining in the midst the image of a God.   190

When in an antechamber every guest
Had felt the cold full sponge to pleasure press'd,
By minist'ring slaves, upon his hands and feet,
And fragrant oils with ceremony meet
Pour'd on his hair, they all mov'd to the feast
In white robes, and themselves in order placed
Around the silken couches, wondering
Whence all this mighty cost and blaze of wealth could spring.

Soft went the music the soft air along,
While fluent Greek a vowel'd undersong   200
Kept up among the guests, discoursing low
At first, for scarcely was the wine at flow;
But when the happy vintage touchd' their brains,
Louder they talk, and louder come the strains
Of powerful instruments: — the gorgeous dyes,
The space, the splendour of the draperies,
The roof of awful richness, nectarous cheer,
Beautiful slaves, and Lamia's self, appear,
Now, when the wine has done its rosy deed,
And every soul from human trammels freed,   210
No more so strange; for merry wine, sweet wine,
Will make Elysian shades not too fair, too divine.
Soon was God Bacchus at meridian height;
Flush'd were their cheeks, and bright eyes double bright:
Garlands of every green, and every scent
From vales deflower'd, or forest-trees branch-rent,
In baskets of bright osier'd gold were brought
High as the handles heap'd, to suit the thought
Of every guest; that each, as he did please,

Might fancy-fit his brows, silk-pillow'd at his ease.   220
    What wreath for Lamia? What for Lycius?
What for the sage, old Apollonius?
Upon her aching forehead be there hung
The leaves of willow and of adder's tongue;
And for the youth, quick, let us strip for him
The thyrsus, that his watching eyes may swim
Into forgetfulness; and, for the sage,
Let spear-grass and the spiteful thistle wage
War on his temples. Do not all charms fly
At the mere touch of cold philosophy?   230
There was an awful rainbow once in heaven:
We know her woof, her texture; she is given
In the dull catalogue of common things.
Philosophy will clip an Angel's wings,
Conquer all mysteries by rule and line,
Empty the haunted air, and gnomed mine —
Unweave a rainbow, as it erewhile made
The tender-person'd Lamia melt into a shade.

    By her glad Lycius sitting, in chief place,
Scarce saw in all the room another face,   240
Till, checking his love trance, a cup he took
Full brimm'd, and opposite sent forth a look
'Cross the broad table, to beseech a glance
From his old teacher's wrinkled countenance,
And pledge him. The bald-head philosopher
Had fix'd his eye, without a twinkle or stir
Full on the alarmed beauty of the bride,
Brow-beating her fair form, and troubling her sweet pride.
Lycius then press'd her hand, with devout touch,
As pale it lay upon the rosy couch: 250
'Twas icy, and the cold ran through his veins;
Then sudden it grew hot, and all the pains
Of an unnatural heat shot to his heart.
"Lamia, what means this? Wherefore dost thou start?
Know'st thou that man?" Poor Lamia answer'd not.
He gaz'd into her eyes, and not a jot
Own'd they the lovelorn piteous appeal:
More, more he gaz'd: his human senses reel:
Some hungry spell that loveliness absorbs;
There was no recognition in those orbs.   260
"Lamia!" he cried — and no soft-toned reply.
The many heard, and the loud revelry
Grew hush; the stately music no more breathes;

The myrtle sicken'd in a thousand wreaths.
By faint degrees, voice, lute, and pleasure ceased;
A deadly silence step by step increased,
Until it seem'd a horrid presence there,
And not a man but felt the terror in his hair.
"Lamia!" he shriek'd; and nothing but the shriek
With its sad echo did the silence break.   270
"Begone, foul dream!" he cried, gazing again
In the bride's face, where now no azure vein
Wander'd on fair-spaced temples; no soft bloom
Misted the cheek; no passion to illume
The deep-recessed vision: — all was blight;
Lamia, no longer fair, there sat a deadly white.
"Shut, shut those juggling eyes, thou ruthless man!
Turn them aside, wretch! or the righteous ban
Of all the Gods, whose dreadful images
Here represent their shadowy presences,   280
May pierce them on the sudden with the thorn
Of painful blindness; leaving thee forlorn,
In trembling dotage to the feeblest fright
Of conscience, for their long offended might,
For all thine impious proud-heart sophistries,
Unlawful magic, and enticing lies.
Corinthians! look upon that gray-beard wretch!
Mark how, possess'd, his lashless eyelids stretch
Around his demon eyes! Corinthians, see!
My sweet bride withers at their potency."   290
"Fool!" said the sophist, in an under-tone
Gruff with contempt; which a death-nighing moan
From Lycius answer'd, as heart-struck and lost,
He sank supine beside the aching ghost.
"Fool! Fool!" repeated he, while his eyes still
Relented not, nor mov'd; "from every ill
Of life have I preserv'd thee to this day,
And shall I see thee made a serpent's prey?"
Then Lamia breath'd death breath; the sophist's eye,
Like a sharp spear, went through her utterly,   300
Keen, cruel, perceant, stinging: she, as well
As her weak hand could any meaning tell,
Motion'd him to be silent; vainly so,
He look'd and look'd again a level — No!
"A Serpent!" echoed he; no sooner said,
Than with a frightful scream she vanished:
And Lycius' arms were empty of delight,
As were his limbs of life, from that same night.
On the high couch he lay! — his friends came round —

Supported him — no pulse, or breath they found,   310
And, in its marriage robe, the heavy body wound.[1]

[1] "Philostratus, in his fourth book *de Vita Apollonii*, hath a memorable instance in this kind, which I may not omit, of one Menippus Lycius, a young man twenty-five years of age, that going betwixt Cenchreas and Corinth, met such a phantasm in the habit of a fair gentlewoman, which taking him by the hand, carried him home to her house, in the suburbs of Corinth, and told him she was a Phœnician by birth, and if he would tarry with her, he should hear her sing and play, and drink such wine as never any drank, and no man should molest him; but she, being fair and lovely, would live and die with him, that was fair and lovely to behold. The young man, a philosopher, otherwise staid and discreet, able to moderate his passions, though not this of love, tarried with her a while to his great content, and at last married her, to whose wedding, amongst other guests, came Apollonius; who, by some probable conjectures, found her out to be a serpent, a lamia; and that all her furniture was, like Tantalus' gold, described by Homer, no substance but mere illusions. When she saw herself descried, she wept, and desired Apollonius to be silent, but he would not be moved, and thereupon she, plate, house, and all that was in it, vanished in an instant: many thousands took notice of this fact, for it was done in the midst of Greece."

Burton's "Anatomy of Melancholy," Part 3. Sect. 2.
Memb. 1. Subs. 1.

KING STEPHEN

A FRAGMENT OF A TRAGEDY

ACT I.

SCENE I. — *Field of Battle.*

Alarum. Enter King STEPHEN, *Knights, and Soldiers.*

  Stephen. If shame can on a soldier's vein-swoll'n front
Spread deeper crimson than the battle's toil,
Blush in your casing helmets! for see, see!
Yonder my chivalry, my pride of war,
Wrench'd with an iron hand from firm array,
Are routed loose about the plashy meads,
Of honour forfeit. O that my known voice
Could reach your dastard ears, and fright you more!
Fly, cowards, fly! Glocester is at your backs!
Throw your slack bridles o'er the flurried manes,   10
Ply well the rowel with faint trembling heels,
Scampering to death at last!
  1st Knight.   The enemy
Bears his flaunt standard close upon their rear.
  2nd Knight. Sure of a bloody prey, seeing the fens
Will swamp them girth-deep.
  Stephen.   Over head and ears.
No matter! 'Tis a gallant enemy;
How like a comet he goes streaming on.
But we must plague him in the flank, — hey, friends?
We are well breath'd, — follow!

Enter Earl BALDWIN *and Soldiers, as defeated.*

  Stephen.   De Redvers!
What is the monstrous bugbear that can fright   20
Baldwin?
  Baldwin. No scarecrow, but the fortunate star
Of boisterous Chester, whose fell truncheon now
Points level to the goal of victory.
This way he comes, and if you would maintain
Your person unaffronted by vile odds,
Take horse, my Lord.
  Stephen.   And which way spur for life?

Now I thank heaven I am in the toils,
That soldiers may bear witness how my arm
Can burst the meshes. Not the eagle more
Loves to beat up against a tyrannous blast,   30
Than I to meet the torrent of my foes.
This is a brag, — be't so, — but if I fall,
Carve it upon my 'scutcheon'd sepulchre.
On, fellow soldiers! Earl of Redvers, back!
Not twenty Earls of Chester shall brow-beat
The diadem.

                                        [*Exeunt. Alarum.*

SCENE II. — *Another part of the Field.*

Trumpets sounding a Victory. Enter GLOCESTER,
Knights, and Forces.

Glocester. Now may we lift our bruised visors up
And take the flattering freshness of the air,
While the wide din of battle dies away
Into times past, yet to be echoed sure
In the silent pages of our chroniclers.
   1st Knight. Will Stephen's death be mark'd there, my good Lord,
Or that we gave him lodging in yon towers?
   Glocester. Fain would I know the great usurper's fate.

Enter two Captains severally.

   1st Captain. My Lord!
   2nd Captain.   Most noble Earl!
                            The King —
   2nd Captain. The Empress greets —
   Glocester. What of the King?
   1st Captain.   He sole and lone maintains   10
A hopeless bustle mid our swarming arms,
And with a nimble savageness attacks,
Escapes, makes fiercer onset, then anew
Eludes death, giving death to most that dare
Trespass within the circuit of his sword!
He must by this have fallen. Baldwin is taken;
And for the Duke of Bretagne, like a stag
He flies, for the Welsh beagles to hunt down.
God save the Empress!
   Glocester.   Now our dreaded Queen:
What message from her Highness?

2nd Captain.   Royal Maud   20
From the throng'd towers of Lincoln hath look'd down,
Like Pallas from the walls of Ilion,
And seen her enemies havock'd at her feet.
She greets most noble Glocester from her heart,
Intreating him, his captains, and brave knights,
To grace a banquet. The high city gates
Are envious which shall see your triumph pass;
The streets are full of music.

Enter 2nd Knight.

Glocester.   Whence come you?
2nd Knight. From Stephen, my good Prince — Stephen! Stephen!
Glocester. Why do you make such echoing of his name?   30
2nd Knight. Because I think, my lord, he is no man,
But a fierce demon, 'nointed safe from wounds,
And misbaptized with a Christian name.
Glocester. A mighty soldier! — Does he still hold out?
2nd Knight. He shames our victory. His valour still
Keeps elbow-room amid our eager swords,
And holds our bladed falchions all aloof.
His gleaming battle-axe, being slaughter-sick,
Smote on the morion of a Flemish knight,
Broke short in his hand; upon the which he flung   40
The heft away with such a vengeful force
It paunch'd the Earl of Chester's horse, who then
Spleen-hearted came in full career at him.
Glocester. Did no one take him at a vantage then?
2nd Knight. Three then with tiger leap upon him flew,
Whom, with his sword swift drawn and nimbly held,
He stung away again, and stood to breathe,
Smiling. Anon upon him rush'd once more
A throng of foes, and in this renew'd strife,
My sword met his and snapp'd off at the hilt.   50
Glocester. Come, lead me to this Mars and let us move
In silence, not insulting his sad doom
With clamorous trumpets. To the Empress bear
My salutation as befits the time.
                              [*Exeunt* GLOCESTER *and Forces.*

SCENE III. — *The Field of Battle. Enter* STEPHEN *unarmed.*

Stephen. Another sword! And what if I could seize
One from Bellona's gleaming armoury,
Or choose the fairest of her sheaved spears!

Where are my enemies? Here, close at hand,
Here come the testy brood. O, for a sword!
I'm faint — a biting sword! A noble sword!
A hedge-stake — or a ponderous stone to hurl
With brawny vengeance, like the labourer Cain.
Come on! Farewell my kingdom, and all hail
Thou superb, plum'd, and helmeted renown!   10
All hail! I would not truck this brilliant day
To rule in Pylos with a Nestor's beard —
Come on!

Enter DE KAIMS *and Knights,* &c.

De Kaims. Is't madness, or a hunger after death,
That makes thee thus unarm'd throw taunts at us?
Yield, Stephen, or my sword's point dips in
The gloomy current of a traitor's heart.
 Stephen. Do it, De Kaims, I will not budge an inch.
 De Kaims. Yes, of thy madness thou shalt take the meed.
 Stephen. Darest thou?
 De Kaims.   How dare, against a man disarm'd?
 Stephen. What weapons has the lion but himself?   20
Come not near me, De Kaims, for by the price
Of all the glory I have won this day,
Being a king, I will not yield alive
To any but the second man of the realm,
Robert of Glocester.
 De Kaims.   Thou shalt vail to me.
 Stephen. Shall I, when I have sworn against it, sir?
Thou think'st it brave to take a breathing king,
That, on a court-day bow'd to haughty Maud,
The awed presence-chamber may be bold
To whisper, there's the man who took alive   30
Stephen — me — prisoner. Certes, De Kaims,
The ambition is a noble one.
 De Kaims.   'Tis true,
And Stephen, I must compass it.
Stephen.   No, no,
Do not tempt me to throttle you on the gorge,
Or with my gauntlet crush your hollow breast,
Just when your knighthood is grown ripe and full
For lordship.
 A Soldier. Is an honest yeoman's spear
Of no use at a need? Take that.
 Stephen.   Ah, dastard!
 De Kaims. What, you are vulnerable! my prisoner!

Stephen. **No, not yet.** I disclaim it, and demand   **40**
Death as a sovereign right unto a king
Who 'sdains to yield to any but his peer,
If not in title, yet in noble deeds,
The Earl of Glocester. Stab to the hilt, De Kaims,
For I will never by mean hands be led
From this so famous field. Do ye hear! Be quick!

            [*Trumpets. Enter the Earl of* CHESTER *and Knights.*

SCENE IV. — *A Presence Chamber. Queen* MAUD *in a Chair of State,
    the Earls of* GLOCESTER *and* CHESTER, *Lords, Attendants.*

Maud. Glocester, no more. I will behold that Boulogne:
Set him before me. Not for the poor sake
Of regal pomp and a vain-glorious hour,
As thou with wary speech, yet near enough,
Hast hinted.
    Glocester. Faithful counsel have I given;
If wary, for your Highness' benefit.
    Maud. The Heavens forbid that I should not think so,
For by thy valour have I won this realm,
Which by thy wisdom I will ever keep.
To sage advisers let me ever bend   **10**
A meek attentive ear, so that they treat
Of the wide kingdom's rule and government,
Not trenching on our actions personal.
Advised, not school'd, I would be; and henceforth
Spoken to in clear, plain, and open terms,
Not side-ways sermon'd at.
    Glocester.   Then, in plain terms,
Once more for the fallen king —
    Maud.   Your pardon, Brother,
I would no more of that; for, as I said,
'Tis not for worldly pomp I wish to see
The rebel, but as dooming judge to give   **20**
A sentence something worthy of his guilt.
    Glocester If't must be so, I'll bring him to your presence.

            [*Exit* GLOCESTER.

    Maud. A meaner summoner might do as well.
My Lord of Chester, is't true what I hear
Of Stephen of Boulogne, our prisoner,
That he, as a fit penance for his crimes,
Eats wholesome, sweet, and palatable food

Off Glocester's golden dishes — drinks pure wine,
Lodges soft?
 Chester. More than that, my gracious Queen,
Has anger'd me. The noble Earl, methinks,   30
Full soldier as he is, and without peer
In counsel, dreams too much among his books.
It may read well, but sure 'tis out of date
To play the Alexander with Darius.
 Maud. Truth! I think so. By Heavens, it shall not last!
 Chester. It would amaze your Highness now to mark
How Glocester overstrains his courtesy
To that crime-loving rebel, that Boulogne —
 Maud. That ingrate!
 Chester.   For whose vast ingratitude
To our late sovereign lord, your noble sire,   40
The generous Earl condoles in his mishaps,
And with a sort of lackeying friendliness
Talks off the mighty frowning from his brow,
Woos him to hold a duet in a smile,
Or, if it please him, play an hour at chess —
 Maud. A perjured slave!
 Chester.   And for his perjury,
Glocester has fit rewards — nay, I believe,
He sets his bustling household's wits at work
For flatteries to ease this Stephen's hours,
And make a heaven of his purgatory;   50
Adorning bondage with the pleasant gloss
Of feasts and music, and all idle shows
Of indoor pageantry; while syren whispers,
Predestined for his ear, 'scape as half-check'd
From lips the courtliest and the rubiest
Of all the realm, admiring of his deeds.
 Maud. A frost upon his summer!
 Chester.   A queen's nod
Can make his June December. Here he comes.

THE FALL OF HYPERION

A DREAM

CANTO I

FANATICS have their dreams, wherewith they weave
A paradise for a sect; the savage, too,
From forth the loftiest fashion of his sleep
Guesses at Heaven; pity these have not
Trac'd upon vellum or wild Indian leaf
The shadows of melodious utterance.
But bare of laurel they live, dream, and die;
For Poesy alone can tell her dreams, —
With the fine spell of words alone can save
Imagination from the sable chain   10
And dumb enchantment. Who alive can say,
"Thou art no Poet — may'st not tell thy dreams"?
Since every man whose soul is not a clod
Hath visions, and would speak, if he had lov'd
And been well nurtured in his mother tongue.
Whether the dream now purpos'd to rehearse
Be poet's or fanatic's will be known
When this warm scribe, my hand, is in the grave.

   Methought I stood where trees of every clime,
Palm, myrtle, oak, and sycamore, and beech,   20
With plantane, and spice-blossoms, made a screen;
In neighbourhood of fountains, by the noise
Soft-showering in mine ears, and, by the touch
Of scent, not far from roses. Turning round,
I saw an arbour with a drooping roof
Of trellis vines, and bells, and larger blooms,
Like floral censers, swinging light in air;
Before its wreathed doorway, on a mound
Of moss, was spread a feast of summer fruits,
Which, nearer seen, seemed refuse of a meal   30
By angel tasted or our Mother Eve;
For empty shells were scatter'd on the grass,
And grape-stalks but half bare, and remnants more,
Sweet-smelling, whose pure kinds I could not know.
Still was more plenty than the fabled horn
Thrice emptied could pour forth, at banqueting
For Proserpine return'd to her own fields,
Where the white heifers low. And appetite,

More yearning than on earth I ever felt,
Growing within, I ate deliciously;
And, after not long, thirsted; for thereby
Stood a cool vessel of transparent juice,
Sipp'd by the wander'd bee, the which I took,
And, pledging all the mortals of the world,
And all the dead whose names are in our lips,
Drank. That full draught is parent of my theme.
No Asian poppy nor elixir fine
Of the soon-fading, jealous Caliphat,
No poison gender'd in close monkish cell,
To thin the scarlet conclave of old men,
Could so have rapt unwilling life away.
Among the fragrant husks and berries crush'd
Upon the grass, I struggled hard against
The domineering potion, but in vain.
The cloudy swoon came on, and down I sunk,
Like a Silenus on an antique vase.
How long I slumber'd 'tis a chance to guess.
When sense of life return'd, I started up
As if with wings, but the fair trees were gone,
The mossy mound and arbour were no more:
I look'd around upon the carved sides
Of an old sanctuary with roof august,
Builded so high, it seem'd that filmed clouds
Might spread beneath, as o'er the stars of heaven.
So old the place was, I remember'd none
The like upon the earth: what I had seen
Of gray cathedrals, buttress'd walls, rent towers,
The superannuations of sunk realms,
Or Nature's rocks toil'd hard in waves and winds,
Seem'd but the faulture of decrepit things
To that eternal domed monument.
Upon the marble at my feet there lay
Store of strange vessels, and large draperies,
Which needs had been of dyed asbestos wove,
Or in that place the moth could not corrupt,
So white the linen, so, in some, distinct
Ran imageries from a sombre loom.
All in a mingled heap confus'd there lay
Robes, golden tongs, censer and chafing-dish,
Girdles, and chains, and holy jewelries.

    Turning from these with awe, once more I rais'd
My eyes to fathom the space every way;
The embossed roof, the silent massy range

Of columns north and south, ending in mist
Of nothing; then to eastward, where black gates
Were shut against the sunrise evermore.
Then to the west I look'd, and saw far off
An image, huge of feature as a cloud,
At level of whose feet an altar slept,
To be approach'd on either side by steps   90
And marble balustrade, and patient travail
To count with toil the innumerable degrees.
Towards the altar sober-pac'd I went,
Repressing haste, as too unholy there;
And, coming nearer, saw beside the shrine
One minist'ring; and there arose a flame.
When in mid-May the sickening east wind
Shifts sudden to the south, the small warm rain
Melts out the frozen incense from all flowers,
And fills the air with so much pleasant health   100
That even the dying man forgets his shroud;
Even so that lofty sacrificial fire,
Sending forth Maian incense, spread around
Forgetfulness of everything but bliss,
And clouded all the altar with soft smoke;
From whose white fragrant curtains thus I heard
Language pronounc'd: "If thou canst not ascend
These steps, die on that marble where thou art.
Thy flesh, near cousin to the common dust,   110
Will parch for lack of nutriment, — thy bones
Will wither in few years, and vanish so
That not the quickest eye could find a grain
Of what thou now art on that pavement cold.
The sands of thy short life are spent this hour,
And no hand in the universe can turn
Thy hourglass, if these gummed leaves be burnt
Ere thou canst mount up these immortal steps."
I heard, I look'd: two senses both at once,
So fine, so subtle, felt the tyranny
Of that fierce threat and the hard task proposed.   120
Prodigious seem'd the toil; the leaves were yet
Burning, — when suddenly a palsied chill
Struck from the paved level up my limbs,
And was ascending quick to put cold grasp
Upon those streams that pulse beside the throat!
I shriek'd, and the sharp anguish of my shriek
Stung my own ears — I strove hard to escape
The numbness, strove to gain the lowest step.
Slow, heavy, deadly was my pace: the cold

Grew stifling, suffocating, at the heart;   130
And when I clasp'd my hands I felt them not.
One minute before death, my iced foot touch'd
The lowest stair; and, as it touch'd, life seem'd
To pour in at the toes: I mounted up,
As once fair angels on a ladder flew
From the green turf to heaven. "Holy Power,"
Cried I, approaching near the horned shrine,
"What am I that should so be saved from death?
What am I that another death come not
To choke my utterance, sacrilegious here?"   140
Then said the veiled Shadow: "Thou hast felt
What 'tis to die and live again before
Thy fated hour; that thou hadst power to do so
Is thy own safety; thou hast dated on
Thy doom." "High Prophetess," said I, "purge off,
Benign, if so it please thee, my mind's film."
"None can usurp this height," returned that shade,
"But those to whom the miseries of the world
Are misery, and will not let them rest.
All else who find a haven in the world,   150
Where they may thoughtless sleep away their days,
If by a chance into this fane they come,
Rot on the pavement where thou rotted'st half."
"Are there not thousands in the world," said I,
Encourag'd by the sooth voice of the shade,
"Who love their fellows even to the death,
Who feel the giant agony of the world,
And more, like slaves to poor humanity,
Labour for mortal good? I sure should see
Other men here, but I am here alone."   160
"Those whom thou spak'st of are no visionaries,"
Rejoin'd that voice, — "they are no dreamers weak;
They seek no wonder but the human face,
No music but a happy-noted voice —
They come not here, they have no thought to come —
And thou art here, for thou art less than they.
What benefit canst thou do, or all thy tribe,
To the great world? Thou art a dreaming thing,
A fever of thyself — think of the earth;
What bliss, even in hope, is there for thee?   170
What haven? every creature hath its home;
Every sole man hath days of joy and pain,
Whether his labours be sublime or low —
The pain alone, the joy alone, distinct:
Only the dreamer venoms all his days,

Bearing more woe than all his sins deserve.
Therefore, that happiness be somewhat shar'd,
Such things as thou art are admitted oft
Into like gardens thou didst pass erewhile,
And suffer'd in these temples: for that cause   180
Thou standest safe beneath this statue's knees."
"That I am favour'd for unworthiness,
By such propitious parley medicin'd
In sickness not ignoble, I rejoice,
Aye, and could weep for love of such award."
So answered I, continuing, "If it please,
[Majestic shadow, tell me: sure not all
Those melodies sung into the world's ear
Are useless: sure a poet is a sage;
A humanist, physician to all men.   190
That I am none I feel, as vultures feel
They are no birds when eagles are abroad.
What am I then: thou spakest of my tribe:
What tribe?" The tall shade veil'd in drooping white
Then spake, so much more earnest, that the breath
Moved the thin linen folds that drooping hung
About a golden censer from the hand
Pendent — "Art thou not of the dreamer tribe?
The poet and the dreamer are distinct,
Diverse, sheer opposite, antipodes.   200
The one pours out a balm upon the world,
The other vexes it." Then shouted I
Spite of myself, and with a Pythia's spleen,
"Apollo! faded! O far-flown Apollo!
Where is thy misty pestilence to creep
Into the dwellings, through the door crannies
Of all mock lyrists, large self-worshippers,
And careless Hectorers in proud bad verse?
Though I breathe death with them it will be life
To see them sprawl before me into graves.]   210
Majestic shadow, tell me where I am,
Whose altar this, for whom this incense curls;
What image this whose face I cannot see
For the broad marble knees; and who thou art,
Of accent feminine so courteous?"

Then the tall shade, in drooping linens veil'd,
Spake out, so much more earnest, that her breath
Stirr'd the thin folds of gauze that drooping hung
About a golden censer, from her hand
Pendent; and by her voice I knew she shed   220

Long-treasured tears. "This temple, sad and lone,
Is all spar'd from the thunder of a war
Foughten long since by giant hierarchy
Against rebellion: this old image here,
Whose carved features wrinkled as he fell,
Is Saturn's; I, Moneta, left supreme,
Sole priestess of his desolation." —
I had no words to answer, for my tongue,
Useless, could find about its roofed home
No syllable of a fit majesty   230
To make rejoinder to Moneta's mourn:
There was a silence, while the altar's blaze
Was fainting for sweet food. I look'd thereon,
And on the paved floor, where nigh were piled
Faggots of cinnamon, and many heaps
Of other crisped spicewood: then again
I look'd upon the altar, and its horns
Whiten'd with ashes, and its lang'rous flame,
And then upon the offerings again;
And so by turns — till sad Moneta cried: 240
"The sacrifice is done, but not the less
Will I be kind to thee for thy good will.
My power, which to me is still a curse,
Shall be to thee a wonder; for the scenes
Still swooning vivid through my globed brain,
With an electral changing misery,
Thou shalt with these dull mortal eyes behold
Free from all pain, if wonder pain thee not."
As near as an immortal's sphered words
Could to a mother's soften, were these last: 250
And yet I had a terror of her robes,
And chiefly of the veils, that from her brow
Hung pale. and curtain'd her in mysteries,
That made my heart too small to hold its blood.
This saw that Goddess, and with sacred hand
Parted the veils. Then saw I a wan face,
Not pined by human sorrows, but bright-blanch'd
By an immortal sickness which kills not;
It works a constant change, which happy death
Can put no end to; deathwards progressing   260
To no death was that visage; it had pass'd
The lily and the snow; and beyond these
I must not think now, though I saw that face.
But for her eyes I should have fled away.
They held me back with a benignant light,
Soft mitigated by divinest lids

Half closed, and visionless entire they seem'd
Of all external things — they saw me not,
But, in blank splendour, beam'd like the mild moon,
Who comforts those she sees not, who knows not   270
What eyes are upward cast. As I had found
A grain of gold upon a mountain's side,
And, twing'd with avarice, strain'd out my eyes
To search its sullen entrails rich with ore,
So, at the view of sad Moneta's brow,
I ached to see what things the hollow brain
Behind enwombed: what high tragedy
In the dark secret chambers of her skull
Was acting, that could give so dread a stress
To her cold lips, and fill with such a light   280
Her planetary eyes, and touch her voice
With such a sorrow. — "Shade of Memory!"
Cried I, with act adorant at her feet,
"By all the gloom hung round thy fallen house,
By this last temple, by the golden age,
By great Apollo, thy dear foster-child,
And by thyself, forlorn divinity,
The pale Omega of a wither'd race,
Let me behold, according as thou saidst,
What in thy brain so ferments to and fro. —"   290
No sooner had this conjuration pass'd
My devout lips, than side by side we stood
(Like a stunt bramble by a solemn pine)
Deep in the shady sadness of a vale
Far sunken from the healthy breath of morn,
Far from the fiery noon and eve's one star.
Onward I look'd beneath the gloomy boughs,
And saw what first I thought an image huge,
Like to the image pedestall'd so high
In Saturn's temple; then Moneta's voice   300
Came brief upon mine ear, — "So Saturn sat
When he had lost his realms — " whereon there grew
A power within me of enormous ken,
To see as a god sees, and take the depth
Of things as nimbly as the outward eye
Can size and shape pervade. The lofty theme
Of those few words hung vast before my mind
With half-unravell'd web. I sat myself
Upon an eagle's watch, that I might see,
And seeing ne'er forget. No stir of life   310
Was in this shrouded vale, not so much air
As in the zoning of a summer's day

Robs not one light seed from the feather'd grass;
But where the dead leaf fell, there did it rest:
A stream went voiceless by, still deaden'd more
By reason of the fallen Divinity
Spreading more shade; the Naiad 'mid her reeds
Press'd her cold finger closer to her lips.

Along the margin sand large footmarks went
No farther than to where old Saturn's feet   320
Had rested, and there slept, how long a sleep!
Degraded, cold, upon the sodden ground
His old right hand lay nerveless, listless, dead,
Unsceptred, and his realmless eyes were clos'd;
While his bow'd head seem'd listening to the Earth,
His antient mother, for some comfort yet.

It seem'd no force could wake him from his place;
But there came one who, with a kindred hand,
Touch'd his wide shoulders, after bending low
With reverence, though to one who knew it not.   330
Then came the griev'd voice of Mnemosyne,
And griev'd I hearken'd. "That divinity
Whom thou saw'st step from yon forlornest wood,
And with slow pace approach our fallen king,
Is Thea, softest-natur'd of our brood."
I mark'd the Goddess, in fair statuary
Surpassing wan Moneta by the head,
And in her sorrow nearer woman's tears.
There was a list'ning fear in her regard,
As if calamity had but begun;   340
As if the vanward clouds of evil days
Had spent their malice, and the sullen rear
Was with its stored thunder labouring up.
One hand she press'd upon that aching spot
Where beats the human heart; as if just there,
Though an immortal, she felt cruel pain;
The other upon Saturn's bended neck
She laid, and to the level of his ear
Leaning with parted lips, some words she spoke
In solemn tenour and deep organ-tone;   350
Some mourning words, which in our feeble tongue
Would come in this like accenting; how frail
To that large utterance of the early Gods!

"Saturn, look up! and for what, poor lost king?
I have no comfort for thee; no — not one;

I cannot cry, *Wherefore thus sleepest thou?*
For Heaven is parted from thee, and the Earth
Knows thee not, so afflicted, for a God.
The Ocean, too, with all its solemn noise,
Has from thy sceptre pass'd; and all the air   360
Is emptied of thine hoary majesty.
Thy thunder, captious at the new command,
Rumbles reluctant o'er our fallen house;
And thy sharp lightning in unpractised hands
Scorches and burns our once serene domain.
With such remorseless speed still come new woes,
That unbelief has not a space to breathe.
Saturn! sleep on: — me thoughtless, why should I
Thus violate thy slumbrous solitude?
Why should I ope thy melancholy eyes?   370
Saturn! sleep on, while at thy feet I weep."

    As when upon a tranced summer night
Forests, branch-charmed by the earnest stars,
Dream, and so dream all night, without a noise,
Save from one gradual solitary gust
Swelling upon the silence; dying off;
As if the ebbing air had but one wave;
So came those words and went; the while in tears
She press'd her fair large forehead to the earth,
Just where her fallen hair might spread in curls,   380
A soft and silken mat for Saturn's feet.
Long, long these two were postured motionless,
Like sculpture builded up upon the grave
Of their own power. A long awful time
I look'd upon them: still they were the same;
The frozen God still bending to the earth,
And the sad Goddess weeping at his feet,
Moneta silent. Without stay or prop,
But my own weak mortality, I bore
The load of this eternal quietude,   390
The unchanging gloom and the three fixed shapes
Ponderous upon my senses, a whole moon;
For by my burning brain I measured sure
Her silver seasons shedded on the night,
And every day by day methought I grew
More gaunt and ghostly. Oftentimes I pray'd
Intense, that death would take me from the vale
And all its burthens — Gasping with despair
Of change, hour after hour I curs'd myself;
Until old Saturn rais'd his faded eyes,   400

And look'd around, and saw his kingdom gone,
And all the gloom and sorrow of the place,
And that fair kneeling Goddess at his feet.
As the moist scent of flowers, and grass, and leaves
Fills forest-dells with a pervading air,
Known to the woodland nostril, so the words
Of Saturn fill'd the mossy glooms around,
Even to the hollows of time-eaten oaks,
And to the windings in the foxes' holes,
With sad, low tones, while thus he spake, and sent   410
Strange musings to the solitary Pan.
"Moan, brethren, moan; for we are swallow'd up
And buried from all godlike exercise
Of influence benign on planets pale,
And peaceful sway above man's harvesting,
And all those acts which Deity supreme
Doth ease its heart of love in. Moan and wail,
Moan, brethren, moan; for lo! the rebel spheres
Spin round, the stars their antient courses keep,
Clouds still with shadowy moisture haunt the earth,   420
Still suck their fill of light from sun and moon,
Still buds the tree, and still the sea-shores murmur.
There is no death in all the universe,
No smell of death — there shall be death — moan, moan;
Moan, Cybele, moan, for thy pernicious babes
Have changed a god into a shaking palsy.
Moan, brethren, moan, for I have no strength left;
Weak as the reed — weak — feeble as my voice —
O, O, the pain, the pain of feebleness.
Moan, moan, for still I thaw — or give me help: 430
Throw down those Imps, and give me victory.
Let me hear other groans; and trumpets blown
Of triumph calm, and hymns of festival,
From the gold peaks of heaven's high piled clouds;
Voices of soft proclaim, and silver stir
Of strings in hollow shells; and let there be
Beautiful things made new, for the surprise
Of the sky-children — " So he feebly ceas'd,
With such a poor and sickly-sounding pause,
Methought I heard some old man of the earth   440
Bewailing earthly loss; nor could my eyes
And ears act with that pleasant unison of sense
Which marries sweet sound with the grace of form,
And dolorous accent from a tragic harp
With large-limb'd visions. More I scrutinized.
Still fix'd he sat beneath the sable trees,

Whose arms spread straggling in wild serpent forms,
With leaves all hush'd; his awful presence there
(Now all was silent) gave a deadly lie
To what I erewhile heard: only his lips   450
Trembled amid the white curls of his beard.
They told the truth, though, round, the snowy locks
Hung nobly, as upon the face of heaven
A mid-day fleece of clouds. Thea arose,
And stretch'd her white arm through the hollow dark,
Pointing some whither: whereat he too rose
Like a vast giant seen by men at sea
To grow pale from the waves at dull midnight.
They melted from my sight into the woods:
Ere I could turn, Moneta cried, "These twain   460
Are speeding to the families of grief,
Where, roof'd in by black rocks, they waste in pain
And darkness for no hope." — And she spake on,
As ye may read who can unwearied pass
Onward from the antechamber of this dream,
Where even at the open doors awhile
I must delay, and glean my memory
Of her high phrase; — perhaps no further dare.

CANTO II

"MORTAL, that thou mayst understand aright,
I humanize my sayings to thine ear,
Making comparisons of earthly things;
Or thou might'st better listen to the wind,
Whose language is to thee a barren noise,
Though it blows legend-laden through the trees —
In melancholy realms big tears are shed,
More sorrow like to this, and such like woe,
Too huge for mortal tongue, or pen of scribe.
The Titans fierce, self-hid or prison-bound,   10
Groan for the old allegiance once more,
Listening in their doom for Saturn's voice.
But one of the whole eagle-brood still keeps
His sov'reignty, and rule, and majesty;
Blazing Hyperion on his orbed fire
Still sits, still snuffs the incense teeming up
From man to the Sun's God — yet unsecure,
For as upon the earth dire prodigies
Fright and perplex, so also shudders he;
Nor at dog's howl, or gloom-bird's even screech,   20

Or the familiar visitings of one
Upon the first toll of his passing bell:
But horrors, portion'd to a giant nerve,
Make great Hyperion ache. His palace bright,
Bastion'd with pyramids of glowing gold,
And touched with shade of bronzed obelisks,
Glares a blood-red through all the thousand courts,
Arches, and domes, and fiery galleries;
And all its curtains of Aurorian clouds
Flush angrily; when he would taste the wreaths   30
Of incense breath'd aloft from sacred hills,
Instead of sweets, his ample palate takes
Savour of poisonous brass and metals sick.
Wherefore when harbour'd in the sleepy west,
After the full completion of fair day,
For rest divine upon exalted couch
And slumber in the arms of melody,
He paces through the pleasant hours of ease,
With strides colossal, on from hall to hall,
While, far within each aisle and deep recess,   40
His winged minions in close clusters stand
Amaz'd, and full of fear; like anxious men,
Who on a wide plain gather in sad troops,
When earthquakes jar their battlements and towers.
Even now while Saturn, roused from icy trance,
Goes, step for step, with Thea from yon woods,
Hyperion, leaving twilight in the rear,
Is sloping to the threshold of the west. —
Thither we tend." Now in clear light I stood,
Relieved from the dusk vale. Mnemosyne   50
Was sitting on a square-edg'd polish'd stone,
That in its lucid depth reflected pure
Her priestess-garments. My quick eyes ran on
From stately nave to nave, from vault to vault,
Through bowers of fragrant and enwreathed light,
And diamond-paved lustrous long arcades.
Anon rush'd by the bright Hyperion;
His flaming robes stream'd out beyond his heels,
And gave a roar, as if of earthly fire,
That scared away the meek ethereal hours,   60
And made their dove-wings tremble. On he flared.

*   *   *   *   *   *   *

TO AUTUMN

[handwritten annotations: "ALTHOUGH THERE SEEMS TO BE A DEATH TO SEASON — LIFE 2 THERE EXISTS LIFE — CYCLING — NOT DOTTED NOT SPECTACULAR"]

[handwritten: "HAS THE MOST TO OFFER of itself"]

I.

Season of mists and mellow fruitfulness,
    Close bosom-friend of the maturing sun;
Conspiring with him how to load and bless
    With fruit the vines that round the thatch-eves run;
To bend with apples the moss'd cottage-trees,
    And fill all fruit with ripeness to the core;
      To swell the gourd, and plump the hazel shells
With a sweet kernel; to set budding more,
    And still more, later flowers for the bees,
    Until they think warm days will never cease,   10
      For Summer has o'er-brimm'd their clammy cells.

II.

Who hath not seen thee oft amid thy store?
    Sometimes whoever seeks abroad may find
Thee sitting careless on a granary floor,
    Thy hair soft-lifted by the winnowing wind;
Or on a half-reap'd furrow sound asleep,
    Drows'd with the fume of poppies, while thy hook
      Spares the next swath and all its twined flowers:
And sometimes like a gleaner thou dost keep
    Steady thy laden head across a brook;   20
    Or by a cyder-press, with patient look,
      Thou watchest the last oozings hours by hours.

III.

Where are the songs of Spring? Ay, where are they?
    Think not of them, thou hast thy music too, —
While barred clouds bloom the soft-dying day,
    And touch the stubble-plains with rosy hue;
Then in a wailful choir the small gnats mourn
    Among the river sallows, borne aloft
      Or sinking as the light wind lives or dies;
And full-grown lambs loud bleat from hilly bourn;   30
    Hedge-crickets sing; and now with treble soft

The red-breast whistles from a garden-croft;
    And gathering swallows twitter in the skies

THE DAY IS GONE

THE day is gone, and all its sweets are gone!
    Sweet voice, sweet lips, soft hand, and softer breast,
Warm breath, light whisper, tender semi-tone,
    Bright eyes, accomplish'd shape, and lang'rous waist!
Faded the flower and all its budded charms,
    Faded the sight of beauty from my eyes,
Faded the shape of beauty from my arms,
    Faded the voice, warmth, whiteness, paradise —
Vanish'd unseasonably at shut of eve,
    When the dusk holiday — or holinight   10
Of fragrant-curtain'd love begins to weave
    The woof of darkness thick, for hid delight;
But, as I've read love's missal through to-day,
He'll let me sleep, seeing I fast and pray.

TO — [FANNY BRAWNE]

WHAT can I do to drive away
Remembrance from my eyes? for they have seen,
Aye, an hour ago, my brilliant Queen!
Touch has a memory. O say, love, say,
What can I do to kill it and be free
In my old liberty?
When every fair one that I saw was fair
Enough to catch me in but half a snare,
Not keep me there:
When, howe'er poor or particolour'd things,   10
My muse had wings,
And ever ready was to take her course
Whither I bent her force,
Unintellectual, yet divine to me; —
Divine, I say! — What sea-bird o'er the sea
Is a philosopher the while he goes
Winging along where the great water throes?

How shall I do
To get anew
Those moulted feathers, and so mount once more   20
Above, above
The reach of fluttering Love,

And make him cower lowly while I soar?
Shall I gulp wine? No, that is vulgarism,
A heresy and schism,
Foisted into the canon law of love; —
No, — wine is only sweet to happy men;
More dismal cares
Seize on me unawares, —
Where shall I learn to get my peace again?   30
To banish thoughts of that most hateful land,
Dungeoner of my friends, that wicked strand
Where they were wreck'd and live a wrecked life;
That monstrous region, whose dull rivers pour,
Ever from their sordid urns unto the shore,
Unown'd of any weedy-haired gods;
Whose winds, all zephyrless, hold scourging rods,
Iced in the great lakes, to afflict mankind;
Whose rank-grown forests, frosted, black, and blind,
Would fright a Dryad; whose harsh herbag'd meads   40
Make lean and lank the starv'd ox while he feeds;
There bad flowers have no scent, birds no sweet song,
And great unerring Nature once seems wrong.

O, for some sunny spell
To dissipate the shadows of this hell!
Say they are gone, — with the new dawning light
Steps forth my lady bright!
O, let me once more rest
My soul upon that dazzling breast!
Let once again these aching arms be plac'd,   50
The tender gaolers of thy waist!
And let me feel that warm breath here and there
To spread a rapture in my very hair, —
O, the sweetness of the pain!
Give me those lips again!
Enough! Enough! it is enough for me
To dream of thee!

I CRY YOUR MERCY

I CRY your mercy — pity — love! — aye, love!
  Merciful love that tantalises not,
One-thoughted, never-wandering, guileless love,
  Unmask'd, and being seen — without a blot!
O! let me have thee whole, — all — all — be mine!
  That shape, that fairness, that sweet minor zest

Of love, your kiss, — those hands, those eyes divine,
   That warm, white, lucent, million-pleasured breast, —
Yourself — your soul — in pity give me all,
   Withhold no atom's atom or I die,   10
Or living on perhaps, your wretched thrall,
   Forget, in the mist of idle misery,
Life's purposes, — the palate of my mind
Losing its gust, and my ambition blind!

[LINES WRITTEN IN THE MS. OF *THE CAP AND BELLS*]

THIS living hand, now warm and capable
Of earnest grasping, would, if it were cold
And in the icy silence of the tomb,
So haunt thy days and chill thy dreaming nights
That thou wouldst wish thine own heart dry of blood
So in my veins red life might stream again,
And thou be conscience-calm'd — see here it is —
I hold it towards you.

LETTERS

TO BENJAMIN ROBERT HAYDON

[10–11 May 1817]
Margate Saturday Eve

MY DEAR HAYDON,

> Let Fame, which all hunt after in their Lives,
> Live register'd upon our brazen tombs,
> And so grace us in the disgrace of death:
> When spite of cormorant devouring time
> The endeavour of this preasent breath may buy
> That Honor which shall bate his Scythe's keen edge
> And make us heirs of all eternity.[1]

To think that I have no right to couple myself with you in this speech would be death to me me so I have e'en written it — and I pray God that our brazen Tombs be nigh neighbors. It cannot be long first the endeavor of this present breath will soon be over — and yet it is as well to breathe freely during our sojourn — it is as well if you have not been teased with that Money affair — that bill-pestilence. However I must think that difficulties nerve the Spirit of a Man — they make our Prime Objects a Refuge as well as a Passion. The Trumpet of Fame is as a tower of Strength the ambitious bloweth it and is safe — I suppose by your telling me not to give way to forebodings George has mentioned to you what I have lately said in my Letters to him — truth is I have been in such a state of Mind as to read over my Lines and hate them. I am "one that gathers Samphire dreadful trade"[2] the Cliff of Poesy Towers above me — yet when, Tom who meets with some of Pope's Homer in Plutarch's Lives reads some of those to me they seem like Mice[3] to mine. I read and write about eight hours a day. There is an old saying well begun is half done" — 't is a bad one. I would use instead — Not begun at all 'till half done" so according to that I have not begun my Poem and consequently (a priori) can say nothing about it. Thank God! I do begin arduously where I leave off, notwithstanding occasional depressions: and I hope for the support of a High Power

---

[1] *Love's Labour's Lost* I.i.1–7.
[2] *King Lear* IV.vi.15.
[3] *Ibid.*, IV.vi.18.

while I clime this little eminence and especially in my Years of more momentous Labor. I remember your saying that you had notions of a good Genius presiding over you — I have of late had the same thought. for things which [I] do half at Random are afterwards confirmed by my judgment in a dozen features of Propriety — Is it too daring to Fancy Shakspeare this Presider? When in the Isle of Whight I met with a Shakspeare in the Passage of the House at which I lodged — it comes nearer to my idea of him than any I have seen — I was but there a Week yet the old Woman made me take it with me though I went off in a hurry — Do you not think this is ominous of good? I am glad you say every Man of great Views is at times tormented as I am —

Sunday Aft. This Morning I received a letter from George by which it appears that Money Troubles are to follow us up for some time to come perhaps for always — these vexations are a great hindrance to one — they are not like Envy and detraction stimulants to further exertion as being immediately relative and reflected on at the same time with the prime object — but rather like a nettle leaf or two in your bed. So now I revoke my Promise of finishing my Poem by the Autumn which I should have done had I gone on as I have done — but I cannot write while my spirit is feavered in a contrary direction and I am now sure of having plenty of it this Summer — At this moment I am in no enviable Situation — I feel that I am not in a Mood to write any to day; and it appears that the loess of it is the beginning of all sorts of irregularities. I am extremely glad that a time must come when every thing will leave not a wrack behind.[4] You tell me never to despair — I wish it was as easy for me to observe the saying — truth is I have a horrid Morbidity of Temperament which has shown itself at intervals — it is I have no doubt the greatest Enemy and stumbling block I have to fear — I may even say that it is likely to be the cause of my disappointment. How ever every ill has its share of good — this very bane would at any time enable me to look with an obstinate eye on the Devil Himself — ay to be as proud of being the lowest of the human race as Alfred could be in being of the highest. I feel confident I should have been a rebel Angel had the opportunity been mine. I am very sure that you do love me as your own Brother — I have seen it in your continual anxiety for me — and I assure you that your wellfare and fame is and will be a chief pleasure to me all my Life. I know no one but you who can be fully sensible of the turmoil and anxiety, the sacrifice of all what is called comfort the readiness to Measure time by what is done and to die in 6 hours could plans be brought to conclusions.

4 *The Tempest* IV.i.155–6.

— the looking upon the Sun the Moon the Stars, the Earth and its contents as materials to form greater things — that is to say ethereal things — but here I am talking like a Madman greater things that [*for* than] our Creator himself made!! I wrote to Hunt yesterday — scar[c]ely know what I said in it — I could not talk about Poetry in the way I should have liked for I was not in humor with either his or mine. His self delusions are very lamentable they have inticed him into a Situation which I should be less eager after than that of a galle₁ Slave — what you observe thereon is very true must be in time. Perhaps it is a self delusion to say so — but I think I could not be be dece[i]ved in the Manner that Hunt is — may I die tomorrow if I am to be. There is no greater Sin after the 7 deadly than to flatter oneself into an idea of being a great Poet — or one of those beings who are privileged to wear out their Lives in the pursuit of Honor — how comfortable a feel it is that such a Crime must bring its heavy Penalty? That if one be a Selfdeluder accounts will be balanced? I am glad you are hard at Work — 't will now soon be done — I long to see Wordsworth's as well as to have mine in: ⁵ but I would rather not show my face in Town till the end of the Year — if that will be time enough — if not I shall be disappointed if you do not write for me even when you think best — I never quite despair and I read Shakspeare — indeed I shall I think never read any other Book much — Now this might lead me into a long Confab but I desist. I am very near Agreeing with Hazlit that Shakspeare is enough for us — By the by what a tremendous Southean Article his last was — I wish he had left out "grey hairs"

✿   ✿   ✿   ✿   ✿   ✿

So now in the Name of Shakespeare Raphael and all our Saints I commend you to the care of heaven!

Your everlasting friend
John Keats —

TO BENJAMIN BAILEY

[28–30 October 1817]

MY DEAR BAILEY,

So you have got a Curacy! good. . . .

✿   ✿   ✿   ✿   ✿   ✿

⁵ Figures in Haydon's painting, *Christ's Entry into Jerusalem,* were given the heads of Wordsworth, Keats, *et al.*

Thus far had I written [1] when I received your last which made me at the sight of the direction caper for despair — but for one thing I am glad that I have been neglectful — and that is, therefrom I have received a proof of your utmost kindness which at this present I feel very much — and I wish I had a heart always open to such sensations — but there is no altering a Man's nature and mine must be radically wrong for it will lie dormant a whole Month — This leads me to suppose that there are no Men thouroughly wicked — so as never to be self spiritualized into a kind of sublime Misery — but alas! 't is but for an Hour — he is the only Man "who has kept watch on Man's Mortality" [2] who has philantrophy enough to overcome the disposition [to] an indolent enjoyment of intellect — who is brave enough to volunteer for uncomfortable hours. You remember in Hazlit's essay on commonplace people — He says they read the Edinburgh and Quarterly and think as they do" Now with respect to Wordsworth's Gipseys I think he is right and yet I think Hazlitt is right [*for* righter?] [3] and yet I think Wordsworth is rightest. Wordsworth had not been idle he had not been without his task — nor had they Gipseys — they in the visible world had been as picturesque an object as he in the invisible. The Smoke of their fire — their attitudes — their Voices were all in harmony with the Evenings — It is a bold thing to say and I would not say it in print — but it seems to me that if Wordsworth had though[t] a little deeper at that Moment he would not have written the Poem at all — I should judge it to ~~has~~ have been written in one of the most comfortable Moods of his Life — it is a kind of sketchy intellectual Landscape — not a search after Truth — nor is it fair to attack him on such a subject — for it is with the Critic as with the poet had Hazlitt thought a little deeper and been in a good temper he would never have spied an imaginary fault there.

❀   ❀   ❀   ❀   ❀   ❀

My Brother Georges kindest wishes to you. My dear Bailey I am
your affectionate friend.
John Keats

[1] Keats had just copied into the letter *Endymion* iv.1–29.
[2] Wordsworth, *Intimations of Immortality* 202.
[3] Rollins, I, 173.

TO BENJAMIN BAILEY

[22 November 1817]

MY DEAR BAILEY,

I will get over the first part of this (*unsaid*) Letter as soon as possible for it relates to the affair of poor Crips — To a Man of your nature, such a Letter as Haydon's must have been extremely cutting — What occasions the greater part of the World's Quarrels? simply this, two Minds meet and do not understand each other time enough to p[r]aevent any shock or surprise at the conduct of either party — As soon as I had known Haydon three days I had got enough of his character not to have been surp[r]ised at such a Letter as he has hurt you with. Nor when I knew it was it a principle with me to drop his acquaintance although with you it would have been an imperious feeling. I wish you knew all that I think about Genius and the Heart — and yet I think you are thoroughly acquainted with my innermost breast in that respect or you could not have known me even thus long and still hold me worthy to be your dear friend. In passing however I must say of one thing that has pressed upon me lately and encreased my Humility and capability of submission and that is this truth — Men of Genius are great as certain ethereal Chemicals operating on the Mass of neutral intellect — by [*for* but] they have not any individuality, any determined Character. I would call the top and head of those who have a proper self Men of Power —

But I am running my head into a Subject which I am certain I could not do justice to under five years s[t]udy and 3 vols octavo — and moreover long to be talking about the Imagination — so my dear Bailey do not think of this unpleasant affair if possible — do not — I defy any ha[r]m to come of it — I defy — I'll shall write to Crips this Week and reque[s]t him to tell me all his goings on from time to time by Letter whererever I may be — it will all go on well — so dont because you have suddenly discover'd a Coldness in Haydon suffer yourself to be teased. Do not my dear fellow. O I wish I was as certain of the end of all your troubles as that of your momentary start about the authenticity of the Imagination. I am certain of nothing but of the holiness of the Heart's affections and the truth of Imagination — What the imagination seizes as Beauty must be truth — whether it existed before or not — for I have the same Idea of all our Passions as of Love they are all in their sublime, creative of

essential Beauty — In a Word, you may know my favorite Speculation by my first Book and the little song I sent in my last [1] — which
is a representation from the fancy of the probable mode of operating
in these Matters — The Imagination may be compared to Adam's
dream [2] — he awoke and found it truth. I am the more zealous in this
affair, because I have never yet been able to perceive how any
thing can be known for truth by consequitive reasoning — and yet it
must be — Can it be that even the greatest Philosopher ever ~~when~~
arrived at his goal without putting aside numerous objections — However it may be, O for a Life of Sensations rather than of Thoughts!
It is 'a Vision in the form of Youth' a Shadow of reality to come —
and this consideration has further conv[i]nced me for it has come as
auxiliary to another favorite Speculation of mine, that we shall enjoy
ourselves here after by having what we called happiness on Earth
repeated in a finer tone and so repeated — And yet such a fate
can only befall those who delight in sensation rather than hunger as
you do after Truth — Adam's dream will do here and seems to be a
conviction that Imagination and its empyreal reflection is the same
as human Life and its spiritual repetition. But as I was saying —
the simple imaginative Mind may have its rewards in the repeti-
[ti]on of its own silent Working coming continually on the spirit
with a fine suddenness — to compare great things with small — have
you never by being surprised with an old Melody — in a delicious
place — by a delicious voice, fe[l]t over again your very speculations and surmises at the time it first operated on your soul — do
you not remember forming to yourself the singer's face more beautiful that [*for* than] it was possible and yet with the elevation of the
Moment you did not think so — even then you were mounted on the
Wings of Imagination so high — that the Prototype must be here
after — that delicious face you will see — What a time! I am continually running away from the subject — sure this cannot be exactly
the case with a complex Mind — one that is imaginative and at the
same time careful of its fruits — who would exist partly on sensation
partly on thought — to whom it is necessary that years should bring
the philosophic Mind [3] — such an one I consider your's and therefore it is necessary to your eternal Happiness that you not only ~~have~~
drink this old Wine of Heaven which I shall call the redigestion of
our most ethereal Musings on Earth; but also increase in knowledge

[1] The first book of *Endymion* and the first five stanzas of the "Ode to
Sorrow," from the fourth book, which Keats had copied in his letter of Nov. 3.
[2] *Paradise Lost* viii. 460–90.
[3] Wordsworth, *Intimations of Immortality* 190.

and know all things. I am glad to hear you are in a fair Way for Easter — you will soon get through your unpleasant reading and then! — but the world is full of troubles and I have not much reason to think myself pesterd with many — I think Jane or Marianne has a better opinion of me than I deserve — for really and truly I do not think my Brothers illness connected with mine — you know more of the real Cause than they do — nor have I any chance of being rack'd as you have been — you perhaps at one time thought there was such a thing as Worldly Happiness to be arrived at, at certain periods of time marked out — you have of necessity from your disposition been thus led away — I scarcely remember counting upon any Happiness — I look not for it if it be not in the present hour — nothing startles me beyond the Moment. The setting sun will always set me to rights — or if a Sparrow come before my Window I take part in its existince and pick about the Gravel. The first thing that strikes me on hea[r]ing a Misfortune having befalled another is this. 'Well it cannot be helped. — he will have the pleasure of trying the resourses of his spirit, and I beg now my dear Bailey that hereafter should you observe any thing cold in me not to but [*for* put] it to the account of heartlessness but abstraction — for I assure you I sometimes feel not the influence of a Passion or Affection during a whole week — and so long this sometimes continues I begin to suspect myself and the genui[ne]ness of my feelings at other times — thinking them a few barren Tragedy-tears — My Brother Tom is much improved — he is going to Devonshire — whither I shall follow him — at present I am just arrived at Dorking to change the Scene — change the Air and give me a spur to wind up my Poem, of which there are wanting 500 Lines. I should have been here a day sooner but the Reynoldses persuaded me to spop [*for* stop] in Town to meet your friend Christie — There were Rice and Martin — we talked about Ghosts — I will have some talk with Taylor and let you know — when please God I come down a[t] Christmas — I will find that Examiner if possible. My best regards to Gleig. My Brothers to you and Mrs Bentley['s]

> Your affectionate friend
> John Keats —

I want to say much more to you — a few hints will set me going
Direct Burford Bridge near dorking

TO GEORGE AND THOMAS KEATS

[21, 27 (?) December 1817]
Hampstead Sunday

MY DEAR BROTHERS,

I must crave your pardon for not having written ere this. °°°
I saw Kean return to the public in Richard III, & finely he did
it, & at the request of Reynolds I went to criticise his Luke in Riches
— the critique is in todays champion, which I send you with the
Examiner in which you will find very proper lamentation on the obso-
letion of christmas Gambols & pastimes: but it was mixed up with so
much egotism of that drivelling nature that pleasure is entirely lost.
Hone the publisher's trial, you must find very amusing; & as Englishmen very ~~amusing~~ encouraging — his *Not Guilty* is a thing, which not
to have been, would have dulled still more Liberty's Emblazoning —
Lord Ellenborough has been paid in his own coin — Wooler & Hone
have done us an essential service [1] — I have had two very pleasant
evenings with Dilke yesterday & today; & am at this moment just come
from him & feel in the humour to go on with this, began in the morning, & from which he came to fetch me. I spent Friday evening with
Wells & went the next morning to see *Death on the Pale horse*. It
is a wonderful picture, when West's [2] age is considered; But there
is nothing to be intense upon; no women one feels mad to kiss; no
face swelling into reality. the excellence of every Art is its intensity,
capable of making all disagreeables evaporate, from their being in
close relationship with Beauty & Truth — Examine King Lear &
you will find this examplified throughout; but in this picture we have
unpleasantness without any momentous depth of speculation excited,
in which to bury its repulsiveness — The picture is larger than Christ
rejected — I dined with Haydon the sunday after you left, & had a
very pleasant day, I dined too (for I have been out too much lately)
with Horace Smith & met his two Brothers with Hill & Kingston & one
Du Bois, they only served to convince me, how superior humour is to
wit in respect to enjoyment — These men say things which make one

[1] Hone and Wooler were liberals who were acquitted of charges of libel.
Lord Ellenborough, Hone's trial judge, had in 1813 sentenced Leigh Hunt
and his brother (Rollins, I, 191–2).
[2] Benjamin West (1738–1820), the American painter and president of the
Royal Academy.

start, without making one feel, they are all alike; their manners are alike; they all know fashionables; they have a mannerism in their very eating & drinking, in their mere handling a Decanter — They talked of Kean & his low company — Would I were with that company instead of yours said I to myself! I know such like acquaintance will never do for me & yet I am going to Reynolds, on wednesday — Brown & Dilke walked with me & back from the Christmas pantomime. I had not a dispute but a disquisition with Dilke, on various subjects; several things dovetailed in my mind, & at once it struck me, what quality went to form a Man of Achievement especially in Literature & which Shakespeare posessed so enormously — I mean *Negative Capability*, that is when man is capable of being in uncertainties, Mysteries, doubts, without any irritable reaching after fact & reason — Coleridge, for instance, would let go by a fine isolated verisimilitude caught from the Penetralium of mystery, from being incapable of remaining content with half knowledge. This pursued through Volumes would perhaps take us no further than this, that with a great poet the sense of Beauty overcomes every other consideration, or rather obliterates all consideration.

Shelley's poem [3] is out, & there are words about its being objected too, as much as Queen Mab was. Poor Shelley I think he has his Quota of good qualities, in sooth la!! Write soon to your most sincere friend & affectionate Brother.

John

TO BENJAMIN BAILEY

Friday Jany 23rd [1818]

MY DEAR BAILEY,

Twelve days have pass'd since your last reached me — what has gone through the myriads of human Minds since the 12th we talk of the immense number of Books, the Volumes ranged thousands by thousands — but perhaps more goes through the human intelligence in 12 days than ever was written. How has that unfortunate Family lived through the twelve? One saying of your's I shall never forget — you may not recollect it — it being perhaps said when you were looking on the surface and seeming of Humanity alone, without a thought of the past or the future — or the deeps of good and evil — you were at the moment estranged from speculation and I think you have arguments ready for the Man who would utter it to you — this is a formidable preface for a simple thing — merely you said; *"Why should*

[3] *Laon and Cythna (The Revolt of Islam).*

Woman suffer?" Aye. Why should she? 'By heavens I'd coin my very
Soul and drop my Blood for Drachmas"! [1] These things are, and he who
feels how incompetent the most skyey Knight errantry its [*for* is] to
heal this bruised fairness is like a sensitive leaf on the hot hand of
thought. Your tearing, my dear friend, a spiritless and gloomy Letter
up ~~and~~ to rewrite to me is what I shall never forget — it was to me a
real thing. Things have happen'd lately of great Perplexity — You
must have heard of them — Reynolds and Haydon retorting and re-
crimminating — and parting for ever — the same thing has happened
between Haydon and Hunt — It is unfortunate — Men should bear
with each other — there lives not the Man who may not be cut up, aye
hashed to pieces on his weakest side. The best of Men have but a portion of good in them — a kind of spiritual yeast in their frames which
creates the ferment of existence — by which a Man is propell'd to act
and strive and buffet with Circumstance. The sure way Bailey, is first
to know a Man's faults, and then be passive, if after that he insensibly
draws you towards him then you have no Power to break the link.
Before I felt interested in either Reynolds or Haydon — I was well
read in their faults yet knowing them I have been cementing gradually
with both — I have an affection for them both for reasons almost opposite — and to both must I of necessity cling — supported always
by the hope that when a little time — a few years shall have tried me
more fully in their esteem I may be able to bring them together — the
time must come because they have both hearts — and they will recollect the best parts of each other when this gust is overblown. * * * * *
* * * * * * * I was at Hunt's the other day, and he surprised me with
a real authenticated Lock of *Milton's Hair.* I know you would like what
I wrote thereon — so here it is — *as they say of a Sheep in a* Nursery
Book

On seeing a Lock of Milton's Hair —
[Here follows the poem.]

This I did at Hunt's at his request — perhaps I should have done
something better alone and at home — I have sent my first book [2] to
the Press — and this afternoon shall begin preparing the second —
my visit to you will be a great spur to quicken the Proceeding —
* * * * * * * * * * My Brother Tom is getting stronger but his Spitting of blood continues — I sat down to read King Lear yesterday, and
felt the greatness of the thing up to the writing of a Sonnet preparatory
thereto — in my next you shall have it There were some miserable re-

[1] *Julius Caesar* IV.iii.72–3.
[2] Of *Endymion.*

ports of Rice's health — I went and lo! Master Jemmy had been to the play the night before and was out at the time — he always comes on his Legs like a Cat — I have seen a good deal of Wordsworth. Hazlitt is lectu[r]ing on Poetry at the Surr[e]y institution — I shall be there next Tuesday.

Your most affectionate Friend
John Keats —

TO JOHN HAMILTON REYNOLDS

[3 February 1818]
Hampstead Tuesday.

MY DEAR REYNOLDS,

I thank you for your dish of Filberts — Would I could get a basket of them by way of des[s]ert every day for the sum of two pence — Would we were a sort of ethereal Pigs, & turn'd loose to feed upon spiritual Mast & Acorns — which would be merely being a squirrel & feed[ing] upon filberts. for what is a squirrel but an airy pig, or a filbert but a sort of archangelical acorn. About the nuts being worth cracking, all I can say is that where there are a throng of delightful Images ready drawn simplicity is the only thing. the first is the best on account of the first line, and the "arrow — foil'd of its antler'd food" — and moreover (and this is the only only word or two I find fault with, the more because I have had so much reason to shun it as a quicksand) the last has "tender and true" — We must cut this, and not be rattle-snaked into any more of the like — It may be said that we ought to read our Contemporaries. that Wordsworth &c should have their due from us. but for the sake of a few fine imaginative or domestic passages, are we to be bullied into a certain Philosophy engendered in the whims of an Egotist — Every man has his speculations, but every man does not brood and peacock over them till he makes a false coinage and deceives himself — Many a man can travel to the very bourne of Heaven, and yet want confidence to put down his halfseeing. Sancho [1] will invent a Journey heavenward as well as any body. We hate poetry that has a palpable design upon us — and if we do not agree, seems to put its hand in its breeches pocket. Poetry should be great & unobtrusive, a thing which enters into one's soul, and does not startle it or amaze it with itself but with its subject. — How beautiful are the retired flowers! how would they lose their beauty were they to throng

[1] Don Quixote's squire.

into the highway crying out, "admire me I am a violet! dote upon me I am a primrose! Modern poets differ from the Elizabethans in this. Each of the moderns like an Elector of Hanover governs his petty state, & knows how many straws are swept daily from the Causeways in all his dominions & has a continual itching that all the Housewives should have their coppers well scoured: the antients were ~~Emperors of large~~ Emperors of vast Provinces, they had only heard of the remote ones and scarcely cared to visit them. — I will cut all this — I will have no more of Wordsworth or Hunt in particular — Why should we be of the tribe of Manasseh, when we can wander with Esau? why should we kick against the Pricks, when we can walk on Roses? Why should we be owls, when we can be Eagles? Why be teased with "nice Eyed wag-tails",[2] when we have in sight "the Cherub Contemplation"?[3] — Why with Wordsworths "Matthew with a bough of wilding in his hand"[4] when we can have Jacques "under an oak &c."?[5] — The secret of the Bough of Wilding will run through your head faster than I can write it — Old Matthew spoke to him some years ago on some nothing, & because he happens in an Evening Walk to imagine the figure of the old man — he must stamp it down in black & white, and it is henceforth sacred — I don't mean to deny Wordsworth's grandeur & Hunt's merit, but I mean to say we need not be teazed with grandeur & merit — when we can have them uncontaminated & unobtrusive. Let us have the old Poets, & robin Hood Your letter and its sonnets gave me more pleasure than will the 4th Book of Childe Harold & the whole of any body's life & opinions. In return for your dish of filberts, I have gathered a few Catkins, I hope they'll look pretty.

[Here follow *Robin Hood* and *Lines on the Mermaid Tavern*]

❖   ❖   ❖   ❖   ❖   ❖

Yr sincere friend and Coscribbler
John Keats.

TO JOHN HAMILTON REYNOLDS

[19 February 1818]

MY DEAR REYNOLDS,

I have an idea that a Man might pass a very pleasant life in this manner — let him on any certain day read a certain Page of full Poesy or

2 Leigh Hunt, *The Nymphs* ii.170.
8 *Il Penseroso* 54.
4 Wordsworth, *The Two April Mornings* 57–60.
5 *As You Like It* II.i.31.

distilled Prose and let him wander with it, and muse upon it, and
reflect from it, and bring home to it, and prophesy upon it, and dream
upon it — untill it becomes stale — but when will it do so? Never —
When Man has arrived at a certain ripeness in intellect any one grand
and spiritual passage serves him as a starting post towards all "the
two-and-thirty Pallaces" How happy is such a "voyage of conception,'
what delicious diligent Indolence! A doze upon a Sofa does not hinder
it, and a nap upon Clover engenders ethereal finger-pointings — the
prattle of a child gives it wings, and the converse of middle age a
strength to beat them — a strain of musick conducts to 'an odd angle
of the Isle' [1] and when the leaves whisper it puts a 'girdle round the
earth.' [2] Nor will this sparing touch of noble Books be any irreverance
to their Writers — for perhaps the honors paid by Man to Man are
trifles in comparison to the Benefit done by great Works to the 'Spirit
and pulse of good' [3] by their mere passive existence. Memory should
not be called knowledge — Many have original minds who do not
think it — they are led away by Custom — Now it appears to me that
almost any Man may like the Spider spin from his own inwards his own
airy Citadel — the points of leaves and twigs on which the Spider begins her work are few and she fills the Air with a beautiful circuiting:
man should be content with as few points to tip with the fine Webb
of his Soul and weave a tapestry empyrean — full of Symbols for his
spiritual eye, of softness for his spiritual touch, of space for his wandering of distinctness for his Luxury — But the Minds of Mortals are so
different and bent on such diverse Journeys that it may at first appear
impossible for any common taste and fellowship to exist ~~bettween~~
between two or three under these suppositions — It is however quite
the contrary — Minds would leave each other in contrary directions,
traverse each other in Numberless points, and all [*for* at] last greet
each other at the Journeys end—An old Man and a child would talk
together and the old Man be led on his Path, and the child left thinking — Man should not dispute or assert but whisper results to his
neighbour, and thus by every germ of Spirit sucking the Sap from
mould ethereal every human might become great, and Humanity instead of being a wide heath of Furse [4] and Briars with here and there a
remote Oak or Pine, would become a grand democracy of Forest Trees.
It has been an old Comparison for our urging on — the Bee hive —
however it seems to me that we should rather be the flower than the
Bee — for it is a false notion that more is gained by receiving than

[1] *The Tempest* I.ii.223.
[2] *A Midsummer Night's Dream* II.i.175.
[3] Wordsworth, *The Old Cumberland Beggar* 77
[4] *The Tempest* I.i.68–9.

giving — no the receiver and the giver are equal in their benefits —
The f[l]ower I doubt not receives a fair guerdon from the Bee — its
leaves blush deeper in the next spring — and who shall say between
Man and Woman which is the most delighted? Now it is more noble
to sit like Jove that [*for* than] to fly like Mercury — let us not therefore go hurrying about and collecting honey-bee like, buzzing here
and there impatiently from a knowledge of what is to be arrived at:
but let us open our leaves like a flower and be passive and receptive —
budding patiently under the eye of Apollo and taking hints from every
noble insect that favors us with a visit — sap will be given us for Meat
and dew for drink — I was led into these thoughts, my dear Reynolds,
by the beauty of the morning operating on a sense of Idleness — I have
not read any Books — the Morning said I was right — I had no Idea
but of the Morning and the Thrush said I was right — seeming to
say —

[Here follows *What the Thrush Said.*]

Now I am sensible all this is a mere sophistication, however it may
neighbour to any truths, to excuse my own indolence — so I will not
deceive myself that Man should be equal with jove — but think himself very well off as a sort of scullion-Mercury or even a humble Bee —
It is not [*for* no] matter whether I am right or wrong either one way
or another, if there is sufficient to lift a little time from your Shoulders.

Your affectionate friend
John Keats —

TO JOHN TAYLOR

[27 February 1818]
Hampstead 27 Feby —
~~London T~~ [*or* L]

MY DEAR TAYLOR,

Your alteration strikes me as being a great improvement — the page
looks much better. And now I will attend to the Punctuations you
speak of — the comma should be at *soberly*,[1] and in the other passage
the comma should follow *quiet,*.[2] I am extremely indebted to you for
this attention and also for your after admonitions — It is a sorry thing
for me that any one should have to overcome Prejudices in reading my

[1] *Endymion* i.149.
[2] *Ibid.*, i.247.

Verses — that affects me more than any hyper-criticism on any particular Passage. In *Endymion* I have most likely but moved into the Go-cart from the leading strings. In Poetry I have a few Axioms, and you will see how far I am from their Centre. 1st I think Poetry should surprise by a fine excess and not by Singularity — it should strike the Reader as a wording of his own highest thoughts, and appear almost a Remembrance — 2nd Its touches of Beauty should never be half way ther[e]by making the reader breathless instead of content: the rise, the progress, the setting of imagery should like the Sun come natural natural too him — shine over him and set soberly although in magnificence leaving him in the Luxury of twilight — but it is easier to think what Poetry should be than to write it — and this leads me on to another axiom. That if Poetry comes not as naturally as the Leaves to a tree it had better not come at all. However it may be with me I cannot help looking into new countries with 'O for a Muse of fire to ascend!' [3] — If Endymion serves me as a Pioneer perhaps I ought to be content. I have great reason to be content, for thank God I can read and perhaps understand Shakspeare to his depths, and I have I am sure many friends, who, if I fail, will attribute any change in my Life and Temper to Humbleness rather than to Pride — to a cowering under the Wings of great Poets rather than to a Bitterness that I am not appreciated. I am anxious to get Endymion printed that I may forget it and proceed. I have coppied the 3rd Book and have begun the 4th. On running my Eye over the Proofs — I saw one Mistake I will notice it presently and also any others if there be any — There should be no comma in 'the raft branch down sweeping from a tall Ash top' [4] — I have besides made one or two alteration[s] and also altered the 13 Line Page 32 to make sense of it as you will see. I will take care the Printer shall not trip up my Heels — There should be no dash after Dryope in this Line 'Dryope's lone lulling of her Child.[5] Remember me to Percy Street.

Your sincere and oblig^d friend
John Keats —

P. S. You shall have a sho[r]t *Preface* in good time —

[3] *Henry V*, Prologue 1.
[4] *Endymion* i 334–5.
[5]*Ibid.*, i.495.

TO BENJAMIN BAILEY

[13 March 1818]
Teignmouth Friday

MY DEAR BAILEY,

      ❋   ❋   ❋   ❋   ❋   ❋

I like, I love England, I like its strong Men — Give me a "long brown
plain" [1] for my Morning [*for* Money?] so I may meet with some of
Edmond Iron side's des[c]endants — Give me a barren mould so I may
meet with some shadowing of Alfred in the shape of a Gipsey, a Huntsman or as [*for* a] Shepherd. Scenery is fine — but human nature is
finer — The Sward is richer for the tread of a real, nervous, english
foot — the eagles nest is finer for the Mountaineer has look'd into it —
Are these facts or prejudices? Whatever they are, for them I shall never
be able to relish entirely any devonshire scenery — Homer is very fine,
Achilles is fine, Diomed is fine, Shakspeare is fine, Hamlet is fine, Lear
is fine, but dwindled englishmen are not fine — Where too the Women
are so passable, and have such english names, such as Ophelia, Cordelia & — that they should have such Paramours or rather Impara-
mours — As for them I cannot, in thought help wishing as did the
cruel Emperour, [2] that they had but one head and I might cut it off to
deliver them from any horrible Courtesy they may do their undeserv-
ing Countrymen — I wonder I meet with no born Monsters — O
Devonshire, last night I thought the Moon had dwindled in heaven —
I have never had your Sermon from Wordsworth but Mrs Dilke lent it
me — You know my ideas about Religion — I do not think myself
more in the right than other people and that nothing in this world is
proveable. I wish I could enter into all your feelings on the subject
merely for one short 10 Minutes and give you a Page or two to your
liking. I am sometimes so very sceptical as to think Poetry itself a mere
Jack a lanthern to amuse whoever may chance to be struck with its
brilliance — As Tradesmen say every thing is worth what it will fetch,
so probably every mental pursuit takes its reality and worth from the
ardour of the pursuer — being in itself a nothing — Ethereal thing[s]
may at least be thus real, divided under three heads — Things real —
things semireal — and no things — Things real — such as existences of
Sun Moon & Stars and passages of Shakspeare — Things semireal such

---

[1] *The Tempest* I.i.68–9.
[2] The Roman emperor Caligula.

as Love, the Clouds &c which require a greeting of the Spirit to make them wholly exist — and Nothings which are made Great and dignified by an ardent pursuit — Which by the by stamps the burgundy mark on the bottles of our Minds, insomuch as they are able to *"consec[r]ate whate'er they look upon"* [3] I have written a Sonnet here of a somewhat collateral nature — so don't imagine it an a propos des bottes.

[Here follows *The Human Seasons* — which was considerably altered before publication.]

Aye this may be carried — but what am I talking of — it is an old maxim of mine and of course must be well known that eve[r]y point of thought is the centre of an intellectual world — the two uppermost thoughts in a Man's mind are the two poles of his World he revolves on them and every thing is southward or northward to him through their means — We take but three steps from feathers to iron. Now my dear fellow I must once for all tell you I have not one Idea of the truth of any of my speculations — I shall never be a Reasoner because I care not to be in the right, when retired from bickering and in a proper philosophical temper — ° ° ° ° ° ° My Brother Tom desires to be remember'd to you — he has just this moment had a spitting of blood poor fellow — Remember me to Greig [*for* Gleig] and Whitehe[a]d —

Your affectionate friend
John Keats —

TO BENJAMIN ROBERT HAYDON

[8 April 1818]
Wednesday —

MY DEAR HAYDON,

I am glad you were pleased with my nonsense and if it so happen that the humour takes me when I have set down to prose to you I will not gainsay it. I should be (god forgive me) ready to swear because I cannot make use of you[r] assistance in going through Devon if I was not in my own Mind determined to visit it thoroughly at some more favorable time of the year. But now Tom (who is getting greatly better) is anxious to be in Town therefore I put off my threading the County. I purpose within a Month to put my knapsack at my back

[3] Shelley, *Hymn to Intellectual Beauty* 13–14.

and make a pedestrian tour through the North of England, and part of Scotland — to make a sort of Prologue to the Life I intend to pursue — that is to write, to study and to see all Europe at the lowest expence. I will clamber through the Clouds and exist. I will get such an accumulation of stupendous recollolections that as I walk through the suburbs of London I may not see them — I will stand upon Mount Blanc and remember this coming Summer when I intend to straddle ben Lomond — with my Soul! — galligaskins are out of the Question — I am nearer myself to hear your Christ is ~~having~~ being tinted into immortality — Believe me Haydon your picture is a part of myself — I have ever been too sensible of the labyrinthian path to eminence in Art (judging from Poetry) ever to think I understood the emphasis of Painting. The innumerable compositions and decompositions which take place between the intellect and its thousand materials before it arrives at that trembling delicate and snail-horn [1] perception of Beauty — I know not you[r] many havens of intenseness — nor ever can know them — but for this I hope no[ugh]t you atchieve is lost upon me: for when a Schoolboy the abstract Idea I had of an heroic painting — was what I cannot describe I saw it somewhat sideways large prominent round and colour'd with magnificence — somewhat like the feel I have of Anthony and Cleopatra. Or of Alcibiades, leaning on his Crimson Couch in his Galley, his broad shoulders imperceptibly heaving with the Sea — That [*for* What] passage in Shakspeare is finer than this

'See how the surly Warwick mans the Wall' [2]

*　*　*　*　*　*

I am affraid Wordsworth went rather huff'd out of Town — I am sorry for it. he cannot expect his fireside Divan to be infallible he cannot expect but that every Man of worth is as proud as himself. * * * *
* * * * * *

Remember me to Hazlitt, and Bewick — Your affectionate friend
John Keats —

---

[1] Cf. Shakespeare, *Venus and Adonis* 1033 f. (which Keats had quoted in a letter to Reynolds, 22 Nov., 1817). Rollins (I, 265) quotes Hazlitt (*Works,* ed. Howe, V, 51): "In Shakspeare there is a continual composition and decomposition of its elements, a fermentation of every particle in the whole mass. . . ."
[2] *3 Henry VI* V.i.17.

TO JOHN HAMILTON REYNOLDS

[3 May 1818]
Teignmouth May 3ᵈ

MY DEAR REYNOLDS.

What I complain of is that I have been in so an uneasy a state of Mind as not to be fit to write to an invalid. I cannot write to any length under a dis-guised feeling. I should have loaded you with an addition of gloom, which I am sure you do not want. I am now thank God in a humour to give you a good groats worth — for Tom, after a Night without a Wink of sleep, and overburdened with fever, has got up after a refreshing day sleep and is better than he has been for a long time; and you I trust have been again round the Common without any effect but refreshment. — As to the Matter I hope I can say with Sir Andrew "I have matter enough in my head" ¹ in your favor And now, in the second place, for I reckon that I have finished my Imprimis, I am glad you blow up the weather — all through your letter there is a leaning towards a climate-curse. and you know what a delicate satisfaction there is in having a vexation anathematized: one would think there has been growing up for these last four thousand years, a grandchild Scion of the old forbidden tree, and that some modern Eve had just violated it; and that there was come with double charge, "Notus and Afer black with thunderous clouds, from Sierra-leona" — ² I shall breathe worsted stockings sooner than I thought for. Tom wants to be in Town — we will have some such days upon the heath like that of last summer and why not with the same book: or what say you to a black Letter Chaucer printed in 1596: aye I've got one huzza! I shall have it bounden gothique a nice sombre binding — it will go a little way to unmodernize. And also I see no reason, because I have been away this last month, why I should not have a peep at your Spencerian — notwithstanding you speak of your office, in my thought a little too early, for I do not see why a Mind like yours is not capable of harbouring and digesting the whole Mystery of Law as easily as Parson Hugh does Pepins ³ — which did not hinder him from his poetic Canary — Were I to study physic or rather Medicine again, — I feel it would not make the least difference in my Poetry; when the Mind is in

¹ Slender, in *Merry Wives of Windsor* I.i.127.
² *Paradise Lost* x.702–3.
³ *Merry Wives of Windsor* I.ii.13.

its infancy a Bias ~~in~~ is in reality a Bias, but when we have acquired more strength, a Bias becomes no Bias. Every department of knowledge we see excellent and calculated towards a great whole. I am so convinced of this, that I am glad at not having given away my medical Books, which I shall again look over to keep alive the little I know thitherwards; and moreover intend through you and Rice to become a sort of Pip-civilian. An extensive knowlege is needful to thinking people — it takes away the heat and fever; and helps, by widening speculation, to ease the Burden of the Mystery: [4] a thing I begin to understand a little, and which weighed upon you in the most gloomy and true sentence in your Letter. The difference of high Sensations with and without knowledge appears to me this — in the latter case we are falling continually ten thousand fathoms deep and being blown up again without wings and with all [the] horror of a ~~Case~~ bare shoulderd Creature — in the former case, our shoulders are fledged, and we go thro' the same ~~Fir~~ air and space without fear.[5] This is running one's rigs on the score of abstracted benefit — when we come to human Life and the affections it is impossible [to know] how a parallel of breast and head can be drawn — (you will forgive me for thus privately ~~heading~~ treading out [of] my depth, and take it for treading as schoolboys ~~head~~ tread the waters) — it is impossible to know how far knowlege will console ~~as~~ us for the death of a friend and the ill "that flesh is heir too" [6] — With respect to the affections and Poetry you must know by a sympathy my thoughts that way; and I dare say these few lines will be but a ratification: I wrote them on May-day — and intend to finish the ode all in good time. —

[Here follows *Fragment of an Ode to Maia*]

You may be anxious to know for fact to what sentence in your Letter I allude. You say "I fear there is little chance of any thing else in this life". You seem by that to have been going through with a more painful and acute ~~test~~ zest the same labyrinth that I have — I have come to the same conclusion thus far. My Branchings out therefrom have been numerous: one of them is the consideration of Wordsworth's genius and as a help, in the manner of gold being the meridian Line of worldly wealth, — how he differs from Milton. — And here I have nothing but surmises, from an uncertainty whether Miltons apparently less anxiety for Humanity proceeds from his seeing further or no than Wordsworth: And whether Wordsworth has in truth epic passions, and

[4] Wordsworth, *Tintern Abbey* 38.
[5] Cf. *Paradise Lost* ii.933f., iii.627.
[6] *Hamlet* III.i.63.

martyrs himself to the human heart, the main region of his song [7] —
In regard to his genius alone — we find what he says true as far as we
have experienced and we can judge no further but by larger experience — for axioms in philosophy are not axioms until they are proved
upon our pulses: We read fine — things but never feel them to the full
until we have gone the same steps as the Author. — I know this is not
plain; you will know exactly my meaning when I say, that now I shall
relish Hamlet more than I ever have done — Or, better — You are
sensible no Man can set down Venery as a bestial or joyless thing until
he is sick of it and therefore all philosophizing on it would be mere
wording. Until we are sick, we understand not; — in fine, as Byron says,
"Knowledge is Sorrow"; [8] and I go on to say that "Sorrow is Wisdom"
— and further for aught we can know for certainty! "Wisdom is folly"
— So you see how I have run away from Wordsworth, and Milton, and
shall still run away from what was in my head, to observe, that some kind
of letters are good squares others handsome ovals, and others some orbi-
cular, others spheroid — and why should there not be another species
with two rough edges like a Rat-trap? I hope you will find all my long
letters of that species, and all will be well; for by merely touching the
spring delicately and etherially, the rough edged will fly immediately
into a proper compactness; and thus you may make a good wholesome
loaf, with your own le[a]ven in it, of my fragments — If you cannot find
this said Rat-trap sufficiently tractable — alas for me, it being an impossibility in grain for my ink to stain otherwise: If I scribble long letters I must play my vagaries. I must be too heavy, or too light, for
whole pages — I must be quaint and free of Tropes and figures — I
must play my draughts as I please, and for my advantage and your
erudition, crown a white with a black, or a black with a white, and
move into black or white, far and near as I please — I must go from
Hazlitt to Patmore, and make Wordsworth and Coleman play at leap-
frog — or keep one of them down a whole half holiday at fly the garter
— "From Gray to Gay, from Little to Shakespeare" [9] — Also, as a long
cause requires two or more sittings of the Court, so a long letter will
require two or more sittings of the Breech wherefore I shall resume
after dinner. —

Have you not seen a Gull, an orc, a Sea Mew,[10] or any thing to bring

[7] Cf. line 41 in the passage from *The Recluse* that Wordsworth quoted in
the preface to *The Excursion.*

[8] Byron, *Manfred* I.i.10.

[9] Apparently a variation on Pope, *Essay on Man* iv.380, "From grave to
gay, from lively to severe." "Thomas Little" was a pseudonym used by
Thomas Moore.

[10] Cf. *Paradise Lost* xi.835.

this Line to a proper length, and also fill up this clear part; that like
the Gull I may *dip* — I hope, not out of sight — and also, like a Gull,
I hope to be lucky in a good sized fish — This crossing a letter is not
without its association — for chequer work leads us naturally to a Milkmaid, a Milkmaid to Hogarth Hogarth to Shakespeare Shakespear to
Hazlitt — Hazlitt to Shakespeare and thus by merely pulling an apron
string we set a pretty peal of Chimes at work — Let them chime on
while, with your patience, — I will return to Wordsworth — whether
or no he has an extended vision or a circumscribed grandeur —
whether he is an eagle in his nest, or on the wing — And to be more
explicit and to show you how tall I stand by the giant, I will put down
a simile of human life as far as I now perceive it; that is, to the point
to which I say we both have arrived at — ' Well — I compare human
life to a large Mansion of Many Apartments, two of which I can only
describe, the doors of the rest being as yet shut upon me — The first
we step into we call the infant or thoughtless Chamber, in which we remain as long as we do not think — We remain there a long while, and
notwithstanding the doors of the second Chamber remain wide open,
showing a bright appearance, we care not to hasten to it; but are at
length imperceptibly impelled by the awakening of the thinking principle — within us — we no sooner get into the second Chamber,
which I shall call the Chamber of Maiden-Thought, than we become
intoxicated with the light and the atmosphere, we see nothing but
pleasant wonders, and think of delaying there for ever in delight: However among the effects this breathing is father of is that tremendous
one of sharpening one's vision into the head heart and nature of Man —
of convincing ones nerves that the World is full of Misery and Heartbreak, Pain, Sickness and oppression — whereby This Chamber of
Maiden Thought becomes gradually darken'd and at the same time on
all sides of it many doors are set open — but all dark — all leading to
dark passages — We see not the ballance of good and evil. We are in a
Mist — *We* are now in that state — We feel the "burden of the Mystery," To this Point was Wordsworth come, as far as I can conceive
when he wrote 'Tintern Abbey' and it seems to me that his Genius is
explorative of those dark Passages. Now if we live, and go on thinking,
we too shall explore them. he is a Genius and superior [to] us, in so far
as he can, more than we, make discoveries, and shed a light in them —
Here I must think Wordsworth is deeper than Milton — though I think
it has depended more upon the general and gregarious advance of
intellect, than individual greatness of Mind — From the Paradise Lost
and the other Works of Milton, I hope it is not too presuming, even
between ourselves to say, his Philosophy, human and divine, may

be tolerably understood by one not much advanced in years, In his time
englishmen were just emancipated from a great superstition — and
Men had got hold of certain points and resting places in reasoning
which were too newly born to be doubted, and too much oppressed opposed by the Mass of Europe not to be thought etherial and authen-
tically divine — who could gainsay his ideas on virtue, vice, and
Chastity in Comus, just at the time of the dismissal of Cod-pieces and
a hundred other disgraces? who would not rest satisfied with his hint-
ings at good and evil in the Paradise Lost, when just free from the
inquisition and burning in Smithfield? The Reformation produced such
immediate and greats benefits, that Protestantism was considered under
the immediate eye of heaven, and its own remaining Dogmas and
superstitions, then, as it were, regenerated, constituted those resting places and seeming sure points of Reasoning — from that I
have mentioned, Milton, whatever he may have thought in the
sequel, appears to have been content with these by his writings —
He did not think into the human heart, as Wordsworth has done —
Yet Milton as a Philosop[h]er, had sure as great powers as Wordsworth — What is then to be inferr'd? O many things — It proves
there is really a grand march of intellect — , It proves that a mighty
providence subdues the mightiest Minds to the service of the time
being, whether it be in human Knowledge or Religion — I have
often pitied a Tutor who has to hear "Nom^e: Musa" — so often
dinn'd into his ears — I hope you may not have the same pain in
this scribbling — I may have read these things before, but I never
had even a thus dim perception of them; and moreover I like to
say my lesson to one who will endure my tediousness for my own
sake — After all there is certainly something real in the World —
Moore's present to Hazlitt is real — I like that Moore, and am glad
that I saw him at the Theatre just before I left Town. Tom has spit a
leetle blood this afternoon, and that is rather a damper — but I
know — the truth is there is something real in the World Your
third Chamber of Life shall be a lucky and a gentle one — stored
with the wine of love — and the Bread of Friendship. When you
see George if he should not have recēd a letter from me tell
him he will find one at home most likely — tell Bailey I hope soon
to see him — Remember me to all The leaves have been out here,
for mony a day — I have written to George for the first stanzas of my
Isabel — I shall have them soon and will copy the whole out for you.

Your affectionate friend

John Keats.

TO BENJAMIN BAILEY

[10 June 1818]
London —

MY DEAR BAILEY,

I have been very much gratified and very much hurt by your Letters
in the Oxford Paper [1]: because indepependant of that unlawful and
mortal feeling of pleasure at praise, there is a glory in enthusia[s]m;
and because the world is malignant enough to chuckle at the most
honorable Simplicity. Yes on my Soul my dear Bailey you are too
simple for the World — and that Idea makes me sick of it — How
is it that by extreme opposites we have as it were got discon[ten]ted
nerves — you have all your Life (I think so) believed every Body
— I have suspected every Body — and although you have been so
deceived you make a simple appeal — the world has something else
to do, and I am glad of it — were it in my choice I would reject a
petrarchal coronation — on accou[n]t of my dying day, and because
women have Cancers. I should not by rights speak in this tone to you
— for it is an incendiary spirit that would do so. Yet I am not old
enough or magnanimous enough to an[n]ihilate self — and it would
perhaps be paying you an ill compliment. I was in hopes some little
time back to be able to releive your dullness by my spirits — to
point out things in the world worth your enjoyment — and now I am
never alone without rejoicing that there is such a thing as death —
without placing my ultimate in the glory of dying for a great human
purpose Perphaps if my affairs were in a different state I should not
have written the above — you shall judge — I have two Brothers one
is driven by the 'burden of Society' to America the other, with an
exquisite love of Life, is in a lingering state — My Love for my
Brothers from the early loss of our parents and even for earlier Misfortunes has grown into a[n] affection 'passing the Love of Women'[2]
— I have been ill temper'd with them, I have vex'd them — but the
thought of them has always stifled the impression that any woman
might otherwise have made upon me — I have a Sister too and may
not follow them, either to America or to the Grave — Life must be

---

[1] In the *Oxford University and City Herald,* May 30 and June 6, 1818,
Bailey printed two letters in a well-meant effort to forestall hostile criticism
of *Endymion.*
[2] 2 Samuel i.26.

undergone, and I certainly derive a consolation from the thought of writing one or two more Poems before it ceases — I have heard some hints of your retireing to scotland — I should like to know your feeling on it — it seems rather remote — perhaps Gle[i]g will have a duty near you. I am not certain whether I shall be able to go my Journey on account of my Brother Tom and a little indisposition of my own — If I do not you shall see me soon — if no[t] on my return — or I'll quarter myself upon you in Scotland next Winter. I had know[n] my sister in Law some time before she was my Sister and was very fond of her. I like her better and better — she is the most disinterrested woman I ever knew — that is to say she goes beyond degree in it. To see an entirelely disinterrested Girl quite happy is the most pleasant and extraordinary thing in the world — it depends upon a thousand Circumstances — on my word 't is extraordinary. Women must want Imagination and they may thank God for it — and so m[a]y we that a delicate being can feel happy without any sense of crime. It puzzles me and I have no sort of Logic to comfort me — I shall think it over. I am not at home and your letter being there I cannot look it over to answer any particular — only I must say I felt that passage of Dante — if I take any book with me it shall be those minute volumes of carey for they will go into the aptest corner. Reynolds is getting I may say robust — his illness has been of service to him — like eny one just recoverd he is high-spirited. I hear also good accounts of Rice — With respect to domestic Literature — the Endinburgh Magasine in another blow up against Hunt calls me 'the amiable Mister Keats' [3] and I have more than a Laurel from the Quarterly Reviewers for they have *smothered* me in 'Foliage' [4] I want to read you my 'Pot of Basil' if you go to scotland I should much like to read it there to you among the Snows of next Winter. My Brothers' remembrances to you.

Your affectionate friend
John Keats —

[3] In a "Letter from Z. to Leigh Hunt, King of the Cockneys," in *Blackwood's Edinburgh Magazine*, III (May, 1818), 197; quoted in MacGillivray, *Keats*, p. 65.

[4] Hunt's *Foliage* was reviewed in the *Quarterly Review*, XVIII (1818), 324–35.

TO JAMES AUGUSTUS HESSEY

[8 October 1818]

MY DEAR HESSEY,

You are very good in sending me the letter from the Chronicle — and I am very bad in not acknowledging such a kindness sooner. — pray forgive me. — It has so chanced that I have had that paper every day — I have seen today's. I cannot but feel indebted to those Gentlemen who have taken my part — As for the rest, I begin to get a little acquainted with my own strength and weakness. — Praise or blame has but a momentary effect on the man whose love of beauty in the abstract makes him a severe critic on his own Works. My own domestic criticism has given me pain without comparison beyond what Blackwood or the ~~Edinburgh~~ Quarterly could possibly inflict. and also when I feel I am right, no external praise can give me such a glow as my own solitary reperception & ratification of what is fine. J. S.[1] is perfectly right in regard to the slip-shod Endymion. That it is so is no fault of mine. — No! — though it may sound a little paradoxical. It is as good as I had power to make it — by myself — Had I been nervous about its being a perfect piece, & with that view asked advice, & trembled over every page, it would not have been written; for it is not in my nature to fumble — I will write independantly. — I have written independently *without Judgment.* — I may write independently & *with judgment* hereafter. — The Genius of Poetry must work out its own salvation in a man: It cannot be matured by law & precept, but by sensation & watchfulness in itself — That which is creative must create itself — In Endymion, I leaped headlong into the Sea, and thereby have become better acquainted with the Soundings, the quicksands, & the rocks, than if I had ~~stayed~~ stayed upon the green shore, and piped a silly pipe, and took tea & comfortable advice. — I was never afraid of failure; for I would sooner fail than not be among the greatest — But I am nigh getting into a rant. So, with remembrances to Taylor and Woodhouse &c I am

Yrs very sincerely
John Keats.

[1] Probably John Scott was the J. S. who sent a letter to the *Morning Chronicle* defending Keats against Croker's attack (Rollins, I, 373).

TO RICHARD WOODHOUSE

[27 October 1818]

MY DEAR WOODHOUSE,

Your Letter gave me a great satisfaction; more on account of its friendliness, than any relish of that matter in it which is accounted so acceptable in the 'genus irritabile'.[1] The best answer I can give you is in a clerklike manner to make some observations on two principle points, which seem to point like indices into the midst of the whole pro and con, about genius, and views and atchievements and ambition and cœtera. 1st As to the poetical Character itself, (I mean that sort of which, if I am any thing, I am a Member; that sort distinguished from the wordsworthian or egotistical sublime; which is a thing per se and stands alone [2]) it is not itself — it has no self — it is every thing and nothing — It has no character — it enjoys light and shade; it lives in gusto, be it foul or fair, high or low, rich or poor, mean or elevated — It has as much delight in conceiving an Iago as an Imogen. What shocks the virtuous philosop[h]er, delights the camelion Poet. It does no harm from its relish of the dark side of things any more than from its taste for the bright one; because they both end in speculation. A Poet is the most unpoetical of any thing in existence; because he has no Identity — he is continually in for — and filling some other Body — The Sun, the Moon, the Sea and Men and Women who are creatures of impulse are poetical and have about them an unchangeable attribute — the poet has none; no identity — he is certainly the most unpoetical of all God's Creatures. If then he has no self, and if I am a Poet, where is the Wonder that I should say I would ~~right~~ write no more? Might I not at that very instant [have] been cogitating on the Characters of saturn and Ops? It is a. wretched thing to confess; but is a very fact that not one word I ever utter can be taken for granted as an opinion growing out of my identical nature — how can it, when I have no nature? When I am in a room with People if I ever am free from speculating on creations of my own brain, then not myself goes home to myself: [3] but the identity of every one in the room begins to [*for so?*] to press upon

---

1 "The irritable tribe [of poets]." Horace, *Epistles* II.ii.102.
2 Cf. Shakespeare, *Troilus and Cressida* I.ii.15f. (Rollins, I,387).
3 Cf. *ibid.*, III.iii.105,107 (Rollins, *l.c.*).

me that, I am in a very little time an[ni]hilated — not only among Men; it would be the same in a Nursery of children: I know not whether I make myself wholly understood: I hope enough so to let you see that no dependence is to be placed on what I said that day.

In the second place I will speak of my views, and of the life I purpose to myself — I am ambitious of doing the world some good: if I should be spared that may be the work of maturer years — in the interval I will assay to reach to as high a summit in Poetry as the nerve bestowed upon me will suffer. The faint conceptions I have of Poems to come brings the blood frequently into my forehead — All I hope is that I may not lose all interest in human affairs — that the solitary indifference I feel for applause even from the finest Spirits, will not blunt any acuteness of vision I may have. I do not think it will — I feel assured I should write from the mere yearning and fondness I have for the Beautiful even if my night's labours should be burnt every morning and no eye ever shine upon them. But even now I am perhaps not speaking from myself; but from some character in whose soul I now live. I am sure however that this next sentence is from myself. I feel your anxiety, good opinion and friendliness in the highest degree, and am

Your's most sincerely
John Keats

TO GEORGE AND GEORGIANA KEATS

[16 December 1818 — 4 January 1819]

MY DEAR BROTHER AND SISTER,

You will have been prepared, before this reaches you for the worst news you could have, nay if Haslam's letter arrives in proper time, I have a consolation in thinking the first shock will be past before you receive this. The last days of poor Tom were of the most distressing nature; but his last moments were not so painful, and his very last was without a pang — I will not enter into any parsonic comments on death — yet the common observations of the commonest people on death are as true as their proverbs. I have scarce a doubt of immortality of some nature of [*for* or] other — neither had Tom. My friends have been exceedingly kind to me every one of them — Brown detained me at his House. I suppose no one could have had their time made smoother than mine has been. During poor Tom's illness I was not able to write and since his death the task of beginning has been a hindrance to me. Within this last Week I have been every where — and I will tell you as nearly as possible how all go on — With Dilke and Brown I am quite thick — with Brown indeed I am going to domesticate — that is, wee shall keep house together — I Shall have the front parlour and he the back one — by which I shall avoid the noise of Bentley's Children — and be the better able to go on with my Studies — which [h]ave been greatly interrupted lately, so that I have not the Shadow of an idea of a book in my head, and my pen seems to have grown too goutty for verse. How are you going on now? The going[s] on of the world make me dizzy — there you are with Birkbeck — here I am with brown — sometimes I fancy an immense separation, and sometimes, as at present, a direct communication of spirit with you. That will be one of the grandeurs of immortality — there will be no space and consequently the only commerce between spirits will be by their intelligence of each other — when they will completely understand each other — while we in this world merely comp[r]ehend each other in different degrees — the higher the degree of good so higher is our Love and friendship — * * * * * * * *

Mrs Brawne who took Brown's house for the Summer, still resides in Hampstead — she is ~~her~~ a very nice woman — and her daughter senior is I think beautiful and elegant, graceful, silly, fashionable and strange we have a little tiff now and then — and she behaves a little better, or I must have sheered off. * * * * * *

[December 18]. * * * Shall I give you Miss Brawn[e]? She is about my height — with a fine style of countenance of the lengthen'd sort — she wants sentiment in every feature — she manages to make her hair look well — her nostrills are fine — though a little painful — he[r] mouth is bad and good — he[r] Profil is better than her full-face which indeed is not full put [*for* but] pale and thin without showing any bone — Her shape is very graceful and so are her movements — her Arms are good her hands badish — her feet tolerable — she is not seventeen — but she is ignorant — monstrous in her behaviour flying out in all directions, calling people such names — that I was forced lately to make use of the term *Minx* — this is I think no[t] from any innate vice but from a penchant she has for acting stylishly. I am however tired of such style and shall decline any more of it. * * * * *

[December 31] * * * The more we know the more inadequacy we discover in the world to satisfy us — this is an old observation; but I have made up my Mind never to take any thing for granted — but even to examine the truth of the commonest proverbs — This however is true — Mrs Tighe and Beattie once delighted me — now I see through them and can find nothing in them — or weakness — and yet how many they still delight! [1] Perhaps a superior being may look upon Shakspeare in the same light — is it possible? * * * * But I'll go no further — I may be speaking sacrilegiously — and on my word I have thought so little that I have not one opinion upon any thing except in matters of taste — I never can feel certain of any truth but from a clear perception of its Beauty — and I find myself very young minded even in that perceptive power — which I hope will encrease — A year ago I could not understand in the slightest degree Raphael's cartoons — now I begin to read them a little — and how did I lea[r]n to do so? By seeing something done in quite an opposite spirit — I mean a picture of Guido's in which all the Saints, instead of that heroic simplicity and unaffected grandeur which they inherit from Raphael, had each of them both in countenance and gesture all the canting, solemn melodramatic mawkishness of Mackenzie's father Nicholas [2] — When I was last at Haydon's I look[ed] over a Book of Prints taken from the fresco of the Church at Milan [3] the name of which I forget — in it are comprised Specimens of the first and second age of art in Italy — I do not think I ever had a greater treat out of Shakspeare — Full of Romance and the most tender feeling — magnificence of draperies beyond any I ever saw not excepting Raphael's — But Grotesque to a curious pitch — yet still making up a fine whole — even finer to me than more accomplish'd works — as there was left so much room for Imagination. * * * *

[Under Jan. 2 Keats copies *Fancy* and "Bards of Passion and of Mirth."]

My dearest brother and sister
Your most affectionate Brother
John —

[1] The *Psyche* (1805) of Mrs. Tighe (1772–1810) is quoted sometimes in the notes. The earlier and more important Spenserian, James Beattie (1735–1803), published *The Minstrel* in 1771–4.

[2] "The Story of Father Nicholas," by the novelist Henry Mackenzie (1745–1831), in *Works* (1808), VI, 238–73.

[3] Actually from the Campo Santo at Pisa (see Rollins' note. II,19).

TO GEORGE AND GEORGIANA KEATS

[14 February–3 May 1819]
sunday Morn Feby 14th

MY DEAR BROTHER & SISTER —

* * * I am still at Wentworth Place — indeed I have kept in doors
lately, resolved if possible to rid myself of my sore throat — consequently, i have not been to see your Mother since my return from
Chichester — but my absence from her has been a great weight upon
me — I say since my return from Chichester — I believe I told you I
was going thither — I was nearly a fortnight at Mr John Snook's and
a few days at old Mr Dilke's — Nothing worth speaking of happened
at either place — I took down some of the thin paper and wrote on it
a little Poem call'd 'St Agnes Eve' — which you shall have as it is
when I have finished the blank part of the rest for you — I went out
twice at Chichester to old Dowager card parties — I see very little
now, and very few Persons — being almost tired of Men and things
— Brown and Dilke are very kind and considerate towards me — The
Miss Reynoldses have been stoppi[n]g next door lately — but all very
dull — Miss Brawne and I have every now and then a chat and a tiff
— Brown and Dilke are walking round their Garden hands in Pockets
making observations. The Literary world I know nothing about —
There is a Poem from Rogers dead born — and another Satire is ex-
pected from Byron call'd Don Giovanni — * * *

In my next Packet as this is one by the by way, I shall send you the
Pot of Basil, St Agnes eve, and if I should have finished it a little thing
call'd the 'eve of St Mark' you see what fine mother Radcliff names I
have — it is not my fault — I did not search for them — I have not
gone on with Hyperion — for to tell the truth I have not been in great
cue for writing lately — I must wait for the sp[r]ing to rouse me up a
little — The only time I went out from Bedhampton was to see a
Chapel consecrated — Brown I and John Snook the boy, went in a
chaise behind a leaden horse Brown drove, but the horse did not mind
him * * * *

Friday Feby 18 [actually February 19] * * * I have not said in
any Letter yet a word about my affairs — in a word I am in no despair
about them — my poem has not at all succeeded — in the course of a
year or so I think I shall try the public again — in a selfish point of
view I should suffer my pride and my contempt of public opinion to

hold me silent — but for your's and fanny's sake I will pluck up a spirit, and try again. I have no doubt of success in a course of years if I persevere — but it must be patience — for the Reviews have enervated and made indolent mens minds — few think for themselves — These Reviews too are getting more and more powerful and especially the Quarterly * * * *

A Man's life of any worth is a continual allegory — and very few eyes can see the Mystery of his life — a life like the scriptures, figurative — which such people can no more make out than they can the hebrew Bible. Lord Byron cuts a figure — but he is not figurative — Shakspeare led a life of Allegory: his works are the comments on it —

* * * * * *

Friday [March] *19ᵗʰ* Yesterday I got a black eye — the first time I took a Cr[icket] bat — Brown who is always one's friend in a disaster [app]lied a le[ech to] the eyelid, and there is no infla[mm]ation this morning though the ball hit me dir[ectl]y on the sight — 't was a white ball — I am glad it was not a clout — This is the second black eye I have had since leaving school — during all my [scho]ol days I never had one at all — we must e[a]t a peck before we die — This morning I am in a sort of temper indolent and supremely careless: I long after a stanza or two of Thompson's Castle of indolence. My passions are all alseep [*for* asleep] from my having slumbered till nearly eleven and weakened the animal fibre all over me to a delightful sensation about three degrees on this side of faintness — if I had teeth of pearl and the breath of lillies I should call it langour — but as I am †
I must call it Laziness — In this state of effeminacy the fibres of the brain are relaxed in common with the rest of the body, and to such a happy degree that pleasure has no show of enticement and pain no unbearable frown. Neither Poetry, nor Ambition, nor Love have any alertness of countenance as they pass by me: they seem rather like three figures on a greek vase — a Man and two women — whom no one but myself could distinguish in their disguisement. This is the only happiness; and is a rare instance of advantage in the body overpowering the Mind. I have this moment received a note from Haslam in which he expects the death of his Father who has been for some time in a state of insensibility — his mother bears up he says very well — I shall go to twon [*for* town] tommorrow to see him. This is the world — thus we cannot expect to give way many hours to pleasure — Circumstances are like Clouds continually gathering and bursting — While we are laughing the seed of some trouble is put into he the wide arable land

† especially as I have a black eye

of events — while we are laughing it sprouts is [*for* it] grows and suddenly bears a poison fruit which we must pluck — Even so we have
leisure to reason on the misfortunes of our friends; our own touch us
too nearly for words. Very few men have ever arrived at a complete disinterestedness of Mind: very few have been influenced by a pure desire
of the benefit of others — in the greater part of the Benefactors ~~of~~ &
to Humanity some meretricious motive has sullied their greatness —
some melodramatic scenery has fa[s]cinated them — From the manner
in which I feel Haslam's misfortune I perceive how far I am from any
humble standard of disinterestedness — Yet this feeling ought to be
carried to its highest pitch, as there is no fear of its ever injuring society
— which it would do I fear pushed to an extremity — For in wild
nature the Hawk would loose his Breakfast of Robins and the Robin his
of Worms The Lion must starve as well as the swallow — The greater
part of Men make their way with the same instinctiveness, the same un-
wandering eye from their purposes, the same animal eagerness as the
Hawk — The Hawk wants a Mate, so does the Man — look at them
both they set about it and procure on[e] in the same manner — They
want both a nest and they both set about one in the same manner —
they get their food in the same manner — The noble animal Man for
his amusement smokes his pipe — the Hawk balances about the Clouds
— that is the only difference of their leisures. This it is that makes the
Amusement of Life — to a speculative Mind. I go among the Feilds
and catch a glimpse of a stoat or a fieldmouse peeping out of the withered grass — the creature hath a purpose and its eyes are bright with
it — I go amongst the buildings of a city and I see a Man hurrying
along — to what? The Creature has a purpose and his eyes are bright
with it. But then as Wordsworth says, "we have all one human heart" [1]
— there is an ellectric fire in human nature tending to purify — so that
among these human creature[s] there is continu[a]lly some birth of
new heroism — The pity is that we must wonder at it: as we should
at finding a pearl in rubbish — I have no doubt that thousands of
people never heard of have had hearts comp[l]etely disinterested: I
can remember but two — Socrates and Jesus — their Histories evince
it — What I heard a little time ago, Taylor observe with respect to
Socrates, may be said of Jesus — That he was so great as man that
though he transmitted no writing of his own to posterity, we have his
Mind and his sayings and his greatness handed to us by others. It is to
be lamented that the history of the latter was written and revised by
Men interested in the pious frauds of Religion. Yet through all this I
see his splendour. Even here though I myself am pursueing the same

[1] *The Old Cumberland Beggar* 153.

instinctive course as the veriest human animal you can think of — I
am however young writing at random — straining at particles of light
in the midst of a great darkness — without knowing the bearing of any
one assertion of any one opinion. Yet may I not in this be free from
sin? May there not be superior beings amused with any graceful,
though instinctive attitude my mind m[a]y fall into, as I am entertained
with the alertness of a Stoat or the anxiety of a Deer? Though a quarrel in the streets is a thing to be hated, the energiies displayed in it are
fine; the commonest Man shows a grace in his quarrel — By a superior
being our reasoning[s] may take the same tone — though erroneous
they may be fine — This is the very thing in which consists poetry;
and if so it is not so fine a thing as philosophy — For the same reason
that an eagle is not so fine a thing as a truth — Give me this credit —
Do you not think I strive — to know myself? Give me this credit —
and you will not think that on my own accou[n]t I repeat Milton's
lines

> "How charming is divine Philosophy
> Not harsh and crabbed as dull fools suppose
> But musical as is Apollo's lute" — 2

No — no[t?] for myself — feeling grateful as I do to have got into
a state of mind to relish them properly — Nothing ever becomes
real till it is experienced — Even a Proverb is no proverb to you till
your Life has illustrated it — I am ever affraid that your anxiety for
me will lead you to fear for the violence of my temperament continually smothered down: for that reason I did not intend to have
sent you the following sonnet — but look over the two last pages
and ask yourselves whether I have not that in me which will well
bear the buffets of the world. It will be the best comment on my sonnet; it will show you that it was written with no Agony but that
of ignorance; with no thirst of any thing but knowledge when pushed
to the point though the first steps to it were throug[h] my human
passions — they went away, and I wrote with my Mind — and perhaps I must confess a little bit of my heart —

[Here follows *Why Did I Laugh Tonight?*]

I went to ~~bead~~ bed, and enjoyed an uninterrupted sleep — Sane I
went to bed and sane I ~~aose~~ arose.

*   *   *   *   *   *

[15 April]. * * * Last Sunday I took a Walk towards highgate and
2 *Comus* 475–7.

in the lane that winds by the side of Lord Mansfield's park I met
Mr Green our Demonstrator at Guy's in conversation with Coleridge
— I joined them, after enquiring by a look whether it would be agree-
able — I walked with him a[t] his alderman-after dinner pace for
near two miles I suppose In those two Miles he broached a thousand
things — let me see if I can give you a list — Nightingales, Poetry —
on Poetical sensation — Metaphysics — Different genera and species
of Dreams — Nightmare — a dream accompanied ~~with~~ by a sense of
touch — single and double touch — A dream related — First and second consciousness — the difference explained between will and Volition
— so m[an]y metaphysicians from a want of smoking the second
consciousness —Monsters — the Kraken — Mermaids — southey be-
lieves in them — southeys belief too much diluted — A Ghost story —
Good morning — I heard his voice as he came towards me — I heard
it as he moved away — I had heard it all the interval — if it may be
called so. He was civil enough to ask me to call on him at Highgate
Good night! * * * * * * *

[In the next few pages Keats copies *On a Dream* and *La Belle Dame
sans Merci*.]

 *   *   *   *   *   *

[21 April]. * * * I have been reading lately two very different books
Robertson's America and Voltaire's Siecle De Louis XIV It is like
walking arm and arm between Pizarro and the great-little Monarch.
In How lementabl[e] a case do we see the great body of the people in
both instances: in the first, where Men might seem to inherit quiet of
Mind from unsophisticated senses; from uncontamination of civilisa-
tion; and especially from their being as it were estranged from the
mutual helps of Society and its mutual injuries — and thereby more
immediately under the Protection of Providence — even there they
had mortal pains to bear as bad; or even worse than Ba[i]liffs, Debts
and Poverties of civilised Life — The whole appears to resolve into
this — that Man is originally 'a poor forked creature' [3] subject to the
same mischances as the beasts of the forest, destined to hardships and
disquietude of some kind or other. If he improves by degrees his bodily
accom[m]odations and comforts — at each stage, at each accent [*for
ascent*] there are waiting for him a fresh set of annoyances — he is
mortal and there is still a heaven with its Stars abov[e] his head. The
most interesting question that can come before us is, How far by the
persevering endeavours of a seldom appearing Socrates Mankind may
be made happy — I can imagine such happiness carried to an extreme

[3] *King Lear* III.iv.112–13.

— but what must it end in? — Death — and who could in such a case bear with death — the whole troubles of life which are now frittered away in a series of years, would the[n] be accumulated for the last days of a being who instead of hailing its approach, would leave this world as Eve left Paradise — But in truth I do not at all believe in this sort of perfectibility — the nature of the world will not admit of it — the inhabitants of the world will correspond to itself — Let the fish philosophise the ice away from the Rivers in winter time and they shall be at continual play in the tepid delight of summer. Look at the Poles and at the sands of Africa, Whirlpools and volcanoes — Let men exterminate them and I will say that they may arrive at earthly Happiness — The point at which Man may arrive is as far as the paral[l]el state in inanimate nature and no further — For instance suppose a rose to have sensation, it blooms on a beautiful morning it enjoys itself — but there comes a cold wind, a hot sun — it can not escape it, it cannot destroy its annoyances — they are as native to the world as itself: no more can man be happy in spite, the world[l]y elements will prey upon his nature — The common cognomen of this world among the misguided and superstitious is 'a vale of tears' from which we are to be redeemed by a certain arbit[r]ary interposition of God and taken to Heaven — What a little circumscribe[d] straightened notion! Call the world if you Please "The vale of Soul-making" Then you will find out the use of the world (I am speaking now in the highest terms for human nature admitting it to be immortal which I will here take for granted for the purpose of showing a thought which has struck me concerning it) I say '*Soul making*' Soul as distinguished from an Intelligence — There may be intelligences or sparks of the divinity in millions — but they are not Souls the till they acquire identities, till each one is personally itself. I[n]telligences are atoms of perception — they know and they see and they are pure, in short they are God — How then are Souls to be made? How then are these sparks which are God to have identity given them — so as ever to possess a bliss peculiar to each ones individual existence? How, but by the medium of a world like this? This point I sincerely wish to consider because I think it a grander system of salvation than the chrystean religion — or rather it is a system of Spirit-creation — This is effected by three grand materials acting the one upon the other for a series of years. These three Materials are the *Intelligence* — the *human heart* (as distinguished from intelligence or Mind) and the *World* or *Elemental space* suited for the proper action of *Mind and Heart* on each other for the purpose of forming the *Soul* or *Intelligence destined to possess the sense of Identity*. I can scarcely express what I but dimly perceive

— and yet I think I perceive it — that you may judge the more clearly I will put it in the most homely form possible — I will call the *world* a School instituted for the purpose of teaching little children to read — I will call the *human heart* the *horn Book* used in that School — and I will call the *Child able to read, the Soul* made from that *school* and its *hornbook*. Do you not see how necessary a World of Pains and troubles is to school an Intelligence and make it a soul? A Place where the heart must feel and suffer in a thousand diverse ways! Not merely is the Heart a Hornbook, It is the Minds Bible, it is the Minds experience, it is the teat from which the Mind or intelligence sucks its identity — As various as the Lives of Men are — so various become their souls, and thus does God make individual beings, Souls, Identical Souls of the sparks of his own essence — This appears to me a faint sketch of a system of Salvation which does not affront our reason and humanity — I am convinced that many difficulties which christians labour under would vanish before it — there is one wh[i]ch even now Strikes me — the Salvation of Children — In them the Spark or intelligence returns to God without any identity — it having had no time to learn of, and be altered by, the heart — or seat of the human Passions — It is pretty generally suspected that the chr[i]stian scheme has been coppied from the ancient persian and greek Philosophers. Why may they not have made this simple thing even more simple for common apprehension by introducing Mediators and Personages in the same manner as in the he[a]then mythology abstractions are personified — Seriously I think it probable that this System of Soul-making — may have been the Parent of all the more palpable and personal Schemes of Redemption, among the Zoroastrians the Christians and the Hindoos. For as one part of the human species must have their carved Jupiter; so another part must have the palpable and named Mediatior and saviour, their Christ their Oromanes and their Vishnu — If what I have said should not be plain enough, as I fear it may not be, I will but [*for* put] you in the place where I began in this series of thoughts — I mean, I began by seeing how man was formed by circumstances — and what are circumstances? — but touchstones of his heart —? and what are touchstones? — but proovings of his hearrt? and what are proovings of his heart but fortifiers or alterers of his nature? and what is his altered nature but his soul? — and what was his soul before it came into the world and had These provings and alterations and perfectionings? – An intelligences — without Identity — and how is this Identity to be made? Through the medium of the Heart? And how is the heart to become this Medium but in a world of Circumstances? * * *

[The last pages include tl e sonnets *On Fame* and *To Sleep*, the *Ode to Psyche*, and *On the Sonnet*.]

. . . this is the 3ᵈ of May & every thing is in delightful forwardness; the violets are not withered, before the peeping of the first rose; You must let me know every thing, how parcels go & come, what papers you have, & what Newspapers you want, & other things — God bless you my dear Brother & Sister

Your ever Affectionate Brother,
John Keats —

TO FANNY BRAWNE

[Isle of Wight, 25 July 1819]
Sunday Night.

MY SWEET GIRL,

I hope you did not blame me much for not obeying your request of a Letter on Saturday: we have had four in our small room playing at cards night and morning leaving me no undisturb'd opportunity to write. Now Rice and Martin are gone I am at liberty. Brown to my sorrow confirms the account you give of your ill health. You cannot conceive how I ache to be with you: how I would die for one hour — for what is in the world? I say you cannot conceive; it is impossible you should look with such eyes upon me as I have upon you: it cannot be. Forgive me if I wander a little this evening, for I have been all day employ'd in a very abstr[a]ct Poem and I am in deep love with you — two things which must excuse me. I have, believe me, not been an age in letting you take possession of me; the very first week I knew you I wrote myself your vassal; but burnt the Letter as the very next time I saw you I thought you manifested some dislike to me. If you should ever feel for Man at the first sight what I did for you, I am lost. Yet I should not quarrel with you, but hate myself if such a thing were to happen — only I should burst if the thing were not as fine as a Man as you are as a Woman. Perhaps I am too vehement, then fancy me on my knees, especially when I mention a part of you[r] Letter which hurt me; you say speaking of Mr. Severn "but you must be satisfied in knowing that I admired you much more than your friend." My dear love, I cannot believe there ever was or ever could be any thing to admire in me especially as far as sight goes — I cannot be admired, I am not a thing to be admired. You are, I love you; all I can bring you is a swooning admiration of your Beauty. I hold that

place among Men which snubnos'd brunettes with meeting eyebrows
do among women — they are trash to me — unless I should find one
among them with a fire in her heart like the one that burns in mine.
You absorb me in spite of myself — you alone: for I look not forward
with any pleasure to what is call'd being settled in the world; I tremble
at domestic cares — yet for you I would meet them, though if it
would leave you the happier I would rather die than do so. I have
two luxuries to brood over in my walks, your Loveliness and the hour
of my death. O that I could have possession of them both in the same
minute. I hate the world: it batters too much the wings of my self-will,
and would I could take a sweet poison from your lips to send me out
of it. From no others would I take it. I am indeed astonish'd to find
myself so careless of all cha[r]ms but yours — rememb[e]ring as I do
the time when even a bit of ribband was a matter of interest with me.
What softer words can I find for you after this — what it is I will not
read. Nor will I say more here, but in a Postscript answer any thing
else you may have mentioned in your Letter in so many words — for
I am distracted with a thousand thoughts. I will imagine you Venus
tonight and pray, pray, pray to your star like a He[a]then.

Your's ever, fair Star,
John Keats

[Postscript omitted]

TO BENJAMIN BAILEY

[14 August 1819]

❋　　❋　　❋　　❋　　❋　　❋

We removed to Winchester for the convenience of a Library and
find it an exceeding pleasant Town, enriched with a beautiful
Cathedrall and surrounded by a fresh-looking country. We are in
tolerably good and cheap Lodgings. Within these two Months I have
written 1500 Lines, most of which besides many more of prior composition you will probably see by next Winter. I have written two
Tales, one from Boccac[c]io call'd the Pot of Basil; and another call'd
St Agnes' Eve on a popular superstition; and a third call'd Lamia —
(half finished — I have also been writing parts of my Hyperion [1] and
completed 4 Acts of a Tragedy. It was the opinion of most of my
friends that I should never be able to write a scene — I will endeavour
to wipe away the prejudice — I sincerely hope you will be pleased
when my Labours since we last saw each other shall reach you — One
of my Ambitions is to make as great a revolution in modern dramatic

---

[1] That is, *The Fall of Hyperion.*

writing as Kean has done in acting — another to upset the drawling of the blue stocking literary world — if in the course of a few years I do these two things I ought to die content — and my friends should drink a dozen of Claret on my Tomb — I am convinced more and more every day that (excepting the human friend Philosopher) a fine writer is the most genuine Being in the World. Shakspeare and the paradise Lost every day become greater wonders to me — I look upon fine Phrases like a Lover — I was glad to see, by a Passage in one of Brown's Letters some time ago from the north that you were in such good Spirits — Since that you have been married and in congra[tu]-lating you I wish you every continuance of them — Present my Respects to Mrs Bailey. This sounds oddly to me, and I dare say I do it awkwardly enough: but I suppose by this time it is nothing new to you — Brown's remembrances to you — As far as I know we shall remain at Winchester for a goodish while —

> Ever your sincere friend
> John Keats.

TO JOHN HAMILTON REYNOLDS

[24 August 1819]
Winchest^r Augt 25th

MY DEAR REYNOLDS,

By this Post I write to Rice who will tell you why we have left Shanklin; and how we like this Place — I have indeed scar[c]ely any thing else to say, leading so monotonous a life except I was to give you a history of sensations, and day-night mares. You would not find me at all unhappy in it; as all my thoughts and feelings which are of the selfish nature, home speculations every day continue to make me more Iron — I am convinced more and more day by day that fine writing is next to fine doing the top thing in the world; the Paradise Lost becomes a greater wonder — The more I know what my diligence may in time probably effect; the more does my heart distend with Pride and Obstinacy [1] — I feel it in my power to become a popular writer — I feel it in my strength to refuse the poisonous suffrage of a public — My own being which I know to be becomes of more consequence to me than the crowds of Shadows in the Shape of Man and women that inhabit a kingdom. The Soul is a world of itself and has enough to do in its own home — Those whom I know already and

[1] Cf. *Paradise Lost* i.571–2.

who have grown as it were a part of myself I could not do without:
but for the rest of Mankind they are as much a dream to me as Miltons
Hierarchies. I think if I had a free and healthy and lasting organisation
of heart and Lungs — as strong as an oxe's — so as to be able [to
bear] unhurt the shock of extreme thought and sensation without
weariness, I could pass my Life very nearly alone though it should
last eighty years. But I feel my Body too weak to support me to the
height; I am obliged continually to check myself and strive to be
nothing. It would be vain for me to endeavour after a more reasonable
manner of writing to you: I have nothing to speak of but myself —
and what can I say but what I feel? If you should have any reason to
regret this state of excitement in me, I will turn the tide of your feelings
in the right channel by mentioning that it is the only state for the best
sort of Poetry — that is all I care for, all I live for. Forgive me for not
filling up the whole sheet; Letters become so irksome to me that the
next time I leave London I shall petition them all to be spar'd me. To
give me credit for constancy and at the same time wa[i]ve letter
writing will be the highest indulgence I can think of.

> Ever your affectionate friend
> John Keats

TO FANNY BRAWNE

[11 October 1819]
College Street.

MY SWEET GIRL,

I am living to day in yesterday: I was in a complete fa[s]cination
all day. I feel myself at your mercy. Write me ever so few lines and
tell you [*for* me] you will never for ever be less kind to me than
yesterday — You dazzled me — There is nothing in the world so
bright and delicate — When Brown came out with that seemingly
true story again[s]t me last night, I felt it would be death to me if you
had ever believed it — though against any one else I could muster
up my obstinacy — Before I knew Brown could disprove it I was for
the moment miserable. When shall we pass a day alone? I have had
a thousand kisses, for which with my whole soul I thank love — but
if you should deny me the thousand and first — 't would put me to the
proof how great a misery I could live through. If you should ever carry
your threat yesterday into execution — believe me 't is not my pride,
my vanity or any petty passion would torment me — really 't would

hurt my heart — I could not bear it. I have seen Mrs Dilke this morning — she says she will come with me any fine day.

Ever yours
John Keats

Ah hertè mine! [1]

TO JOHN TAYLOR

[17 November 1819]
Wentworth Place
Wednesday

MY DEAR TAYLOR,

I have come to a determination not to publish any thing I have now ready written; but for all that to publish a Poem before long and that I hope to make a fine one. As the marvellous is the most enticing and the surest guarantee of harmonious numbers [1] I have been endeavouring to persuade myself to untether Fancy and let her manage for herself — I and myself cannot agree about this at all. Wonders are no wonders to me. I am more at home amongst Men and women. I would rather read Chaucer than Ariosto — The little dramatic skill I may as yet have however badly it might show in a Drama would I think be sufficient for a Poem — I wish to diffuse the colouring of St Agnes eve throughout a Poem in which Character and Sentiment would be the figures to such drapery — Two or three such Poems, if God should spare me, written in the course of the next six years, would be a famous gradus ad Parnassum altissimum [2] — I mean they would nerve me up to the writing of a few fine Plays — my greatest ambition — when I do feel ambitious. I am sorry to say that is very seldom. The subject we have once or twice talked of appears a promising one, The Earl of Leicester's historry. I am this morning reading Holingshed's Elisabeth,[3] You had some Books awhile ago, you promised to lend me, illustrative of my Subject. If you can lay hold of them or any others which may be serviceable to me I know you will encourage my low-spirited Muse by sending them — or rather by letting me know when our Errand cart Man shall call with my little Box. I will endeavour to set my self selfishly at work on this Poem that is to be —

Your sincere friend
John Keats —

[1] "Herte myn" recurs often in Chaucer's *Troilus and Criseyde*, especially in Book iii.
[1] *Paradise Lost* iii.38.
[2] Ladder to the peak of Parnassus.
[3] Raphael Holinshed's *Chronicles of England* (1577), reprinted in 1807–8.

TO JAMES RICE

[14–16 February 1820]
Wentworth Place
Monday Morn.

MY DEAR RICE,

I have not been well enough to make any tolerable rejoinder to your kind Letter. I will as you advise be very chary of my health and spirits. I am sorry to hear of your relapse and hypochondriac symptoms attending it. Let us hope for the best as you say. I shall follow your example in looking to the future good rather than brooding upon present ill. I have not been so worn with lengthen'd illnesses as you have therefore cannot answer you on your own ground with respect to those haunting and deformed thoughts and feelings you speak of. When I have been or supposed myself in health I have had my share of them, especially within this last year. I may say that for 6 Months before I was taken ill I had not passed a tranquil day — Either that gloom overspre[a]d me or I was suffering under some passionate feeling, or if I turn'd to versify that acerbated the poison of either sensation. The Beauties of Nature had lost their power over me. How astonishingly (here I must premise that illness as far as I can judge in so short a time has relieved my Mind of a load of deceptive thoughts and images and makes me perceive things in a truer light) — How astonishingly does the chance of leaving the world impress a sense of its natural beauties on us. Like poor Falstaff, though I do not babble, I think of green fields.[1] I muse with the greatest affection on every flower I have known from my infancy — their shapes and coulours are as new to me as if I had just created them with a superhuman fancy — It is because they are connected with the most thoughtless and happiest moments of our Lives — I have seen foreign flowers in hothouses of the most beautiful nature, but I do not care a straw for them. The simple flowers of our sp[r]ing are what I want to see again.

❁ ❁ ❁ ❁ ❁ ❁

I am
my dear Rice
ever most sincer[e]ly yours
John Keats

[1] *Henry* V, II.iii.17.

I have broken this open to let you know I was surprised at seeing it on the table this morning; thinking it had gone long ago.

TO FANNY BRAWNE

[February (?), 1820]

MY DEAR FANNY,

Do not let your mother suppose that you hurt me by writing at night. For some reason or other your last night's note was not so treasureable as former ones. I would fain that you call me *Love* still. To see you happy and in high spirits is a great consolation to me — still let me believe that you are not half so happy as my restoration would make you. I am nervous, I own, and may think myself worse than I really am; if so you must indulge me, and pamper with that sort of tenderness you have manifested towards me in different Letters. My sweet creature when I look back upon the pains and torments I have suffer'd for you from the day I left you to go to the Isle of Wight; the ecstasies in which I have pass'd some days and the miseries in their turn, I wonder the more at the Beauty which has kept up the spell so fervently. When I send this round I shall be in the front parlour watching to see you show yourself for a minute in the garden. How illness stands as a barrier betwixt me and you! Even if I was well — I must make myself as good a Philosopher as possible. Now I have had opportunities of passing nights anxious and awake I have found other thoughts intrude upon me. "If I should die," said I to myself, "I have left no immortal work behind me — nothing to make my friends proud of my memory — but I have lov'd the principle of beauty in all things, and if I had had time I would have made myself remember'd." Thoughts like these came very feebly whilst I was in health and every pulse beat for you — now you divide with this (may *I* say it?) "last infirmity of noble minds"[1] all my reflection.

God bless you, Love.
J. Keats

TO FANNY BRAWNE

[March (?), 1820]

My dearest Fanny, I slept well last night and am no worse this morning for it. Day by day if I am not deceived I get a more un-

[1] *Lycidas* 71.

restrain'd use of my Chest. The nearer a racer gets to the Goal the more his anxiety becomes so I lingering upon the borders of health feel my impatience increase. Perhaps on your account I have imagined my illness more serious than it is: how horrid was the chance of slipping into the ground instead of into your arms — the difference is amazing Love. Death must come at last; Man must die, as Shallow says [1]; but before that is my fate I feign [*for* fain] would try what more pleasures than you have given so sweet a creature as you can give. Let me have another op[p]ortunity of years before me and I will not die without being remember'd. Take care of yourself dear that we may both be well in the Summer. I do not at all fatigue myself with writing, having merely to put a line or two here and there, a Task which would worry a stout state of the body and mind, but which just suits me as I can do no more.

Your affectionate
J. K —

TO PERCY BYSSHE SHELLEY

[16 August 1820]
Hampstead August 16th

MY DEAR SHELLEY,

I am very much gratified that you, in a foreign country, and with a mind almost over occupied, should write to me in the strain of the Letter beside me. If I do not take advantage of your invitation it will be prevented by a circumstance I have very much at heart to prophesy — There is no doubt that an english winter would put an end to me, and do so in a lingering hateful manner, therefore I must either voyage or journey to Italy as a soldier marches up to a battery. My nerves at present are the worst part of me, yet they feel soothed when I think that come what extreme may, I shall not be destined to remain in one spot long enough to take a hatred of any four particular bed-posts. I am glad you take any pleasure in my poor Poem; — which I would willingly take the trouble to unwrite, if possible, did I care so much as I have done about Reputation. I received a copy of the Cenci, as from yourself from Hunt. There is only one part of it I am judge of; the Poetry, and dramatic effect, which by many spirits now a days is considered the mammon. A modern work it is said must have a purpose, which may be the God — *an artist* must serve Mammon —

[1] *2 Henry IV*, III.ii.42.

he must have "self concentration" selfishness perhaps. You I am sure will forgive me for sincerely remarking that you might curb your magnanimity and be more of an artist, and 'load every rift' of your subject with ore.[1] The thought of such discipline must fall like cold chains upon you, who perhaps never sat with your wings furl'd for six Months together. And is not this extraordina[r]y talk for the writer of Endymion? whose mind was like a pack of scattered cards— I am pick'd up and sorted to a pip. My Imagination is a Monastry and I am its Monk — you must explain my metap^{cs} [*for* metaphysics] to yourself. I am in expectation of Prometheus every day. Could I have my own wish for its interest effected you would have it still in manuscript — or be but now putting an end to the second act. I remember you advising me not to publish my first-blights, on Hampstead heath — I am returning advice upon your hands. Most of the Poems in the volume [2] I send you have been written above two years, and would never have been publish'd but from a hope of gain; so you see I am inclined enough to take your advice now. I must exp[r]ess once more my deep sense of your kindness, adding my sincere thanks and respects for Mrs Shelley. In the hope of soon seeing you I remain

most sincerely yours,
John Keats —

TO CHARLES BROWN

Rome, 30 November 1820

MY DEAR BROWN,

'Tis the most difficult thing in the world ~~for~~ to me to write a letter. My stomach continues so bad, that I feel it worse on opening any book, — yet I am much better than I was in Quarantine. Then I am afraid to encounter the proing and conning of any thing interesting to me in England. I have an habitual feeling of my real life having past, and that I am leading a posthumous existence. God knows how it would have been — but it appears to me — however, I will not speak of that subject. I must have been at Bedhampton nearly at the time you were writing to me from Chichester — how unfortunate — and to pass on the river too! There was my star predominant! I cannot answer any thing in your letter, which followed me from Naples to Rome, because I am afraid to look it over again. I am so weak (in mind) that I

[1] *The Faerie Queene* II.vii.28.5.
[2] Keats's volume of 1820.

cannot bear the sight of any hand writing of a friend I love so much as I do you. Yet I ride the little horse, — and, at my worst, even in Quarantine, summoned up more puns, in a sort of desperation, in one week than in any year of my life. There is one thought enough to kill me — I have been well, healthy, alert &c, walking with her — and now — the knowledge of contrast, feeling for light and shade, all that information (primitive sense) necessary for a poem are great enemies to the recovery of the stomach. There, you rogue, I put you to the torture, — but you must bring your philosophy to bear — as I do mine, really — or how should I be able to live? D͏r Clarke is very attentive to me; he says, there is very little the matter with my lungs, but my stomach, he says, is very bad. I am well disappointed in hearing good news from George, — for it runs in my head we shall all die young. I have not written to * * * * * 1 yet, which he must think very neglectful; being anxious to send him a good account of my health, I have delayed it from week to week. If I recover, I will do all in my power to correct the mistakes made during sickness; and if I should not, all my faults will be forgiven. I shall write to * * * to-morrow, or next day. I will write to * * * * * in the middle of next week. Severn is very well, though he leads so dull a life with me. Remember me to all friends, and tell * * * * I should not have left London without taking leave of him, but from being so low in body and mind. Write to George as soon as you receive this, and tell him how I am, as far as you can guess; and also a note to my sister — who walks about my imagination like a ghost — she is so like Tom. I can scarcely bid you good bye even in a letter. I always made an awkward bow.

God bless you!
John Keats.

JOSEPH SEVERN TO CHARLES BROWN 2
Rome. 27 February 1821.

MY DEAR BROWN,

He is gone — he died with the most perfect ease — he seemed to go to sleep. On the 23͏rd, about 4, the approaches of death came on. "Severn — I — lift me up — I am dying — I shall die easy — don't be frightened — be firm, and thank God it has come!" I lifted him up in my arms. The phlegm seemed boiling in his throat, and increased

1 The names of Keats's friends were deleted by Brown, from whose *Life of John Keats* the letter is taken (Rollins, *K.C.*, II, 85f.; Rollins, II, 359–60).

2 Rollins, *K.C.*, II, 94.

until 11, when he gradually sunk into death — so quiet — that I still thought he slept. I cannot say now — I am broken down from four nights' watching, and no sleep since, and my poor Keats gone. Three days since, the body was opened; the lungs were completely gone. The Doctors could not conceive by what means he had lived these two months. I followed his poor body to the grave on Monday, with many English. They take such care of me here — that I must, else, have gone into a fever. I am better now — but still quite disabled.

The Police have been. The furniture, the walls, the floor, every thing must be destroyed by order of the law. But this is well looked to by D^r C.

The letters I put into the coffin with my own hand.

I must leave off.

T. S.

SELECT BIBLIOGRAPHY

LIST OF ABBREVIATIONS

NOTES

INDEX OF POEMS

SELECT BIBLIOGRAPHY [1]

EDITIONS

Poems, by John Keats. London: C. & J. Ollier, 1817.

Endymion: A Poetic Romance. By John Keats. London: Taylor and Hessey, 1818.

Lamia, Isabella, The Eve of St. Agnes, and Other Poems. By John Keats London: Taylor and Hessey, 1820.

Life, Letters, and Literary Remains, of John Keats, ed. Richard Monckton Milnes. 2 vols. London, 1848. (Houghton)

Life and Letters of John Keats. By Lord Houghton. A New Edition. London, 1867.

The Poetical Works of John Keats. Chronologically Arranged and Edited, with a Memoir, by Lord Houghton. Third Edition. London, 1883.

Poems of John Keats, ed. G. Thorn-Drury. With an Introduction by Robert Bridges. Muses' Library. 2 vols. London, 1896. (Bridges)

Complete Works of John Keats, ed. H. B. Forman. 5 vols. Glasgow, 1900–1901.

Poems of John Keats, ed. Ernest de Selincourt. Fifth Edition. London, 1926. (De Selincourt)

John Keats: Complete Poems and Selected Letters, ed. Clarence D. Thorpe. New York, 1935. (Thorpe)

The Keats Circle: Letters and Papers 1816–1878, ed. Hyder E. Rollins. 2 vols. Cambridge, Mass., 1948. (Rollins, *K.C.*)

Complete Poetry and Selected Prose of John Keats, ed. Harold E. Briggs. New York, 1951.

Selected Letters of John Keats, ed. Lionel Trilling. New York, 1951.

The Letters of John Keats, ed. Maurice B. Forman. Fourth Edition. Oxford, 1952.

More Letters and Poems of the Keats Circle, ed. Hyder E. Rollins. Cambridge, Mass., 1955.

Poetical Works of John Keats, ed. H. W. Garrod. Oxford Standard Authors. London, 1956. (Garrod, *OSA*)

Poetical Works of John Keats, ed. H. W. Garrod. Second Edition. Oxford, 1958. (Garrod)

The Letters of John Keats 1814–1821, ed. Hyder E. Rollins. 2 vols. Cambridge, Mass., 1958. (Rollins)

[1] Abbreviations used in the notes are given in parentheses after various titles. See also the List of Abbreviations that follows the Bibliography.

BIOGRAPHY AND CRITICISM

MacGillivray, J. R. *Keats: A Bibliography and Reference Guide with an Essay on Keats' Reputation.* Toronto, 1949.

Bate, Walter Jackson. *Negative Capability: The Intuitive Approach in Keats.* Cambridge, Mass., 1939.

Bate, Walter Jackson. *The Stylistic Development of Keats.* New York, 1945. (Bate)

Beyer, Werner W. *Keats and the Daemon King.* New York, 1947. (Beyer)

Caldwell, James Ralston. *John Keats' Fancy: The Effect on Keats of the Psychology of his Day.* Ithaca, 1945.

Colvin, Sir Sidney. *John Keats: His Life and Poetry, His Friends, Critics, and After-Fame.* Third Edition. New York, 1925. (Colvin)

Finney, Claude Lee. *The Evolution of Keats's Poetry.* 2 vols. Cambridge, Mass., 1936. (Finney)

Fogle, Richard Harter. *The Imagery of Keats and Shelley: A Comparative Study.* Chapel Hill, 1949.

Ford, George H. *Keats and the Victorians: A Study of His Influence and Rise to Fame, 1821–1895.* New Haven, 1944.

Ford, Newell F. *The Prefigurative Imagination of John Keats: A Study of the Beauty-Truth Identification and Its Implications.* Stanford University, 1951.

Gittings, Robert. *John Keats: The Living Year.* Cambridge, Mass., 1954. (Gittings, *J.K.*)

Gittings, Robert. *The Mask of Keats: A Study of Problems.* Cambridge, Mass., 1956. (Gittings, *Mask*)

Hewlett, Dorothy. *A Life of John Keats.* Second Edition. London, 1950. (D. Hewlett)

James, D. G. *Scepticism and Poetry: An Essay on the Poetic Imagination.* London, 1937.

James, D. G. *The Romantic Comedy.* London, 1948.

Leavis, F. R. "Keats." *Revaluation.* London, 1936.

Lowell, Amy. *John Keats.* 2 vols. Boston, 1925. (A. Lowell)

Murry, John Middleton. *Keats.* New York, 1955. (Enlarged and altered from *Studies in Keats,* 1930; *Studies in Keats New and Old,* 1939; *The Mystery of Keats,* 1949.)

Perkins, David D. *The Quest for Permanence: the Symbolism of Wordsworth, Shelley, and Keats.* Cambridge, Mass., 1959 (forthcoming).

Ridley, M. R. *Keats' Craftsmanship: A Study in Poetic Development.* Oxford, 1933. (Ridley)

Sherwood, Margaret. "Keats' Imaginative Approach to Myth." *Undercurrents of Influence in English Romantic Poetry.* Cambridge, Mass., 1934.

Thorpe, Clarence D. *The Mind of John Keats.* New York, 1926.

Thorpe, Clarence D. "Keats." *The English Romantic Poets. A Review of Research,* ed. Thomas M. Raysor. Revised Edition. New York, 1956.

Wasserman, Earl R. *The Finer Tone: Keats' Major Poems.* Baltimore, 1953.

LIST OF ABBREVIATIONS

USED IN THE NOTES

In addition to the list below, see some abbreviations, in parentheses, in the preceding Select Bibliography.

Aen.: Virgil, *Aeneid.*

Baldwin: Edward Baldwin (i.e., William Godwin), *The Pantheon: or Ancient History of the Gods of Greece and Rome* (London, 1806).

Brit. Past.: William Browne, *Britannia's Pastorals,* in *Poems,* ed. G. Goodwin (2 vols., London, 1894).

Cary, *Inf., Purg., Parad.*: *The Vision; or Hell, Purgatory, and Paradise, of Dante Alighieri,* tr. Henry F. Cary (2nd ed., 3 vols., London, 1819).

C.I.: James Thomson, *The Castle of Indolence,* in *Poetical Works,* ed. J. L. Robertson (Oxford, 1908).

ELH: ELH: A Journal of English Literary History.

Exc.: Wordsworth, *The Excursion.*

F.Q.: Spenser, *The Faerie Queene.*

Il P.: Milton, *Il Penseroso.*

I Stood: Keats, *I Stood Tip-toe upon a Little Hill.*

K-SJ: Keats-Shelley Journal.

Lay: Scott, *The Lay of the Last Minstrel.*

Lempriere: John Lempriere, *A Classical Dictionary . . . Sixth Edition* (London, 1806).

Lyc.: Milton, *Lycidas.*

MLN: Modern Language Notes.

MLQ: Modern Language Quarterly.

Oberon: Wieland, *Oberon,* tr. W. Sotheby (2 vols., Boston, 1810).

PDJ: Plymouth and Devonport Weekly Journal (cited, *passim,* in Garrod, 1958 ed.).

P.L.: Milton, *Paradise Lost.*

Potter: John Potter, *Archaeologia Graeca, or the Antiquities of Greece* (2 vols., Edinburgh, 1818). (First pub. 1697–8.)

PMLA: Publications of the Modern Language Association of America.

Sandys: *Ovid's Metamorphosis,* tr. George Sandys [with the allegorical commentary] (London, 1640).

S. and P.: Keats, *Sleep and Poetry.*

M. Tighe: *Psyche,* in *Keats and Mary Tighe: The poems of Mary Tighe with parallel passages from the work of John Keats,* ed. E. V. Weller (New York, 1928).

TLS: London Times Literary Supplement.

Udolpho: Ann Radcliffe, *The Mysteries of Udolpho* (2 vols., Everyman's Library).

NOTES

Imitation of Spenser *Page 3*

Printed in *Poems*, 1817; Keats's first poetical effort, according to his friend Charles Brown. Although by this time — early in 1814? (Garrod, *OSA*, dates 1812) — Keats had some acquaintance with Spenser, this piece has almost nothing Spenserian except the stanza; a few observed images are embedded in the pallid elegance of eighteenth-century Spenserianism and conventional verse of the early nineteenth century.

3. amber flame: cf. Milton, *L'Allegro* 61.   **14 f.** Keats's friend Richard Woodhouse cited *P.L.* vii.438 f.; cf. Thomson, *Spring* 778 f.   **22. teen:** woe.   **27. cœrulean:** azure.   **36. Flora:** the Roman goddess of flowers.

To Lord Byron *Page 4*

Printed by Houghton, 1848; written in December, 1814. While Coleridge and Wordsworth had few admirers among either critics or general public, Byron was already the great poet and glamorous personality. Keats's sentimental sonnet presents the stock view of the romantic, melancholy sufferer; the mature Keats turned strongly against both the egoist and the satirist. The sonnet contains his first reference to what was to be so potent in his imagination, the moon.

To Chatterton *Page 4*

Printed by Houghton; written in 1815 (January?). Chatterton, who committed suicide when he was less than 18 (1770), was for Coleridge (*Monody*), Wordsworth (*Resolution and Independence* 43-4), and Shelley (*Adonais* 399-401) a symbol of unfulfilled genius. This weak sonnet is Keats's first expression of his high esteem; he later thought of Chatterton's pseudo-Middle-English as pure in contrast with Chaucer's Gallicism and Milton's Latinism. Chatterton's rather meagre influence on Keats is discussed by De Selincourt, p. 610 and notes; Gittings, *Mask*, pp. 88-97 (also in *K-SJ* IV, 1955); and N. T. Ting, *K-SJ* V (1956).

8. amate: daunt, overcome (in Chatterton and Spenser).

Written on the Day That Mr. Leigh Hunt Left Prison *Page 4*

Printed in *Poems*, 1817; written on Feb. 2, 1815. Early in 1813 Hunt had been imprisoned for two years for ridiculing in his paper, the *Examiner*, the *Morning Post's* adulation of the Prince Regent (later George IV); Hunt's truer picture of a libertine and parasite was adjudged libelous. Keats had absorbed Hunt's liberalism at school through reading the *Examiner* and through the sympathetic Clarkes. This earnest though badly written tribute sharpened Tory reviewers' hostility to Keats. As the sonnet says, Hunt had not allowed prison to cut him off from poetry.

Ode to Apollo   *Page 5*

Printed by Houghton; written in February, 1815. Keats's first celebration of the god of poetry is a forcible-feeble attempt at the kind of declamatory ode written by Dryden, Gray, and others. But the eighteenth-century clichés embody ardent devotion to poetry (and the first line partly anticipates the first line of the sonnet on Chapman's *Homer*).

1–2. Cf. Collins, *To Evening* 5–6; Jonson, *Queen and Huntress* 3–4. **7. nervous:** strong.   **11–12.** Cf. Keats's sonnet *To Homer*.   **14.** Virgil's name was Publius Vergilius Maro.   **34.** Cf. Thomson, *C.I.* I.xl–xli. **42. the Nine:** the Muses.

To Solitude   *Page 6*

Keats's first published poem, printed in Hunt's *Examiner*, May 5, 1816 (included, with no title, in *Poems*, 1817). It was written in November, 1815, while Keats was living as a medical student in the dingy Borough and cherishing hours of escape into unspoiled nature and communion with a kindred spirit, such as G. F. Mathew, to whom the sonnet was apparently addressed (see the note on the following poem). The texture of the sonnet, though mainly artificial, has some Huntian "naturalness"; and along with the urban realism of 2–3 there is the rural realism of line 8, a bit of fresh observation and probably also an echo of Wordsworth (*Nuns Fret Not at their Convent's Narrow Room* 5–7).

To George Felton Mathew   *Page 7*

Printed in *Poems*, 1817; written in November, 1815. Mathew was a small versifier and a rather priggish, sentimental devotee of poetry with whom — and with whose female relations — Keats for a time enjoyed associating. Keats's poem was a reply to one Mathew addressed to him (Murry, *Studies in Keats New and Old*, p. 4; see also Rollins, *K.C.*, II, 186–8, and Rollins, I, 100). This was Keats's first poem in heroic couplets and the first of several epistles perhaps modeled on Michael Drayton's; more concrete evidence of his growing interest in Elizabethan and Jacobean poetry is the epigraph prefixed to the group of epistles, taken from William Browne's *Britannia's Pastorals*, ii.3.748–50. But the young Keats's familiar style, a combination of colloquial looseness (with many double rhymes) and plush elegance, is less akin to Browne than to Hunt. Amid all the bad writing there emerge, faintly, some characteristic attitudes — political liberalism, devotion to poetry, direct observation of nature, and the fusion of nature with classical myth.

5. brother Poets: Beaumont and Fletcher.   **18.** "Lydian airs": *L'Allegro* 136.   **24. a rapt seraph.** Cf. Pope, *Essay on Man* i. 278: "As the rapt seraph that adores and burns"; Coleridge, *Ancient Mariner* 490–6.

40. blowing: blossoming.   **75. "a sun-shine . . . place":** from Spenser's picture of Una, *F.Q.* I.iii.4.8.   **83.** The rays of Apollo, the sun. **93. Naiad's pearly hands:** cf. the water-nymphs' "pearled wrists," *Comus* 834.

How Many Bards   *Page 9*

Printed in *Poems*, 1817; written in March, 1816. Another linking of the beauties of poetry (octave) and the kindred beauties of nature (sestet). It is a question if, at this date, the arresting metrical irregularity of the first line is conscious art or unwitting awkwardness.

1. Cf. Coleridge, *To the Nightingale* 2: "How many Bards in city garret pent."   **9–13.** Cf. *Udolpho* I, 6–7: "till the lonely sound of a sheep-bell, or the distant bark of a watch-dog, were all that broke the stillness of the evening. Then, the gloom of the woods; the trembling of their leaves, at intervals, in the breeze . . . groves, and hamlets, and villas — their outlines softened by distance."   **11–12. bell . . . sound:** cf. *Il P.* 74–6.

To One Who Has Been Long in City Pent   *Page 9*

Printed in *Poems*, 1817; written in June, 1816.

1. Cf. *P.L.* ix.445: "As one who long in populous city pent"; and the line from Coleridge cited under *How Many Bards.*   **7–8.** Probably Hunt's *Story of Rimini*, published in February, 1816.

To My Brother George   *Page 10*

Printed in *Poems*, 1817. This sonnet and the epistle following were written at Margate in August, 1816, shortly after Keats had received his Apothecaries' Certificate.

3. laurel'd peers: "poets in Heaven" (Woodhouse); cf. *Ode to Apollo* 20, *To G. F. Mathew* 58.   **5 f.** Keats was having his first sight of the sea. **10–12.** Cf. Cynthia (the moon) and her bridal night in *I Stood.*

To My Brother George   *Page 11*

Printed in *Poems*, 1817. See the preceding introductory note and the one on *To G. F. Mathew.*

19. bay: laurel, the symbol of Apollo and poetry.   **24. Libertas:** Leigh Hunt (see the sonnet on Hunt's leaving prison).   **51–2.** Cf. *P.L.* vii.405–6.   **66. spell:** put under a spell.   **73–4.** Cf. Coleridge, *Monody on . . . Chatterton* 64–5: "And now in wrath he grasps the patriot steel, And her own iron rod he makes Oppression feel."   **81–2.** Woodhouse cited Spenser, *Colin Clout's Come Home Again* 640–3.   **85 f.** Cf. *F.Q.* VI.ix.7–8; Thomson, *Summer* 400 f.   **105–6.** Cf. Gray, *Progress of Poesy* 114–16.

To Charles Cowden Clarke   *Page 15*

Printed in *Poems*, 1817; written in September, 1816. A grateful tribute to the young teacher and literary mentor of Keats's schooldays, who remained a friend.

6. Zephyr: the West Wind.   **17.** Cf. Cowper, *On the Receipt of My Mother's Picture* 103: "Sails ript, seams op'ning wide, and compass lost." **27. Helicon:** the mountain, with its fountains, sacred to the Muses. **29. Baiæ:** a famous ancient resort near Naples.   **31. Armida:** the enchantress of Tasso's *Jerusalem Delivered*.   **33–7. Mulla:** a river near Spenser's Irish home. With 34, cf. *Epithalamion* 175: "Her brest like to a bowle of creame uncrudded." Una is the heroine of the *F.Q.*, bk. I; Belphoebe appears in II.iii and III–IV; Archimago, the wicked magician, is prominent in I.   **40. Titania:** the fairy queen of both Shakespeare and Wieland's *Oberon;* "sequester'd haunts" is in *Oberon* iii.4 (Beyer, pp. 71, 321).   **41. Urania:** originally the Muse of astronomy; later, as in *P.L.*, of exalted poetry.   **44–7.** See the note on the sonnet to Hunt, above, and *To My Brother George* 24. Lines 44–5 refer especially to Hunt's *Feast of the Poets*, 46–7 to his *Story of Rimini*.   **58–9.** A very eighteenth-century view of *P.L.*   **63. Atlas:** the Titan who held up the sky on his shoulders. **68. Clio:** the Muse of history.   **70. the shaft of Tell:** in Campbell, *Pleasures of Hope* (ed. 1815), p. 35; on pp. 34–5 Brutus is named.   **92. corn:** grain.   **111.** Thomas Arne (1710–78), composer of operas, etc., and of the music for *Rule, Britannia*.   **112.** The *Irish Melodies* of Thomas Moore, which Keats imitated in some of his worst early verses.   **113. music:** piano.   **117–18.** Commentators cite the same rhyme — though *got* has a different sense — in Drayton's epistle to Henry Reynolds, lines 7–8.

On First Looking into Chapman's Homer   *Page 18*

Printed in the *Examiner*, Dec. 1, 1816, and in *Poems*, 1817. Written in October, 1816, near Keats's twenty-first birthday, this sonnet represents a poetic coming of age; it is the grand expression in English of the discovery of a new world. Although Keats was still to write much poor verse, this sonnet stands out among his early poems because, for once, high emotion was matched by imaginative symbols, form, and style. Clarke, having been lent a folio copy of Chapman's translation, invited Keats to share the feast. They stayed up most of the night savoring the "famousest" passages, including that of Odysseus' shipwreck. At dawn Keats walked home the long distance from Clerkenwell to the Borough and by ten o'clock that morning Clarke received the sonnet (two later revisions are indicated below). The thought of voyaging, and his own ardor for poetry, crystallized in Keats's mind a number of floating associations — Apollo's "western halls of gold," the accounts in Robertson's *History of America* (ed. 1803, I, 284 f.), which he had read as a schoolboy, of the Spanish quest for treasure and of Balboa's first sight of the Pacific from Darien (Panama), the eyes of Cortez in Titian's portrait, and Bonnycastle's story (in the book Keats had won as a school prize) of Herschel's discovery of the planet Uranus in 1781. But excitement is under perfect control. Cortez may have been a slip of the memory (he is much more prominent in Robertson than Balboa); C. C. Walcutt suggests (*Explicator*, V, 1947, no. 8) that Keats thought of Cortez' first sight (from Mexico) of an ocean he had heard about, as he himself had heard about Chapman. In addition to Finney, I, 120–8, some earlier special studies are those of Murry (*Keats* and earlier edns.), J. W. Beach, *PMLA* XLIX (1934), and Sir Ifor Evans, *Essays and Studies . . . of the English Association,* XVI (1931).

7. pure serene: probably from Coleridge, *Hymn before Sun-rise, in the Vale of Chamouni* 72. On the first version of the line, "Yet could I never judge what men could mean," Keats's comment was "bald, and too simply wondering." **10.** Cf. *I Stood* 113–15. **11. eagle:** originally "wond'ring." **13.** Cf. Thomson, *Liberty* iv.38, "wild surmises"; Shakespeare, *Lucrece* 83–4.

Keen, Fitful Gusts — Page 18

Printed in *Poems,* 1817. The sonnet was evidently composed on Keats's way home, in late autumn or early winter (1816), from a literary evening at Hunt's house in Hampstead.

To My Brothers — Page 18

Printed in *Poems,* 1817; written on Nov. 18, 1816. De Selincourt (p. 398) cites Wordsworth's sonnets, *Personal Talk,* for a similar contrast between everyday delights and those of the poetic life, and for a parallel use (iii.10) of *voluble;* Finney (I, 138) cites Hunt's more genial sonnets to friends. Keats's line 5 reminds us of the often strained rhyme words in his early verse, e.g., *lair* in the preceding sonnet.

Addressed to the Same [Second Sonnet to Haydon] — Page 19

In *Poems,* 1817, this sonnet followed one *Addressed to Haydon,* which is omitted here. Keats wrote the second sonnet when wrought up by an evening (Nov. 19, 1816) with Haydon; the young poet, for all the bad writing, feels the significance of the romantic movement. Benjamin Haydon (1786–1846), an intensely ambitious and unsuccessful historical painter, lives now as the friend of Keats (whose life-mask he made), as the author of a highly colored autobiography, and as the champion of the Elgin Marbles against orthodox opinion. He introduced Keats to the Marbles, to Raphael's cartoons, and to Wordsworth. His artistic ardor, on the heroic scale, and his eager encouragement were of value, but later friendship cooled because of his egoism and his willingness to sponge on the financially harassed Keats.

1. Cf. Wordsworth's sonnet, *Great men have been among us.* **2–4.** Wordsworth. **5–6.** Hunt. **7–8.** Haydon. **9–10.** Keats and others.

13. The line at first read "Of mighty workings in a distant Mart," but was truncated at Haydon's suggestion.

On the Grasshopper and Cricket   *Page 19*

Printed in *Poems*, 1817; written Dec. 30, 1816, in friendly competition with Hunt, who suggested the subject. Hunt praised the "prosperous opening" and, at "when the frost Has wrought a silence," exclaimed "Ah! that's perfect. Bravo Keats!"

I Stood Tip-toe   *Page 20*

The opening poem in the 1817 volume; begun, perhaps, in early summer and finished in December, 1816. It was Keats's first attempt to deal with the myth of Endymion (he referred to it by that title). Though uneven and often bad, the poem has felicities, and as a whole is Keats's most promising meditation so far on his favorite themes. From a lingering catalogue of nature's luxuries — as observed on Hampstead Heath — and the inspiration of nature, it moves into the realm of myth and poetry, of nature humanized and spiritualized by the imagination. In his review of the book Hunt noted that Keats's conception of myth was akin to that of Wordsworth (*Exc.* iv.718–62, 847–87); Hunt himself held a similar if less philosophical view of myth and would exert a similar influence.

7. The conceit goes back to the myth of the dew as the tears of Aurora (the Dawn) weeping for the death of her son Memnon.   **68. chequer'd shadows:** in Hunt, *Politics and Poetics* 80; cf. *L'Allegro* 96, "chequer'd shade."   **147.** Cf. M. Tighe, *Psyche* i.45; "Increasing wonder filled her ravished soul." The young Keats had a liking for this lush allegorical romance (published in 1811), but most of the Keatsian parallels cited by its editor, E. V. Weller (1928), are unconvincing.   **153. Fauns:** minor rural deities akin to Pan.   **Dryades:** wood-nymphs.   **157–62.** The amorous goat-god pursued the nymph Syrinx; she was changed into a reed, of which Pan made a flute.   **163 f.** While Keats would have met many allusions to Narcissus in Elizabethan poetry, his friend Woodhouse cited Sandys' *Ovid*, p. 50 in the 1640 edition, which contained a full allegorical commentary; Keats apparently drew a number of mythological hints from this work.   **185–6.** Cf. *Exc.* iv.1144: "Authentic tidings of invisible things." Beyer (p. 92) cites *Oberon* viii.26: "rob'd in heavenly light Shapes of the viewless world his soul responsive call."   **190.** A direct statement of Keats's — and other romantic poets' — central quest, the attaining, through the imagination, of supra-human or supra-rational intuitions of spiritual reality.   **193 f.** The myth of the love between Cynthia (Diana, the moon) and Endymion had been traditionally allegorized as the celestial contemplation of an astronomer.   **211–40.** An excess of particulars somewhat obscures the idea that the love and union of Endymion and Cynthia are attended by a new birth of love and sympathy in men and women.   **217.** Probably an echo of Chapman's preface to his translation of the *Iliad*

("Of Homer"), in which the young Homer is said to have volunteered for action (M. Boddy, *TLS*, Feb. 2, 1933, p. 76). **218.** The Apollo Belvedere. Cf. Joseph Spence, *Polymetis* (abridged ed., 1802), p. 21 and Plate V; and Thomson, *Liberty* iv.163 f. **220.** The Venus de' Medici. Cf. Spence, p. 13 and Plate III; and Thomson, *Liberty* iv.177 f.

Sleep and Poetry   *Page 26*

Printed in *Poems*, 1817; written in November and December, 1816. The immediate occasion of the poem was a night spent under Hunt's roof (350 f.). Here, as in later poems, sleep, or a half-waking state, is seen as conducive to poetic insight. In the way of artistry, this poem has youthful virtues and defects akin to those of *I Stood Tip-toe*, which Keats finished about the same time; defects are perhaps more conspicuous here because, in trying to grapple with abstract ideas, Keats can be turgid or doubtfully articulate. As a document, a poetic stock-taking, *Sleep and Poetry* is his most important utterance before *Endymion*. The young poet of nature's luxuries is now a happy denizen of the realm of Flora and old Pan, but he is impelled to look beyond that to "a nobler life," to poetry which, like Wordsworth's, deals with "the agonies, the strife Of human hearts." This is the first clear revelation of what was to be a continuing conflict and was to have its last expression in *The Fall of Hyperion*. Here Keats rises above his personal predicament and ambitions to a somewhat cloudy but vehement defense of the imagination, a manifesto on behalf of romantic poetry. Lines 181–206, a concrete attack on the Popeian tradition, on the neoclassical rationalism represented by the heroic couplet, angered the conservative critics (and Byron); this, and the whole proclamation, show the influence of Wordsworth, Hunt, and Hazlitt, but the young Keats himself is already "the true voice of feeling."

The epigraph is from *The Flower and the Leaf* (then supposed to be Chaucer's), on which Keats later wrote a sonnet. **5. blowing:** blossoming. **27–8. thunder . . . under:** cf. Milton, *Vacation Exercise* 41–2. **66–7.** Cf. *Comus* 118–20. **69–71.** Woodhouse cited Wordsworth, *To the Daisy* 70–2. **74. Meander:** the famous winding river in Asia Minor. **84.** Cf. *I Stood* 190 and note. **89. Montmorenci:** the river, with a deep waterfall, in Quebec. **90–125.** Critics have seen a parallel with the three stages of Wordsworth's development as described in *Tintern Abbey*, and with Keats's letter of May 3, 1818 (printed below). Though the images in 90–5 picture the brevity of life in general, the last ones recall Wordsworth's first stage, "The coarser pleasures of my boyish days, And their glad animal movements" (*T.A.* 73–4). **101–21.** While very Keatsian in substance and manner, these lines correspond to Wordsworth's second stage, that of purely aesthetic passion for natural beauty (*T.A.* 75–85). **122–5.** Wordsworth's third stage (*T.A.* 83 f.) brought sympathy with human suffering and a sense of a universal spirit in nature and man. Wordsworth was then looking back on a state already achieved; Keats, instinctively attached to the sensuous, has to force himself to look forward to the poetry of the human heart. **125–54.** The chariot of the imagination is an image more characteristic of Shelley than of Keats (cf. *The Daemon of the World,* 1816, lines 56 f.). Symbolic details seem to move from sense and fancy to such shapes of mystery and fear as Collins had evoked in some of his odes. **155–9.** The disillusionment of a relapse into actuality after an ideal vision. **171–80.** Chaucer and the Elizabethan poets. **185–7.** In his essay, "On Milton's Versification" (1815), Hazlitt said: "Dr. Johnson and Pope would have converted his [Milton's] vaulting Pegasus into a rocking-horse" (*Works,* ed. Howe, IV, 40). Cf. Chatterton, *Letter to . . . Mastre Canynge* 31–2: "Instead of mounting on a wingèd horse, You on a cart-horse drive in doleful course." **188–90.** A significant echo of Wordsworth's *The World Is Too Much with Us* 5–7. **198.** Jacob's wit: Gen. xxx.31–43. Keats's "certain wands" is from Shylock's version, *Merchant of Venice* I.iii.85. **202. the bright Lyrist:** Apollo. **206.** Hunt and others thought of the English Augustans, Dryden, Pope, *et al.,* as "the French school," because English neoclassicism owed much to that of France, of which Boileau (1636–1711) was the high priest. Keats's tirade is of course unjust to Augustan poetry, as poets commonly are to a tradition they are rebelling against. **209. boundly:** boundless? bounden? Apparently a Keatsian coinage, one of many infelicities in Keats's early verse engendered by a desire for smoothness, freshness, or familiar ease. **218–19.** Chatterton. **224–6.** Wordsworth. He and Coleridge and Southey were commonly known as the Lake poets. **226–9.** Hunt. **230–5.** These lines, usually regarded as a condemnation of Byronic Titanism, Hunt, in reviewing the volume, took as a censure of "the morbidity that taints the productions of the Lake Poets" (*Examiner,* July 13, 1817; Finney, I, 170–1); Keats is clearly criticizing their faults. Homer's Polyphemus threw, not his club (with which Odysseus had put out his eye), but a fragment of rock, into the sea in the effort to wreck Odysseus' ship; Keats's image may be a slip of memory or a conscious alteration. **237.** Cf. Coleridge, *Eolian Harp* 33: "Is Music slumbering on her instrument"; Campbell, *Pleasures of Hope* (ed. 1815), p. 35: "The might that slumbers in a peasant's arm." **248–69.** This relapse into sensuous luxuries, and lines 58–9, 101–21, 346–7, may be inconsistent with the high aspirations of 81–4 and 122–54, but, in Keats's present phase, such wavering between instinct and ambition is natural enough. **248–9. myrtle . . . Paphos:** associated with Venus. **257. Yeaned:** brought forth. **279.** Cf. *Il P.* 66. **303.** Daedalus made wax wings for himself and his son Icarus, but Icarus flew too near the sun, his wings melted, and he fell into the sea. **312–404.** After straining to conceive of the highest reaches of the imagination, Keats subsides into the more substantial attractions of friendship and nature and Hunt's pictures. **334–6.** Keats's first allusion to Titian's *Bacchus and Ariadne;* he would know the myth from Ovid, etc. **348. poppy:** as an opiate, associated with sleep (*Othello* III.iii.30). **354. a poet's house.** A bed had been made up for Keats in Hunt's study, which was adorned with busts and prints. **364.**

liny: veined.   **379. unshent:** unharmed, unspoiled.   **387.** Kosciusko, the Polish patriot, died in 1817. Keats wrote a sonnet on him in December, 1816.

Dedication. To Leigh Hunt, Esq.   *Page 36*

The dedicatory sonnet in *Poems,* 1817; written in February. Clarke records that it was composed extempore, amid a buzz of talk, when the last proof sheet was delivered; the subject may have been in Keats's mind earlier, as Clarke says (Rollins, *K.C.,* II, 150). The second quatrain recalls the opening of Spenser's May eclogue; and cf. *Brit. Past.* i.2.671 f.

On Seeing the Elgin Marbles   *Page 36*

This sonnet, and one addressed to Haydon that accompanied it, were printed in the *Examiner,* March 9, 1817, and in the *Champion* of the same date, in a review by Reynolds of the newly published *Poems;* Haydon, a week before, had introduced Keats to the Marbles at the British Museum (Rollins, *Studies in Honor of A.H.R. Fairchild,* 1946, and *Harvard Library Bulletin,* VI, 1952). These figures and friezes from the Athenian Parthenon had been acquired from the Turks by Lord Elgin (the "g" is hard), whose offer to sell them to the nation started violent controversy. His action, though it saved the Marbles from almost inevitable destruction, and cost him a great deal of money, was denounced by some as vandalism (see Byron's *Curse of Minerva*); and the Marbles themselves were commonly condemned by critics as postclassical and crudely "natural." Haydon, the most fervent champion of their Phidian authenticity and greatness, had eventually prevailed. (See S. A. Larrabee, *English Bards and Grecian Marbles,* 1943.) At the moment Keats is overwhelmed by a new kind of beauty, but the Marbles worked on his imagination and had their effect on *Hyperion* and the *Grecian Urn.* While the sonnet has some typical early weakness, it is moving away from the Huntian toward the Shakespearian manner (Finney, I, 184–5).

On an Engraved Gem of Leander   *Page 36*

Printed in Thomas Hood's *The Gem, a Literary Annual,* 1829; written probably in March, 1817. Another poem inspired by art, of a kind at the opposite pole from the Elgin Marbles.

7. Cf. *Julius Caesar* V.iii.61: "in thy red rays thou dost sink to night."
14. Cf. Chatterton, *Ælla* 709: "They leap into the sea, and bubbling yield their breath."

On Leigh Hunt's Poem
"The Story of Rimini"   *Page 37*

Printed by Houghton; written in March, 1817. This pallid sonnet is included only as Keats's most explicit — and last — tribute to a work (published in February, 1816) which, for a time, he admired and which encouraged his own early manner and faults of style and taste.

6. Hesperus: the evening star.   **8.** The moon as Diana the huntress.

On the Sea   *Page 37*

Printed in the *Champion*, Aug. 17, 1817, and by Houghton. The sea links itself with the Elgin Marbles as a grand object of contemplation, in contrast with the beauties of Hampstead Heath. In a letter to Reynolds of April 17, 1817, from the Isle of Wight, the letter containing the sonnet, Keats said he had been haunted intensely by the passage in *King Lear*, "Do you not hear the sea?" (misquoted from IV.vi.4, "Hark! do you hear the sea?"). The strength of the sonnet is in the first quatrain.

4. Hecate: the underworld goddess of witchcraft; here the moon-goddess drawing the tides. Cf. *King Lear* I.i.112.

Endymion: A Poetic Romance   *Page 38*

Endymion (written during April–November, 1817, and published in April, 1818) was an ambitious effort to express the thoughts and feelings about the nature of the poet and the poetic senses and imagination that Keats had partly adumbrated in *I Stood Tip-toe* and *Sleep and Poetry*. A few critics — Amy Lowell, N. F. Ford, E. C. Pettet — deny the presence of any allegory or parable, though they can hardly be said to face the difficulties of such a denial; most critics find it impossible to explain away the manifest development of a theme and the clear relation of that theme to Keats's earlier poems. That is not to say that he worked out a coherent "Platonic" doctrine. Whatever Platonic or Neoplatonic hints he might have absorbed from such Elizabethans as Spenser, his "Platonism" was compounded of two elements, neither of which required any philosophic knowledge: first, the timeless idealism that is a matter of instinct and temperament; and, secondly, the specifically romantic idealism set forth in the much-quoted letter to Benjamin Bailey of November 22, which Keats wrote when he had nearly finished the poem:

> I am certain of nothing but of the holiness of the Heart's affections and the truth of Imagination — What the imagination seizes as Beauty must be truth — whether it existed before or not — for I have the same idea of all our Passions as of Love they are all in their sublime, creative of essential Beauty. In a Word, you may know my favorite Speculation by my first Book and the little song I sent in my last . . . The Imagination may be compared to Adam's dream — he awoke and found it truth.

As M. R. Ridley remarks (p. 4), we may come nearer Keats's meaning if we substitute "reality" for the "truth" that is beauty.

The orthodox view of Keats's fable may be baldly outlined. Endymion, the leader of his people, has fallen into a strange lassitude that disturbs his sister Peona, who represents the ordinary values of society. He tells her of his several visions of a goddess and of his feeling impelled to give up his active responsibilities and seek his mysterious immortal love. In Book II he is led through an underworld where he witnesses the annual reunion of Venus and Adonis, and he himself experiences "Love's madness" in union with the object of his quest. At the end of the book he feels sympathy with the lovers Alpheus and Arethusa and prays to his goddess to make them happy. Early in Book III (142 f.), Endymion apostrophizes the Moon (Cynthia, Diana), who had been his first love, the symbol of all beauty in nature and art and life; but she had faded when he came under the spell of his dream-goddess (he does not know that they are the same). In the elaborate episode of Glaucus, Endymion's altruistic sympathy is carried further into humanitarian service, his revival of the host of dead lovers. In Book IV, Endymion comes upon a forlorn Indian maid, left behind by the followers of Bacchus, and, to his agonized dismay, he falls in love with her. From now on he is torn between his dream-goddess, his celestial ideal, and his flesh-and-blood companion. At the end, when in despair he would abandon both, the Indian maid reveals herself as Cynthia. In other words, the direct apprehension of the abstract ideal is beyond mortal powers; the way to the ideal lies through the earthly, the real. The "holiness of the Heart's affections" and "the truth of Imagination" are one.

The lack of coherence and clarity in the poem has a number of obvious causes. Narrative and descriptive elements, small and large, are so continually introduced or over-elaborated that the significant and the insignificant are out of proportion and the theme at times is obscured. This wayward profuseness was a natural failing in a young poet of the romantic period, and it was encouraged by Keats's unfortunate resolve to "make 4000 Lines of one bare circumstance," a resolve based on the idea that a long poem is a test of invention and offers the reader a world of variety and fresh surprise. Then, while Keats must at the start have had some general plan in his head, it was modified as he went along in accordance with new impulses and insights. Also, though nothing is more central in Keats's development than his faith in imaginative intuition, the desire to "burst our mortal bars" (*I Stood* 190), the attempt in *Endymion* to set forth this inevitably nebulous idealism led the young poet — as it might lead a mature one — beyond his experience. Passages describing nature, or the hero's lapses into disillusionment, have in their different ways an authenticity that is more or less wanting in depictions of the ideal; and the final revelation of the Indian maid as Cynthia is only a bit of "Platonic" algebra, not an equation felt on the pulses.

This brings up another aspect of Keats's rendering of the ideal which seems mainly responsible for some critics' refusal to see any parable in the poem: that is, that Endymion's encounters with his dream-goddess are more fleshly than abstract, so that the whole poem is seen as a young poet's celebration of sexual love. This view invites three comments (in addition to what has been said already). First, the experience of passion is a designed part of Endymion's spiritual pilgrimage (the usual badness of the writing in these passages has no bearing on this point). Secondly, it is altogether natural that, in a youthful poem by an intensely sensuous poet, the passionate elements should sometimes override the "Platonic," however sincere the Platonic intention. Thirdly, Keats's erotic instincts both colored and clouded the later development of his parable: sympathy with Alpheus and Arethusa, the restoration to life of dead lovers, and love for the Indian maid were, as symbols, by no means clearly expressive of growth toward Wordsworthian poetry, "the agonies, the strife Of human hearts." But there is a large difference between total lack of purpose and somewhat oblique execution.

Whether or not *Endymion* was in part a conscious or half-conscious reply to Shelley's *Alastor* (1816), these early works illustrate both the "romantic" affinity and the distance between the two young poets. Shelley's poet-hero, though blamed in the preface for turning away from humanity, in the poem is glorified for his uniqueness, his single-hearted and fatal pursuit of the ideal, and there is no hint of possible reconciliation of the visionary with the actual; Keats's aim, at least, is realistic. And Shelley's scenic background is a remote, unreal phantasmagoria, while Keats revels in the concrete beauties of earth, of southern England.

Shelley, though he saw defects in *Endymion*, thought it "full of some of the highest and the finest gleams of poetry." The length and the narrative faults of the poem may try a reader's patience, and Keats has by no means cured his early stylistic and metrical weaknesses, yet his frequent felicities, exuberant or sober, are fresh and inviting, sometimes even powerful, and the very unevenness provides a continual exercise in discernment and taste.

Keats's central situation and theme had a close parallel in Drayton's "Platonic" fable of the ideal and the actual, *Endimion and Phoebe* (1595): Phoebe, disguised as a nymph, wins Endymion's love away from her divine self and then reveals her identity. But, while Keats had some knowledge of Drayton, this book was extremely rare, and, though one of the several extant copies was in the library at Westminster Abbey, it seems unlikely that Keats would have known of it. Drayton's *Man in the Moon* may have contributed some things, although this radical revision of *Endimion and Phoebe* left out the central "plot." De Selincourt (pp. 416–17) suggested that the framework of *Endymion* was indebted to allegorical verses prefixed to a book Keats knew, Sandys' *Ovid:* these verses described the four elements, fire, air, earth, and water as united by love, and the mythological symbolism of the human will and desires. Beyer has seen the pervasive influence of Wieland's *Oberon.* D. Hewlett (p. 170) cites "the travels through earth, water and air in Southey's *The Curse of Kehama.*" If Keats had a clear pattern in mind, and not merely variety of scene, Endymion's normal world, his flights through the sky, and his underworld journey might be related to the familiar triple functions of Cynthia as "Queen of Earth, and Heaven, and Hell" (Keats's sonnet *To Homer*).

The general books on Keats usually include discussion of *Endymion.* Finney's full study (I, 209–322) is helpful, though some reservations must be lodged. An elaborate comparison with *Alastor* was made by Leonard

Brown, *Studies in Philology,* XXX (1933). The various conceptions of the myth before, in, and after Keats are described by E. S. LeComte, *Endymion in England* (1944). The "personal, Romantic allegory" of *Endymion* is defended by J. D. Wigod, *PMLA* LXVIII (1953); and see G. O. Allen, "The Fall of Endymion," *K–SJ* VI (1957), 37–57.

The epigraph is from Shakespeare, Sonnet xvii.

Book i. **23. immortal drink.** "Immortal" and "mortal" are recurrent and significant words; cf. *I Stood* 190, "burst our mortal bars." The senses and imagination may lead to that apprehension of reality which is for mortals a kind of immortal knowledge. **25. essences.** Another significant word in Keats's vocabulary. It seems to mean things of nature, myth, and art experienced through the senses and imagination and remaining in the memory as vital nourishment (25–33); cf. Wordsworth, *Tintern Abbey* 22 f. See N. F. Ford, *PMLA* LXII (1947) and *The Prefigurative Imagination of John Keats* (1951). **50. vermeil:** a favorite word; cf. *Comus* 752, *F.Q.* III.i.46. **63.** In the myth Cynthia visited Endymion on Mount Latmos in Caria, in Asia Minor. **89 f.** The idea of beginning with a feast of Pan may have come from Drayton's *Man in the Moon.* **89. pleasantness.** Potter, I, 233, on the placing of ancient altars in groves, says "the pleasantness of such places was apt to allure the people." **121.** Cf. Coleridge, *Eolian Harp* 11: "The stilly murmur of the distant Sea"; Chatterton, *Goddwyn* 19, "a surgy sea." **139.** Cf. *The Tempest* IV.i.134. **141–4.** Apollo was compelled for a year to be herdsman to King Admetus of Thessaly. Cf. Baldwin, p. 314: "here he taught to the shepherds of Admetus the use of the pipe and other instruments of music; and these pastoral people, who had before led a savage life, became so happy, that the Gods, fearful lest mortals should become happier than themselves, suddenly recalled Apollo to Heaven." **154. mingled wine:** cf. Potter, I, 251–2. **157–8.** Jove made love to Leda in the form of a swan, whose special whiteness was proverbial (e.g., Spenser, *Prothalamion* 42). **170.** Ganymede, a beautiful Trojan youth, was taken to heaven by Jove to be his cupbearer. **174. nervy:** strong. **177. groves Elysian:** in Wordsworth, *Exc.,* Prospectus, lines 47–8. **182.** Cf. Coleridge, *Ancient Mariner* 533–7, *Frost at Midnight* 2. **206. old Triton's horn.** See the note on *Lamia* i.15; and Wordsworth's echo of Spenser in *The World Is Too Much with Us.* **228–9.** Cf. Theocritus ii.28–9 (tr. Fawkes): "this laurel . . . fumes and crackles in the blaze." **229. frankincense:** cf. Potter, I, 253, 271. **232 f.** The Hymn to Pan, despite some flaws of diction, may be called the first of Keats's great odes. The details of Pan's activities, gathered chiefly from Elizabethan poets (Finney, I, 260 f.), are enriched and marshaled in a crescendo of both sound and significance. The goat-god, the tutelary divinity of shepherds, had long been allegorized on various levels, from Christ to "Universall Nature" (Sandys, p. 267); here he becomes the symbol of the romantic imagination, of supra-mortal knowledge. Wordsworth, on hearing Keats read the hymn, pronounced it "A very pretty piece of paganism" — although its reinterpretation of myth was quite in the spirit of his own (see the prefatory note on *I Stood*). **241. pipy:** of tubular shape. **243. Syrinx:** see *I Stood* 157–62 and note. **275–6.** Cf. Theocritus v.98 and vi.10 (tr. Fawkes). **285–7.** Cf. Baldwin, p. 104: "All the strange, mysterious and unaccountable sounds which were heard in solitary places, were attributed to Pan, the God of rural scenery." **290.** Pan was, in some accounts, the son of Hermes (Mercury) and Dryope (*Homeric Hymn to Pan;* Lempriere). **293 f.** De Selincourt (p. 422) cites Marston, *I Antonio and Mellida* IV.i.18–22. **298. ethereal:** a favorite and significant word, which links itself with "essence" (see i.25 and note). See below the letter to Haydon of May 10–11, 1817, and also the letters to Bailey of Nov. 22, 1817, and March 13, 1818. **318. Thermopylæ:** the scene of Leonidas' heroic stand against the Persian invaders of Greece. **328–9.** Apollo accidentally killed Hyacinthus, a youth he loved, when they were playing at quoits. Keats uses the version given in Lempriere in which the jealous Zephyr, the West Wind, blew the quoit against the boy's head. **334. raft:** torn off. **338.** Niobe, for boasting of her children, saw them slain before her eyes by the arrows of Apollo and Artemis. **347–53.** Perhaps based on passages in Apollonius Rhodius' *Argonautica*, tr. W. Preston (J. L. Lowes, *TLS*, Sept. 28, 1933, p. 651). **360–97.** Guesses at more than mortal knowledge — of which Endymion has had glimpses. **394.** Cf. *The Tempest* I.ii.408, *Pericles* III.ii.99–101. **405–6.** The town of petrified people is in "The Story of Zobeide" ("The Sixty-third Night"), in *Arabian Nights Entertainments* (1792), I, 182; ditto, ed. J. Scott (1811), I, 307; *Tales of the East,* ed. H. Weber (1812), I, 62. **411.** In deleting 13 lines Keats left this one rhymeless. **453 f.** Various passages rest on the idea of sleep as a trance-like state or symbol of imaginative activity; cf. *S. and P.* **477–86.** The conflicting claims of social action and contemplative detachment. Peona (715–60) upholds the former against her brother. **495.** Dryope bore a child to Apollo (Sandys, pp. 166, 180). **501. melt away and thaw.** Cf. *Hamlet* I.ii.129–30; *Exc.* iv.145. Most of the Shakespearian echoes in *Endymion* are from the outdoor plays, *The Tempest* and *A Midsummer Night's Dream* (C. Spurgeon, *Keats's Shakespeare,* pp. 5–16). **531. Lucifer:** the morning star (Sandys, p. 36). **555. ditamy:** dittany. Cf. Lempriere ("Diana"): "Among plants the poppy and the ditamy were sacred to her." **562–3.** Mercury, as a herald, carried a wand or *caduceus,* entwined at one end with two serpents (cf. *F.Q.* II.xii.41, *P.L.* xi.130–3, Sandys, p. 42). **595. argent:** silvery (*P.L.* iii.460; Chatterton). **614. gordian'd:** coiled, like the Gordian Knot (cf. *P.L.* iv.348). **620–2.** The first of a number of disillusioned relapses into actuality after a glimpse of the ideal; cf. 691–706, etc., and *S. and P.* 157–9. **625. bluely vein'd:** cf. Coleridge, *Christabel* 63, "Her blue-veined feet." **627–8.** R. D. Cornelius (*MLQ* V, 1944) reproduces and discusses Spence's picture (*Polymetis,* ed. 1755, pp. 184, 199) of Diana approaching Endymion and holding a fluttering scarf above her head (the picture is not in the abridged *Polymetis* of 1802). **629–30.** Cf. *P.L.* xi.130. **633. Dream within dream!** Peona seems to refer to the goddess' appearing (601 f.) within the dream that began at 572. **655.** Keats's recurring idea of

ecstatic passion as an approach to death — here a prelude to new life.
683. ouzel: a European blackbird or variety of thrush.   **691–2.** Cf.
Alastor 196–7: "Whither have fled The hues of heaven . . . ?"   **749.** Cf.
The Tempest IV.i.156–8.

i.777–81. On Jan. 30, 1818, when *Endymion* was in the press, Keats
sent his publisher, John Taylor, the present version of these lines, saying
that "such a preface is necessary to the Subject," and proceeding:

> The whole thing must I think have appeared to you, who are a con-
> sequitive Man, as a thing almost of mere words — but I assure you that
> when I wrote it, it was a regular stepping of the Imagination towards a
> Truth. My having written that Argument will perhaps be of the greatest
> Service to me of any thing I ever did — It set before me at once the
> gradations of Happiness even like a kind of Pleasure Thermometer —
> and is my first Step towards the chief Attempt in the Drama — the
> playing of different Natures with Joy and Sorrow.

In the Platonic–Romantic–Keatsian "Pleasure Thermometer" of i.777 f.,
"The clear religion of heaven," Keats's version of Wordsworth's view of
nature, is linked (as in the opening paragraph of the poem) with art. Experience of beautiful objects, natural and artistic, brings "A fellowship with
essence" (cf. i.25 and note), "a sort of oneness" with the universe and man,
the sense of organic unity which is so central for Coleridge and Wordsworth
but here carries Keats's sensuous and aesthetic emphasis. The two suc-
cessively higher stages are more outgoing, "More self-destroying": "friendship" or humanitarian sympathy and action, and love. Lines 816–42 (and cf.
ii.1 f.) seem to make love between man and woman the dynamic life-force
of the world, and Keats's friend Bailey saw in *Endymion* an "approaching in-
clination . . . to that abominable principle of *Shelley's* — that *Sensual Love*
is the principle of *things*." "Of this," Bailey went on, "I believe him [Keats]
to be unconscious, & can see how by a process of imagination he might arrive at so false, delusive, & dangerous conclusion" (Rollins, *K.C.*, I, 34–5).
But even earthly love is allied with contemplation as against the life of
action, and the topmost stage, the mortal Endymion's love for an immortal,
includes but transcends sexual passion (843 f.). It is no reflection on the sin-
cerity of Keats's "Platonism" to say that, while he could speak of "the
eternal Being, the Principle of Beauty" (letter to Reynolds, April 9, 1818)
and of "The mighty abstract Idea I have of Beauty in all things" (letter to
George and Georgiana Keats, Oct. 21, 1818), he is generally more aware of
the Many than of the One; his instincts are concrete.

i.796. One of several unexplained rhymeless lines.   **806. orbed:** in
Shakespeare, *passim; P.L.* vi.543.   **831.** Cf. *Romeo and Juliet* III.v.10 and
Comus 188.   **862.** Latona gave birth to Apollo and Cynthia on the island
of Delos (966).   **903–5.** See the note on i.655.   **924. amber studs:**
from Marlowe's *Come live with me*.   **944.** Proserpine was carried off by
Pluto from the Sicilian vale of Enna to be queen of Hades; cf. *P.L.* iv.268–
72.   **947–51. Echo:** a nymph who pined away for love of Narcissus; cf.
I Stood 163 f. and note.   **948. thorough:** through.   **975–7.** Cf. *Il P.*
32 and 167 f.

320 · *Notes*

Book ii. The introduction, 1–43, celebrates earthly or sexual love, the main theme of this book, as higher than the active life; cf. i.777–81 and note.   13. close: embrace (*Twelfth Night* V.i.161; *Troilus* III.ii.51).   22–3. Plutarch's anecdote (*Themistocles*) of the owl accepted as a good omen for battle is repeated in Potter, I, 379–80; Potter refers, pp. 378, 380, to Alexander, but Keats's allusion suggests a misty recollection of Robertson's *History of America* (1803), I, 20 f.   31–2. Hero: *Much Ado About Nothing.*   Imogen: *Cymbeline.*   Pastorella: *F.Q.* VI.ix–xii.   39. chaffing: chafing. .   60. pight: placed, fixed (Spenser, Shakespeare, Chatterton).   70 f. One of Keats's felicitous pictures of quietude.   91. mealy gold: cf. *Troilus* III.iii.78–9.   109. Amphitrite: a sea-goddess, wife of Neptune.   168–70. Endymion is not aware that his "thrice-seen love" is Cynthia.   197. Deucalion, the Noah of classical myth, and his wife Pyrrha repeopled the earth by casting behind them stones that turned into human beings.   198. Orion, a giant and hunter, blinded by Oenopion, was to regain his sight if he journeyed toward the rising sun. Hazlitt took this great line as an epigraph for his essay, "On a Landscape of Nicolas Poussin" (1821), in which he described Poussin's picture of Orion; Keats may have heard Hazlitt talk about it (De Selincourt, p. 431).   213. Cf. *Comus* 208.   230. antre: cave (*Othello* I.iii.140).   245. fray; see *Eve of St. Agnes* 198 and note.   275–80. On the return to "self," see the note on i.777–81.   277. the fog-born elf: the will o' the wisp (*Midsummer Night's Dream* II.i.39; *L'Allegro* 104 f.; *P.L.* ix.634–42).   302 f. With this prayer to Diana (Cynthia), cf. *Exc.* iv.861 f. (Colvin, p. 233).   360. Arion, a musician, cast overboard by sailors, was rescued by dolphins that enjoyed his music (cf. *F.Q.* IV.xi.23).   387 f. Adonis, killed by a boar, was so lamented by Venus that for half of every year he was allowed to leave the underworld and be with her. Keats would know Shakespeare's poem, *F.Q.* III.i.34–9, vi.46–9, and Ovid, *Met.* x, including Sandys' commentary, pp. 201–2, but his picture of the awakening and the reunion seems to be largely original.   400. tenting: like the top of a tent (cf. Marlowe, *Hero and Leander* ii.264).   419 f. The Cupids might be partly suggested by Fawkes's translation of Moschus, iii.95–6; Bion, *Adonis* 10, 80, 114 f.; Theocritus xv.176 (Fawkes's line numbers).   443. As the wife of Bacchus, Ariadne is associated with wine.   445. Vertumnus, an Italian deity of fruits, loved Pomona.   448. Amalthea: a Cretan princess who nursed the infant Jupiter on goat's milk.   453. Hesperides: the nymphs who guarded the golden apples given to Juno on her marriage with Jupiter.   461. fond: foolish.   475–6. Cf. *Il P.* 107.   492. Cythera was the island near which, in some myths, Cytherea (Aphrodite, Venus) rose from the sea.   494. clamant: cf. Thomson, *Autumn* 350.   533. coy excuse: in *Lyc.* 18.   537. quell: power.   563. fringed lids: cf. i.394 and note, and "fring'd eye-lids" in Hunt, *Juvenilia* (ed. 1803), p. 16.   585. The volcanic eruptions of Etna were the heavings of Typhon, the rebel giant whom Zeus imprisoned under it.   611. Thetis: a sea-nymph, mother of Achilles.   640 f. This impressive if not clearly relevant picture of the Mother of the Gods seems to echo Sandys, pp. 191, 201 (De Selincourt, pp

433–4).   657–8. The eagle is the bird of Jupiter.   674. **Hesperean:**
the word (cf. Sandys, p. 204) seems to mean "Hesperidean": "as if he were
in the garden of the Hesperides."   688. Apparently the Hours. Cf. *F.Q.*
VII.vii.45 and the note below on iv.421–4.   689–90. The constellation of
the Pleiades, the seven daughters of Atlas.   691. Cf. *Comus* 873.   775–
805. Endymion's dream-goddess virtually reveals herself as Cynthia, though
he is too excited to understand.   842. **centinel:** sentinel.   875. **Alecto:**
one of the Furies, who had serpents instead of hair, or twined in their hair.
876–7. Hermes (Mercury) with his music lulled to sleep and then beheaded
the hundred-eyed Argus, whom Hera (Juno) made guardian of Io after
changing her into a cow. Cf. *P.L.* xi.128–33.   905. **essences:** see the note
on i.25.   936. Arethusa, a nymph of Diana, was loved and pursued by
the river-god Alpheus and, praying to Diana, was changed into a fountain
(Baldwin, pp. 114–15; Sandys, pp. 92, 102).   973–4. Cf. i.485.   996.
mealy sweets: see the note on ii.91.

   Book iii.1 f. The theme of humanitarian service in this book may war-
rant an attack on the blind vanity of officialdom, though the writing is very
bad.   7–8. **foxes:** see Judges xv.4–5.   10. **dight:** clothed (Spenser,
Milton, Chatterton).   21. **Chaldeans:** ancient masters of prophecy (cf.
Exc. iv.694 f.).   25. **ethereal:** see the note on i.298.   42. **thy Sister:**
Cynthia, Diana, the Moon. Cf. i.28–9 and iii.142–74.   69. **monstrous:**
inhabited by monsters (*Lyc.* 158).   70. **spooming:** foaming.   71.
Tellus: the Earth.   78. **Vesper:** Venus as the evening star.   97–8.
Leander and Orpheus, though stock examples of the venturesome lover, may
have been suggested by Spenser's *Hymn to Love* 231 f.   99. **Pluto:** see
the note on i.944.   123–36. The picture of undersea relics, suggestive of
human history, seems to combine details from *Richard III* I.iv.21–33 and
Aen. vii.183–6. Sandys (p. 153), translating the Virgilian lines, has "brazen
beakes"; the epithet is not in Virgil.   133. **Nox:** a classical personification
of Night (*P.L.* ii.970, 986).   134. **behemoth . . . leviathan:** cf. Job xl.15,
xli.1; *P.L.* vii.412, 471.   142–74. Critics compare Wordsworth's various
accounts of his response to nature, Coleridge's *The Nightingale* 96–105, etc.,
but Keats's ardent conception, which embraces nature, art, friendship, heroic
action, and sensuous pleasure, is his own. Cf. i.1–35, 777 f.   157. **mesh:**
entwine?   172. **essence:** see the note on i.25.   175–84. In the chronology of Endymion's experience, though not of the narrative, his first
passion was for the moon, but this faded with his new passion for his dream-
goddess; he does not know that they are the same.   196–209. Glaucus'
symbolic mantle may be modeled on Cynthia's in Drayton's *Man in the
Moon* (Colvin, p. 170).   221–2. Cf. Sandys, p. 252 (on Glaucus): "thick
and arched eye-browes which touch one another."   243–4. See the note
on ii.585.   251. **Sisters three:** the Fates.   254. Cf. *Macbeth* I.iii.23.
265. **magian:** magical.   269. **Tartarus:** Hades.   271. Cf. *Cymbeline*
V.v.263.   314 f. Glaucus' experience, altered and elaborated from Ovid,
Met. xiii–xiv, seems intended as a partial parallel to Endymion's, though it is
not consistently so. He had been a contented child of nature (318–71), but
longed for a larger life in the ocean, fell in love with the unresponsive

Scylla, appealed for aid to the enchantress Circe, succumbed to her sensual charms, discovered her evil character and fled; but Circe doomed him to 1000 years of life and put Scylla to death. Circe as a sensual symbol is conspicuous in Sandys' commentary, pp. 261, 264–5. Glaucus' sentence might have been suggested by the fate of the Sibyl in Sandys, p. 254 (J. Grundy, *Notes and Queries*, II, 1955) and of Aswad in Southey's *Thalaba* i.577f. (a poem Keats echoes in *End.* iii.833 and *Isabella*).   **364. Æthon:** one of the horses of the sun-god Apollo.   **405–6.** The same rhyme words as in *Lyc.* 94–5 and the first couplet of Hunt's *Bacchus, or the Pirates* (1814).   **406–7.** Hercules' relieving Atlas of the burden of holding up the sky Sandys (p. 177) calls his "last labour"; Hercules had "travelled to the uttermost bounds of the Earth to increase his knowledge by conferring with Atlas."   **414. Phœbus' daughter:** Circe, who lived on the isle of Æœa (Sandys, p. 265), off the coast of Italy.   **461.** Amphion's music built the walls of Thebes; here, and in 1002, Keats seems to mean Arion (ii.360 and note).   **503–4.** Charon ferried the dead across the Styx.   **515.** A recollection of hospital training?   **530–1. huge Python:** the serpent killed by Apollo (the phrase is in *P.L.* x.531 and Sandys, p. 5).   **Boreas:** the North Wind.   **546. ruddy drops:** in *Julius Caesar* II.i.289.   **565.** Cf. *Comus* 349.   **567. Dis:** Pluto (*P.L.* iv.270).   **593. vast:** cf. Shakespeare, *Pericles* III.i.1.   **615–6.** Cf. *P.L.* xi.494–5.   **638.** See the note on *Hyp.* i.18.   **648. A gallant vessel:** cf. *The Tempest* I.ii.6.   **653. Æolus:** god of the winds.   **701 f.** The humanitarian act of collecting the bodies of drowned lovers, whom Endymion will be able to restore to life, may have been suggested by Jonson's *Masque of Lethe*.   **762. charactery:** writing (Shakespeare).   **806 f.** The festival at Neptune's palace may owe something to Jonson's masque, *Neptune's Triumph*.   **833. the palace of his pride:** in Southey, *Thalaba* i.238, 363.   **851. Iris:** goddess of the rainbow.   **853. Paphian army:** army of lovers (see the note on i.510). **865. Beauty's paragon:** Venus.   **899. Nais:** mother of Glaucus.   **906–7.** Cf. *I Stood* 190, *End.* i.23, 293f., etc., and Fletcher, *Faithful Shepherdess* I.ii.104–5: "to make them free From dying flesh and dull mortality." **912. one of heaven:** Cynthia.   **918.** The text as commonly printed, "Visit my Cytherea," confuses one of Venus' names with the name of her island (a mistake made in Tooke's *Pantheon*, ed. 1781, p. 111). The mistake is corrected in the draft reading supplied by Woodhouse (De Selincourt, p. 441; Garrod, p. 154), and the text is accordingly emended. "Cytherea" is used correctly in ii.492.   **927–30. pleach'd . . . coverture:** cf. *Much Ado About Nothing* III.i.7 and 30.   **957–9.** Cf. Milton, *Vacation Exercise* 34–8.   **978.** Cupid.   **993–1004.** Editors compare *F.Q.* IV.xi.11, 12, and 18.   **1000. Doris:** wife of Nereus and mother of the sea-nymphs. **1002.** See the note on iii.461.

Book iv.1 f. The theme of this book is Endymion's spiritual (and poetic) fulfilment through union with Cynthia; the introduction takes, rather unexpectedly, the form of a sketch of the history of poetry.   **10. eastern voice:** biblical poetry.   **11. the Nine:** the Muses.   **15. Ausonia:** Italy (as in Virgil), here represented apparently by Virgil and Dante. **30–37, 44–51, 66–85.** Spoken by the Indian maiden, who has been left behind by Bacchus and his throng on their westward march. She is a symbol of human love and experience, in opposition to the dream-goddess — but a decidedly romantic, not to say coquettish, embodiment of actuality. Cf. the Arab maiden in *Alastor* 129 f., whom Shelley's poet-hero ignores. **56–7. Phœbe:** Cynthia. **66.** See the note on i.562. **68. Hyacinthus: see the** note on i.328. **95. A triple soul:** Endymion had first loved the moon, then his dream-goddess (who at the end of book iii had assured him of their union), and he now loves the Indian maid. **121. Erebus:** Hades. **146–290.** Keats's reference, in the letter to Bailey of Nov. 22, 1817, to "the little song" (the first five stanzas of this ode) indicates his serious conception of sorrow as strengthening the creative imagination, but this idea is rendered much more adequately in his later poetry and prose; it hardly comes through the pretty images and lilting rhythms of these stanzas. **157. spry:** a variant of "spray" (e.g., Sandys, p. 207). **167–8.** Cf. *Comus* 897–9. **182–272.** The description of the Bacchic march is a notable orchestration of image and sound, but, compared with the Hymn to Pan, it remains merely pictorial. The main suggestions may have come from Sandys, pp. 53, 61–5, 73–5, Baldwin, pp. 225–30 (his Bacchus is "plump"), and Titian's *Bacchus and Ariadne;* details from Milton's *Nativity* and *Lycidas,* the *Ancient Mariner* and *Kubla Khan,* Landor's *Gebir,* Lempriere, etc., and possibly Rabelais, V.39–40, and Booth's translation of Diodorus Siculus (Finney, I, 272–91). **215. Silenus:** a satyr companion of Bacchus (Lempriere; Baldwin, pp. 229–30; Sandys, pp. 61–2, 75, 204). **245–9.** Cf. *Antony and Cleopatra* II.ii.199–214; *Gebir* iv.157–8: "Crown'd were tame crocodiles, and boys white-robed Guided their creaking crests across the stream." **257–63.** Cf. Baldwin, pp. 228–9: Bacchus was fused with "an Asiatic conqueror, who extended his triumphant progress over Egypt, Ethiopia, Arabia and many other countries, who planted a colony on the banks of the Indus . . . The Egyptians relate his history under the name of Osiris." **265–7.** Cf. Milton, *Nativity* 173 f.; Campbell, *Pleasures of Hope* (ed. 1815), references to "Brama" on pp. 41–4, e.g., p. 44: "He comes! dread Brama shakes the sunless sky With murmuring wrath, and thunders from on high!" **343. two steeds:** symbols of rekindled imagination? In the *Arabian Nights* ("The Sixty-second Night"), just before the tale alluded to in *End.* i.405–6, there is a winged black horse that carries its rider aloft and brings him back to earth: see *Arabian Nights Entertainments* (1792), I, 175; ditto, ed. J. Scott (1811), I, 296; *Tales of the East,* ed. H. Weber (1812), I, 60. **365. Snuff:** cf. *P.L.* x.272. **370.** Cf. *Comus* 553–4. **374. aloof:** cf. *P.L.* iii.577. **376. a young man:** Endymion. **378. empyreal:** heavenly (*P.L., passim*). **385. litter:** cf. *Comus* 554. **394.** Cf. "old Skiddaw," Wordsworth, *To Joanna* 62. **413. Pallas:** Athene, goddess of wisdom and war. **415. Hebe:** cupbearer to Jove and goddess of youth. **421–5.** Cf. Ovid's description of the palace of the Sun, *Met.* ii.1 f. (Sandys, p. 25), and *F.Q.* VII.vii.28–31. **430–2.** Now, in his dream, Endymion first realizes that

his dream-goddess is Cynthia.   **441–3. Icarus:** see the note on *S. and P.*
303.   **459. dædale:** labyrinthine, cunning; the word, from the ingenious
Daedalus, Spenser uses for "skillful" (*F.Q.* III, proem, ii.4) or "fruitful"
(IV.x.45).   **470. she:** Cynthia.   **476–7.** The experience of love was to
be "More self-destroying" (i.799) than response to nature and art.   **485.
throe:** be in throes (*Antony and Cleopatra* III.vii.81; *Tempest* II.i.231).
500. Cf. *Comus* 333.   **512–48.** Murry (*Keats*, pp. 166 f. and earlier edns.)
interprets the Cave of Quietude as a state of profound content, beyond sorrow and joy: "in this calm ecstasy of despair" the sufferer's whole being is
reborn. But the passage — which Murry sees as the psychological culmina-
tion of the poem — dwells much more on misery and apathy than on re-
newal, and Endymion continues to feel the pangs of a divided soul.   **536.
Semele:** mother of Bacchus.   **563–611.** A choric song in honor of Diana's
approaching marriage to Endymion. Critics cite the description of the signs
of the zodiac in Spence's *Polymetis* (ed. 1802), pp. 60 f.; cf. Sandys, pp. 10,
25 f., etc.   **599. shent:** disgraced (Spenser).   **606. Danae's son:** Perseus, who saved Andromeda from the sea-monster.   **611.** Daphne, loved
and pursued by Apollo, was changed into a laurel.   **623–4.** The Indian
maid, who had vanished in lines 509–12.   **626–69.** Endymion's human
instincts cry out for human experience and against pursuit of a celestial
ideal.   **638–43.** Cf. i.13–24.   **650. too thin breathing:** cf. i.751, and
Exc. iv.140–5.   **651–2.** Cf. ii.199–214.   **670–721.** In the tradition of
the pastoral "invitation to love," e.g., Ovid, *Met.* xiii.789 f. (Sandys, pp.
242–3); here, contentment with simple earthly life and love.   **701. Vesta:**
the Roman goddess of the hearth.   **730. feather'd tyrant:** Cupid.   **764.**
See the note on *Hyp.* i.18.   **769. cirque:** circle (cf. *Exc.* iii.50).   **774.**
Apollo, the hero of *Hyperion.* For other indications of the poem to come,
see ii.994, iii.129, 993 f., iv.943, 956.   **790. charactery:** see iii.762.
792. fear'd: frightened (Spenser; Shakespeare).   **804–46.** Peona wel-
comes Endymion back to his role of leader and benefactor of his people.
849–72. Endymion, rejecting union with the Indian maid for contemplative
solitude, seems to revert to his earlier idealism; if his attitude here and in
975–6 represents the final extinction of "self" (cf. i.799), it is not very clearly
rendered.   **878–9.** Cf. *Hamlet* V.ii.231; Matt. x.29.   **943. Titan's foe:**
Jupiter (see the note on iv.774).   **950. seemlihed:** seemliness.   **953.
Rhadamanthus:** one of the judges of Hades.   **955.** Prometheus, who stole
fire from heaven, made man of clay (*F.Q.* II.x.70; Sandys, p. 13; Baldwin,
p. 92).   **971.** Cf. Collins, "Spring, with dewy fingers cold" (*How Sleep
the Brave*).   **986.** On the identity of Cynthia and the Indian maid, see
the introduction to the poem.

In Drear-Nighted December   *Page 131*

Written in December, 1817, when Keats had just finished *Endymion.*
There are variations in the early printed versions (*Literary Gazette*, Sept. 19,
1829; etc.) and transcripts. The problems are discussed by A. Whitley

(*Harvard Library Bulletin*, V, 1951; see also Garrod, *OSA*, pp. 470–1), who prints a text from a newly discovered autograph copy; this is reproduced above, with corrections in spelling and punctuation. The metrical pattern apparently came from the song *Farewell, ungrateful traitor* in Dryden's *Spanish Friar* V.i.

15. **petting**: sulking, complaining.   21. In the first three printed versions, and two transcripts, the line reads "To know the change and feel it"; and, in the autograph copy cited above, this reading — not in Keats's hand — is added as an alternative. Like Colvin (p. 160), Murry (*Keats*, pp. 119 f., and earlier edns.) defends "The feel of not to feel it," relating the line to the occasional moods of spiritual torpor, "sublime misery," that Keats was aware of in himself. Cf., in this volume, the letters to Bailey of Oct. 28–30 and Nov. 22, 1817.

On Seeing a Lock of Milton's Hair   Page 131

Printed in *PDJ*, Nov. 15, 1838, and by Houghton; written on Jan. 21, 1818. See below the letter of Jan. 23 to Bailey (with whom Keats had read Milton some months before). Lines 30–1 are Keats's first distinct declaration on the need of knowledge along with "sensation" (Thorpe, *Mind*, pp. 65–6).

5–6. Cf. Coleridge, *Dejection* 42–3: "It were a vain endeavour, Though I should gaze for ever. . . ."   18. **Delian**: see the note on *End.* i.862.

On Sitting Down to Read *King Lear* Once Again   Page 132

Printed in *PDJ*, Nov. 8, 1838, and by Houghton; written on Jan. 22, 1818. For comments on *King Lear* and the sonnet, see below Keats's letters of Dec. 21 (–27?), 1817 to his brothers and of Jan. 23, 1818, to Bailey. "Romance" was equated by Woodhouse with *Endymion*, by Colvin (p. 257) and De Selincourt (p. 542) with *The Faerie Queene*. The reference may be general; on the threshold of a supreme tragedy, Keats may be dismissing all poetry of less reality. But, since he is now revising *Endymion* for the press — as he writes to his brothers on Jan. 23, in the letter containing the sonnet — he may be putting aside his own poem, subtitled "A Poetic Romance," and based on ancient myth ("olden pages"). Logic suggests that line 11 should mean "When I have finished *Lear*," although the image of the oak forest points rather to *Endymion* (and in the sonnet *To Spenser* of Feb. 5 a forest symbolizes *The Faerie Queene*, romance). The last four lines might mean "When I am done with *Endymion*, let me be re-created by the fire of Shakespeare." (See H. E. Briggs, *MLN* LVIII, 1943.) The last line, by the way, is an Alexandrine (12 syllables).

When I Have Fears   Page 133

Printed by Houghton; written late in January, 1818. This sonnet, one of Keats's best, is his first in the Shakespearian form, and in something like the Shakespearian style. The most elaborate analysis is by M. A. Goldberg, *MLQ* XVIII (1957), 125–31.

3. **charact'ry**: see *End.* iii.762 and note.   5–6. Cf. *S. and P.* 10, *End.* iii.1021.   9. **fair creature of an hour.** Cf. below, *To a Lady Seen for a Few Moments*, and — if Keats had read in Cary's *Dante* at this time — Cary, *Purg.* xxix.25, "Woman, the creature of an hour."   12. **unreflecting love**: one aspect of the tension remarked upon in the note on the poem next below.

God of the Meridian   *Page 133*

Printed by Houghton; written Jan. 31, 1818, in a letter to Reynolds. Although the letter contains two pieces of light verse, this third one, addressed to Apollo, is serious, and links itself with significant utterances in other poems and letters. The "division" described in the opening lines recalls the prolonged and many-sided tension in Keats between "thought" and "sensation," and the last lines are one of his affirmations on the side of philosophic knowledge, ethical wisdom. Lines 9 f. touch the problem so earnestly probed a little later in the *Epistle to Reynolds* 78 f.

Lines on the Mermaid Tavern   *Page 134*

Printed in the 1820 volume; written Feb. 1–3, 1818. See the introductory note to *Robin Hood* just below. Keats may have known some of the convivial pieces by Jonson, Francis Beaumont, and others.

12. Cf. *F.Q.* I.iv.22.6–7, "a bouzing can Of which he supt."

Robin Hood: To a Friend   *Page 135*

Printed in the 1820 volume. This and the preceding poem were included in a letter to Reynolds of Feb. 3, 1818; Keats was writing "In answer to his Robin Hood Sonnets." The two poems reflect the sentiments of the letter; Keats was in one of his moods of revulsion against the obtrusive didacticism and introspectiveness of Wordsworth (he also censured Byron and Hunt).

10. Reynolds was shortly to become a lawyer; cf. 47–8.   18. **forest drear**: cf. *Il P.* 119.   36. **"grenè shawe"**; from Chaucer, *Friar's Tale* 1386.

To a Lady Seen for a Few Moments
at Vauxhall   *Page 136*

Printed in *Hood's Magazine*, September, 1844; written Feb. 4, 1818. We may agree with De Selincourt (p. 544) that this "is probably the most Shakespearian sonnet that Keats ever wrote," without sharing Robert Bridges' quite extravagant opinion that it "might have been written by Shakespeare." Only a few lines can be called more or less Shakespearian.

Vauxhall: public gardens in London, on the south bank of the Thames; long a popular place of entertainment.

12. **in . . . sense**: through hearing.

What the Thrush Said   *Page 137*

Printed by Houghton; included in a letter to Reynolds, Feb. 19, 1818.
This unrhymed quatorzain is one of Keats's statements about one side of his
nature, belief in the potential creativeness of passive receptivity, as opposed
to the also recurrent desire to gain intellectual knowledge. Line 8 is presumably a paradox corresponding to line 4; "triple" seems to be a general intensive
prompted by the "supreme darkness" of human ignorance and meditation.

The Human Seasons   *Page 137*

Printed, in a revised version (given here), in Hunt's *Literary Pocket
Book*, 1819; the original version was included in a letter to Bailey of
March 13, 1818 (Rollins, I, 243). The theme may owe something to *Exc.*
v.390 f. (Finney, I, 383), but the moods are Keats's own — and partly akin
to those of *What the Thrush Said* and the *Epistle to Reynolds.*

7–8. nigh His. If Keats wrote "nigh," it seems a rather strained use of the
word as an infinitive. For "nigh His" Houghton read "high Is."

Epistle to John Hamilton Reynolds   *Page 138*

Printed by Houghton; written March 25, 1818, from Devon. These im-
promptu verses start from the confused fancies of a wakeful night and turn
from forced jocularity to the world of serene imagination and romance, and
then to a vehement questioning of the power of imagination confronted with
actuality, in particular the cruelty of nature. The contrast may remind us of
Wordsworth's *Elegiac Stanzas* (Finney, I, 391). Though the writing is, as
Keats said, "careless" and ragged, the ideas suggest the measure of his
growth since the pretty poetizing of the epistles of 1815–16.

10. The novelist, Maria Edgeworth (1767–1849).   **11–12.** The actor,
Junius Brutus Booth (1796–1852). **so so:** tipsy. **Soho:** a dubious district
of London.   **16. tushes:** tusks.   **19–25.** Claude Lorrain's painting,
Sacrifice to Apollo (reproduced in Colvin, p. 264). Keats had seen it in 1816
at the British Institution, hung beside Titian's *Europa* — hence his slip here.
21. the milk-white heifer lows. Cf. *End.* i.214; Theocritus ix.13 (tr. Fawkes):
"the soft skins of milk-white heifers"; M. Tighe, i.33: "The milk-white bull
they to the altar lead"; and the note on the *Grecian Urn* 31 f.   **22.** Cf.
Southey, *Hymn to the Penates* 240: "The rich libation flowed"; Potter, I,
277: "the mix'd libation flows."   **26.** *The Enchanted Castle* is another
painting by Claude. See the notes on the *Nightingale* 69–70.   **29. Urganda's sword.** In *Amadis of Gaul, by Vasco Lobeira* (London, 1803), Bk. I,
c. 12 (I, 104), etc.; mentioned also in Keats's letter of May 16, 1817, to his
publishers Taylor and Hessey.   **42. Santon:** holy man, perhaps from William Beckford's *Vathek* (ed. R. Garnett, 1893, pp. 79, 132–6, 218; Gittings,
Mask, p. 101) or *Childe Harold* ii.56.   **44. Cuthbert:** Keats's invention?
46. Lapland was a traditional home of witches (*P.L.* ii.665; Sandys, p. 133).
75. Lore of good and ill. Critics have debated over "lore" and Houghton's

reading, "love" (De Selincourt, p. 586), but in printing the verse-letter from Woodhouse's transcript Rollins (I, 262), like Forman and Garrod, gives "lore." **76–7.** Do these lines mean that the harsh actualities of life cannot be overcome by the will or imagination but harass us beyond endurance or solution? Or if, as we might expect, "tease us out of thought" has more or less the same meaning as in the *Grecian Urn* 44, the rough sense would be: "Our dreamings cannot alter actuality but they are a means of escape from it." Cf. *End.* i.6–13. **78–85.** The conviction forced upon Endymion (iv.636–59); cf. *What the Thrush Said.* But the defect of this alternative is that the imagination has no absolutes to appeal to. Some reflections partly akin to this whole passage appear in the letter to James Rice of March 24, the day before this verse-letter was written. **88. lampit:** limpet. **88– 92.** The setting happens to resemble a beach on which William Paley, the great exponent of the theological "argument from design," saw multitudes of shrimps leaping in sheer exuberance of happiness (*Natural Theology*, 1803, p. 492; quoted in D. Bush, *Science and English Poetry*, pp. 105–6). **93 f.** Keats's account of "Nature red in tooth and claw" grows out of his mature thought and feeling, as some letters illustrate, and, more immediately, out of the fact that he is at the moment in Devon nursing his consumptive brother Tom. This view of nature has been traced from antiquity down through Voltaire and Erasmus Darwin by H. N. Fairchild, *PMLA* LXIV (1949). D. B. Green (*Notes and Queries*, CXCV, 1950, pp. 410–12) finds in Keats the special influence of a passage in Goethe's *Sorrows of Werter*, tr. 1783, I, 144–5. **104. pard:** leopard. **ounce:** lynx. **108.** Keats's allusion to Kamchatka may have been suggested by reading in Buffon's *Natural History* and Robertson's *History of America* (Rollins, I, 263). **111. new romance:** *Isabella?* **113. "here follows prose":** *Twelfth Night* II.v.154.

Isabella; or, The Pot of Basil   *Page 141*

Printed in the 1820 volume; written February–April, 1818. Keats and Reynolds planned a collection of tales versified from Boccaccio's *Decameron* — an enterprise lately suggested by Hazlitt in a lecture on Dryden in which he mentioned the story of Isabella (Day IV, Novel 5). Keats's source was a translation of 1620 (in its fifth edition of 1684), which somewhat softened and idealized the love story, and he carried on the process (H. G. Wright, *TLS*, April 17, 1943, p. 192; *Boccaccio in England*, 1957, pp. 397– 407). Keats's model for the *ottava rima* seems to have been Edward Fairfax's translation of Tasso (1600), of which he owned a copy; but he made his own modifications. Lamb, very oddly, thought *Isabella* the finest poem in the 1820 volume. Matthew Arnold, though condemning it for feebleness of action and structure and excess of decoration, affirmed that it "contains, perhaps, a greater number of happy single expressions which one could quote than all the extant tragedies of Sophocles" (Preface to *Poems*, 1853). Keats himself came to see the poem as weak in comparison with *Lamia* and

The Eve of St. Agnes (letter to Woodhouse, Sept. 21–2, 1819). Modern readers are likely to see a few fine bits — notably stanzas 35–8 — in a general tissue of sentimental pathos and, especially in the first third of the poem, much bad writing. It seems strange that the author of the sonnet on *King Lear* and the *Epistle to Reynolds* could, in the same few months, produce *Isabella;* but the conventions of romantic narrative had been shifting from Scott and Byron to the tepid luxuriance of Hunt, Mrs. Hemans, and "Barry Cornwall." Ridley has a full critique, pp. 18–56. F. E. L. Priestley (*MLQ* V, 1944) sees Chaucerian influence in *Isabella*, as contrasted with *Endymion*, in closer narrative structure, the attempt at a character's psychology, and pathos achieved through realistic simplicity.

2. palmer: cf. *Romeo and Juliet* I.v.95–103. 62. fear: frighten. 91. fee: compensation. 95. Theseus' spouse: Ariadne, deserted by the lover she had enabled to overcome the Minotaur. 99. under-grove: forest in the underworld (*Aen.* vi.450 f.). 105–20. This sudden anti-capitalist utterance (which led G. B. Shaw to see Keats as a potential Marxist) evidently drew upon Dryden's *Annus Mirabilis* iii and Southey's *Thalaba* i.239 f., and perhaps Robertson's accounts, in his *History of America*, of Spanish oppression of the natives. 107. swelt: faint (Chaucer, *Knight's Tale* 1356; *F.Q.* IV.vii.9). 109. proud-quiver'd: "which once proudly bore quivers" (Finney, I, 378). Cf. Campbell, *Pleasures of Hope* (ed. 1815, p. 39): "The quiver'd chief of Congo loved to reign." 133. Ready to swoop like hawks on incoming vessels. 145. An apostrophe in Chaucer's manner, e.g., *Knight's Tale* 1623. 150. ghittern: guitar (Chaucer, *Miller's Tale* 3333, 3353, etc.). 167–8. This mercenary motive is Keats's invention, in keeping with 105–20. In Boccaccio the brothers' motive for murder is that Lorenzo, their employee, has seduced their sister; this is glossed over in the version Keats used. 209 f. From here on, in general, the narrative and texture are stronger. 238. made . . . moan: cf. Chaucer, *Knight's Tale* 1366, "makynge his mone"; Spenser *passim*. 262. Hinnom's vale: a place of human sacrifice, near Jerusalem (2 Kings xxiii.10; 2 Chron. xxviii.3; *P.L.* i.404). 272. In Southey's *Curse of Kehama*, "fire in heart and brain" is a recurrent phrase (Ridley, p. 41). 393–4. Perseus slew the Gorgon Medusa. 432. leafits: apparently from Coleridge's *Nightingale* 65 (Coleridge later substituted *leaflets*). 442. Melpomene: the Muse of Tragedy. 451. Baälites: worshipers of the Philistine sun-god Baal.

To Homer Page 157

Printed by Houghton; written in April, 1818?
2. Cyclades: a cluster of Aegean islands encircling Delos. 5. the veil was rent: Matt. xxvii.51, Mark xv.38, Luke xxiii.45. 5–8. Homer is seen as a poet of natural, not "bookish," inspiration; cf. *What the Thrush Said*, the *Ode to Maia*, and the letter enclosing the *Ode*. 12. triple. The word looks back to the heaven, sea, and earth of Jupiter, Neptune, and Pan, and

forward to Diana, the *dea triformis,* as the huntress of earth, the Moon (Luna, Selene), and the queen of hell (Proserpine, Hecate) (Sandys, p. 133; Lempriere; Baldwin, p. 159). Keats doubtless had Milton in mind as well as Homer.

Fragment of an Ode to Maia   *Page 157*

Printed by Houghton; written May 1, 1818, and copied in the notable letter to Reynolds of May 3. This fragment — which needs nothing more — is one of Keats's most serene and felicitous affirmations on the side of passive, non-intellectual receptivity to concrete impressions. Cf. *What the Thrush Said* (also sent to Reynolds).

3. Baiæ: see the note on *To C. C. Clarke* 29. In regard to the rhyme with Maia, "Baia" is used several times by Mrs. Radcliffe in her *Sicilian Romance* (Ridley, p. 104, n.) and by Thomson, *Liberty* i.58.   **5. earlier Sicilian:** the manner of Theocritus.

On Visiting the Tomb of Burns   *Page 157*

Printed by Houghton. Copying the sonnet in a letter to Tom, July 1, 1818, Keats said he wrote it "in a strange mood, half asleep. I know not how it is, the Clouds, the sky, the Houses, all seem anti Grecian & anti Charlemagnish." Somewhat different interpretations, based on somewhat different texts, are given by Murry ("The Feel of *Not* to Feel it," *Keats,* pp. 199 f., and earlier edns.), who follows the traditional text (but with a question mark after "upon it," line 12), and J. C. Maxwell (*K–SJ* IV, 1955), who printed, more accurately than Forman did in the *Letters,* the transcript by John Jeffrey, Georgiana Keats's second husband. Murry sees Keats suffering from his recurrent mood of unresponsive torpor; for Maxwell, Keats is associating the apprehension of beauty with pain. The former view would link the sonnet with Coleridge's *Dejection,* the latter with Keats's *Ode on Melancholy.* Neither Forman nor Maxwell has any punctuation after "done" (8), where editors have put a colon; and Maxwell reads "Through" for "Though" (7) and "Fickly" ("fickle") for "Sickly" (11). See Rollins, I, 308–9. The text and sense remain problematical.

9. Minos: one of the judges of the underworld (cf. Cary, *Inf.* v.4 f.; Keats had Cary in his knapsack); here, absolute judgment, uncolored by mood or circumstance.   **11–12.** Keats may be thinking not only of his own mood but of Hunt's capacity for "making fine things petty and beautiful things hateful," which "perplexes one in the standard of Beauty" (journal-letter of Dec., 1818–Jan., 1819, to George and Georgiana Keats, the section of Dec. 17, 1818).

Meg Merrilies   *Page 158*

Printed in *PDJ,* Nov. 22, 1838, by Brown in 1840 (Rollins, I, 438), and in *Hood's Magazine,* June, 1844; included in letters of July 2–5 and 3–9,

1818, to Fanny Keats and Tom. As Keats and Brown walked through the country of *Guy Mannering*, which Keats had not read, he was much taken with Brown's account of Scott's gipsy.

25. Margaret: queen of Henry VI (see Shakespeare).   **28. chip:** strips of woody fibre.

Staffa   *Page 159*

Printed in *PDJ*, Sept. 20, 1838, and by Houghton; included in a letter to Tom, July 23–26, with a prose account of the island of Staffa and Fingal's Cave.

1. Aladdin: from one of the best-known tales in the *Arabian Nights*. **3. wizard of the Dee.** Keats may be thinking of the changes in the river's flow which, in old tradition, foretold good or ill for England and Wales (cf. *Lyc.* 55).   **5–8. St. John:** see Rev. i.4, 9, etc.   **11 f.** The use of *Lycidas* may have been prompted by his becoming "the Genius of the shore" as well as by Milton's allusion to the Hebrides.   **29. mighty waters:** Wordsworth, *Intimations of Immortality* 171.   **31–4.** In ancient tradition dolphins were fond of music; cf. *Lyc.* 164.   **44. Proteus:** the Old Man of the Sea (*F.Q.* III.viii.29 f.; Sandys, pp. 149, 160).   **50–4.** These lines, included in the version in Keats's letter, are omitted by some editors, not without reason. In copying the poem in September for George and Georgiana (Rollins, II, 199–200), Keats himself omitted lines 7–8 and 45–57.

Written upon the Top of Ben Nevis   *Page 160*

Printed in *PDJ*, Sept. 6, 1838, and by Houghton; written Aug. 2, 1818. For Keats's mood, see the note on *On Visiting the Tomb of Burns,* and *The Human Seasons* 13–14.

Hyperion: A Fragment   *Page 161*

Printed in the 1820 volume. A bad cold had compelled Keats to give up the Scottish tour and return to London in mid-August, 1818. During the early autumn he began the epic *Hyperion* which had been in his mind at least since Sept. 28, 1817, when he wrote to Haydon about "a new Romance which I have in my eye for next summer"; and the last two books of *Endymion* contained some allusions to characters of the projected work (see the note on *End.* iv.774). Keats's preface to *Endymion* and later comments in his letters reveal his dissatisfaction with that poem, and *Hyperion* — which was referred to in the preface — was to be of a different kind. He wrote to Haydon on Jan. 23, 1818:

> . . . in Endymion I think you may have many bits of the deep and sentimental cast — the nature of *Hyperion* will lead me to treat it in a more naked and grecian Manner — and the march of passion and endeavour will be undeviating — and one great contrast between them

will be — that the Hero of the written tale being mortal is led on, like Buonaparte, by circumstance; whereas the Apollo in Hyperion being a fore-seeing God will shape his actions like one.

Keats abandoned *Hyperion* in April, 1819, and gave the manuscript of the fragment to his friend Woodhouse. That devoted admirer's account of the plan of the whole (De Selincourt, p. 486) embraces matters that are much more epical than Keatsian and that could hardly have been added to the portion we have; De Selincourt (pp. 488–9) argued plausibly that Keats had changed his mind and planned a much shorter poem, perhaps in four books. Moreover, the remarks to Haydon, quoted above, do not fit the Apollo of the fragmentary third book.

In ancient as well as modern literature there had been confusion over the identities and the wars of the Titans and the Giants, and Keats's mixture was in the tradition — though the Titans in his list all had some authority (Finney, II, 498). In any case Keats's handling of his subject, the dethronement of Saturn and his fellow Titans by the gods, was so largely original that he needed no great body of data. He owned such works of reference as Lempriere, the *Pantheon* (1806 and later editions) of "Edward Baldwin" (Godwin the philosopher), and *Auctores Mythographi Latini* (Leyden, 1742); and Sandys' *Ovid*, the 1640 edition with the commentary, was evidently available, as it had been before. Keats would probably read a translation, such as Thomas Cooke's, of so central a document as Hesiod's *Theogony*. Numerous allusions, such as *Paradise Lost* i.510 f. and suggestive bits in Chapman's *Iliad* (viii.420–4, xiv.229–30: quoted in De Selincourt, p. xlvi), were within his range of reading. A number of miscellaneous items are cited in the notes.

Critics have seen both external and internal reasons for Keats's inability to finish the poem. In August and September appeared the reviews of *Endymion* which, though they did not prevent his beginning *Hyperion*, might gnaw at the vitals of any young poet, however gifted and stout-hearted. The time of most active composition was also the time when Keats was nursing Tom through the last stages of tuberculosis (he died on Dec. 1). "His identity," he wrote to Dilke on Sept. 20–1,

> presses upon me so all day that I am obliged to go out — and although I intended to have given some time to study alone I am obliged to write, and plunge into abstract images to ease myself of his countenance his voice and feebleness — so that I live now in a continual fever — it must be poisonous to life although I feel well. . . .

In spite of this last statement, Keats's own health continued to suffer from the effects of the northern tour. Then on Sept. 22 (?) he wrote to Reynolds about being haunted for two days by "the voice and the shape of a Woman" (Jane Cox, a cousin of the Reynoldses) and of "the feverous relief of Poetry":

> This morning Poetry has conquered — I have relapsed into those abstractions which are my only life — I feel escaped from a new strange

and threatening sorrow. — And I am thankful for it — There is an awful warmth about my heart like a load of Immortality.

Poor Tom — that woman — and Poetry were ringing changes in my senses.

Finally, acquaintance with Fanny Brawne soon developed into a passion, and, in January, inspired poetry more appropriate than epic for a lover, *The Eve of St. Agnes.*

Keats's chosen subject and mode of treatment involved perhaps insuperable difficulties. Since the poem begins when the epic action is over, there was the problem of sustaining further action; the narrative, so far as it goes, is nearly static, a grand façade or frieze — in W. M. Rossetti's phrase, "a Stonehenge of reverberance." It is a question, too, if Keats is not somewhat uncertain in his conception of the Titans: do they exemplify serene beneficence of world-sovereignty, now overthrown (i.106–12, 316–18, 329–31, ii.208–11, 335–8), or, in defeat, the weakness of self-centered human passions and appeal to mere force (i.248–50, 328–38, ii.68–72, 92–8, 173–6, 309–45), or a deliberately imagined mixture of beneficence and immaturity? The germinal idea of beneficence may have been a mythological datum Keats could not have failed to know, the golden age of Saturn's reign in Italy (De Selincourt, p. 499), though his own use of it is a departure from the crude myth of the Titans. At any rate, the chief Titans are so majestic that it would have been hard — even granted the high place they are given in evolutionary progress (ii.188 f.) — to show the superiority of the gods; and that problem becomes most acute in regard to Keats's essential theme. This theme is centered in Apollo, who is to supersede the one undefeated Titan, Hyperion, but Apollo's deification at the end of the fragment is the birth of a true poet through his imaginative apprehension of the pain and mystery of life — an experience difficult to render in epic 'erms. Moreover, while this central theme — a reworking of the central theme of *Endymion* — must surely, in some form, have been in Keats's mind from the beginning, in the poem we have it seems to be almost superimposed upon, or at least not fused with, another theme, the idea of progress set forth in the speech of Oceanus (ii.173 f.). Even the wise Oceanus as well as Clymene presents what may be called a romantic conception of beauty; the beauty Apollo's illumination affirms is Keats's more mature and tragic reading of life.

Finally, the massive, elevated style was a continuing difficulty as well as an extraordinary achievement. Not to mention Shelley's high admiration, even Byron, who had foamed at the mouth against Keats, pronounced *Hyperion* "as sublime as Æschylus." And most modern readers have in some degree concurred — though there is a parallel between *Hyperion* and *The Eve of St. Agnes,* in that we are moved less by the experience of the characters than we are by the incidental and innumerable beauties of descriptive phrase and rhythm. Doubtless *Hyperion* could not have been without *Paradise Lost,* and Keats does use Miltonic diction and rhetorical devices (summarized in De Selincourt, pp. 490–3), yet the label "Miltonic" does much less than justice to Keats's original powers of imagination and artistry. For example, his slow tempo, in which the normal rhythmic unit is the heavily weighted single line, is not much like Milton's intricate, forward-moving paragraph. The trouble is that, even if Keats's magnificence is only partly Miltonic, it is only partly Keatsian too; it is, for him, an unnatural tour de force. And indeed his epic grandeur, which suffers multiplying lapses as the poem proceeds, breaks down almost completely in the third book; here Keats is resolved, before he gives up, to get his theme expressed, and he must do so in something like his own voice.

Study of Keats's revisions of details richly illuminates the nature of his sensibility and craftsmanship (Ridley, pp. 57–95; Bate, pp. 66–91). Along with the standard books may be mentioned Kenneth Muir's "The Meaning of *Hyperion*," *Essays in Criticism*, II (1952), 54–75.

Book i.1–14. A signal example of revision, as the critics show; for an apprentice effort at a picture of stillness, cf. *I Stood* 1–14. **2.** Cf. Thomson, *C.I.* II.vi: "Deep in the winding bosom of a lawn"; "shady vale," in *Paradise Regained* i.304 and Hesiod, *Works and Days,* tr. Cooke, ii.14, 211. In his notes on Milton, Keats expressed a special liking for the word "vale" (*Works,* ed. H. B. Forman, III, 258). **2. breath of morn:** in *P.L.* iv.641. **5. lair.** With this finely appropriate use, cf. *To One . . . Pent* 6 and *Keen, Fitful Gusts* 8. **11. voiceless.** The first "Miltonic" use of an adjective for the more ordinary adverb, but probably from *Exc.* iii.92, "Voiceless the stream descends." **16.** The "stray'd" of the 1820 text should probably be "stay'd," as in the Woodhouse transcript; cf. the *Fall* 321, "rested" (Ridley, p. 275), *End.* iii.107–8, and Cary, *Inf.* xiv.13, "Our steps we stay'd." **18. nerveless, listless, dead.** Cf. Chatterton, *Excelent Balade of Charitie* 23, "withered, sapless, dead"; and *End.* iv.764, *Eve of St. Agnes* 12 (De Selincourt, p. 495). **21. some comfort yet:** cf. *Comus* 348. **23. one:** Thea, wife of Hyperion. **28.** Cf. *P.L.* i.575, 771–81. **30.** Ixion, for an offence against Juno, was bound to a turning wheel in Hades. **31. Memphian sphinx.** Egyptian influence in *Hyperion* has been ascribed by H. Darbishire (*Review of English Studies,* III, 1927; De Selincourt, p. 514) chiefly to articles in *Annals of the Fine Arts;* her data and inferences have been modified by B. Garlitz (*Philological Quarterly,* XXXIV, 1955), who suggests other sources for Keats's not very extensive knowledge. In the review of Light's *Travels in Egypt* (*Quarterly Review,* XIX, 1818, pp. 178–204) — which immediately preceded Croker's review of *Endymion* — we have, e.g., "The common Egyptian sphinx . . . Headless statues . . . of gigantic size . . . In the western court, in front of the great portico, . . . is an upright headless statue of one block of granite" (p. 187); and there follows a discussion of statues of Memnon. Writing to George and Georgiana, probably on March 3, 1819, Keats said he had just seen, for the first time, a giant sphinx at the Museum. **33.** For this not uncommon item one may cite Potter, I, 217, and the "Discourse" appended to Cooke's *Hesiod.* **35–6.** The first Miltonic "turn," or repetition with variations. For the idea, cf. Southey, *Thalaba* xi.383–4: "Her face was sorrowful, but sure More beautiful for sorrow"; Sandys, p. 129: "She still was sad: yet lovelier none then she, Even in that sadnesse"; Landor, *Gebir* i.68–71 (quoted in De Selincourt, p. 496).   **52. poor old King.** Here and elsewhere Saturn recalls King Lear (De Selincourt, p. 496; Gittings, *Mask*, pp. 23 f.).   **61. reluctant:** cf. *P.L.* vi.58, x.515, and Keats's comment (*Works*, ed. Forman, III, 264).   **72–8.** An epic simile Miltonic in elaboration but wholly Keatsian in feeling and language (for earlier versions, see De Selincourt, pp. 497–8.)   **83. alteration slow:** the first instance of the Miltonic inverted adjective.   **86.** A reminder of the many sculpturesque effects in the poem; cf. *Staffa* 38. In the letter (July 23–26, 1818) containing *Staffa* and describing Fingal's Cave, Keats said that the black columns might have been set up by "the Giants who rebelled against Jove" and that "For solemnity and grandeur it far surpasses the finest Cathedrall"; he spoke also of the loud noise of the water.   **90. faded eyes:** in *Gebir* v.57. Cf. *P.L.* i.602, "faded cheek"; iv.870, "faded splendor wan." With an earlier version, "faint-blue eyes," cf. *Gebir* i.109: "This faint blue lustre under both thine eyes."   **94. horrid:** rough, bristling, in the Latin sense; cf. *F.Q.* I.vii.31; *P.L.* ii.710, etc.   **98–102.** Cf. *King Lear* I.iv.246–50.   **102. Peers . . . Saturn:** cf. *Hamlet* III.iv.56, *Winter's Tale* IV.iv.3.   **105. nervous:** strong.   **116. spot of earth:** cf. *Comus* 5–6.   **129. gold clouds metropolitan:** the Miltonic use of a noun between adjectives. For the second one, of dubious value here, cf. Wordsworth, *Exc.*, Prospectus 86, and *P.L.* iii.549–51.   **137. Druid locks:** Keats owned Edward Davies' *Celtic Researches* (1804), which tried to link the Titans and Celts (De Selincourt, p. 580; Ridley, pp. 64–5, 76).   **147. The rebel three:** Jupiter, Neptune, Pluto.   **166. Hyperion:** strictly the father of the sun-god, but commonly the sun-god himself. The accent is properly on *i*; Keats followed Elizabethan pronunciation.   **167. snuff'd:** cf. *End.* iv.365 and note.   **169–85.** The omens are mainly adapted from Shakespeare (Finney, II, 519 f.; De Selincourt, pp. 580–1).   **172–3.** Keats may be recalling the custom of sending the bellman or town crier to a criminal before his execution, or the ringing of a church bell when someone was dying (De Selincourt, p. 500); cf. *Macbeth* II.ii.3–4.   **176 f.** For Hyperion's palace, Gittings (*Mask*, p. 104) quotes from Beckford's *Vathek* the description of the halls of Eblis; cf. *Exc.* ii.839 f.   **181. Aurorian:** from Aurora, the Dawn; cf. *Romeo and Juliet* I.i.143.   **184. neighing steeds:** in *Gebir* vii.97; cf. *Julius Caesar* II.ii.23.   **195. stride colossal:** cf. *Gebir* iii.18, "the parting Sun's gigantic strides"; *Julius Caesar* I.ii.135–6.   **204. slope:** cf. *Comus* 98, *P.L.* iv.261, 591; *Oberon* iv.30, "the sun's slope wheels."   **211. inlet:** cf. *Comus* 839.   **216. Hours:** see the note on *End.* ii.688.   **219–21.** Cf. *Vathek* (under 176 f. above); *Udolpho*, I, 212 and 331, "long arcades"; 214, "an open cupola," "fragrance," "brilliant light," "lustre."   **230.** Cf. *Gebir* iii.202–10: "the marshes, yellow-flower'd . . . with black weeds besmear'd . . . dull-ear'd miscreant."   **232. essence:** cf. *P.L.* i.425, ii.215.   **235–9.** Cf. *P.L.* i.242–5.   **238.** Cf. *Exc.* ii.842, "serene pavilions bright."   **239.**

lucent: cf. *P.L.* iii.589; Cary *passim.*   **246. Tellus:** the Earth (cf. *End.* iii.71).   **258–70.** Cf. *P.L.* ix.53–75, 158–60, 179–82.   **265. season due:** in *Lyc.* 7.   **274. colure:** cf. *P.L.* ix.66.   **284. argent.** See the note on *End.* i.595 and cf. *End.* iii.186, *Eve of St. Agnes* 37, *Lamia* i.163. **307. Cœlus:** Uranus, the Sky, father of the Titans.   **323. my first-born:** Saturn.

Book ii. The Titans are named in various books Keats knew, e.g., Baldwin, pp. 45–6: "The names of the Titans were Oceanus, Cœus, Creus, Hyperion, Iapetus, Cottus, Gyges and Briareus: they had an equal number of sisters with whom they married, Oceanus to Tethys, Cœus to Phœbe, Hyperion to Theia, and Iapetus to Clymene"; cf. Hesiod, *Theogony,* tr. Cooke, 214 f. In the Woodhouse MS., opposite ii.19–20, are written, apparently in Keats's hand, references to pages in Sandys (25, 90, 108) for some of the Titans (De Selincourt, p. 505). For other sources see De Selincourt's notes, pp. 495 f., 579 f., and Finney, II, 494 f. The fallen Titans' council, though inspired by that of the fallen angels in *P.L.* ii, is obviously quite different. De Selincourt (p. xlvi) cites a suggestive phrase from Chapman, *Iliad* xiv.229–30: "all the gods of the infernall state Which circle Saturne."

4. Cybele (cf. *End.* ii.639–48) is properly the wife of Saturn and mother of the gods (as she is in the *Fall* i.425); see the note on *Hyp.* ii.389. **7–8.** See the note on i.86.   **13.** Cf. *Comus* 205.   **15–16.** Cf. "flinty couch" in *Gebir* vi.207 and Scott, *Lady of the Lake* III.xxix.722.   **17.** Cf. *King John* IV.i.67.   **28. gurge:** whirlpool (*P.L.* xii.41).   **29. Mnemosyne:** Memory, mother of the Muses (Sandys, p. 95); a daughter of Coelus. **30. Phœbe:** Keats seems to confuse the goddess of the moon with her grandmother, the wife of Coeus.   **34–5.** Keats had seen such stones near Keswick in the Lake country; cf. his letter to Tom, June 29, 1818, and the note on *End.* iv.769.   **36. at shut of eve:** cf. *P.L.* ix.278.   **44–6.** Cf. Southey, *Thalaba* v.347–9: "He . . . oft would seize Their swelling necks, and in his giant grasp Bruise them"; 367–8: "roll'd out Their undulating length"; *Gebir* v.230–1: "nor fear'd to squeeze The viscous poison from his glowing gums."   **45. plashy:** marked as if splashed with color.   **53. Asia:** properly the daughter of Oceanus and Tethys and wife of Iapetus; Keats's Caf apparently came from *Vathek* (De Selincourt, p. 581; Gittings, *Mask,* pp. 98–107).   **54.** Cf. *P.L.* iv.271.   **57–60.** Cf. Lempriere ("Asia"): "This part of the globe has given birth to many of the greatest monarchies of the universe, and to the ancient inhabitants of Asia we are indebted for most of the arts and sciences."   **61. Hope . . . anchor:** a traditional "emblem" (*F.Q.* I.x.14; *Exc.* v.333–6; Baldwin, p. 192).   **66–72.** Keats follows the tradition that identifies Enceladus with Typhon (see the note on *End.* ii.585; *End.* iii.243–4; Sandys, pp. 96–7; Lempriere; Baldwin, p. 88; De Selincourt, p. 508).   **71–2.** Cf. Baldwin, pp. 88–9.   **76. Clymene:** not the mother of Phaethon in Ovid, *Met.* ii, though perhaps partly based on her, but the daughter of Oceanus and wife of Iapetus, commonly identified with Asia.   **77. Themis:** daughter of Coelus, a personification of law (Sandys, pp. 19–20; Baldwin, p. 173).   **78. Ops: the** same as Cybele (ii.4).   **79. No shape distinguishable:** cf. *P.L.* ii.667–8. **80. night confounds:** in Chapman, *Iliad* viii.421 (De Selincourt, pp. xlvi, 509).   **93–5.** Cf. *P.L.* iv.114–15.   **97. mortal oil:** human weakness. **134. Uranus:** see the note on i.307.   **135. shores of darkness:** cf. *To Homer* 9.   **165. astonied:** astonished (cf. Job xvii.8, xviii.20; *F.Q.* VII.vi.28.6; *P.L.* ix.890).   **168. Sophist:** here apparently used in a favorable sense, "wise."   **170. locks not oozy:** cf. *End.* iii.993 and *Lyc.* 175. **171. first-endeavouring tongue:** in Milton, *Vacation Exercise* 2.   **181 f.** This speech is the *locus classicus* (along with passages in the letters, e.g., May 3, 1818) for Keats as a child of the revolutionary age; but his faith in progress was realistic and moderate, and he was wholly skeptical regarding Godwin's ideas of perfectibility.   **183. atom-universe:** cf. *End.* iii.700. **203–5.** This ethical ideal is a constant theme of the *Excursion* (e.g., iii.381– 6, iv.69–73) and, increasingly, of Keats's letters. Here it is only a parenthetical prelude to the delivery of bad news, but it goes along with other passages, including Oceanus' opening lines, as a condemnation of the Titans' lapse into human rage and passion.   **232. God of the Seas:** Neptune. **244. poz'd:** puzzled, shaken.   **266. soft delicious warmth:** cf. *P.L.* ii.400, 601.   **270–1.** Cf. *Exc.* iv.1135, "a smooth-lipped shell" (and the whole passage); *Gebir* i.177.   **281. a living death:** cf. *End.* i.655 and note; *Nightingale* 51 f.   **293–5.** Apollo's voice crying his own name. **317. blows . . . buffets:** cf. *Macbeth* III.i.109.   **318. a youngling arm:** cf. *Titus Andronicus* IV.ii.93.   **358–61.** Cf. *Hamlet* I.iv.70–1, "the cliff That beetles o'er his base"; Thomson, *C.I.* I.xlvi: "black gulfs where sullen waters sleep . . . On beetling cliffs"; *Udolpho*, I, 37: "a rock of granite shot up . . . the dashing of torrents . . . the long sullen murmur of the breeze . . . the beetling cliff"; 43: "the thunder of the torrent"; Wordsworth, *Intimations* 25: "The cataracts blow their trumpets from the steep."   **367–8.** An example of what Keats, in his notes on *P.L.*, called "stationing," the placing of figures in relation to solid objects (*Works*, ed. Forman, III, 264–5). **374–6.** Memnon, son of Tithonus and Aurora, was slain by Achilles. His supposed statue, in Egyptian Thebes, was said, when touched by the sun's rays, to "render a mournefull sound" (Sandys, p. 248; cf. Baldwin, p. 344, Lempriere).   **389. Mother of the Gods:** Cybele (see the note on ii.4). Throughout, apparently (cf. i.26, 51, etc., ii.379, 390), Keats uses "Gods" or "God" simply with regard to the divine nature and without regard to the difference, and the war, between gods and Titans.

Book iii. This fragmentary book may have been written in the late winter of 1818–19 (Murry, *Keats*, p. 36; Gittings, *J.K.*, p. 101).   **5–6.** Keats is aware that he is turning from epic objectivity to the subjective. Cf. Wordsworth, *Exc.*, Prospectus 76–7: "Must hear Humanity in fields and groves Pipe solitary anguish."   **12. Dorian flute:** cf. *P.L.* i.550–1.   **13. Father of all verse:** Apollo.   **29–30. Giant of the Sun:** Hyperion, in ii.356 f.   **31– 2. mother:** Leto (Latona); cf. *End.* i.862. **twin-sister:** Diana.   **41.** Cf. *Udolpho* I, 216, "green recesses."   **46. Goddess:** Mnemosyne (ii.29).

68–79, 82–110, and cf. ii.275 f. The young Apollo has so far been only a singer of beauty. He has — in the image of Keats's letter of May 3, 1818 — been in the Chamber of Maiden Thought, which is now becoming darkened; he is vaguely unhappy, vaguely aware that life is not all lovely. **82 f.** Keats told Woodhouse that Apollo's speech "seemed to come by chance or magic — to be as it were something given to him" (Rollins, *K.C.,* I, 129). **86. dark, dark:** cf. *Samson Agonistes* 80. **111–12.** Cf. *Exc.* i.204–5, ii.40–1 (Murry, *Keats,* pp. 273–4). **113–20.** "Knowledge," as the context indicates, means, not intellectual attainment, but the sympathetic understanding of the human condition which Keats, in *S. and P.,* had looked forward to as his highest aim (cf. such letters as that of May 3, 1818, to Reynolds, and that of Feb. 14–May 3, 1819, to George and Georgiana). In becoming a god Apollo becomes a mature poet. Keats here directly states his main theme, and there would appear to be little left for epic dramatization, since we can hardly envisage an open conflict between Apollo and Hyperion. **115. sovran:** Milton's spelling. **120.** Cf. *I Stood* 190 and *Endymion passim.* **126.** Cf. *Gebir* vii.241: "He seems to struggle from the grasp of death" (De Selincourt, p. 514). **130. Die into life:** a Keatsian and poetic parallel to the Christian paradox.

Fancy   *Page 181*

Fancy and the following *Ode* were printed in the 1820 volume; they were included in the journal-letter to George and Georgiana of December–January, 1818–19, in the section dated Jan. 2. Gittings (*J.K.,* p. 46) thinks both poems were written Dec. 17, 1818. *L'Allegro* was evidently in Keats's mind, though his *Fancy* is more sensuous and poetic than Milton's embodiment of social and decorous mirth. Possible echoes of Herrick are suggested by J. H. Wagenblass, "Keats's Roaming Fancy" (*Harvard Studies and Notes in Philology and Literature,* XX, 1938), of Chatterton by N. T. Ting (*K–SJ* V, 1956).

1–2. Cf. Herrick, *To his Muse* 1–2: "Whither Mad maiden wilt thou roame? Farre safer 'twere to stay at home." **10.** Cf. Herrick, *A Country Life* 140: "For seldome use commends the pleasure." **21. shoon:** shoes (*Hamlet* IV.v.26). **22–4.** Cf. Herrick, *Upon a black Twist* 5–8, *His Protestation to Perilla* 1, 4. **29.** Cf. *Exc.* iv.769, "Mad Fancy's favourite vassals." **53–4.** Cf. Herrick, *Upon Roses* 5–6: ". . . look'd more fresh then flowers Quickned of late by Pearly showers." **58. sunny bank:** cf. N. Breton, *Who Can Live* 25, "On a bank for sunny place." **81. Ceres' daughter:** Proserpine. **85. Hebe:** see *End.* iv.415 and note, and Lempriere.

Ode [Bards of Passion]   *Page 183*

"Written on the blank page before Beaumont and Fletcher's Tragi-comedy 'The Fair Maid of the Inn.'" See the note on *Fancy* above. The theme, as Keats said in his letter, is "the double immortality of Poets."

8. parle: speech.

The Eve of St. Agnes *Page 184*

Printed in the 1820 volume; written in January and February, 1819, after Keats had fallen in love with Fanny Brawne and largely given up *Hyperion.* According to Woodhouse, the subject was suggested by a friend, a Mrs. Isabella Jones. (Gittings' unpleasant theory about her, Keats, and the *Eve* is pulverized by Murry, *Keats,* pp. 130–44.) The germ of the story is the superstition — in the poem turned from dream into actuality — that a girl who performed certain rites on St. Agnes' Eve (January 20) would have a vision of her future husband. For central or peripheral elements and atmosphere many sources have been suggested, of varying degrees of likelihood: Boccaccio's *Filocolo* (see De Selincourt, p. 575: even in a French version this seems most unlikely), Chaucer's *Troilus* (Priestley, *MLQ* V, 1944), Wieland's *Oberon* (Beyer), Mrs. Radcliffe's *Mysteries of Udolpho* (see De Selincourt, p. 576), *Christabel,* etc. In writing of young lovers from hostile families Keats could not help recalling *Romeo and Juliet.* Scott's *Lay of the Last Minstrel* included a similar situation, the love of Margaret and Lord Cranstoun, and apparently contributed a number of miscellaneous details (the fullest discussion is in E. C. Pettet, *On the Poetry of Keats,* 1957, pp. 18–29.). Parallels with other poets are noted by R. K. Gordon (*Modern Language Review,* XLI, 1946). Gittings (*J.K.,* pp. 70 f.) finds items from the architecture of Chichester and the Chapel at nearby Stansted, which Keats saw while at work on the poem. Keats's uncommonly full revisions show him eliminating weakness and in various ways achieving stronger intensity (Ridley, pp. 96–190; Bate, pp. 91–117).

The Eve of St. Agnes is obviously a great advance upon *Isabella;* and the Spenserian stanza is a congenial vehicle that invites Spenserian richness of texture. Keats makes potent use of contrast: winter and withered age and death, and family feud, are set against the warmth of young love, the cold outer world against the interior scenes, and harsh actuality casts shadows over romance and mystery. Madeline and Porphyro are, to be sure, only romantic silhouettes, and we may respond less to their passion than to the intensely vivid sensations of cold, color, and the like that belong to the setting. The poem is usually taken as opulent romantic tapestry, but R. H. Fogle (*College English,* VI, 1944–5), Wasserman, and R. A. Foakes (in *The Romantic Assertion,* 1958) urge a more serious and symbolic reading.

5 f. The Beadsman may owe something to Scott's Minstrel and Monk of St. Mary's aisle in the *Lay.* 26–7. Cf. *F.Q.* I.iii.14.1–3. 34. carved angels: cf. *Christabel* 178–80. 47. The phrase "vision(s) of delight" recurs in *Oberon* v.6 and 76, xi.42. 49. Cf. *Measure for Measure* IV.i.35, "Upon the heavy middle of the night"; *Julius Caesar* II.i.230, "the honey-heavy dew of slumber." 58. train: skirts sweeping the floor. 61. high disdain: in *P.L.* i.98, *Christabel* 416, and *Lay* I.ix.86. 70. all amort: as if dead (in *Taming of the Shrew* IV.iii.36). 71. her lambs unshorn. On St. Agnes' Day wool was offered at Mass while the *Agnus* was chanted, and then spun and woven by nuns. 81. touch, kiss: cf. *Cymbeline* II.ii.16–17.

91 f. Angela may be partly drawn from Juliet's old nurse, Angelica; there is an Angela in *Oberon*.   109–10. Cf. *Lay* II.iii.35–7.   117. Cf. the note on 71.   126. **mickle:** much (*Comus* 31; Chatterton).   127. Cf. Scott, *Lady of the Lake* IV.xxvii.640, "feebly laughed."   129. **aged crone:** in *Oberon* iv.35.   130. Keats might be recalling Prospero's magic books and the "Mighty Book" of Michael Scott (*Lay* II.xv, etc.).   133. **brook:** properly "endure," not, as here, "check." Scott had used the word similarly in *Marmion* I.x.149.   168. Cf. Milton, *Vacation Exercise* 59–64; *Romeo and Juliet* I.iv.71.   171. The usual explanation (H.B. Forman, *Works*, II, 74; cf. De Selincourt, p. 468; Ridley, pp. 135–8; R. P. Basler, *Explicator*, III, 1944, no. 1) is that the magician, the son of a demon, paid the monstrous debt of his own existence when Vivien, whom he loved, brought about his imprisonment and death in a cave by means of one of his own spells; see *The History of the Renowned Prince Arthur* (1816), I, 104–6 — which may be the Arthurian *History* Keats owned — and *F.Q.* III.iii.10–13, Ariosto, *Orlando* iii.10. There is also the story, summarized in Daniel's *Musophilus* 349 f., of how the stones of Stonehenge "were by the devil's force" transported from Africa to Ireland "in a night," and thence to Brittany, "From giants' hands redeemed by Merlin's sleight."   174. **tambour:** a frame for embroidery.   194. Cf. *Oberon* v.63: "Like a commission'd angel of the skies."   198. **fray'd:** frightened. Cf. *End.* ii.245; *F.Q.* V.xii.5.9; *Lay* II.xxxiv.411.   204. Cf. *Oberon* vi.17: "When mute the tongue, how voluble the heart!"   208 f. Cf. *Udolpho* I, 249, "high-arched casements"; *Lay* II.xi.113 f. and II.viii.80–3.   218. **gules:** red (from heraldry). The moonlight would not be colored by the window, but Scott had taken the same liberty with fact in the *Lay* II.xi.127–8.   223–4. Cf. *Romeo and Juliet* II.ii.26–8.   226 f. This picture may be indebted to *Brit. Past.* i.5.807 f. (quoted in De Selincourt, p. 470).   241. "Clasp'd like a missal in a land of *Pagans:* that is to say, where Christian prayer-books must not be seen, and are, therefore, doubly cherished for the danger" (Leigh Hunt, *Imagination and Fancy*, ed. 1870, p. 306). In the *Lay* (II.xxi, III.ix) the magic book has iron clasps which are hard to open, and Keats's different use of "clasp" may have started from, or included, the idea of closeness and secrecy (Pettet, p. 28). In addition to the Paynims of the *F.Q.*, the passages of the *Lay* that Keats has in mind contain the line "For Paynim countries I have trod" (II.xii.133).   246–7. Cf. *Cymbeline* II.ii.18–19.   251 (and 285, 360). Carpets are an anachronism in a medieval tale — not that it matters.   257. **Morphean:** see the note on *End.* i.559.   261. Keats told C. C. Clarke that he was recalling his schooldays, when, in bed, he heard Clarke's piano.   264 f. As the poem stands, Porphyro's unused banquet seems meaningless, but a stanza omitted between vi and vii had made such a banquet, offered "as sacrifice," part of the maiden's dream. Cf. *P.L.* v.341–7.   262. **azure-lidded;** 267. **tinct:** tinctured. Cf. *Cymbeline* II.ii.20–3: "her lids . . . white and azure lac'd With blue of heaven's own tinct"; Cary, *Purg.* xxvi.5, "azure tinct."   266. **soother:** softer, more soothing.   269. **spiced dainties.** Cf. *F.Q.* I.v.4, "daintie spices fetcht from furthest Ynd."   269–70. **Fez, Samarcand:** cf. *P.L.* xi.389, 403.   277.

eremite: hermit.   **292.** A poem by the medieval poet Alain Chartier, formerly supposed to have been translated by Chaucer.   **296. affrayed:** see the note on 198.   **309. tuneable . . . sweetest:** cf. *P.L.* v.151–2. **313–16. immortal . . . mortal.** Though these words link themselves with earlier phrases in *Endymion,* etc., about transcending mortal knowledge, they seem here to be incidental overtones.   **346, 349** (and cf. the kettle-drum of 259): cf. *Hamlet* I.iv.8–12 and III.iv.182.   **357. chain-droop'd lamp:** cf. *Christabel* 182; *Marmion* II.xviii.350.   **363–4.** Cf. the porter in *Macbeth* and Thomson, *C.I.* I.xxiv: "A comely full-spread porter, swoln with sleep."   **365.** Cf. *Christabel* 145 f.; *Lay* II.xxvi–ii.   **370–1.** The lines put this particular story into a long perspective, the successive generations of young lovers.   **376. meagre face deform:** cf. *F.Q.* IV.viii.12.6.

The Eve of Saint Mark   *Page 195*

Printed by Houghton; written Feb. 13–17, 1819, soon after Keats's visit to the cathedral town of Chichester. Both meter and manner recall *Christabel,* Chatterton's *The Unknown Knight,* and Scott's *Lay* — for example,

> So passed the day — the evening fell,
> 'T was near the time of curfew bell (*Lay* III.xxiv.305–6) —

but in its atmosphere and its quiet, delicate purity and precision of detail the poem — or the first part of it — has seemed to critics to be, in anticipation, the quintessence of Pre-Raphaelitism. Unlike *The Eve of St. Agnes,* this poem has a modern setting and modern heroine; medievalism is confined to the book, the legendary life of St. Mark, which has kept Bertha fascinated. Keats's only comment— apart from one on his "fine mother Radcliff" titles — is in his letter of Sept. 20 to George and Georgiana (Rollins, II, 201): "Some time since I began a Poem call'd 'the Eve of St Mark quite in the spirit of Town quietude. I th[i]nk it will give you the sensation of walking about an old county Town in a coolish evening. I know not yet whether I shall ever finish it." After copying it and speaking of his attempt at Middle English, he added: "I hope you will like this for all its Carelessness." In this poem, as in *The Eve of St. Agnes,* contrast is most effective: commonplace present and romantic past, the cool Sunday evening and church-going people in an English town and the biblical and exotic images that swarm from the book and the screen into Bertha's imagination, heightened by the play of light and shadow in her room. Gittings (*J.K.,* pp. 75 f., 87 f.) has connected some of those images with the windows of Stansted Chapel; Keats had attended the consecration on Jan. 25.*

---

* Some debatable matters may be crowded into a note. The traditional view of the poem, which still holds sway, has been Rossetti's (De Selincourt, p. 525), that Keats's story would have turned on a superstition connected with St. Mark's Eve (St. Mark's Day is April 25): that, if one stood near a church porch in twilight, one would see going into church the apparitions of those people of

17. Cf. *Il P.* 32.   24. The name Bertha probably came from Chatterton's *Ælla.*   33. Different readings suggest some confusion in Keats's mind between Aaron and Moses (see the note in Garrod, p. 450), perhaps due to mixed recollections of Exod. xxv.7 and xxviii.4 f.   33–4. See Rev. i.12–13; cf. *Staffa* 5–8.   35. St. Mark was the patron saint of Venice and the lion a traditional emblem.   36. **Covenantal Ark:** see Exod. xxv, etc.   38. **Cherubim:** Exod. xxv.19 f.   38. **golden mice:** 1 Sam. vi.4, 11, 18.   66. **drowsy chimes:** cf. *Il P.* 83.   67–8. **gloom . . . room:** cf. *ibid.,* 79–80.   69. **poor cheated soul.** Because the light had failed (M. A. E. Steele)? Because she was dreaming of martyrdom (Houghton)?   79. **Lima mice:** see Gittings' suggestion, *J.K.,* pp. 90–1.   80. Cf. Coleridge, *Eolian Harp* 24: "Footless and wild, like birds of Paradise."   81. **Avadavat:** Japanese love bird.   99 f. Keats's Middle English, doubtless prompted by Chatterton's, has been dismissed as if inevitably bad, but F. E. L. Priestley (*MLQ* V, 1944) praises its comparative accuracy, evidently based on study of Chaucer.   99. **Als:** also.   **swevenis:** dreams.   102. **crimped:** pinched, crinkled?   103. **mote:** may.   105. **Gif:** if.   112. **Somdel:** somewhat.   117. Houghton quotes the account of the martyrdom of St. Mark from *The Golden Legend, or Lives of the Saints as Englished by William Caxton* (1900), III, 136–7.   117–18. Cf. Milton, *Nativity* 202.

Bright Star   *Page 198*

Printed in *PDJ,* Sept. 27, 1838, and by Houghton. This sonnet, in its revised and much improved version, Keats copied in his volume of Shakespeare *c.* Oct. 1, 1820, when he and Severn were on their way to Italy. Brown's draft of the first version was dated 1819, but conjectural dates within that year include February, April, July, and autumn. One need not linger over Gittings' notion (*J.K.,* pp. 25–36, 156–8; *Mask,* pp. 54–68) that the sonnet was written in October, 1818, and inspired by the inevitable Mrs. Jones (see Murry, *Keats,* pp. 104–30). Aileen Ward (*Studies in Philology,* LII, 1955), after a review of the several theories, supports and elaborates

---

the parish who during the coming year would be seriously ill, or, if they did not come out again, would die. But this conjecture has no legitimate bearing on our reading of the unfinished poem we have, although it has become solidified in criticism and although it seemed, fifty years ago, to be confirmed by the discovery of some hitherto unknown lines. In 1906 there was found a MS. leaf containing 16 lines of pseudo-Middle-English which described the superstition; and later Woodhouse's transcript of these lines turned up. But there is no ground for inserting the lines between 98 and 99. All that we know is that the superstition was an after-thought, and that, while Keats wrote the lines for possible use, he did not incorporate them in the poem. Finney (II, 565) thinks the lines were written as late as September, as Murry had, less precisely, suggested (*Poems and Verses of John Keats,* 1930, II, 584). W. E. Houghton (*ELH* XIII, 1946) elaborated the case against the superstition as Keats's presumed theme and urged instead Bertha's preoccupation with the life and martyrdom of St. Mark; he also developed the aesthetic contrasts of the poem. Gittings (*J.K.,* pp. 91–2) thinks that Keats was unable to finish the poem because it, unlike his others, was "made" out of impressions of recent actual scenes, which he had exhausted.

De Selincourt's suggestion (p. 588) of July, a time when Keats was in the Isle of Wight working in the hope of making enough money to marry, and trying vainly to keep Fanny Brawne out of his mind. The arguments for July may, or may not, seem less unsubstantial than those for February (or some other winter month). The phrases in Keats's letter to Fanny of July 25, which are cited by De Selincourt and Miss Ward, might just as well be echoes of the sonnet as immediate parallels (the letter is included in this book). The fall of snow on Feb. 24–25 (Colvin, p. 335) is a point. And even if lines 7–8 can be said to approach anticlimactic padding, is an image of snow (and specifically "new" snow) likely to occur to a poet, above all a poet in England, writing in July? Finally, Keats's wishful mood is surely not that of tormented separation but rather of quiet and serene contentment. The present commentator can only say that he has less misgiving about winter than about midsummer.

1 f. Cf. the extract, in the introduction to this volume, from Keats's letter to Tom of June 25–27, 1818, in which he said that scenes in the Lake country "refine one's sensual vision into a sort of north star. . . ."   4. Eremite: cf. *Eve of St. Agnes* 277; Byron, *Childe Harold* ii.27; Cary, *Parad.* xxi.100, "the lonely Eremite."

Why Did I Laugh To-night?   *Page 198*

Printed by Houghton; copied in Keats's journal-letter of February–May, 1819, to George and Georgiana, in the section dated March 19 (see the letters below). Cf. *Written upon the Top of Ben Nevis.*
11. Cf. the *Nightingale* 55–6.   13–14. Cf. *When I Have Fears* 12–14.

On a Dream   *Page 199*

Printed in Hunt's *Indicator*, June 28, 1820; written in early April, 1819. The genesis of the sonnet was described in Keats's letter cited in the preceding note, in the section of April 16:

> The fifth canto of Dante pleases me more and more — it is that one in which he meets with Paulo and Franchesca — I had passed many days in rather a low state of mind and in the midst of them I dreamt of being in that region of Hell. The dream was one of the most delightful enjoyments I ever had in my life — I floated about the whirling atmosphere as it is described with a beautiful figure to whose lips mine were joined at [*for* as] it seem'd for an age — and in the midst of all this cold and darkness I was warm — even flowery tree tops sprung up and we rested on them sometimes with the lightness of a cloud till the wind blew us away again — I tried a Sonnet upon it — there are fourteen lines but nothing of what I felt in it — o that I could dream it every night.

1–2. Hermes . . . Argus. See the note on *End.* ii.876–7.   4. Cf. *End.* ii.685.   7. Ida: the mountain celebrated in Trojan story.   8. Tempe:

the valley in Thessaly often referred to as an idyllic scene. Keats may have thought of Jove's falling in love with Io and thereby incurring Juno's displeasure, a tale that follows the mention of Tempe in Ovid, *Met.* i.568 f. **9–14.** Cary, *Inf.* v.73 f. This was the story unhappily expanded by Hunt into the romance, *The Story of Rimini.* Gittings (*Mask,* p. 29) notes that it is the third circle of hell (*Inf.* vi) that is cold and wet. **14.** An Alexandrine.

La Belle Dame sans Merci   *Pages 199, 201*

The first version was written for George and Georgiana in Keats's journal-letter of February–May, 1819, in the section of April 21; it was printed by Houghton. The revised version was printed in Hunt's *Indicator,* May 10, 1820. Keats's second thoughts were not, as they usually were, his best. The ballad has no connection beyond the title with Chartier's poem (*Eve of St. Agnes* 292 and note). The story of a mortal's being loved by a beautiful and baleful goddess or fay is as old as Homer's Calypso and Circe and takes its canonical form in popular ballads. Some critics have seen in Keats's poem only a ballad of romantic diablerie; some, his ambivalent feelings about Fanny Brawne; and some a symbol of beauty or poetry.

As the following notes suggest, Keats's most immediate source for details was probably *The Faerie Queene.* Critics have cited the picture of Cymochles and Phaedria (*F.Q.* II.vi.14) and the false Florimel of Books III–IV, but two other episodes provide more and closer parallels — the witch Duessa's seduction of the Red Cross Knight (I.ii.28 f.) and Arthur's wholly inspiring vision of the Faerie Queene (I.ix.13 f.). The very effective short last line of each stanza is commonly ascribed to Browne's "Let no bird sing" (*Brit. Past.* ii.1.244).

1 f. Cf. Peacock, *Rhododaphne* i (*Works,* VII, 13): "What ails thee, stranger? Leaves are sear, And flowers are dead, and fields are drear . . . And streams are bright, and sweet birds sing." The question "What ails thee, youth?" is repeated twice.   **10.** Cf. *End.* iii.568–9; *Oberon* i.16: "Fear stands upon his brow in dew-drops chill"; Cary, *Inf.* iii.122–3: "with clammy dews Fear chills my brow."   **11.** Cf. M. Tighe, i.29, "The fading roses of her cheek"; Bion, *Adonis* 18 (tr. Fawkes): "And on his lips the roses fade away."   **16.** Cf. Wordsworth, *Her Eyes Are Wild.*   **17.** Cf. *F.Q.* I.ii.30: "And thinking of those braunches greene to frame A girlond for her dainty forehead fit"; Chaucer, *Knight's Tale* 1054: "To make a subtil gerland for hire hede."   **19–20.** Cf. *F.Q.* I.ii.14: "With faire disport and courting dalliaunce She intertainde her lover all the way"; *ibid.,* I.ix.14: "Most goodly glee and lovely blandishment She to me made, and bad me love her deare, For dearely sure her love was to me bent"; and the note on *Isabella* 238. **21.** Cf. *F.Q.* I.ii.45: "with trembling cheare Her up he tooke, too simple and too trew, And oft her kist. At length all passed feare, He set her on her steede, and forward forth did beare."   **26.** honey . . . dew: cf. *End.* i.766; *Kubla Khan* 53.   **29. f.** Cf. *F.Q.* II.vi.14, and I.ix.13: "Me seemed, by my side a royall Mayd Her daintie limbes full softly down did lay." **33.** Cf. *F.Q.* II.vi.18: "By this she had him lulled fast a sleepe."   **37 f.**

Cf. *On a Dream* 11–13; *F.Q.* III.xi.29 and 46.   43–4. Cf. *F.Q.* I.ix.15: "When I awoke, and found her place devoyd, And nought but pressed gras, where she had lyen, I sorrowed all so much, as earst I joyd, And washed all her place with watry eyen."

To Sleep   *Page 202*

Printed in *PDJ*, Oct. 11, 1838, and by Houghton; written in April, 1819. See the introductory note to *On the Sonnet*, below.
1–4. Cf. *2 Henry IV*, III.i.5 f.   5. soothest: softest, most soothing (cf. *Eve of St. Agnes* 266).   7. poppy: see the note on S. *and P.* 348.   11. lords. Some editors, following one of Woodhouse's two copies, read "hoards," which makes more obvious sense but has no authority. The word is "lords" in Keats's journal-letter (April 30) to George and Georgiana, in Brown's transcript, and in one of Woodhouse's copies which Keats passed with one change ("lulling" for "dewy"). See Garrod, *OSA*, p. 467; Garrod, citing *End*. ii.891, remarks that "lords" in the sonnet means "marshals," "arrays." 13. Gittings (*Mask*, p. 32) notes that the image and "wards" are in Cary, *Inf*. xiii.60–2, a passage Keats had marked.

On Fame   *Page 202*

The second of two sonnets on Fame; both written in April, 1819, and printed by Houghton. See the introductory note to the next sonnet.
14. miscreed: the false belief that ambition is commendable.

On the Sonnet   *Page 203*

Printed by Houghton; written in April, 1819. The theme and pattern of this sonnet, and the patterns of the two preceding sonnets, illustrate Keats's technical concern with this form — out of which, apparently, grew the stanza forms of the odes. At the end of the journal-letter of February–May, 1819, to George and Georgiana, after copying the *Ode to Psyche* and just before copying *On the Sonnet*, Keats said: "I have been endeavouring to discover a better sonnet stanza than we have. The legitimate does not suit the language over-well from the pouncing rhymes — the other kind appears too elegaiac — and the couplet at the end of it has seldom a pleasing effect — I do not pretend to have succeeded." By "legitimate" Keats means the Petrarchan sonnet, by "the other kind" the Shakespearian (see Bate, 118 f., 125 f.).
2. Andromeda: see the note on *End*. iv.606.

Ode to Psyche   *Page 203*

Printed, with slight revision, in the 1820 volume; written in late April, 1819. In the journal-letter of February–May to George and Georgiana, in the section dated April 30, Keats said:

The following Poem — the last I have written is the first and the only one with which I have taken even moderate pains — I have for the most part dash'd of[f] my lines in a hurry — This I have done leisurely — I think it reads the more richly for it and will I hope encourage me to write other thing[s] in even a more peac[e]able and healthy spirit. You must recollect that Psyche was not embodied as a goddess before the time of Apulieus [*sic*] the Platonist who lived afteir the A[u]gustan age, and consequently the Goddess was never worshipped or sacrificed to with any of the ancient fervour — and perhaps never thought of in the old religion — I am more orthodox that [*for* than] to let a he[a]then Goddess be so neglected.

The information about Psyche, evidently from Lempriere, doubtless gave Keats his cue for conceiving himself in the role of Psyche's priest. While in the *Nightingale* and the *Grecian Urn* the thematic object is given, here the poet virtually creates it, and his enjoyment is untroubled by thoughts of actuality. In this ode there seems to be no tension, unless some is implied in his nostalgia — akin to that of the *Ode to Maia* — for the happy pieties of a simpler and richer world of consciousness than these days permit. Keats's ideal of creative contemplation is not in itself low or thin, yet the real strength and beauty of the poem have a touch of his earlier softness and prettiness; the texture, if not the conception, might give some color to the old charge of cloistered aestheticism. With the varied rhyme-schemes of the stanzas may be compared those of the sonnets in the preceding pages (see the introductory note to *On the Sonnet* and Bate, pp. 129 f.).

2. Cf. M. Tighe, i.1, "dear remembrance"; *Lyc.* 6.   4. soft-conched: like a soft shell.   5. Cf. Spenser, *Amoretti* lxxvii: "Was it a dreame, or did I see it playne. . .?"   7 f. Perhaps partly suggested by Adlington's translation of Apuleius (quoted in Finney, II, 615) and certainly by Milton's idyllic picture of Adam and Eve.   9. two fair creatures: in *P.L.* iv.790. side by side: in *P.L.* iv.741.   10. "Roof," substituted for "fan," was left rhymeless.   14. Tyrian. Ancient Tyre produced a famous purple dye. 20. aurorean: cf. *End.* ii.696, *Hyp.* i.181.   22–3. Cf. M. Tighe, ii.3: "Oh, Psyche, happy in thine ignorance. . . . Pure spotless dove!"   26. Phœbe: Diana, the moon.   sapphire-region'd star: cf. *Eve of St. Agnes* 319; *P.L.* iv.604–5; D. Perkins, *K–SJ* II (1953), 54–5.   27. Vesper: cf. *End.* iii.78; Coleridge, *Nightingale* 68–9: "while many a glow-worm in the shade Lights up her love-torch."   28. Cf. *P.L.* i.492–3.   29. Cf. Potter, I, 249, 253, 267.   30. virgin-choir: in M. Tighe, i.37, v.34.   make . . . moan: see the note on *Isabella* 238, and Milton, *Nativity* 191.   32–5. Cf. *Nativity* 173–80.   32. pipe: cf. Potter, I, 273, "playing upon a pipe at a sacrifice."   incense: cf. M. Tighe, iii.48, "censer . . . incense"; Potter, I, 253. 34. shrine . . . grove: cf. Potter, I, 233–4.   39. water . . . fire: cf. Potter, I, 261.   50–4. Cf. Spenser, *Amoretti* xxii.5–8: "Her temple fayre is built within my mind. . . ."   50–2. fane . . . pain: cf. M. Tighe, i.10, "fanes . . . pains."   51. untrodden: cf. M. Tighe, i.1, "untrodden forests"; iii.15, "paths untrodden."   52. pleasant pain: a weak cliché, e.g., in Hunt, *The Palace of Pleasure*, stanza 47 (*Juvenilia*, ed. 1803, p. 174); cf. Gray, *Bard*

129, "pleasing pain." **54–5.** These lines cannot be injured by a heap of "parallels": *End.* i.86; the letter to Tom of June 29, 1818: "perpendicular Rocks, all fledged with Ash & other beautiful trees"; *P.L.* iii.627, vii.420; *Udolpho,* I, 228: "among the pine-forests, steep rose over steep, the mountains seemed to multiply"; 229: "Still vast pine-forests . . . crowned the ridgy precipice"; 229: "Mountains, whose shaggy steeps . . . their ridges clothed with pines"; 230: "the opposite steeps . . . clustering towers . . . The extent and darkness of these tall woods"; 245: "Alpine steeps . . . dark with woods"; *The Italian* (ed. 1797), II, 222–3: "as far as the eye could reach, appeared pointed mountains, darkened with forests, rising ridge over ridge in many successions. Ellena, as she surveyed this wild scenery. . . ." **66–7.** Keats evidently conceives of his Psyche as no longer required to receive Cupid ("Love") in darkness. Cf. Coleridge, quoted under 27 above; and studies of the ode by K. Allott, *Essays in Criticism,* VI (1956), 278–301, and G. Yost, *Philological Quarterly,* XXXVI (1957), 496–500.

Ode to a Nightingale   *Page 205*

The ode was printed in *Annals of the Fine Arts,* IV, no. 13, 1819, and in the 1820 volume. We do not know the order in which this and the following three odes were written; presumably they all belong to May, 1819. Charles Brown, with whom Keats was living in Hampstead, many years later gave an account of the composition of the poem which may be true in regard to the setting, if not in some particulars (*Life of John Keats,* 1937, pp. 53–4; Rollins, *K.C.,* II, 65):

> In the spring of 1819 a nightingale had built her nest near my house. Keats felt a tranquil and continual joy in her song; and one morning he took his chair from the breakfast-table to the grass-plot under a plum-tree, where he sat for two or three hours. When he came into the house, I perceived he had some scraps of paper in his hand, and these he was quietly thrusting behind the books. On inquiry, I found those scraps, four or five in number, contained his poetic feeling on the song of our nightingale.

This ode, and the *Grecian Urn,* have been so much discussed of late years that any attempt at a brief comment would be foolish. But it may be said that, while traditional criticism was inclined to see a single-hearted celebration of the immortal beauty of art as contrasted with fleeting experience, modern criticism has emphasized and analyzed the complex tensions at work, tensions that create the structure and inform individual words and phrases. Among critical essays are those of H. M. McLuhan, *University of Toronto Quarterly,* XII (1943); Allen Tate, *The American Scholar,* XV (1945–6) and *On the Limits of Poetry* (1948); Janet Spens, *Review of English Studies,* III (1952); R. H. Fogle, *PMLA* LXVIII (1953); Wasserman (1953).

1–2. Cf. *P.L.* viii.288–9; Horace, *Epod.* xiv.1–4; Marlowe, *Ovid's Elegies* iii.6.13, "as if cold hemlock I had drunk"; M. Tighe, vi.16.   **4. Lethe:**

the mythological river of forgetfulness. **5.** Cf. *Brit. Past.* i.3.163–4: "Sweet Philomela . . . I do not envy thy sweet carolling"; Ronsard, *L'Alouette* 1–2: "Hé! Dieu! que je porte d'envie Aux felicités de ta vie." **11–14.** Cf. Keats's letter to his sister, May 1 (?), 1819: "and, please heaven, a little claret-wine cool out of a cellar a mile deep . . . a strawberry bed to say your prayers to Flora in"; and D. Perkins, *K–SJ* II (1953), 56–7. *Udolpho* has a number of Provençal vignettes of peasants dancing, some of them associated with "vintage" (I, 3, 61–2, 67–8, 74, 99: Ridley, p. 219); the nightingale is heard, e.g., on pp. 5, 7, 99. **12. deep-delved:** in Cary, *Purg.* xxiv.6; cf. *F.Q.* III.iii.7, "In a deep delve." **14. sunburnt mirth:** cf. *The Tempest* IV.i.134–5. **16. Hippocrene:** the fountain of the Muses on Mount Helicon. **18.** Cf. Horace, *Odes* III.iii.12, *purpureo bibet ore nectar*. **20. forest dim:** in *Isabella* 175. **21. dissolve:** cf. *P.L.* viii.291. **23.** Cf. Wordsworth, *Tintern Abbey* 52–3; *Macbeth* III.ii.22. **26.** Keats would be thinking of Tom's death and probably of *Exc.* iv.760: "While man grows old, and dwindles, and decays." **32. pards:** leopards. See the note on *S. and P.* 334–6 and *End.* iv.241. **33.** Cf. Milton, *Passion* 50, "viewless wing." **34.** Cf. "Sensations" versus "Thoughts." **35.** Cf. Milton, *Nativity* 61: "But peaceful was the night." Keats's ode began in sunshine; now it is night; in 56 it is midnight. **37.** Cf. *End.* ii.184–5, iii.50–1. **39–40.** Cf. *F.Q.* I.i.7: "loftie trees . . . Did spred so broad, that heavens light did hide"; Coleridge, *Nightingale* 4–11, 26, 52–7. **42.** Cf. *The Tempest* V.i.94, "the blossom that hangs on the bough." **49.** Cf. *Meg Merrilies* 7. **50.** Cf. *F.Q.* I.i.23, II.xi.16. **51. Darkling:** in the dark; cf. *P.L.* iii.39. **55.** Cf. *Why Did I Laugh To-night* 11. **61 f.** There is no doubt a logical confusion here, since the singing bird is no less mortal than the human poet, but in Keats's mind the bird has become the disembodied and immortal voice of poetry. **62.** Cf. *Exc.* iv.761–2: "And countless generations of mankind Depart; and leave no vestige where they trod"; v.465–7: "Is Man A child of hope? Do generations press On generations, without progress made?" **66–7.** Along with the biblical picture of Ruth, Keats may have remembered Wordsworth's *The Solitary Reaper*. **69–70.** Critics cite the lines on Claude's *Enchanted Castle* in the *Epistle to Reynolds* (26–66), and *Udolpho*, which is full of casements, some of them opening on foam or the sea (I, 245; II, 140); see De Selincourt, pp. 577–8, Ridley, pp. 228–9, Finney, II, 631. Cf. Coleridge, *Fears in Solitude* 87, "perilous seas" (N. F. Ford, *MLQ* VIII, 456); Cary, *Inf.* i.22–3: "'scap'd from sea to shore, Turns to the perilous wide waste." **71 f.** The disillusioned return to reality, after a glimpse of the ideal, had troubled Endymion. Cf. "elf" here and in *End.* ii.277. **73–4.** Cf. *Fancy*. **75. plaintive.** Keats's emotional experience has altered his reaction to the bird's joyous song; cf. *The Solitary Reaper* 18, "the plaintive numbers." **79–80.** Keats may have remembered such diverse things as Wordsworth, *Yarrow Visited* 3, "a waking dream"; *Exc.* ii.833, "By waking sense or by the dreaming soul"; *Merry Wives of Windsor* III.v.141: "Hum! ha! Is this a vision? Is this a dream? Do I sleep?"; Hazlitt, "On Chaucer and Spenser" (*Works*, ed. Howe, V, 44): "Spenser was the poet of our waking dreams . . . lulling the senses into a deep oblivion of the jarring noises of the world, from which we have no wish to be ever recalled."

Ode on a Grecian Urn   *Page 207*

Printed in *Annals of the Fine Arts,* IV, no. 15, 1820, and in the 1820 volume; written apparently in May, 1819. Keats may have had several urns in mind (Colvin, pp. 415–17); and the sacrificial procession of stanza iv has a number of possible "sources," artistic and literary. The symbol of enduring art is here not a bird but a really "immortal" artifact. And here the conflict between transiency and the desire for permanence is focused almost wholly on youthful, sensuous passion. The fourth stanza is a digression from that line, and, though it begins with the suggestion of communal piety and happiness, it ends with a picture of desolation inspired by the negative side of Keats's theme; as in the *Nightingale,* painful actuality intrudes. Moreover, while in the *Nightingale* the second-last stanza purported to be a resolution of the central tension, in the final stanza the imaginative experience of an eternal reality was acknowledged to be illusory or transitory. In the *Grecian Urn* the last stanza, especially the last distich, purports to be a positive resolution, in accord with the conscious argument of the poem; yet it hardly maintains itself against the half-unconscious testimony of the whole ode in favor of the fleeting human experience with all its pains. Keats is an older and wiser Endymion, but he would still choose the Indian maid. The modern reader inevitably compares Yeats's *Sailing to Byzantium.*

Among critical studies are: J. M. Murry (*Keats,* 1955, and earlier editions); Kenneth Burke, *A Grammar of Motives* (1945); Cleanth Brooks, *The Well Wrought Urn* (1947); Wasserman (1953); Leo Spitzer, *Comparative Literature,* VII (1955). H. T. Lyon has collected and edited many critiques of the ode in *Keats' Well-Read Urn* (1958).

7. **Tempe.** Cf. Collins, *The Passions* 86–8: "They saw in Tempe's vale her native maids, Amid the festal sounding shades, To some unwearied minstrel dancing." **Arcady:** Arcadia, a state of ancient Greece, but traditionally a symbol of pastoral idyllicism. **15–16, 23–4.** Cf. *Brit. Past.* ii.2.33–5: "a lovely shepherd's boy Sits piping on a hill, as if his joy Would still endure." **27.** Cf. Thomson, *Summer* 1220–2: "on the marble tomb . . . For ever silent and for ever sad." **28.** In prose order, "Far above all breathing human passion." **30.** Cf. *End.* ii.319. **31 f.** In addition to the sacrificial procession of the Elgin Marbles, with its "lowing heifer," Keats may have recalled Claude's *Sacrifice to Apollo* (which he had used in the *Epistle to Reynolds* 19 f.); details about sacrifices in Potter, I, 267–8; and Sandys, p. 47: "She [a heifer] made a stand; to heaven her fore-head cast, With loftie horns most exquisitely faire; Then, with repeated lowings fill'd the ayre." Keats may also have seen Raphael's cartoon, *The Sacrifice at Lystra,* which was on exhibit at the British Gallery during this spring and on which Haydon published an essay; this essay appeared in both the *Examiner,* May 2 and 9, and *Annals of the Fine Arts* IV, no. 13. Raphael's cartoon depicted "the temple *outside* the city (Acts xiv.13), the crowd which had

come to the sacrifice, and the priest and garlanded victim at the altar" (J. R. MacGillivray, *TLS*, July 9, 1938, p. 465: cf. W. Roberts, *ibid.*, Aug. 20, p. 544). **40. desolate:** Lempriere, describing the Spartan festival of Hyacinthia, says: "During this latter part of the festivity, all were eager to be present at the games, and the city was almost desolate, and without inhabitants." **41. brede:** embroidery (Collins, *To Evening* 7). **44. tease us out of thought.** Cf. *Epistle to Reynolds* 77 and note. In the ode the phrase might express either — or both — of two characteristically Keatsian ideas: "raise us above merely intellectual speculation to the level of intuition" (cf. the similar antithesis in the *Nightingale* 33–4); "carry us beyond the sorrows of life" (cf. *ibid.* 27). **45.** "Cold Pastoral" may be thought an unwitting revelation of Keats's incomplete acceptance of his own argument. The urn is immortal, but it is also cold and inhuman (cf. "cold Beauty" in *On Visiting the Tomb of Burns*); if he had said "Cool Pastoral," the idea of refreshment would have sustained his ostensible thesis. **49– 50.** These much-discussed lines have been sometimes censured as dubious doctrine, or as an illogical conclusion to this poem, or as the superimposition of an abstract statement upon a poem of dramatic concreteness. At any rate one may dispute the common reading, which puts the first five words in quotation marks, even though the lines were so printed in the 1820 volume. In the *Annals* — for which Keats probably supplied the copy (Rollins, *K.C.*, II, 142; Stillinger, below) — and in the transcripts of George Keats, Brown, Dilke, and Woodhouse, there are no quotation marks at all. But the problem is too complex for discussion here: see A. Whitley, *Keats-Shelley Memorial Bulletin*, V (1953), 1–3, and J. Stillinger, *PMLA* LXXIII (1958), 447–8. The reading in the 1820 volume makes the last line and a half a comment by the poet; even if Keats read proof of this poem (we do not know that he did), he surely overlooked this item, since the whole two lines must be the imagined declaration of the urn to people contemplating it. The poet could not himself address his fellow creatures as "Ye . . . on earth" when, in this very stanza, he has just been speaking of them in terms of "us" and "ours." In the present text, accordingly, the punctuation is altered. Keats's meaning, it may be added, becomes clearer if we take "truth" as "reality."

Ode on Melancholy   *Page 209*

Printed in the 1820 volume; written apparently in May, 1819. The ode originally opened with a stanza of macabre extravagance (it is quoted along with the text). The present first stanza may be thought to suffer somewhat from the same quality. And although, like the opening of *L'Allegro*, this stanza is banishing a spurious or unwanted kind of melancholy, it consumes a third of the poem without taking positive hold of the subject (even if "wakeful anguish" turns out to be a main clue); the parallel lines 1–4 of the *Nightingale* are kept in due proportion. The ode as a whole — not to mention such a lapse as line 19 — obviously lacks the full curve of the greater odes; and while the third stanza is a potent statement or resolution of the problem set forth in the *Nightingale* and the *Grecian Urn* — melancholy being seen as inseparable from the most intense joy — the conception here seems, in comparison, to be less richly and broadly human, to be, in spite of its energy, in the vein of an aestheticism at once luxuriant and thin.

1. Lethe: see the note on the *Nightingale* 4. **2. Wolf's-bane** and the other herbs are traditional poisons and symbols of death. **6–7.** Keats may be recalling such an item as is given in Lempriere: "Psyche is generally represented with the wings of a butterfly to intimate the lightness of the soul, of which the butterfly is the symbol, and on that account, among the ancients, when a man had just expired, a butterfly appeared fluttering above, as if rising from the mouth of the deceased." **12–15.** Cf. Thomas Carew, *To the Countess of Anglesey* 1–3: "Madam, men say you keep with dropping eyes Your sorrows fresh, wat'ring the rose that lies Fall'n from your cheeks upon your dear lord's hearse"; and "Glutting your sorrows" (*ibid.*, 25). For Keats's strong, crude "glut," valuable here, cf. also *Othello* I.iii.57: "it engluts and swallows other sorrows." **23–6.** Cf. *End.* ii.823–4. Critics quote a book Keats liked, Burton's *Anatomy of Melancholy* (I.ii.3.5): "in the Calends of January Angerona had her holy day, to whom in the Temple of Volupia, or Goddess of Pleasure, their Augurs and Bishops did yearly sacrifice"; Angerona is identified with Melancholy in *ibid.*, II.i.3. D. Perkins (*K–SJ* II, 52) quotes Hazlitt's "On Poetry in General" (*Works*, ed. Howe, V, 3–4): "Through poetry, the 'uneasy' sense of beauty, says Hazlitt, seeks to '*enshrine* itself . . . in the highest forms of fancy, and to relieve the *aching* sense of *pleasure* by expressing it in the boldest manner.'" **27–8.** Cf. Shakespeare, *Troilus* III.ii.21 f.: "What will it be When that the wat'ry palates taste indeed Love's thrice-repured nectar? Death, I fear me; Sounding destruction; or some joy too fine, Too subtile-potent, tun'd too sharp in sweetness For the capacity of my ruder powers." **30.** Cf. Shakespeare, Sonnet xxxi: "Thou art the grave where buried love doth live, Hung with the trophies of my lovers gone"; Carew (*l.c.*, 84–6): "so the pen . . . Shall sing the trophies of your conquering eye."

Ode on Indolence   *Page 210*

In printing this ode Houghton apparently changed the order of stanzas 3–5; they are given here in the order adopted by Garrod (1958 ed., p. 447; *OSA*, pp. 355, 465). This was probably the last of the odes written in April–May, 1819 (Colvin, p. 353; A. Lowell, II, 257–60), although the vision that provided the material had been described in Keats's journal-letter to George and Georgiana of February–May in the section dated March 19 (printed below among the letters). Earlier passages of verse have illustrated two kinds of "indolence" that visited Keats, one a sterile and unhappy torpor, the other a passive receptivity which was rather a fallow phase of creativeness.

10. Phidias was the great sculptor of Periclean Athens. **18.** Cf. a phrase in the letter cited above, and *End.* iv.526. **39. maiden most unmeek:** a negative version of a phrase traditionally used of the Virgin Mary. **44.** See the note on the *Nightingale* 23. **48. annoy:** pain, harm (Spenser, Shakespeare, Cary). **52.** Cf. *Ode to Psyche* 15.

Lamia *Page 212*

Printed in the 1820 volume. Composition was begun apparently at the end of June, 1819; Part I was finished by July 11, Part II by September 5. On September 18 Keats wrote to George and Georgiana that he was certain there was "that sort of fire in it which must take hold of people in some way — give them either pleasant or unpleasant sensation. What they want is a sensation of some sort." He hoped that this poem might win more popularity than he had so far achieved. There have been widely divergent interpretations of the significance Keats gave or intended to give to Burton's anecdote of diablerie (which is quoted at the end of the text, where Keats put it). *Lamia* has been seen as an allegory of his ecstatic and tortured feelings about Fanny Brawne; as a condemnation — by the man or by the poet —of the blighting philosophic intellect or of the senses or of the unreconcilable antagonism between them; or as an incoherent picture of unresolved tensions in the poet's own mind. No other poem of Keats's evokes, in regard to its central theme, such conflicting views (there are only two opposed notions of *Endymion*), and they indicate the presence in the poem of conflicting elements. It is perhaps most probable that *Lamia* is a sort of *Endymion* in reverse, a much elaborated *Belle Dame sans Merci*, that Lycius' senses are enthralled by a beauty that is corrupt and sterile — although Lamia and Lycius do not always seem to be condemned and although philosophic wisdom, in the person of Apollonius, is hardly presented with sympathy (he is, to be sure, seen through their eyes, but Keats does little to counteract their hostile fear). The conception of the serpent-woman and baleful love may have been colored by *Christabel* and by the *Rhododaphne* (1818) of Shelley's friend, Thomas Love Peacock. Beyer (pp. 192–238) sees the predominant influence of Wieland's *Oberon*. Among recent critics are Wasserman (1953), pp. 158–74; B. Slote, *Keats and the Dramatic Principle* (1958), pp. 138–92; G. S. Dunbar, *K–SJ* VIII (1959); and especially D. D. Perkins, *The Quest for Permanence* (1959).

While the theme, whatever it was, arose from central Keatsian tensions, *Lamia* displays a marked concern with craftsmanship. In comparison with *Endymion*, the handling of both narrative and the couplet shows that Keats's early waywardness has given place to well-proportioned, forward-moving rapidity, his loose versification, with its chirpy feminine rhymes, to masculine firmness of control. His Huntian-Elizabethan manner has been — apart from a few bad lapses —corrected and strengthened by study of the crisply translated tales in Dryden's *Fables* (see Bate, pp. 142–71); and Sandys' *Ovid*, with which he had long been acquainted, may have contributed to the same effect. On the whole, *Lamia* has "fire" and does produce sensations, but its somewhat hard brilliance may be thought less attractive, less fully and genuinely Keatsian, than *The Eve of St. Agnes* or even *Hyperion*.

Part i.1–6. Cf. Sandys, p. 3 ("Our Demi-gods, Nymphs," etc.), and Burton, *Anatomy* I.ii.1.2 (both quoted in De Selincourt, pp. 454–5), and the opening of Chaucer's *Wife of Bath's Tale*. **3. Oberon.** Keats may be thinking of both Shakespeare and Wieland's *Oberon* (Beyer, p. 203).

5. **Fauns:** see the note on *I Stood* 153.   14. **Satyrs:** cf. Una among the Satyrs, *F.Q.* I.vi.7 f.   15. **Tritons.** Triton was a minor sea-divinity, Neptune's trumpeter; sometimes referred to in the plural.   22–6. Cf. Sandys, p. 31: "Love-struck, he burnes as in the Ayre he hung," etc. Hermes' love for the nymph may have been developed from the tale in Sandys, pp. 31–2, of Mercury, Herse, and Aglauros. Wasserman interprets the episode as an example of a perfect, immortal love, to be contrasted with the human love of Lycius and Lamia (cf. E. T. Norris, *ELH* II, 1935).   26. The first of numerous Alexandrines, a device of Dryden's to vary pentameter uniformity and create an expectant pause (Ridley, p. 249).   46. **cirque-couchant:** lying in coils (cf. *P.L.* iv.406).   47. **gordian:** see the note on *End.* i.614. The picture in 47 f., perhaps overdone to suggest Lamia's double nature, may owe something to *P.L.* ix.494 f. and *Aen.* v.84 f.   58. Ariadne, after her marriage to Bacchus, was made a constellation; a circlet of stars ("tiar": tiara) appears in the sky above her in Titian's painting (see the note on *S. and P.* 334–6).   61–3. The first of Keats's Drydenesque triplets.   63. **Proserpine:** see the note on *End.* i.944.   78. **Phœbean dart:** ray of the sun.   81. **the star of Lethe.** One of Hermes' functions was to conduct the spirits of the dead to Hades. Lamb, in his review of the 1820 volume, cited the words as "one of those prodigal phrases which Mr Keats abounds in, which are each a poem in a word, and which in this instance lays open to us at once, like a picture, all the dim regions and their inhabitants, and the sudden coming of a celestial among them."   81–2. **not delay'd . . . eloquence:** Miltonic.   114. **psalterian:** "like the utterance of a psalm," or from psaltery, a stringed instrument.   133. **Cåducean:** see the note on *End.* i.562–3.   144. **green-recessed woods:** cf. *Hyp.* iii.41.   148. **besprent:** besprinkled (*Comus* 542).   158. **brede:** cf. the *Grecian Urn* 41 and note.   163. **rubious-argent:** silvery red.   174. Cenchreae was the eastern harbor of Corinth, on the Saronic Gulf. 189–90. **the lore Of love:** in *F.Q.* III.vi.51; M. Tighe, Proem i; and Cary, *Purg.* xxiv.51.   191. **sciential:** cf. *P.L.* ix.837, "sciential sap."   192. Cf. *End.* ii.823–4 and *Melancholy* 21 f.   193. **pettish:** properly "petulant"; here, "uncertain," "easily confused"?   198. **unshent:** cf. *S. and P.* 379. 202–5. In his note on *P.L.* ix.179–91 (*Works,* ed. Forman, III, 265), Keats said: "Whose head is not dizzy at the possible speculations of Satan in the serpent prison? No passage of poetry ever can give a greater pain of suffocation."   207. Cf. *End.* iii.624–5, and Jonson, *Neptune's Triumph* 419–20: "Or laying forth their tresses all along Upon the glassy waves." 208. **Thetis:** see *End.* ii.611.   211. **palatine:** palatial.   212. **Mulciber:** Vulcan (*F.Q.* III.xi.26; *P.L.* i.740).   244. **syllabling:** cf. *Comus* 208. 248. Orpheus, having won his wife's release from Hades, disobeyed Pluto's command not to look back at her and thereby lost her again.   265. **Pleiad:** see the note on *End.* ii.688.   275. **nice:** accurate.   278. See the note on 22–6.   279. **Thou . . . scholar:** in *Hamlet* I.i.42.   317–20. Cf. Potter, I, 422, on the feast of Adonis.   327. **unperplex'd delight:** cf. 192 and "unreflecting love" (*When I Have Fears* 10).   328–32. The worst lines in the poem, whether consciously Byronic or unconsciously

Huntian. Peris were fairy-like beings of Persian mythology. **333. Pyrrha's pebbles:** see the note on *End.* ii.197. **334.** Cf. *F.Q.* I.vii.49.9. **352.** Potter (II, 304) says that "Corinth is remarkable for being a nursery of harlots," and speaks of temple prostitutes. Cf. Burton, *Anatomy* III.ii.2.1. **355–61.** Cf. *Eve of St. Mark* 13–22. **370.** Cf. Shakespeare, *Venus and Adonis* 143–4.

Part ii.1 f. Perhaps an attempt at the Byronic manner. See Beyer, pp. 197 f. **26. slope:** cf. *Hyp.* i.204 and note. **28. trumpets:** a symbol of active life (cf. *End.* i.737). **36. empery:** empire. **48. My silver planet:** cf. i.265 f. **94–5.** Cf. Potter, II, 215 f. **106–10.** Cf. Potter, II, 280–5. **160. daft:** baffled. **161–2. thaw . . . melt:** cf. the note on *End.* i.501. **173–202.** Most of the concrete details evidently came from Potter, II, 364 f. These items are quoted in D. Bush, *PMLA* L (1935),786 f., and *Mythology and the Romantic Tradition*, pp. 113–14, and in Finney, II, 674 f. Peacock's *Rhododaphne* (cantos vi–vii) described a palace erected by magic and a sumptuous banquet room; the enchantress who seduced the hero was destroyed by Uranian Love. D. B. Green (*MLN* LXVI, 1951) quotes a passage from Schiller's *Ghost-Seer*, a work Keats referred to in September, 1819. **187. Ceres' horn.** The horn of plenty is usually associated with Amalthea (*End.* ii.448; *Fall* i.35 and note). **224. adder's tongue:** a kind of fern. **226. thyrsus:** the vine-leaved staff carried by devotees of Bacchus; here a symbol of intoxication. **229–37.** At Haydon's "immortal dinner," Dec. 28, 1817, Keats and Lamb agreed that Newton had destroyed all the poetry of the rainbow by reducing it to its prismatic colors, and all — doubtless a bit "high" — drank Newton's health and confusion to mathematics (Haydon, *Autobiography*, ed. A. Huxley, I, 269; Colvin, p. 247; De Selincourt, pp. 458–9). The lines here partake of Keats's occasional anti-intellectualism (cf. *What the Thrush Said*, etc.), but Apollonius hardly represents his mature view of "knowledge" and "philosophy," nor are Lycius and Lamia adequate exemplars of the sensuous and imaginative intuition, still less the full humanity, that Keats commonly exalts. **231. awful:** inspiring awe. **234.** Keats may be echoing a phrase from Hazlitt's first lecture on "The English Poets" (*Works,* ed. Howe, V, 9): ". . . the progress of knowledge and refinement has a tendency to circumscribe the limits of the imagination, and to clip the wings of poetry." This idea was much in the air in the period. **271 f.** Keats alters Burton's conclusion. The picture of Lamia writhing under the sage's eye may owe something to the punishment of Aglauros in the Ovidian tale cited under i.22–6. **301. perceant:** piercing (cf. *F.Q.* I.x.47; Chatterton, *Ælla* 558).

King Stephen   *Page 229*

Printed by Houghton. In July and August, 1819, Keats — who had long cherished dramatic ambitions, inspired by Shakespeare, the actor Edmund Kean, and, lately, the need of money — collaborated with Brown in the play *Otho the Great;* Keats wrote up the dialogue as Brown ladled out the material, and the result was not very successful. In the fragment *King Stephen* (August? November?), Keats, while accepting Brown's suggestion of the subject, worked independently. He of course had Shakespeare's history plays in mind, but *King Stephen* is not merely Shakespearian pastiche. He may have given up the play because of news that Kean was going on an American tour.

i.13. flaunt: flaunting.   **ii.22–3.** Keats may be thinking in particular of Chapman's *Iliad* vii.17–18 (though Pallas is not standing on the walls of Ilion).   **iii.2. Bellona:** goddess of war (cf. *Macbeth* I.ii.54).   **iii.3. sheaved spears:** cf. *P.L.* iv.980–5.   **iii.11. truck:** exchange.   **iii.12. Nestor:** the old chief and counselor in the Greek army at Troy.   **iv.34.** The mother, wife, and daughters of King Darius, when captured by Alexander, were treated with uncommon magnanimity.   **iv.55. rubiest:** reddest.

The Fall of Hyperion: A Dream   *Page 235*

This work, first printed by Lord Houghton in *Miscellanies of the Philobiblon Society*, III (1856), became generally accessible only when reprinted in the 1867 edition of his *Life and Letters of John Keats*. The poet seems to have been intermittently engaged with the *Fall* during the late summer of 1819. In a letter to Reynolds (Sept. 21), after praising Chatterton as the purest writer in English, he said:

> I have given up Hyperion — there were too many Miltonic inversions in it — Miltonic verse can not be written but in an artful or rather artist's humour. I wish to give myself up to other sensations. English ought to be kept up. It may be interesting to you to pick out some lines from Hyperion and put a mark × to the false beauty proceeding from art, and one ‖ to the true voice of feeling. Upon my soul 'twas imagination I cannot make the distinction — Every now & then there is a Miltonic intonation — But I cannot make the division properly.

On the same day Keats wrote to Woodhouse quoting at length from the *Fall* (referred to merely as "Hyperion"). It has therefore been inferred that the *Hyperion* he told Reynolds he had given up was the *Fall;* but Muir (pp. 54–5, 74) argues that Reynolds had no copy of the *Fall,* that Keats must have meant the first *Hyperion*, and hence that he had abandoned both versions (he did some further tinkering up into December). The reason he clutches at in writing to Reynolds would apply better to the first *Hyperion*, since in the recasting he eliminated many Miltonisms (though he added some too).

The real reasons were largely and deeper, as indeed his comment suggests. The subjective induction (lines 1–293) constitutes, as critics have fully recognized, a new and distinctive phase, both spiritual and technical, in Keats's development; and the attempt to achieve "the true voice of feeling" seems to go along with a partial shift of masters, from Milton to Dante. The chief evidence is the personal form of the introductory vision — perhaps one should rather say the use of a *persona* that is at once personal and impersonal — which is carried over into the revised epic narrative.* Presumably Keats was still dependent, or mainly dependent, on Cary's rather Miltonic translation, though some critics have argued for his assimilating something of Dante's own quality — for example, Bridges, p. xlviii; Lowes (*TLS*, Jan. 11, 1936, p. 35), who, along with many parallels in detail, saw the *Purgatorio* as the structural background of the induction; and F. R. Leavis (*Revaluation*, pp. 269–70). At any rate Keats's new style has more individual naturalness and more severely functional expressiveness than that of *Hyperion*, and less "poetical" luxuriance than we associate with the typical Keats. The change becomes most apparent, of course, in the partial revision of the epic fragment. Critics have been increasingly inclined to stress the gains achieved in revision rather than the losses incurred. However, notwithstanding the drastic alterations in conception and style, most of the possible reasons for Keats's inability to finish *Hyperion* would still obstruct the finishing of the *Fall;* and along with them there was the further difficulty of fusing the old with the new. And Keats "had already used up the climax of the first poem in the first canto of the second version" (Muir, p. 74). But the induction especially is one of Keats's most serious and moving utterances, even if difficulties of interpretation abound — difficulties apparently born of his acute and complex tensions.

Reference may be made to De Selincourt's notes, pp. 515–24, 582–4; Ridley, pp. 266–80; Bate, pp. 171–82; Muir (see the introduction to *Hyperion*), and, for problems of interpretation, to Murry, "The Poet and the Dreamer" (*Keats*, and earlier edns.); D. G. James, *The Romantic Comedy*, especially pp. 134–54; and B. Wicker, "The Disputed Lines in *The Fall of Hyperion*," *Essays in Criticism*, VII (1957), 28–41.

i.1–7. Cf. Pope, *Essay on Man* i.99 f.: "Lo, the poor Indian," etc.; *Exc.* iv.1275 f.   7–15. Cf. *Exc.* i.77 f.: "Oh! many are the Poets that are sown By Nature; men endowed with highest gifts, The vision and the faculty divine; Yet wanting the accomplishment of verse. . . ."   19–136. Keats's preoccupation, from *I Stood* onward, with the nature and development of the poet, and his conception of Apollo's growth in *Hyperion*, warrant our assuming that the symbolism here has to do with that general theme, though the interpretation of details is uncertain. We think of *S. and P.* 90–125 (see the note), of *Endymion*, of the letter on the "Mansion of Life" (May 3, 1818), and the passage on the "vale of Soul-making" in the journal-letter to George and Georgiana of February–May, 1819 (the section written April 21); but the symbolism of the *Fall* has much more complexity and personal urgency and it moves up to what has been called the sacramental level.   19–40. Cf. the realm of Flora and old Pan (*S. and P.* 101–2), the "infant or thoughtless Chamber."   31. Cf. *P.L.* v.321–49 — which seems to color lines 24–34 and 52 and to suggest the innocence and beauty of Eden.   35. **fabled horn:** a horn, broken off the head of the goat with whose milk Amalthea fed the infant Jupiter (*End.* ii.448), be-

---

* In a Harvard thesis (1958–9), Stuart M. Sperry, in a suggestive analysis of the induction, finds a new and deeper response in Keats to Milton's tragic vision of Eden, the fall, and human history.

came a magical cornucopia or horn of plenty.   **45.** Apparently poets —
but they are linked (44) with all humanity.   **46.** This real elixir — cf.
the simile of *Hyp.* iii.118–20 (Wicker, p. 40) — is presumably the poetic
imagination, advancing from the sensuous toward the poetry of "knowledge."   **47.** poppy: see *S. and P.* 348 and note.   **48.** A council of
Caliphs, Arabian rulers, plotting to poison one another.   **50.** The College
of Cardinals.   **55.** Cf. the "trances" of Endymion.   **56.** Silenus: cf.
End. iv.215–17.   **62 f.** A temple of knowledge and art, the whole texture
of human history and life?   **36 f.** See the letter cited under *Hyp.* i.86.
75. Cf. Matt. vi.19.   **76–80.** Potter, I, 277, lists among offerings made
to the gods "crowns and garlands, garments, cups of gold, or other valuable
metals, and any other thing which conduced to the ornament or the en-
riching of the temples . . . they sometimes were laid on the floor, sometimes hung upon the walls, doors, pillars. . . ." Lowes (*PMLA LI,* 1111)
cites biblical parallels.   **83.** embossed . . . massy: cf. *Il P.* 157–8; *Exc.*
v.145.   **85–7.** eastward . . . west: past and future? the progress of
poetry from the east to the west? Cf. *End.* ii.359–63, 723–8, iv.1 f. Potter,
I, 224, speaks of temples built to face the rising sun, so that worshipers
faced the west.   **93–107.** Lowes (p. 1008) gives biblical parallels.
96. One minist'ring: the Roman Moneta, derived — like the Dolor of *Hyp.*
ii.20 — from a book Keats owned, *Auctores Mythographi Latini* (Leyden,
1742), I, 3–4. Moneta replaces the Mnemosyne of *Hyperion;* in her ad-
monitory function she is closer to Dante's Virgil — and she reflects Keats's
inner conflicts.   **97–9.** Cf. Cary, *Purg.* xxiv.142–7.   **98.** small warm
rain: cf. the "small rain" of Job xxxvii.6 and (Lowes, p. 1111) of the famous
early lyric, *O western wind.*   **103.** Maian: cf. the *Ode to Maia.*   **107–
17.** The steps — probably suggested by Dante, *Purg.* iv, ix, xii–iii (Ridley,
p. 271; Lowes, *TLS,* Jan. 11, 1936) — may stand for the climactic stage in
the ascent from the realm of sense to that of "truth," tragic understanding,
akin to the changes wrought in Endymion and Apollo.   **129–30.** Cf. Cary,
Purg. xxx.97–100: "then, the ice, Congeal'd about my bosom, turn'd itself
To spirit and water."   **135.** Cf. Jacob's vision, Gen. xxviii.12, *P.L.* iii.510–
15.   **142–3.** Cf. *Hyp.* iii.130, "Die into life."   **145–6.** Cf. *P.L.* xi.411–
15.   **147–53.** The first division of mankind is between men — not merely
poets — who feel the miseries of the world and those who do not. De Selincourt (p. 583) quotes the similar division in Shelley's preface to *Alastor.*
On this whole dialogue, see Wicker's essay (cited in the introductory note).
154–60. Still speaking of men in general, the poet asks about active benefactors of mankind. In letters, e.g., August 14, 24, Keats reaffirms his conviction that well-doing is the only thing in the world above good writing.
161–81. A second division is made by Moneta between active benefactors
and mere dreamers; among the latter she includes the poet-speaker and all
his tribe. Active servants of mankind are not here because they find full
happiness in well-doing. All active men, whether imaginative or not, experience distinct joys and pains; only the inactive dreamer never has joy
unmixed with pain. Is this the obverse side of the "negative capability" that
the younger Keats had considered the supreme, the Shakespearian, endow-

ment, the artist's non-moral capacity to enter into all characters and experience, to live all men's lives? De Selincourt (p. 521) cites Keats's letter to Miss Jeffrey of June 9, 1819: "He [Boiardo] was a noble Poet of Romance; not a miserable and mighty Poet of the human Heart. The middle age of Shakespeare was all c[l]ouded over; his days were not more happy than Hamlet's who is perhaps more like Shakespeare himself in his common every day Life than any other of his Characters." With the word "dreamers," cf. *Exc.* i.634 f., iii.333 f.   **187–210.** These lines are bracketed because Woodhouse said that Keats intended to erase them and because, even if he did not intend to delete the whole, he would certainly have revised it (as indeed he had already), since lines 187 and 194–8 are almost identical with 211 and 216–20. Murry ("The Poet and the Dreamer") argues against keeping 187–210 in the text on the grounds that Keats had replaced them and that he had got beyond the view of himself as a mere dreamer, being separated from the dreamer tribe by the experience indicated in 141–5. Yet Keats wrote the lines, he had felt the self-lacerating doubts of 198–210 (and 166 f.), even if he made the partial defense of 187–90 and repudiated the whole, and the rejected lines may be taken as "the key to the understanding of the poem" (Wicker, p. 28, n.).   **189.** a sage. Cf. Dante's address to Virgil, "thou illustrious sage" (Cary, *Inf.* i.85).   **207–08.** Keats could, in a hostile mood, see most contemporary poets in these terms. See the note on *S. and P.* 230–5 and the headnote on *Robin Hood.*   **256 f.** Keats's association of death with aesthetic ecstasy here gives way to a deeper conception of the artist's supra-mortal understanding of human experience in its tragic fullness. In the wisdom revealed in Moneta's face D. G. James (*Romantic Comedy*, p. 150) and Wicker (p. 41) see a kind of parallel to Christ's taking upon himself the sins of the world — this is not mere "negative capability." Cf. Cary, *Purg.* xxxi.117 f. In this scene, and throughout the induction, J. L. N. O'Loughlin found the influence of the "Allegoric Vision" prefixed to Coleridge's *Lay Sermon* of 1817 (*TLS*, Dec. 6, 1934, p. 875). **274.** Cf. *P.L.* i.687.   **276.** Cf. Apollo's "aching ignorance," *Hyp.* iii.107. **288.** Omega: the last letter of the Greek alphabet, hence the last of anything; cf. Rev. i.8, 11; Cary, *Parad.* xxvi.19, "That Alpha and Omega is."   **294 f.** Keats here takes up the original *Hyperion* and proceeds, with many changes; the poet now becomes an observer of the epic action.   **302–6.** Cf. *Hyp.* iii.112–19.   **310 f.** Cf. *Hyp.* i.7 f.   **312.** zoning: course, circuit? **331.** Mnemosyne: a slip for Moneta.   **372–7.** Cf. *Hyp.* i.72–8. The simile has lost some mystery and magic but is more strictly functional (Ridley, pp. 276–7; Muir, p. 69).   **382–3.** Cf. *Hyp.* i.85–6. The revised simile is more relevant to the theme. Cf. Cary, *Purg.* xii.14–16: "As, in memorial of the buried, drawn Upon earth-level tombs, the sculptur'd form Of what was once, appears."   **412–38.** Critics, comparing this speech with *Hyp.* i.95–134, have found it weak and querulous. The reason may be that "Saturn is humanized, because in the plan of the poem his sorrows are the sorrows of humanity" (Muir, p. 72), or that he is incapable of true understanding of humanity; lines 438–41 might support either view but perhaps favor the second.   **425. Cybele: see the** notes on *Hyp.* ii.4, 389. 462–3. Cf. Cary, *Inf.* iv.

ii.1–3. Cf. similar apologies in *P.L.* v.571–4, etc.   **7–61.** Cf. *Hyp.* i.158–217.   **51–3.** Cf. Cary, *Purg.* ix.85–7: "The lowest stair was marble white, so smooth And polish'd, that therein my mirror'd form Distinct I saw."

To Autumn   *Page 247*

Printed in the 1820 volume; written Sept. 19, 1819. On Sept. 21 Keats wrote to Reynolds from Winchester:

> How beautiful the season is now — How fine the air. A temperate sharpness about it. Really, without joking, chaste weather — Dian skies — I never lik'd stubble fields so much as now — Aye better than the chilly green of the spring. Somehow a stubble plain looks warm — in the same way that some pictures look warm — this struck me so much in my sunday's walk that I composed upon it.

He goes on in the same letter (see the introduction to *The Fall of Hyperion*) to say that he is abandoning his epic because of its Miltonic artfulness: "I wish to give myself up to other sensations." Of those "other sensations" *To Autumn* is the supreme expression, the most flawless — and impersonal — of the great odes. Keats turns from the inner turmoil and distress of the induction to the *Fall* and lives, for the moment, in sensuous content with overflowing ripeness — even if ripeness carries with it the suggestion of decay and thus links this ode with the odes of the spring. Among critical studies are: Ridley, pp. 280–90; Bate, pp. 182–6; E. J. Lovell, *University of Texas Studies in English*, XXIX (1950); L. Unger, *Western Review*, XIV (1950) and *The Man in the Name* (Minneapolis, 1956); R. A. Brower, *The Fields of Light* (1951), pp. 38–41.

1 f. Cf. Theocritus vii.155 f. (tr. Fawkes); *End.* i.250–5, iii.38–40.   **5.** Cf. Chatterton, *Ælla* 184–5: "When the fair apple, red as even sky, Do bend the tree unto the fruitful ground." In the letter cited above, Keats remarks: "I always somehow associate Chatterton with autumn."   **9–10.** Cf. Chatterton, *l.c.* 160, "The budding flowerets."   **11.** Cf. *Aen.* i.433. **12 f.** The personifications of autumn may owe something to *F.Q.* VII.vii.30, 38, 39 (Thorpe, p. 377).   **26.** Cf. *Udolpho* I, 44: "the snowy points of the mountains, still reflecting a rosy hue"; I, 126: "touched their snowy tops with a roseate hue"; and II, 138; and Campbell, *Pleasures of Hope* (ed. 1815), p. 15, "clouds of rosy hue."   **27. wailful choir:** cf. *End.* i.450; B. L. Woodruff, *MLN* LXVIII (1953), 217–20.   **30.** Cf. Thomson, *C.I.* I.iv: "And flocks loud-bleating from the distant hills."

The Day Is Gone   *Page 248*

This — first printed in *PDJ*, Oct. 4, 1838 — and the two following pieces (first printed by Houghton) are included partly as poems, partly as per-

sonal documents (the *Ode to Fanny* — "Physician Nature!" — is omitted).
They were apparently written during the autumn of 1819. Keats was again
in London, seeing Fanny Brawne, and they may at this time have become
formally engaged; but passion, intensified by his state of health and by lack
of the money needed for marriage (and for George), kept him in a fever
of ecstasy or misery. De Selincourt (p. 287) prints a somewhat different
version of this sonnet (cf. *ibid.*, p. 550; Garrod, p. 473).

9. **at shut of eve:** see the note on *Hyp.* ii.36.   14. **He:** Love.

—— To —— [Fanny Brawne]   *Page 248*

See the note on the preceding poem. Some scholars have dated these lines
in April, 1819, but the autumn seems almost certain. Lines 31 f. clearly refer
to George's financial misfortunes in the United States, of which Keats learned
on Sept. 10 (Finney, II, 687). Keats's earlier, general anxiety about his
brother and sister-in-law could surely not have occasioned such a violent
outburst without such a specific cause as the news that George had been
swindled out of his money.

1 f. Keats's letters show his craving to retain his "old liberty" even while
overmastered by love. Brought hurriedly from Winchester to London by
George's bad news, and in a much disturbed state, Keats said in a letter of
Sept. 13 to Fanny: "I love you too much to venture to Hampstead, I feel
it is not paying a visit, but venturing into a fire . . . Knowing well that my
life must be passed in fatigue and trouble, I have been endeavouring to
wean myself from you. . . ."   17. **throes:** is in throes.   31 f. H. E.
Briggs (*PMLA* LIX, 1944) showed that the materials of Keats's diatribe
came probably from his recollections of Robertson's *History of America.*

I Cry Your Mercy   *Page 249*

See the note on *The Day Is Gone.*

[Lines Written in the MS. of   *Page 250*
The Cap and Bells]

Printed by H. B. Forman, 1898. If, as scholars assume, these lines were
composed by Keats, they presumably belong to the period of his long satire,
that is, October (?)–January (?), 1819–20. While it is generally agreed
that Fanny Brawne and the impossibility of marriage were at the center of
Keats's feverish unhappiness during this autumn, there has been some questioning of the assumption that these lines were written to or about Fanny;
they may have been personal or they may have been "a scrap of dialogue
for a projected play" (D. Hewlett, p. 283; cf. Colvin, p. 455; Murry, *Keats*,
p. 49). For that reason I have ventured to give them a new and non-
committal title.

1–3. Cf. *Fall of Hyperion* i.18.

INDEX OF POEMS